T0196881

UNSUSPECTING SOULS

UNSUSPECTING SOULS

THE DISAPPEARANCE
OF THE HUMAN BEING

BARRY SANDERS

COUNTERPOINT

BERKELEY

Copyright © 2009 by Barry Sanders. All rights reserved under International and Pan-American Copyright Conventions.

Library of Congress Cataloging-in-Publication Data

Sanders, Barry, 1938-
Unsuspecting souls : the disappearance of the human being / Barry Sanders.
p. cm.
1. Mass society—History. 2. Individuality—History. 3. Conformity—History.
4. Social problems—History. 5. Popular culture—History. I. Title.
HM621.S2274 2009
302.5'45091821—dc22

2008050536

ISBN 978-1-58243-589-3

Cover design by Anita van de Ven
Interior design by Megan Cooney
Printed in the United States of America

COUNTERPOINT
2560 Ninth Street
Suite 318
Berkeley, CA 94710

www.counterpointpress.com

For two dear friends,
Lew Ellenhorn and Al Schwartz

CONTENTS

INTRODUCTION | Pictures at a Deposition

> God himself, who has disappeared . . .
> has left us his judgment that still hovers over us like
> the grin of the famous Cheshire Cat in *Alice in Wonderland*.
>
> —JEAN BAUDRILLARD, *EXILES FROM DIALOGUE*

E DGAR ALLAN POE and Arthur Conan Doyle created two of history's most memorable detectives: C. Auguste Dupin and Sherlock Holmes. Detectives so captured the imagination in the nineteenth century that writers borrowed the word *sleuth*, which originally referred to the dog that did all the nose work, the bloodhound, for that new superhuman, the detective. Those two nineteenth-century sleuths, Dupin and Holmes, came up with solutions for the most intricately plotted crimes—mostly acts of grisly murder. But the greatest crime of the century took place, over a period of time, right under their highly calibrated noses: the slow and deliberate disappearance of the human being.

The clues were shockingly evident. At the very outset of the century, the scaffolding of religious belief that held human beings in their elevated position collapsed. People no longer knew who they were, or what they were. Over the course of the century, the idea of the human being changed radically, and took with it traditional human sensibilities. Science and philosophy tried to resuscitate the human being, but to no avail. And then, the rising corporations—oil and railroads—took charge of everyday life. Armies of professionals followed, defining our lives for us and telling us what would make us happy and healthy and handsome.

This book examines the radical transformation of the matrices of living. The story of the resurrection of Christ redirected people's attention in the most fundamental ways, collapsing the two extremes of birth and death through the power of theology and imagery—ashes to ashes, dust to dust. No longer could ordinary people imagine those two events in the same way. From its inception, the Church defined the human experience. Then, just after the middle of the nineteenth century, with the publication of Darwin's *On the Origin of Species by Means of Natural Selection,* the Church lost its grip. And the human being underwent a new and radical redefinition, evident once again at the fundamental levels of birth and death. The coming of Christ gave way to the coming of science.

In the end, the human being that history had known for so many centuries simply disappeared. Such a profound loss makes any horror not just possible, but plausible. It alone does not produce holocausts, but it makes thinkable and thereby doable wholesale human slaughter and extermination.

Niall Ferguson opens his book *The War of the World* by pointing out that the "hundred years after 1900 were without question the bloodiest century in modern history." But the victims, in particular eleven million Jews and Romani and homosexual men in Germany and Eastern Europe, whom the Nazis reduced to mere numbers in the wholesale and systematic operation of death called the "Final Solution," died, for the most part, out of sight. What remains are various Holocaust museums, an assortment of documentary photographs, relics, and a raft of films. Periodically, the names and stories of actual victims or survivors will surface in the news. For a brief moment or two, the general public will applaud their fortitude and even their heroism. Elie Wiesel will periodically step forward to receive another award, while a few nuts hang in the back screaming that the

Holocaust was a hoax. But what persists, above all else, is a number: eleven million. As a stand-in for monumental horror, the world focuses on that staggering number, eleven million. It has become a catchword—shorthand for the attempted extermination of an entire people.

In the twentieth and twenty-first centuries, human beings do not die. The Nazis did not see humans when they looked at Jews, but rather vermin and cockroaches. They saw a multitude of pests in desperate need of wholesale extermination. Following that same tradition, in the more recent past, we read of entire villages of Vietnamese "pacified"; Tutsis and Serbs "ethnically cleansed"; men, women, and the youngest of children in Darfur and Chad "lost to religious strife." On September 11, 2001, Muslim extremists flew their airplanes into the Twin Towers and the Pentagon, their intense hatred of those symbols of American might forcing them to convert the human beings inside the buildings into mere incidental objects—into poor and benighted "capitalist dupes." We read about entire Iraqi neighborhoods of insurgents "eliminated with all deliberate speed," and of suspected al-Qaeda members whisked off in the middle of the night in black helicopters to destinations unknown, in a program with a name intended to hide its brutality and terrifying finality: "extreme rendition."

In that shadow world—and the word *shadow* runs through this entire book—death leaves its mark through body counts, body bags, collateral damage, friendly fire, fragging, benchmark numbers—and, most recently, through the rising scores on video games with names like Operation Desert Storm and Enduring Freedom. How did we arrive at a state of affairs so catastrophic that fathers, sons, husbands, wives, daughters, lovers, and friends—the rag and bone of human existence—could have collapsed so conclusively into images, pixels, ciphers, ghosts, gross numbers, into the palatable euphemisms of death? Why does virtually every loss of human life now resemble that frightening model of anonymity from the inner city, the drive-by random assassination, where, once again, victims do not die

3

but get "dusted," "wasted," "popped," or "blown away," and nobody is responsible? Under every hoodie, we have begun to believe, lurks a hoodlum: a case of our own fear turning us into racial profilers at the level of the street.

We walk our neighborhoods unarmed, most of us, but still feeling trigger-happy. We drive the streets feeling somewhat safe, but still shaking in our shoes. Ghosts haunt us in the airport and at the supermarket; they stalk us on the sidewalks and in the shadows. Just past the edges of our well-tended lawns, a clash of civilizations, a war of terror, rages endlessly. We live in fear, and come alive in anger. How did we lose our substance and our identities so immaculately? Where have all the human beings gone? In short, when did we stop caring?

A good many historians say that most of the world, and especially Americans, move through history suffering from a case of "historical amnesia." People too easily forget the last disaster and lose track of the last atrocity. But we do not forget because of some bout of amnesia—because of some blow on the head or because of too much alcohol. Something deeper and more radical eats away at us. In a sense, we have been programmed to experience "amnesia." Despite the insistence from Freud that the pleasure principle drives people's behavior, everything around us encourages turning aside from tragedy to just have a good time.

Some critics argue, Well, the numbers are just too overwhelming, the scale just too huge, for anyone to even begin to feel the pain and shock of death. Forty thousand die in a mudslide in Central America, another sixty thousand in a tsunami in Indonesia, perhaps one million or more in Darfur, and tens of millions of human beings from AIDS worldwide. I say the numbers matter little. Something more basic shapes today's attitude toward such a ghostly way of dying. Beneath those euphemisms of death lies a grim reality; but to really see it, we first have to hold in our minds the concept of the human being as something vital and crucial. Human beings first have to come fully alive for us, before we can consider them dead. (In order to truly

4

fall asleep, we must first come fully awake.) And, for a great many people, living seems just too confusing, too remote, or, worse yet, too difficult. The "isness" of being eludes us. A life is easy to come by, but living seems to remain just out of reach. We owe this strange state of affairs to a legacy we inherited from the nineteenth century.

Something new started in the nineteenth century: For the first time, people "had" lives. Which meant that they were in possession of an entity that one professional or agency or corporation could then manage and direct. Life existed as a concept outside of being alive, or simply living. One could objectify "life," analyze it, make plans for its improvement. One could even redirect its course and redefine its goals.

President George Bush marked the first anniversary of his inauguration, on January 20, 2006, by reinforcing a national holiday called the National Sanctity of Human Life Day. (Note: It is only human life here that we celebrate; other animals can agitate for their own special day). The proclamation reads, in part, that on this day "we underscore our commitment to building a culture of life where all individuals are welcomed in life and protected in law." If that sentence makes any sense at all, and I am not convinced that it does, then the sentiment sounds like something churned out by an ad agency announcing the arrival of the latest model car, one that comes complete with a lifetime guarantee. But as odd and bizarre as the proclamation sounds, it describes our current condition, where phrases like *a culture of life* and *welcomed in life* look like they might refer to something significant, or describe some actual reality, but on closer inspection point to nothing at all.

In 2008, after two years into its movement for sanctity, the White House made slight changes to the proclamation: "On National Sanctity of Human Life Day and throughout the year, we help strengthen the culture of life in America and work for the day when every child is welcomed in life and protected in law." The White House, in order to display its much larger ambitions, had added "and throughout the year." No more one-day sanctity for this administration. The White House also replaced the phrase "building a culture of life" with the more realistic "work for the day when . . . " (President Bush may have found it hard to talk about building a sanctity of life after so many years of killing civilians in Iraq and Afghanistan.) And finally, whereas the 2006 proclamation made reference to "all individuals," two years later the president had lowered his sights to focus instead on "every child."

Perhaps abortion activists on both sides feel free to argue the question, "When does human life begin?" because we are so unsure, these days, of what or who is human, and what or who is alive. A great many of us, I would argue, have a difficult time knowing what it feels like to be alive. The minute we get out of bed in the morning, we confront a barrage of advertisers and professionals just waiting to sell something to us, prescribe something to us, and repeat some durable commercial mantra in our ears. To ask the question, "When does life begin?" lays bare a conception of life as something mechanistic, a process that supposes a millisecond when a switch gets thrown and that certain something called a "life" begins. Ironically, under those artificial conditions, people acquire a life from which, inevitably, all living has been drained. In the eyes of the commercial and professional world, we walk about as nothing but bipeds fitted with monstrous and greedy appetites. Who can satisfy us? No one, it seems, even though many keep us enticed and tantalized and fully distracted. But, again as the advertisers instruct, we must keep on trying; we must keep on buying and consuming.

We pay a stiff price for the erosion of human essence. Today's whole-sale torture and killing almost everywhere we look has been made easier because of the erosion of human sensibilities in the nineteenth century. Although no one talks about this, when members of the CIA torture prisoners, they no longer torture actual human beings. A radical shift in the nature of the human being, at the beginning of the nineteenth century, emptied ordinary people of their philosophical and psychic essence; and in the end made this task much easier. I locate this shift, in great part, in the collapse of the Great Chain of Being and the subsequent birth of evolutionary theory. I also point to other eroding factors, like the rise of the machine and the explosion of a capital economy. I give a name to this peculiar phenomenon of loss: the *disappearance* of the human being.

Loss at such a basic level produces a disregard not just for other human beings, it appears, but for all living things. According to the evolutionary biologist E. O. Wilson, by the twenty-first century's end half of all species could vanish, resulting in what he calls the Eremozoic age—an age of hermetic loneliness. One way that we might begin to reverse such an unthinkably dangerous and tragic course is by understanding the disintegration of the human being—disembodying in its broadest sense—that began in the nineteenth century. In its power to shatter traditional meaning at the most basic level, the nineteenth century marks the beginning of the modern condition and carries the seeds for the consciousness associated with postmodernism.

As people began to lose the certainty of their own sentience, nineteenth-century philosophers, artists, and the new social scientists took as their task the recalculation of what it meant to be a human being. Professionals in the emerging academic disciplines and in the laboratory sciences tried to define the basic qualities of humanness, to locate the core of human essence. It is hard to talk about the nature of experimentation because so much of the modern apparatus of science comes into being just at this time. Even the word we take so much for granted, *scientist,* to refer to the person and the concept, does not enter the English language until about 1840; and even then the examples intrigue and baffle. This citation from *Blackwood's Magazine*, for instance, gives one pause: "Leonardo was mentally a seeker after truth—a scientist; Coreggio was an assertor of truth—an artist." A difference in manner or attitude or style, it seems, is enough to separate the artist from the true scientist.

As I hope to show in the following chapters, the close connection between science and art makes sense. The human body, in all its forms and permutations, states of aliveness and shades of decay, took on the same kind of fascination for various kinds of emerging scientists as it did for poets and writers. London physicians began dissecting cadavers, many times before large audiences, and pursued their slicing and chopping at such a furious pace that members of a new underground profession, grave robbers, came to their aid. Under the spell of the late Luigi Galvani, the Italian physicist, doctors all over Europe and in America tried their skill at reanimating the recently dead. Parisian high society gathered at a newly opened institution, the morgue, for extended evenings of gawking, gossiping, and sipping wine and champagne. Americans ate their summer dinners on the great green lawns of cemeteries in the 1830s.

Effigies, mannequins, automatons, wax models, talking dolls—the ordinary person grew hungry to gaze at the human in all of its disembodied, lifeless forms, and to render it in all its horrendous beauty on canvases and on the pages of novels and poems. Madame Tussaud, who thought of herself as an entrepreneur and artist, showed two lavish and detailed examples, fashioned in perfect detail out of wax, of the period's iconic image "The Sleeping Beauty." (Were we all just waiting for the right kiss, to be aroused from our slumbers?) People began to view the body as something detached and clinical, as something removed from themselves. They went to operating theaters to look at flesh investigated, probed, poked, and sketched. The body, like life itself, turned into something that people "had."

As the human being disappeared, ghosts and shades began taking their place; and they mouthed off—making their presence known with shouts and murmurs, screams and curious clatterings and bangings, from this side and from the beyond. Fictional characters, too, filled the pages as shapeshifters. Some characters made their presence known as invisible beings. Others walked the city in their sleep or in their half-awake state, while still others prowled under the influence of the full moon. They hovered, like Christ on the cross, off the ground, neither fully on earth nor yet in heaven, pulled between this world and the one beyond. Characters fell into comas and trances and drifted into a special nineteenth-century state called "suspended animation." Real people succumbed to hypnotic suggestions; others fell into deep trances. And in the world of fiction, still others moved about as specters, poltergeists, zombies, shadows, and doppelgängers. They lived in coffins, loved in graveyards, and, most powerfully, took up residence in the popular imagination.

Edgar Allan Poe embraced every last weird creature—those barely half-alive, those trying to come to life, and those fully disembodied. For him, every house was haunted; every soul was tainted. Each of his stories seemed to explore with a kind of otherworldly delight some paranormal part of the age. Poe rose to worldwide prominence as the poet of death and the macabre. Only America, in the darkest part of the nineteenth century, could have produced such a writer.

To see his spirit up close, I mention only one story here, the satirical "The Man That Was Used Up: A Tale of the Late Bugaboo and Kickapoo Campaign," which Poe published in 1839. In it, he recounts the story of a rather stout military commander, Brevet Brigadier General John A. B. C. Smith, who gets torn almost completely apart by battle. On meeting with the unnamed narrator, Smith reconstructs himself, part by part and limb by limb, ending with eyes, ears, toes, teeth, and tongue, until he stands before the narrator, Poe tells the reader with piercing irony, "whole." (The general's character resembles that ambulating machine from Karel Čapek's 1921 play *R.U.R.*, a creature so strange and so foreign that Čapek had to coin a new word to describe it, a *robot.*)

Poe published that story before he reached thirty years of age; but he was prescient. The traditional notion of the human being got used up. It was a thrilling, liberating idea—anything was possible—and, at the same time, a hopelessly depressing one. What would people finally become? Who were they? How could they be reconstituted? More important, what would finally become of each one of *us*, the heirs to that nineteenth-century seismic shift? Could we find someone to put all our Humpty Dumpty pieces back together again?

Virginia Woolf famously wrote, with her usual sense of assurance, that "on or about December 1910, human character changed."[1] Some literary historians have pointed to the publication, in 1914, of W. B. Yeats's collection of poetry *Responsibilities* as a document that records, on the eve of the First World War, the radical change in human nature. One of the more familiar poems in that volume, "The Magi," gets at the new sensibility through the theme of disappearance: "Now as at all times I can see in the mind's eye,/In their stiff, painted clothes, the pale unsatisfied ones/Appear and disappear in the blue depth of the sky." As telling as these writers are, the dates, for me, come too late. For me, the change began as soon as the nineteenth century opened.

The disappearance of the "pale unsatisfied ones" continues to clog the imagination. The Bush administration brought to the world "ghost prisoners" in Guantánamo Bay, Cuba, at Abu Ghraib in Iraq, and at Bagram prison in Afghanistan. We hear of "the disappeared" in Latin America; the "ghosts of war" in Vietnam; and the "ghost fighters" in Lebanon. The CIA refers to its own clandestine operatives as "spooks." We also periodically learn about those disappeared souls who have undergone extreme rendition, and who have been sent to who knows where, for who knows what kind of treatment. The Pentagon designated its prisoners at Guantánamo and Abu Ghraib as "security detainees" or "unlawful combatants," thus denying them prisoner of war status and allowing the United States to hold them indefinitely without judicial rights or privileges.

One of the images burned into the popular imagination shows a prisoner at Abu Ghraib, a pointed hood covering his head and a loose-fitting gown draping most of his body, his arms outstretched, electrical wires dangling from his arms, his whole being seeming to float on top of a box—a ghostly, spectral nineteenth-century icon from a twenty-first-century war.

Even while film itself has disappeared, we have in the Iraq War the first digital images of horror.

How easy the United States military makes it for us to forget that the wired-up prisoner began the year as someone's husband or brother or fiancé; that under the hood and gown one can find flesh and bone and blood. How gross that we need reminding that the outline we see is not something called a "security detainee"—whatever that might mean exactly—but a human being; not a stuffed mannequin but a live human being. How horrid that we have to remind the torturer—and us—that he is applying electrodes to one of his own kind.

Such atrocities do not just happen at our military prisons, but in our civilian prisons, and in our detention centers as well. *The New York Times,* in a May 6, 2008, editorial titled "Death by Detention," detailed the horror of what the newspaper calls an "undocumented foreigner." It seems that an immigrant from Guinea, Boubacar Bah, overstayed his tourist visa. Immigration authorities picked him up in 2007 and incarcerated him in the Elizabeth, New Jersey, detention center. As with most of our prisons in America, a private company runs the Elizabeth detention center. While incarcerated, Mr. Bah purportedly fell and fractured his skull and, although he was "gravely ill," guards shackled and locked him in a "disciplinary cell." As the *Times* reports: "He was left alone—unconscious and occasionally foaming at the mouth—for more than 13 hours. He was eventually taken to the hospital and died after four months in a coma."

Those in charge of such facilities—prisons, detention centers, military brigs, and compounds—invest the word *immigrant,* in effect, with the same evil as the words *prisoner* or *enemy combatant* or *suspected terrorist.* As with prisoners at Guantánamo or Bagram or Abu Ghraib, immigrants in federal custody have no right to legal representation; most of them cannot defend themselves; many do not even speak English, and thus have no idea of the charges leveled against them.

Using the nineteenth century as its foundation, *Unsuspecting Souls* tries to figure out how we got to such a bizarre state of affairs—especially in this country—where the idea of *immigrant* went from marking the greatness of this country to becoming a stand-in term for *freeloader and felon*. The book explores what it means to be a modern human being, the assumptions on which that definition rests, and where those assumptions came from. The book also entertains ideas about where we may be heading. It shows how even the most ridiculed theories of the nineteenth century shaped our own interior lives, and created who we are today. Seen against the backdrop of the nineteenth century, key cultural artifacts that once seemed odd and complicated fall more neatly into place. For instance, only a radical alteration in attitude toward the human being could bring about something as revolutionary as nonrepresentational art, whose beginnings point to the late-nineteenth-century Russian artist Kazimir Malevich. Imagine: canvas after canvas without a single person, in a time when artists made their reputations painting the human figure. If people disappeared from the canvas, the loss of human essence helps explain, in great part, why they left—even if we do not know where they went. We might well ask, Have we all become unsuspecting victims in that great caper called disappearance? Are we all, in effect, nonrepresentational?

The erosion of human essence continues at a furious pace. If we hope for change in the world, we must regain our sense of being, our sentience. What *does* it mean to be alive, to be human, in this, the twenty-first century? Philosophers and artists, writers and teachers have always asked such questions. Nowadays, we also hear it from politicians and corporate executives, from advertising mavens and design engineers. But these latter types, who enjoy positions of authority and power, of course, have ulterior motives and hidden agendas. And their answers demean and simplify. They define our lives only in the narrowest of ways—as voracious consumers, fragile immune systems, frightened political subjects, and finally as cogs in a high-powered, relentless machine, over which the average person has utterly no control. We confuse the fact of their power and authority with outright intelligence. We believe that they know better than we what we need. That is not the case. And so, we need to be asking those fundamental questions ourselves: Who are we and what can we become?

Unsuspecting Souls shows the frightening price we pay in not questioning prevailing assumptions and attitudes toward the life and death of other people—the minority, the poor, the vagrant, the person of color, the outsider, the so-called enemy, and the so-called stranger. For reasons I hope to make clear, this drift toward insubstantiality and disappearance has particularly victimized Americans. The rough-and-tumble way we negotiate with people, with the environment, with the other, and particularly the way America has over the years dealt with other countries—the assumptions of overwhelming force and power, the disregard of human rights—owe their insistence, in great part, to those transfiguring events of the nineteenth century. But then so does the current resurgence of evangelical fundamentalism and the renewed debate between evolution and creationism. In fact, these two things, the ferocity of America's foreign policy and the tenacious commitment, by many, to fundamental religions, forged their intimate relationship in the nineteenth century.

In the course of this book's writing, the Marine Corps charged five of its men with plotting and carrying out the rape of a young Iraqi woman, dousing her body with gasoline, and setting her on fire, in the Iraqi city of Haditha on November 19, 2005. The men then allegedly killed the rest of the family and, for good measure, burned their house to the ground. Immediately after setting the house ablaze, the supposed ringleader is said to have announced in a matter-of-fact way, "They're dead. All of them. They were bad people."

How bad could they have been? Bad enough, it seems, that those Marines no longer counted the Iraqi civilians as human beings. In fact, the military refers to all Iraqis as "Hajis," a reference to those who have made the hajj, a pilgrimage to Mecca. I have heard them called worse things by GIs—"ragheads," "desert monkeys," and even "sand niggers." Iraq and Afghanistan just present the most recent examples in the endless process of the United States denigrating people we perceive as the other, in anticipation of our attacking them, or in our outright killing of them. In good nineteenth-century fashion, the fact that the overwhelming majority of America's enemies turn out to be people of color makes the process of denigration a much easier task, since people of color already occupy a lower place in the ordering of races.

To understand events like Haditha, we need to know the history of that most lethal erasure that brought us to such a state of affairs, the disappearance of human sensibilities that began in the nineteenth century. We need to address the problem at its base, for the erosion of human essence runs very deep and very powerfully throughout our past. Toughness and power, strength and force, have become in our own time valued and privileged personal virtues. We are all, in the face of such a well-hidden but insidious force of erosion, unsuspecting and unwitting victims. Can a society hang together as one extended fight club, or one unending cage fight? We should not conceive of life as an extreme sport.

If we are to regain our senses, atrocities like Haditha must no longer seem like routine acts in a ruthless world. They must, once again, surprise and repulse us. I know that, with minimal effort, we can make sense of such events—we are at war; soldiers are young and jumpy; and on and on—but the logic of Haditha and Hamdaniya and Mahmoudiya and a host of atrocities at other, similar places—not to mention those prisons both known and secret—must confound normal logic and once again disgust the great majority of us. And we must remain disgusted: Torture and this country's commitment to it must replace the latest TV show and film as major topics of concern and interest.

We must return the inhuman treatment of others to the nineteenth-century category from which it escaped—*the aberrant*. To argue about what constitutes torture should seem extraordinary and extrahuman to us. We simply cannot raise waterboarding, say, to a level where we parse its grisly elements to determine if it is truly torture or not. We must laugh out loud at the Justice Department's argument that if GIs carry out humiliating and harsh treatment of prisoners suspected of being members of al-Qaeda, then no torture has taken place. We cannot allow the Justice Department to make people disappear twice—once as prisoners and once more as suspected terrorists. Torture is barbaric and beyond the boundaries of decent discourse.

Many historians have seen the nineteenth century as the beginning of the modern world. Someone like Tony Judt, writing in *The New York Review of Books,* has taken as his signposts on the road to modernity innovations like "neoclassical economics, liberalism, Marxism (and its Communist stepchild), 'revolution,' the bourgeoisie and the proletariat, imperialism, and 'industrialism'—the building blocks of the twentieth-century political world."[2] But typically what is left out of the description is that the "isms" helped drive out the people, the theories helped displace the humans. Put another way, the "isms" would not have been so easy to implement if the human beings had not disappeared first. And thus I want to focus on the human "building blocks." I want to discover what happened to them.

In 1866, Cyrus West Field succeeded in laying the transatlantic cable. Samuel F. B. Morse, the inventor of the telegraph, witnessed its completion. (Morse's first tapped-out message on May 24, 1844, to his assistant Alfred Vail, reverberates through the rest of the century: "What hath God wrought?") The *New York Tribune* said the cable would bring about "a more sympathetic connection of the nations of the world than has yet existed in history."[3] Morse himself saw bigger things. He predicted the cable would signal an end to war "in a not too distant future."[4] Today, nearly one hundred and fifty years later, we have upped the technology and use the Internet to make that same sympathetic connection with other nations. Still, the drive to destroy the enemy continues; and still the number of enemies proliferates. Technology will not fix our human condition. Only a change in attitude can truly affect social problems. And that requires not high-level technological know-how but only the most basic technical skills—reading, analyzing, and understanding.

This book rests on a firm belief: that human beings carry the capacity for continual self-critique and wholehearted renewal. We must once again recognize ourselves as actors and agents in the shaping of both political and social ideas, not just so as to rescue ourselves, but also to broaden the community we share with others. I see no other way to put a halt to the current fascination with torment and torture and the threat of total annihilation of the planet—people, plants, and animals—through war. H. G. Wells warned of the end of civilization in his 1898 novel, *The War of the Worlds,* about the attack of England by aliens from Mars. More than one hundred years later, Niall Ferguson took his title for his new book from Wells's tale of science fiction, for very much the same reasons—this country seems to have been invaded by aliens, motivated solely by arrogance, might, imperial hubris, and a thorough disregard for the other. Science fiction has become fact.

Others have viewed the nineteenth century as a series of disparate events, or have focused on one small topic. I see a crucial, overarching theme in the century's seemingly unrelated discoveries, innovations, and inventions: the desperate struggle to find the heart of human essence before time ran out. My hope, the hope of this book, is that by understanding that erosion of basic humanness in the nineteenth century, we can reclaim our own sense of being in this, the twenty-first century. Looking back may be the best way to move forward. To move the arrow forward means having to draw the bow back.

One way of looking back, and the best way of doing it over and over again whenever we desire, is with one of the key inventions of the nineteenth century, the camera. Shortly after its introduction in the middle of the nineteenth century, the camera pushed actual events aside and made people pay strict attention to the reproduction of the real thing: The image took charge over the actual. The camera very quickly became a popular household appliance, a plaything for middle- to upper-class families. It also very quickly got consigned for specialized tasks, so that at every major crime scene, for example, some photographer stood by, ready to document and frame, to catch details that the eye could not possibly take in, and of course to create a permanent record of the evidence.

Driven by the desire to capture the look and feel of actual experience, technological advances quickly made the images in the still camera move, giving the illusion that one was watching real life; and suddenly inventors brought it to little tent theaters in Europe: moving pictures, or motion pictures, or what we more commonly call today *film*. The camera of course exploded in the next century into a succession of screens—besides film, we have TV, the computer, various sorts of electronic games, and a variety of handheld devices—BlackBerrys and personal digital assistants—each with its own tiny touch screen. Even with all that innovation and invention, I grant the old and familiar still camera center stage in this book. I will spend an appreciable amount of time talking about the camera's importance in shaping perception in the nineteenth century. But, equally as important, I also use the camera as a tool for converting the succession of chapters in this book into a more graspable reality.

I ask the reader to consider each chapter as a "snapshot," a term that first described a way of hunting, dating from 1808, which involved a hurried shot at a bird in flight, in which the hunter does not have enough time to take perfect aim. Sir John Herschel, who coined the word "photographic," applied the phrase *snapshot*, in 1860, to capturing events, in a hurried and offhand style, with a still camera. Here's the first instance of the word in the *Oxford English Dictionary*: "The possibility of taking a photograph, as it were by a snap-shot—of securing a picture in a tenth of a second of time." For Herschel, time is crucial—do not think, just shoot. By 1894, the phrase had made it into newspapers and journals, and into the recognized organ of the profession, the *American Annual of Photography:* "Many think it is just the thing to commence with a detective camera and snap-shot."

An odd locution, the "detective camera," but by 1860, when Herschel used the phrase, cameras had become small enough and light enough so that even amateurs could use them with agility and speed. Manufacturers designed the Concealed Vest Camera, one inch thick and five inches long, so a person could hide it under a coat or jacket with the lens poking through some small opening in the cloth, with the idea that one could use such a camera for all kinds of detective work—professional and amateur—in sleuthing or where the person wanted to capture real candid situations. The camera, in a sense, disappeared from sight.

The camera captures shadows, the dreamy images that make up so much of experience. The phrase "shadow catcher" got attached to the photographer and ethnographer Edward Sheriff Curtis, who set out in the 1890s to document the rapidly vanishing American Indians. He attempted to make a permanent record of some eighty tribes across North America that he saw disappearing in his own time. William Henry Fox Talbot, who invented the negative and positive technique for taking and developing photographs, so intimately connected with the early days of the camera, says, not so much about Curtis, but about the process of taking photographs itself: "The most transitory of things, a shadow . . . may be fettered by the spells of our 'natural magic,' and may be fixed forever in the position which it seemed only destined for a single instant to occupy."[5]

It is all about shadows, about the past. We can try to capture the past with some specificity, but events come to us only as shadows. The camera captures this better than any other appliance, certainly better than any other nineteenth-century invention. This is especially true of the detective camera, working its magic while completely out of view. I have tried, myself, to recede as much as possible in order for the extraordinary events of the nineteenth century to fully display themselves.

I offer the reader a series of snapshots, a quick and spontaneous look at some key events and ideas and inventions of the nineteenth century, of which there seem to be almost an endless supply. I do not intend this book as detailed history. It is rather the history of an idea, the disappearance of human essence. As the reader moves through these chapters, I hope that these stills, as they did in the nineteenth century, will begin to take on an animated life, creating a kind of moving picture with a clear narrative—that is, a more complex and flowing and continuous story about the period.

As Curtis did with Native Americans, I am trying to record a record of disappearance—no easy feat. I am trying to offer up a positive that I have developed out of a negative. The original has long since vanished. I can only click and snap, knowing full well that I am dealing with perhaps the most evanescent subject imaginable, disappearance. Jean Baudrillard, the French critic, talks about what he calls the "genealogy of disappearance." He argues that "it's when things disappear that you seek to verify them . . . and the more you verify, the more reality fades . . . Things present their credentials through language. But that merely holds up a mirror to their disappearance."[6] I attempt here; I try. My project is one of reconstruction and assemblage. I work with remnants and scraps of information: I am sleuthing.

As photography records shadows, this book opens just as the century dawned, in 1800, with a shadow falling across Great Britain, Europe, and America, and growing longer and longer as the years went by. The book closes with a story of a wandering young man, in a German fairy tale, who sells his shadow to a magician. In the middle looms the dark outline of the Civil War, the horrendous struggle over black and white—the substance and form of writing with light, but not the kind of ghost writing we do with the word processor. I refer to one much older, to the nineteenth-century invention called photography, also an immersion, etymologically, in writing with light: *phos* (light) + *graphia* (writing).

I have chosen as a title for this introduction "Pictures at a Deposition." My title plays, of course, with Modest Mussorgsky's *Pictures at an Exhibition,* which Mussorgsky wrote in 1874 as a series of piano pieces in homage to his architect friend Viktor Hartmann. Mussorgsky intended his music to replicate the rhythm and pace of a visitor walking through the galleries of an art museum and pausing periodically to look at works of art. And while Mussorgsky's title refers to paintings, his use of the word *pictures* also deliberately echoes the new technology of reproduction, the camera.

And finally, I have changed the exhibition to a deposition, shifted the scene from the gallery to the courthouse, from the painter to the policeman, from art to the art of killing. I am trying in this book to make sense out of a terribly violent and important crime scene—the murder of the human being. In a certain sense, I want to interrogate the evidence—as Sherlock Holmes or Sigmund Freud, or a perceptive art historian like Giovanni Morelli, might do—to reach the truth of things, to uncover a revealing theme from the period. I do it not for the sake of the nineteenth century alone, but for what the clues might tell us about our own time and our own condition. I do it so that we might learn something about what we are doing wrong in this period. I am troubled by the violence and terror of our own period and, by understanding it, I hope to change it.

Over the course of these pages, we are witness to a deposition, then, an inquiry about the meaning of this mass disappearance of the human being in an attempt to finger the culprit or culprits. At a deposition, witnesses give testimony under oath. We listen to what they say, and we try to determine if they are telling the truth. We do not necessarily take all witnesses at their word. We look for details and listen for alibis. We concern ourselves with consistencies and inconsistencies. This requires close reading and careful listening, and it also involves a good deal of very careful looking. Body language offers a glimpse at honesty—gestures and expressions, too. For—to continue with my controlling image—the camera does lie. It's a recording machine, but it does indeed lie. We need to be on guard. Consider our iconic prisoner from earlier in this introduction, the one draped in his pointed hood and with electrical wires dangling from his hands.

We now know his name. Or at least we know his nickname. Thanks to an essay by Philip Gourevitch and Errol Morris titled "Exposure: The

Woman Behind the Camera at Abu Ghraib," in *The New Yorker*, we know that his captors, for some reason, called him Gilligan. Nicknames that the GIs gave their prisoners, like Claw, Shank, Mr. Clean, Slash, Thumby, and so on, made them "more like cartoon characters, which kept them comfortably unreal when it was time to mete out punishment." And so, perhaps, we have here a passing reference to *Gilligan's Island*. We also learn, according to an Army sergeant named Javal Davis, that almost "everyone in theatre had a digital camera" and sent hundreds of thousands of snapshots back home. Davis said that GIs took pictures of everything,

> from detainees to death. . . . I mean, when you're surrounded by death and carnage and violence twenty-four hours a day, seven days a week, it absorbs you. You walk down the street and you see a dead body on the road, whereas a couple months ago, you would have been like, "Oh, my God, a dead body," today you're like, "Damn, he got messed up, let's go get something to eat." You could watch someone running down the street burning on fire, as long as it's not an American soldier, it's "Somebody needs to go put that guy out."

The star of *The New Yorker* piece, the one who took more pictures than anyone else, was a twenty-six-year-old specialist named Sabrina Harman, who served as an MP at Abu Ghraib. She took her pictures, she says, because she couldn't believe the horrific assaults by MPs against the prisoners. Like her buddies, Sabrina liked to have a good time, and the camera made the torture and degradation fun. Or, at least she tried to make it so. The encounter with Gilligan turns out to be a mock electrocution—the wires carried no electricity. Gilligan knew a bit of English and so perhaps he understood they had nothing but fun and games in mind—"besides, the whole mock-electrocution business had not lasted more than ten or fifteen minutes—just long enough for a photo session." Harman explains, "He was laughing at us towards the end of the night, maybe because he knew we couldn't break him." To borrow a bit of the lighthearted spirit from *King Lear*, "As flies to wanton boys are we to the gods; they kill us for their sport."

This should not surprise us, that the most iconic picture from the Iraq War is a staged one. One hears the same thing about the group of GIs raising the flag on Mount Suribachi on Iwo Jima in the Second World War. The camera begs for staging and props; the photograph leaves us with a version of the truth: We must read the images with care and skepticism. Gourevitch and Morris end their essay with a cogent analysis of the immediacy of that photograph of Gilligan:

> The image of Gilligan achieves its power from the fact that it does not show the human form laid bare and reduced to raw matter but creates instead an original image of inhumanity that admits no immediately self-evident reading. Its fascination resides, in large part, in its mystery and inscrutability—in all that is concealed by all that it reveals. It is an image of carnival weirdness: this upright body shrouded from head to foot; those wires; that pose; and the peaked hood that carries so many vague and ghoulish associations. The pose is obviously contrived and theatrical, a deliberate invention that appears to belong to some dark ritual, a primal scene of martyrdom. The picture transfixes us because it looks like the truth, but, looking at it, we can only imagine what that truth is: torture, execution, a scene staged for the camera? So we seize on the figure of Gilligan as a symbol that stands for all that we know was wrong at Abu Ghraib and all that we cannot—or do not want to—understand about how it came to this.

We react to this photograph, Morris wants to say, in part because of the disappearance of the human form. The photograph allows us to imagine and ponder the inhumanity of human being to human being. Harman and her buddies staged it just that way because that is the situation they wanted—that's the one they hoped for in their imagination and in their mind's eye. In a sense, it is pornographic, as much a fantasy as a prostitute in a maid's dress or a nurse's uniform. In a serious distortion of reality, the photograph of Gilligan gives us a more perverse look at Guantánamo than if the photograph shot the truth. Harman and her buddies did more than torture the prisoners. They tortured the truth. In their staged presentation, they offer a candid view of themselves.

How it came to this: a staged photograph, "an image of carnival weirdness." Harman and her MP cohort saw torture as entertainment, Abu Ghraib as an amusement park, except that some poor unfortunate souls wound up losing their minds, destroyed for all time as functioning human beings. Of course, others got horribly mutilated and even died. The single iconic piece of evidence for an investigation of Abu Ghraib turns out to be a result of that instrument from the nineteenth century, a series of photographs taken with detective cameras. Entertainment, disappearance, and torture all meet at that place where human rights received a wholesale suspension, Abu Ghraib. It is the end of the road in a journey toward disappearance that begins in the nineteenth century.

ONE | What Is Life?

W ITH THE ARRIVAL of the new century, in 1800, the world, like a Humpty Dumpty egg, cracked wide open. Every belief and construct that held reality together simply loosened its grip. Even that most basic of entities, the human being, gave up its old, enduring definitions and fell in line as just another construct in need of serious rethinking. The century owes that radical shift, in part, not to a scholar, but to a little known pediatrician, Charles White, who published a treatise in 1799 that took on monumental importance, titled *An Account of the Regular Gradation in Man, and in Different Animals and Vegetables; and from the Former to the Latter.* In his *Account,* White predicted that the longest lasting and most static of philosophical ideas, the Great Chain of Being, would soon give way to something much more dynamic. Though he did not yet call it by name, we know it as the theory of evolution by natural selection.

The Chain had provided a schematic on which the Church hung the entirety of God's created universe. Everything had its assigned place on that imagined Chain, starting with God and followed by nine levels of angels, then human beings, birds, animals, and finally rocks and stones. Under the new schema, human beings would no longer occupy their elevated position. To the contrary, God did not make man in His image, as we read in Genesis, but rather man evolved through accidental and competitive forces. We shared that same kind of birth with all the other animals. In this scheme, humans might thus wind up having no higher claim in the kingdom of created things than the apes and the chimps. "The Devil under form of Baboon is our grandfather!" Darwin wrote in his notebooks in 1885. The cosmic egg had decidedly shattered, and human essence slowly disappeared.

But that was just the beginning—or, in some significant ways, the end. In hindsight, one can sense the enormity of other basic changes in the air—the railroad would move people farther and faster than they had ever gone before and, along with the cinema, would utterly destroy the way the average person experienced time and space. The human voice, disembodied from the person, would soon move long distances over a system of telephone lines. The incandescent bulb would push daylight deep into the night. The list of advances and innovations that would occur in the nineteenth century seemed endless: the telegraph (1837), the steam locomotive (1840), inexpensive photographic equipment (1840s), the transoceanic cablegram (1844), anesthesia (1846), the phonograph (1878), radio (1896), and new and cheaper methods of industrial production. The list seemed to go on and on.

If all that were not bewildering enough for ordinary people, they would confront a further revolution in technology that would change forever the way they performed the most ordinary tasks. Typewriters arrived on the market in the 1870s. Bell invented the telephone in 1876; a year later Edison invented the phonograph. Cheap eyeglasses, made of steel, first appeared in 1843, but took another three or four decades to be affordable to the masses. The 1870s and 1880s saw the discovery of radio waves, the electric motor, the National Baseball League, and dynamite. By the end of the 1880s, everyday people could buy their first Kodak cameras. Guglielmo Marconi, the Italian inventor, received his first patent in 1896, for sending radio messages. With the invention of the internal combustion engine, scores of people would soon become auto-mobile. At the same time, the time clock would gradually fix every person to a tighter schedule. Modernity, like a mighty wind, swept across England, much of Europe, and the United States, blowing aside virtually every received idea. How to cope with the overwhelming enormity of so much change at such a fundamental level?

And then the absolutely unthinkable: God would die, or at least the idea of God would cease to define common, agreed-upon experience. The Chain *and* its maker both disappeared. When Nietzsche wrote his obituary for God in *Also Sprach Zarathustra* (1887), he meant a lot of things. But one thing in particular stands out. For almost two thousand years, the Church provided the definition of the human being. All of creation lay in God's hands, including human beings, and every stitch of nature stayed radiantly alive through God's constant, creative support, remaking all of existence second by second. Before the nineteenth century opened, God was not just alive in nature. He filled the world with His imminent presence. By the 1880s, such thinking, at least for intellectuals, no longer had vibrancy. God had opened his hands. And men and women and children—all his creatures, really—fell out of the comfort of his grip to fend for themselves. Without God's constant attention, the contingent, imminent life, which had burned like a small flame, went out. Science took over the task of defining human existence. It could not hold a candle—or a Bunsen burner—to the Church.

Everything—all the usual, settled parameters of people's day-to-day lives—would present themselves, one by one, as ripe for redefinition. It was a freeing time, an exhilarating time of prolonged experimentation and occasional moments of delight. The age promised power and pleasure, growth and the transformation of the self. But it also threatened to destroy everything people knew—more fundamentally, everything they were. It prompted Karl Marx, in his 1856 speech on the anniversary of the *People's Paper*, to call for a new kind of human being: "[T]he newfangled forces of society . . . only want to be mastered by newfangled men." Nietzsche, too, responded to the changes of the period by demanding a wholly new person, what he called "the man of tomorrow and the day after tomorrow."

As Charles White had insisted, a static and fairly secure past would have to make way for a dynamic present—to say nothing of a wildly unpredictable future. The two towering intellects of the period, Marx and Nietzsche, held a fairly dim view of the fate of humankind. For, just as with our own technological revolution today, they both recognized the negative fallout from their own machine age. In fact, some historians argue that the discipline of sociology came into being in the nineteenth century through the efforts of Émile Durkheim, Max Weber, and Georg Simmel, because all three shared a general pessimism about the downward spiral of the social order, or as Simmel more succinctly described the times, "the tragic nature of social experience."[1] In his novel *Fathers and Sons* (1862), the Russian Ivan Turgenev described the philosophy of his radical hero Bazarov with a new word quickly co-opted by the philosophers: *nihilism.* Nietzsche expanded on the idea in his *Will to Power* (1885) and, a few years later, in 1888, in *Ecce Homo,* offered his ironically upbeat strategy for surviving the new modernism: "Nothing avails, one *must* go forward—step by step further into decadence (that is *my* definition of modern 'progress')."

When thinking about the mounting gloom in the nineteenth century, we should keep in mind that the term historians use to describe the century's last years, *fin de siècle,* came from the title of a French play by F. de Jouvenot and H. Micard. First performed in Paris on April 17, 1888, *Fin de Siècle* chronicles the moral degradation that had been building in the century and which culminated around 1880. The playwrights intended the term to refer to the *end:* the end of human beings, as we know them, and the end of moral and spiritual progress. The play is a statement of anti-modernism, of despair and decadence, in which characters long for the good times of the past and deathly fear the horrors of the future.

Everything was up for grabs—which made the nineteenth century a period of tremendous uncertainty, or, more accurately, of indeterminacy. Lewis Carroll got it right—nobody, neither horses nor men, seemed able to put the world back together again. Even with all the prompting from

Nietzsche and Marx, the future, perhaps for the first time in any significant way, began to collapse onto the present. The chasm separating *now* from *then* narrowed. No one knew what unsettling events lay ahead, what explosions might occur in traditionally familiar and stable areas, like travel, work, and recreation, but changes started coming at a faster and faster pace. The newly invented sweep-second hand kept unwinding the present until the future just seemed to disappear. The machine, without announcing itself or without, in many cases, being invited, bullied its way into the home and the office, and took charge. Nothing was off limits.

Near the end of the century, Louis and Auguste Lumière, pioneering brothers of the art form called cinema, produced a very short film titled *La Charcuterie Mécanique.* Louis described it this way: "We showed a sausage machine; a pig was put in at one end and the sausages came out at the other, and vice versa. My brother and I had great fun making the fictitious machine."[2] The film offers a potent allegory on mechanical production and technological innovation, the sausage machine perhaps even standing for motion picture cameras and projectors. But the brothers also joke about the way people get ground up and spit out at the whim of every new innovation and contraption. Surely, they also intended their viewers to think about the connection of swinishness with gross consumption—self-indulgence, gluttony, and materialism—and the numbing uniformity of the sausage links. Whatever the case, the Lumières do not present a very pretty or charming picture of the living and working conditions of the average person. Even with that most exuberant, most magical of all the new machines, the motion picture camera, the Lumières created what may be the first black comedy: a world of gloom and despair, in which individuals get reduced to their essence—to meat.

Alongside the invasion of privacy by that impolitic intruder, the Industrial Revolution, Sigmund Freud was busy taking people's guarded secrets out of their innermost sanctum, the bedroom, and examining each one with the calculating eye of the scientist. In fact, Freud helped his patients confess all their secrets, no matter the content, in the bright light of day. Rooting about in the darkest recesses of life, Freud illuminated human behavior by making case studies, not out of the average, but out of the oddest and most bizarre individuals he could find. Just what are the boundaries of the human endeavor? What is the range of emotions that supposedly elevate us from animals to human beings? In his zeal to define human essence, Freud wrote about strange characters like the Rat Man and the Wolf Man. Like Oliver Sacks today, Freud took great delight and found great wisdom in all sorts of anomalies. He wrote about a man who dreamed of wolves hiding in trees and of another who spent his days and nights in sewers. We must look at the edges, he seemed to be saying, in order to find the rock-solid center.

The general public, forever curious about its own kind, heartily agreed. The noun *freak,* to describe characters, say, who look like they came out of a Diane Arbus photograph, comes into the language in the nineteenth century in the phrase "a freak of nature." More recently, we know freaks, perhaps, as longhaired, unkempt hippies (who even turned the word into a verb by "freaking out"), or those from that same period whom we remember as Jesus freaks. At P. T. Barnum's American Museum, an extremely popular fixture of the middle to late decades of the century in downtown Manhattan, at the corner of Broadway and Ann Street, more visitors filed into the sideshow, or the freak show, than into the big top for the main attraction. Barnum offered for public viewing bizarre creatures with names similar to Freud's own cases: the Bearded Lady, the Lobster Boy, the Human Giant, and a host of other strange wonderments.

All this attention on the fringe and the freak and the underground resulted in a shockingly new aesthetics. Standards of decorum in behavior and dress and actions turned bizarre, outlandish—at times even revolting. Perhaps one of the biggest secrets a society holds is its criminals, its deviants and aberrant castoffs, which it prefers to keep safely tucked away in the shadows—in cells, in darkened chambers—anywhere, away from public view. Those lowlifes, too, became not just the darlings of the emerging avant-garde of the nineteenth century, but at times even models of the most powerful, unrestrained behavior. Imagine, thieves and prostitutes helping to define the idea of what it means to be human. Darwin's theory of natural selection presented problems for the idea of moral development; in fact, they seemed at odds. While we may find such ideas outlandish, we need only think of Dostoevsky's nineteenth-century tale of existential angst, *Notes from Underground,* whose antihero prefers to take aim at modern life from deep under the earth, in his dank dungeon. Thus, someone like Rudyard Kipling, who in a poem titled "The White Man's Burden" harped about making good and morally upright citizens out of "your new-caught, sullen peoples,/Half devil and half child"—which should have been a snap for an imperial nation like Great Britain in the nineteenth century.

America and England suddenly were introduced to a new player from the demimonde, the con artist. The con artist could pull off sleight-of-hand tricks with the deftness of the best magician; rather than performing onstage, he or she preferred working the streets. Melville paid homage to the type in his novel *The Confidence-Man.* When the French symbolist poet Paul Verlaine shot his lover Arthur Rimbaud, in 1873, the press glorified Verlaine, particularly after he moved to England, calling him "the convict poet." One century more and we get to Chris Burden, the American artist, shooting himself, not with a camera but with a rifle, in an art gallery, or, even more ghastly, having some random spectator shoot him. When we ask, "What is art?" we are also asking, "What are the limits of creativity, of human impulse?"

In the 1880s, leading lights in the demimonde enthroned Oscar Wilde as the reigning figure in an outlier aesthetic movement of the marginal that held a view of culture every bit as pessimistic as the sociologists'. To reveal their own character with total clarity, they named themselves, with a directness that startles, the decadents. These new aesthetes cultivated *un esprit décadent,* reflected in their profound distaste for bourgeois society and much of mass culture, and in their sympathetic embrace of the disreputable. Preferring to spend their leisure time in working-class hangouts, like music halls, theaters, and pubs—*un mauvais lieu,* as the poet Baudelaire put it—the decadents painted and wrote about the nefarious life that started up well after the sun went down. The decadents cozied up to thieves, ladies of the streets, and addicts of all kinds, and perhaps explored the most forbidden territory of all—homosexual love. Liberal psychologists in the period termed such lovers "inverts," since their love tended to invert the normal and accepted order of society.

One can trace a fairly straight line from the decadents and underworld deviants of the nineteenth century to the thug and gangster aesthetic of the twenty-first century. If society declares certain people undesirable, not really fit for humanity, then outcasts can defuse the category by appropriating the term and using it for their own advantage. As a case in point, some black artists, kept out of white society for several centuries, turned the categories "outcast" and "criminal" and "loser" back on themselves, exploiting all the power and fear that the rest of the population found in those names. You call us thugs? Well, then, we will dress and act and talk like thugs, and with intensity. We will capitalize on the fear that you find in us; that way we can materialize, feel that we have some substance and meaning. Even our musical groups, with names like Niggaz With Attitude, they announced, will shock and disgust. We'll even call our recording company Death Row Records.

The decadents' outlandish, offensive behavior, some of it perhaps not even at a fully conscious level, formed part of an important nineteenth-century strategy of psychic survival. For example, Nietzsche declared that people could best develop their own potential by tapping into "the powers of the underground." Not in the garden of earthly delights, but deep in the root cellar of humanity do people find the strength to move beyond all the accepted boundaries, categories, and definitions. No one wants to pass through life as one of the Lumières' sausage people. By diving deep

underground, ordinary people could transform, like mythological figures, into unpredictable human beings. Such wild strategies led Nietzsche
to broadcast his own declaration of independence, in the name of the
Übermensch, or the superman.

The new aesthetes did for art what Darwin and the demise of the Chain
of Being did for the human psyche. They cracked wide open the old definitions of what was normal and abnormal, moral and immoral. They pushed
the boundaries of gender, confounded the notion of correct and acceptable
subjects for art, and refused all standard definitions and categories. No one
would dictate to them where art stopped and music began, or where music
stopped and dance began. They paved the way, in our own times, for the
mixed-up objects that Robert Rauschenberg called his Combines, constructions that blasted apart finicky fifties definitions by combining sculpture
and art, or art and dance, and so on. They granted Rauschenberg the lib-
erty of gluing bits of newspaper cartoons, old advertising clips, and sections
of menus onto large canvases. The new aesthetic made possible Cornell's
boxes, Picasso's cubes, and contemporary mashups of all sorts.

The decadents wore funny clothes and smoked weird drugs. The fanci-
est dressers among them went by the name *dandies.* Only the beats or the
hippies or the yippies could match them in their disruptive exuberance.
Ginsberg owes his poetic life to that nineteenth-century soul force—Walt
Whitman, yes, but with a nod, certainly, to Oscar Wilde as well. And like
the free spirits of the late fifties and sixties, many nineteenth-century aesthetes, Wilde chief among them, spent time in jail or prison for their off-
beat, deep-seated beliefs. Modern politics of conviction starts in earnest
with Wilde's *The Ballad of Reading Gaol* and ranges to Martin Luther
King's "Letter from Birmingham Jail" and Eldridge Cleaver's *Soul on Ice.*
You shall know us by our acts of disobedience. *We* shall find ourselves
through such acts. Can it work? Can placing one's body in front of the
great inexorable machine accomplish anything serious and important and
long lasting? Can it make a single person step out of line and confront what

it means to be a thinking, fully alive human being? Well, just ask that other outspoken and feisty nineteenth-century jailbird, Henry David Thoreau.

Both the artist and the criminal stood outside society—today we would use the phrase *alienated from society*—that hung on for dear life to an old and tired set of values. And so they both, criminal and artist, aimed at blowing apart the status quo. Professionals in the nineteenth century, in their passion for categorizing everything in creation, saddled both the avant-garde artist and the petty thief with a new name, the *deviant*. In England, an emerging capitalist society led to the passage of new laws, covering a broad range of punishable offenses, most of which had to do with new bourgeois concepts of property. Authorities came to define a wider range of criminality within the growing class struggle, requiring a new penal system that carried with it longer and harsher sentences. This new social arrangement prompted British authorities to build many more prisons and asylums.

Prison, as many reformers argue, produces a criminal class. Recidivism rates in the United States today hover around seventy-eight percent. This idea of the repeat offender developed in Paris around 1870; by the nineteenth century's end almost fifty percent of all trials in France involved repeat offenders. And so the demand to identify every convict, behind bars and free, got folded into the century's own drive for finding humanity's basic identity. The phrase "Round up the usual suspects" comes from this period, which means, in effect, "Bring in the poor people, the people of color, the out of work, the feeble and insane. Bring me those who have had to resort to petty theft in order to survive." Taking the idea of identification several steps further, authorities wanted to finger the criminal type *before* he or she ever conceived of committing a crime. That's the idea, expressed more than a century later, at the heart of the 2002 film *Minority Report*.

•◉•

HAVELOCK ELLIS, the respected and well-known psychologist, wrote a nontechnical study in 1890, titled *The Criminal,* in which he derides thugs and artists as nothing more than petulant adolescents. While Ellis articulates the general attitude in the nineteenth century toward anyone or anything that appeared to defy its natural category, his prose reveals, at the same time, a bit of envy or jealousy for the criminal's wholesale freedom to engage with life. One can sense a struggle within Ellis, even in this brief passage, with what it means to be fully alive. Abnormal may not be so off-putting as Ellis makes it out to be. Notice the way Ellis compares criminals with artists:

> The vanity of criminals is at once an intellectual and an emotional fact. It witnesses at once to their false estimate of life and of themselves, and to their egotistic delight in admiration. They share this character with a large proportion of artists and literary men, though, as Lombroso remarks, they decidedly excel them in this respect. The vanity of the artist and literary man marks the abnormal elements, the tendency in them to degeneration. It reveals in them the weak point of mental organization, which at other points is highly developed. Vanity may exist in the well-developed man, but it is unobtrusive; in its extreme forms it marks the abnormal man, the man of unbalanced mental organisation, artist or criminal.

Later in this chapter I will come back to the criminal and to Cesare Lombroso, an important figure in confining the deviant to a very narrow and stifling category.

Not only the criminal and the artist, but the deranged, as well, rose to the level of seer in the nineteenth century. The madman and the fool took their solid place, in art and literature, as the embodiment of wisdom and insight. On the other side, in a desire to lock up so-called crazies and get them out of the way, the British Parliament passed its first act establishing public lunatic asylums in 1808. At the beginning of the century, England could count no more than a few thousand lunatics confined in its various institutions; by century's end, that number had exploded to about 100,000.

Authorities defined that troubling category, *insane,* more and more broadly, slipping it like a noose around the necks of more and more unsuspecting British citizens.

But the increase in numbers only added to the lure of the lurid. Whatever festered away, sometimes hidden from the direct line of sight—the criminal, the crazy, and the beggar—artists and writers dragged into full view. Two archetypal narratives got played out in the period: Orpheus descending into the underworld and returning to the world of the heroic and the unexpected; and Alice dropping down the rabbit hole of possibility, only to return to the land of the normal and the expected.

Both Orpheus and Alice descend beneath the earth, and return home radically altered. Both their stories prompted the same questions: Who are we? What does it mean to be a human being? Who is alive, or more alive? Who is really dead? Does the deviant live life more fully, know death more intimately, than so-called normal persons? Do things have meaning only when the Red Queen says they do? Many intellectuals confronted the century as such a bafflement. Henry David Thoreau gives us this account of an unsettling dream, mid-century, in *Walden*: "After a still winter night I awoke with the impression that some question had been put to me, which I had been endeavoring in vain to answer in my sleep, as what—how—when—where?"

In the context of the nineteenth-century search for deep meaning, Thoreau's refusal to pay six years of delinquent poll tax in protest of the Mexican-American War and slavery takes him one more step in his journey to answer those nagging questions—what? when? how? where? In July 1846, a judge sentenced Thoreau to a night in jail as punishment for his actions. To refuse the tax, to "Say no in thunder!" in the words of Herman Melville, is to say yes to oneself. In the face of the machine bearing down, a person must resist at whatever level he or she finds.

The question remains, "How can I maintain the autonomy of my own self?" For Thoreau, it meant refusing to pay a tax. It also meant publishing his ideas in an essay, in 1849, titled "Civil Disobedience." By *civil*, he did not mean polite; he meant the private as opposed to the government. Theories of civil disobedience—the stirrings of one body against the machine of government—start here with Thoreau. Such resistance provides one way of maintaining the autonomy of the self. Thoreau offers a kind of self-controlled deviance.

Scientists, philosophers, artists and even educators believed that they could only arrive at answers to Thoreau's dreamy questions by finding the bedrock of human essence, but through means other than civil disobedience. For some, that meant finding deep meaning through experiments with drugs. For others, the secret lay in fingerprints, or genes, or in the words we use, or in the images we dream. No matter—whatever the defining characteristic a person might choose, the quest betrays a great irony. Human beings, undergoing vast changes in their own nature, were trying, at the same time, to define what was essential about themselves—something akin to a person attempting to draw a self-portrait while staring into a distorted mirror. No one could see things clearly. There was no foundation, no starting place, and certainly no solid ground on which people could stand to define that elusive creature, the human being.

As a result, experts often conflated the process and the product. They substituted the search for the answer. So, for example, in their experiments with drugs, chemists confused feelings of euphoria with essential change. Instead of claiming that heroin, say, had altered perception, the alteration itself served as proof, for them, that they had finally found the secret of life. Scientists never discussed how heroin actually interacted with the brain. Chemical reactions did not matter. Alteration and change were all. Such experiments had the look of someone trying to throw a ball off the wrong foot: The whole enterprise lacked grace and accuracy, the trajectory off target by a wide margin. Worse yet, no one could get a clear bead on the target.

The move to define human essence, in a great many instances, took on a coarseness and grossness. The century did not interest itself in the meaning of life, but more in what it meant to be alive. It did not ask, *What is life?* Instead, it went after *What is aliveness?* Early in the nineteenth century, only drugs could deliver the philosopher's stone—opium and morphine and heroin serving as the alchemical key to universal understanding. Scientists confined their questions to matters of control—could they induce feelings of euphoria, say, and then reduce them, suspend them? They framed their questions the only way they knew how, for theirs was fast becoming a material and mechanical age, or rather, an age falling more and more under the sway of one machine or another. If machines produced, people would have to consume. And consume they did. And while people did not want to think or act like machines, the process of mechanization moved at a rapid clip, and exerted too much power for anyone to stop its advance. People did not, in many cases, know it, but the machine was clearly getting under their skin. It altered their perception. It framed their thinking.

As commerce raced rapidly forward and religion receded in people's lives, science eroded faith, as well, by describing nature clicking away like some well-oiled engine. Consider Darwin's theory of random, materialistic forces propelling life on its course. He even reduced human emotions and behavior to a series of chemical reactions in the brain. If chemists or psychologists could push a button or throw a switch, and with such an act activate the secret of life, that would have satisfied their urge. T. H. Huxley, the biologist, known in his day as "Darwin's bulldog," and who coined the word *agnostic,* described the new evolutionary world in this thoroughly mechanistic way: Man is "mere dust in the cosmic machinery, a bubble on the surface of the ocean of things both in magnitude and duration, a by-product of cosmic chemistry. He fits more or less well into this machinery, or it would crush him, but the machinery has no more special reference to him than to other living beings."

One of the Grimm brothers, Jacob, had retold the sixteenth-century story of the golem in 1808. Grimm was prescient. By 1808, he could already see that the golem perfectly captured the philosophical spirit of the age. In the original Jewish legend, a famed rabbi named Judah Low of Prague breathes life into a lump of clay, just as God had done with Adam, but, instead of creating human life, produces a creature called the golem. While the rabbi intends the golem to protect the Jews against attacks from the gentiles, in Jacob Grimm's retelling, the golem assumes its own life, then grows monstrously large and out of control, so that its creator must eventually destroy it. Grimm had Goethe in mind, specifically his "Sorcerer's Apprentice," a 1797 ballad based loosely on the legend of the golem. In the "Apprentice," a scientist's supernatural powers, which he uses to animate inert life, once again lurch wildly out of control. Both Goethe and Grimm offered warnings to whoever would listen.

But neither Goethe nor Grimm seized the popular imagination. Mary Wollstonecraft Shelley did; and I want to spend some time with her story here, for she frames the period so well. In some ways, the search for the secret of life, as it must inevitably be, was naïve and immature. And that's one reason, at least, that a young person, Shelley, could see with such astonishing clarity into the heart of the period. Shelley published her popular novel, *Frankenstein; or, The Modern Prometheus,* in 1818, at barely nineteen years of age, and settled on Prometheus for her subtitle with good reason, for she had written an allegory about an act of cosmic disobedience—stealing fire from the gods, or, in the context of the novel, discovering how to create life from inert matter. We can thus read *Frankenstein* as the ultimate pursuit for that one grand prize, life itself. But, like Grimm and Goethe before her, she also wanted her novel to serve as a warning, alerting scientists that they were chasing after the wrong thing, and that, in the end, the pursuit would ultimately destroy them. Shelley, who spent two years writing her book, invested *Frankenstein* with a great deal of humor and ironic detachment. She begs us to read her narrative in anything but a straightforward way. She makes us see the silliness in the search.

The search for the secret of life, because of its forbidden nature, found little favor with the general public and sank to the level of underground activity, pure and simple. Shelley understood that. Doctor Victor Frankenstein leaves home and follows his obsession and, in so doing, resembles many of the period's own scientists: "From this day natural philosophy, and particularly chemistry, in the most comprehensive sense of the term, became nearly my sole occupation. . . . My application was at first fluctuating and uncertain; it gained strength as I proceeded, and soon became so ardent and eager, that the stars often disappeared in the light of morning whilst I was yet engaged in my laboratory."

As Victor plunges deeper into his studies in natural philosophy, he moves more and more to the edges—becoming a fringe character—and, at the same time, deeper and deeper underground. The light goes out in the novel: Most of the action takes place at night, for Victor sees most clearly, he believes, by the dull reflected illumination of the moon. Like Dostoevsky's underground man, Victor remains out of sight, working behind closed doors, in muted light, in hiding. He might as well work away at the center of the earth. Isolated and alone, he gives himself over to one scientific pursuit only, to the exclusion of everything else—family, friends, nature, even love—a pursuit that usurps God's role: the creation of life. And so he asks himself the question that consumed the scientific community in the nineteenth century: "Whence . . . did the principle of life proceed? It was a bold question, and one which has ever been considered as a mystery; yet with how many things are we upon the brink of becoming acquainted, if cowardice or carelessness did not restrain our inquiries." Nothing can turn aside the obsessive genius, for the person blinded by such overweening pride, by definition, has to resist as flat-out silliness any warning to steer clear of forbidden knowledge. The ego can become the world's insult.

And so, like Doctor Faustus, some three hundred years earlier, Doctor Victor Frankenstein defies every accepted boundary of knowledge. His misguided ego demands that he possess all knowledge, starting with the creation of life and ending with the elimination of death:

"Life and death appeared to me ideal bounds, which I should first break through, and pour a torrent of light into our dark world. A new species would bless me as its creator and source; many happy and excellent natures would owe their being to me. . . . if I could bestow animation upon lifeless matter, I might in process of time (although I now found it impossible) renew life where death had apparently devoted the body to corruption."

He succeeds in achieving the first half of his dream, the secret of life: "After days and nights of incredible labour and fatigue, I succeeded in discovering the cause of generation and life; nay, more, I became myself capable of bestowing animation upon lifeless matter." He has not realized the second and more crucial half of his dream: the creation of life. And, for a brief moment, he's not certain he wants to open that door. He hesitates. The story teeters; it can go either way. But that momentary pause, freighted with centuries of metaphysical meaning, passes like a heartbeat.

What follows may not be the very first passage in the new genre of science fiction, but it surely counts as one of the earliest, and Shelley gives it to us with a recognizable amount of tongue in cheek. In fact, this singular event has all the trappings of a parody of the gothic romance—a dark and rainy night, a candle nearly burned out, the dreary fall of the year, a woods both deep and creepy. At precisely one in the morning—with every solid citizen fast asleep—as the rain begins pattering against the windowpanes, Frankenstein "collected the instruments of life around me, that I might infuse a spark of being into the lifeless thing that lay at my feet." And then Doctor Victor Frankenstein does what only up to this point God has done. He creates life: "By the glimmer of the half-extinguished light, I saw the dull yellow eye of the creature open; it breathed hard, and a convulsive motion agitated its limbs."

But Victor's elation is shockingly short-lived. One brief paragraph later, Victor yearns to undo his miracle work: "Now that I had finished, the beauty of the dream vanished, and breathless horror and disgust filled my heart. Unable to endure the aspect of the being I had created, I rushed out of the room . . . I beheld the wretch—the miserable monster whom I had created."

Frankenstein's creature has a life—of sorts. But he lacks a soul. He faces the world as a lonely and baffled outsider—the ultimate deviant—desperately in need of a female partner. The monster (who remains un-named throughout the novel) begs his creator for a soul mate, so that he, too, can create life—normal life. But the doctor recoils at the prospect of creating yet another aberration, another freak of nature. Suddenly, for the first time, Frankenstein looks his creation in the eyes, and offers us his only full-blown account of that alien, animated being. The description, once again, rivals any parody of the gothic:

> Oh! no mortal could support the horror of that countenance. A mummy again imbued with animation could not be hideous as that wretch. I had gazed on him while unfinished; he was ugly then; but when those muscles and joints were rendered capable of motion, it became a thing such as even Dante could not have conceived.

Throughout the rest of the novel, Victor flees from what he has done, only to have the monster confront him in the last several pages. Each thinks the other heartless, soulless, cruel, and wicked. Creator and creation merge, the reader recognizing them—doctor and monster—perhaps for the first time, as twin aspects of each other. Such merging must always take place, for whatever the endeavor, one cannot help but replicate oneself. What else is there? That's why, when readers confuse the doctor with the monster, and refer to the latter as Frankenstein, they reveal a basic truth: The doctor and the monster live in effect, really, as one—opposing characteristics of a single, whole person.

Mary Shelley hints at this idea in her subtitle, *The Modern Prometheus*. For one cannot invoke Prometheus without raising the specter of his twin brother, Epimetheus. Where Prometheus stands for foresight, for a certain degree of prophesying, Epimetheus represents hindsight. That's the only way he can see clearly, for he is befuddled by reality, and continually misinterprets the present. He promises to marry Pandora, but in keeping his word manages to let loose on the earth every evil known to humankind. He bumbles.

Victor, as I have said, exists both as himself and monster, creator and creation, light side and dark side, victor and victim—a seeming prophet, but in reality a man unwittingly bent on ruining everything he holds dear. According to Carl Gustav Jung, the Swiss psychiatrist who founded analytical psychology at the end of the nineteenth century, we are all twins, all of us in need of integrating the two halves of our divided soul. When Rimbaud writes, "*Je est un autre,*" he reminds us that, like Victor, we all live as part solid citizen and part monster, sometimes buoyed by brightness, and sometimes dragged down deep into our shadow selves.

The nineteenth century gives birth to a great number of twins because, as with Jung, many writers and philosophers find our basic human nature in that twinning: We pass our days as schizophrenic creatures. I offer only a few examples: Robert Louis Stevenson's *Strange Case of Dr. Jekyll and Mr. Hyde,* Oscar Wilde's *The Picture of Dorian Gray,* Fyodor Dostoevsky's *Double,* Poe's "William Wilson" and "Black Cat," Kipling's "Dream of Duncan Parrenness," Guy de Maupassant's "Horla," and a good deal of the work of E. T. A. Hoffmann. The age courted so many doubles it needed a new word to describe the phenomenon, so the British Folklore Society fashioned one out of German and introduced it in 1895: *doppelgänger,* the "double-walker."

We know the nineteenth century itself, as I said at the outset of this chapter, as a formidable and mighty twin—a century characterized by an energetic, lighter, and upbeat side, and a darker, more tragic one. That dichotomy helped fuel the search for meaning throughout the entirety of the nineteenth century, for in a large sense, meaning usually results in a degree of resolution. In the end, in a world more perfect, the nineteenth century, perhaps, might have reached some sublime integration.

But the age wanted little if any of that. We bump up against exceptions, of course—Thoreau, Emerson, Whitman—but for the most part professionals, from businessperson to biologist, craved Frankenstein's power. That legacy has helped to shape the twentieth century, and it has gathered momentum in the first few years of the twenty-first century, in our avaricious political appetite for power and control and all-out victory at any cost. Mary Shelley's warning about creating monsters and then having to live with them has gone unheeded. That's the problem with nineteen-year-olds. No one listens to them. While generations of readers have embraced her novel as pure horror, Hollywood, of all industries, seems to have gotten it right. It read her story not just as horror, but horror leavened with a good deal of dark, sometimes very dark, humor. *Frankenstein* has provided solid material for both the prince of gore, Boris Karloff, as well as for those sillies Abbott and Costello and Mel Brooks. The formula has proved highly successful: Since 1931, Hollywood has released forty-six separate movies based on Mary Shelley's teenage novel.

And even if Hollywood never releases another film about Frankenstein, the monster will never really die—on the screen or off—for, as we shall see, he keeps reappearing, in many different forms, all through the course of the nineteenth and twentieth centuries. He certainly stalks our own times. He is, many would argue, *us*. Which is to say that we have all had a hand not just in creating him. We have also done our part in keeping him alive.

Very early in the nineteenth century, physicians got infected with Victor Frankenstein's vision, and radically changed the underlying philosophy of medicine. From the ancient world on, doctors had aimed at restoring patients to health. Then, in the last decades of the nineteenth century, the profession assumed a radically different goal: the prolongation of life—no, the extension of life—sometimes beyond a time when it made good medical sense. (This desire, too, has been passed down to us in the twenty-first century.) Well-known and respected surgeons in London even believed that they could reanimate the recently dead, as if the longer one remained dead the harder it would be wake up. This is no less than what Victor Frankenstein and hundreds of real scientists and writers also pursued in the period, expending their time and their souls in the pursuit of some special elixir, a magic potion, that would unlock that key secret of the universe: mastery over death or, turned another way, a hold on eternal life. But first there was that deep-seated, elemental spark to discover—as Victor Frankenstein put it—the "cause of generation and life."

How different, Frankenstein from Pinocchio, but also how similar. "In 1849, before he became Carlo Collodi, Carlo Lorenzini described the Florentine street kid as the incarnation of the revolutionary spirit. Whenever there is a demonstration, said Lorenzini, the street kid 'will squeeze himself through the crowd, shove, push and kick until he makes it to the front.' Only then will he ask what slogan he must shout, and 'whether it is "long live" or "down with"' is a matter of indifference."[3] This passage is from a review of a book about the creation at the center of Collodi's immensely popular and perdurable book, *Pinocchio*. Collodi imparted that revolutionary spirit to the heart of the children's book when Geppetto, the lowly artisan, starts carving his puppet out of a block of wood only to pull off the ultimate miracle of the period—bringing Pinocchio to life as a young boy.

Collodi published his *Pinocchio* in 1881. It has been ever since one of Italy's most treasured books: Italo Calvino, the great fantastical writer, confessed that *Pinocchio* had influenced his writing career his entire life. Toward the end of the story, Pinocchio begins to read and write. Through those two activities, he transforms into a *"ragazzo per bene,"* literally "a respectable boy," or idiomatically, "a real live boy." He looks at "his new self" in a mirror—a traditional way of representing self-reflection—and feels a *"grandissima compiacenza,"* which has been translated as simply "pleased." Pinocchio is of course far from Frankenstein's monster, but he arises out of the inertness of matter—in this case, out of wood. He begins as a puppet—controlled and manipulated and directed—but his master, Geppetto, imbues him with that revolutionary fervor of the street kid, a perfect blending of the political, the scientific, and the spiritual, in keeping with the interests of the late nineteenth century. Pinocchio "comes alive" in the broadest sense. The prize for his good deeds in the book is *consciousness,* the seat and secret of all life.

In the opening days of the new century—January 6, 1800, to be exact—Britain's old and very staid Royal Academy got the search for the secret of life started. The Academy signaled both its approval and support for the quest in a peculiar way by announcing a prize of fifty guineas and a gold medal for the first person who could produce twenty pounds of raw opium from five acres of land. Settling on opium for its own experiments, the Academy had chosen a most ancient drug. In fact, the nineteenth century could have easily installed Paracelsus, the sixteenth-century physician, as patron saint of opium. According to legend, Paracelsus carried a sword with a hollow pommel in which he kept the elixir of life. Historians conjecture that the potion may indeed have been opium, which he affectionately called "the stone of immortality." A contemporary description of his healing method links him closely with opium and connects him with the nineteenth-century belief in the essentialist qualities of that drug:

> In curing [intestinal] ulcers he did miracles where others had given up. He never forbade his patients food or drink. On the contrary, he frequently stayed all night in their company, drinking and eating with them. He said he cured them when their stomachs were full. He had pills which he called laudanum which looked like pieces of mouse shit but used them only in cases of extreme illness. He boasted he could, with these pills, wake up the dead and certainly he proved this to be true, for patients who appeared dead suddenly arose.[4]

This is the sort of resurrective magic that drove scientific interest in the magical properties of opium.

An enterprising laboratory assistant named Thomas Jones claimed the prize money just after the century opened, by producing twenty-one pounds of opium from five acres that he had planted near Enfield, north of London.

And the race was on. Opium tapped into some center of sensation, but no one knew for certain how, or where; and no one seemed able to control its effect. Nonetheless, from this moment on, chemists and physicians took the cessation of pain as the principal piece of evidence that they had homed in on that hidden center of power. The nineteenth century was shaping up as the century of the anodyne to such a degree that many scientists considered their experiments a success if they could eliminate pain in their subjects and maximize their pleasure. Even before Freud popularized the pleasure principle, the nineteenth century was hard at work putting that idea into practice.

Like every drug in this period, opium quickly moved out of the laboratory and into the streets. Doctors recommended it for virtually every illness, from a simple headache to tuberculosis to menstrual cramps. Up to the time of the first opium wars in the late 1830s, a British subject could freely buy opium plasters, candy, drops, lozenges, pills, and so on, at the local greengrocer's. The English took to smoking opium, or ingesting a tincture called laudanum (from the Latin *laudere,* "to praise"), available, quite readily, at corner apothecary shops. Since laudanum sold for less than a bottle of gin or wine, many working-class people ingested it for sheer pleasure.

Some people, like the Victorian novelist Thomas De Quincey, perhaps smoked a bit too much. De Quincey started taking opium in 1804, and four years later found himself addicted. Even so, he could not stop himself from praising its exquisite pleasures. In 1821, he published his *Confessions of an English Opium-Eater,* in which he makes clear exactly what the scientists had hoped to accomplish. But his experience went well beyond science, and sounds, in its images of rebirth, vaguely like Paracelsus: "What a revulsion! what an upheaving, from its lowest depths, of inner spirit! what an apocalypse of the world within me! That my pains had vanished was now a trifle in my eyes: this negative effect was swallowed up . . . in the abyss of the divine enjoyment thus suddenly revealed. Here was a panacea . . . for all human woes; here was the secret of happiness . . . "

America had no De Quincey. No one championed opium as the gateway to insight. Americans went after opium purely for enjoyment and recreation. And so, helped along in great part by the Chinese, who opened smoking dens in great numbers in the Far West during the 1849 rush for gold, opium attracted more users in America than in England. In 1870, in the United States, opium was more widely available than tobacco was in 1970. The Union Army issued over ten million opium pills and two million ounces of powdered opium to its soldiers. Both Kit Carson and Wild Bill Hickock wrote in their diaries how they passed many pleasant hours in those opium dens, much preferring smoking opium to drinking whiskey. Smoking left them with no hangover and, as a bonus, sharpened their shooting and roping skills to such a point, Hickock claimed, that he could perform their sometimes dangerous cowboy shows with not a trace of fear. In fact, he claimed invisibility on the stage. At the end of the nineteenth century, even the distinguished Canadian physician Sir William Osler, professor of medicine at Oxford, declared opium "God's own medicine," for, he said, it could perform miracles, not the least of which was curing all of the world's ills.

Shortly after the Academy awarded its prize, a German chemist named Friedrich Wilhelm Sertürner, eager to find in that magic poppy the active ingredient—termed its "essence" or "basic principle"—isolated an alkaloid from raw opium in 1805. He named it "morphium," after Morpheus, the god of dreams; later it became known as morphine. For many years, Sertürner experimented on himself, trumpeting the drug's ability to eliminate all worry and pain. At one moment, Sertürner wrote, morphine could induce feelings of a state so foreign and so elusive that the philosophers had to coin a new word to describe it, *euphoria.* But, he added, sounding a bit like De Quincey, the very next moment it could make him feel "outright terrible"[5]—pitching him into a depression so dark and heavy and deep that it resembled a near-death experience. And then there it was again, something powerful, almost magnetic, pulling him back up to the heights of ecstasy.

Oh, to be born and die and be reborn over and over again. It was the experience of the century—and, for a moment or two, a victory for the chemist in his laboratory that he could not help broadcasting to the rest of the world.

So much did Sertürner crave the morphine experience, and so much was he a product of his own century, that he demanded a faster way to get the drug into his bloodstream. After all, speed was one of the great side benefits of the Industrial Revolution—faster travel, faster communication, and faster consumption. Sertürner read the zeitgeist; he wanted the high, and he wanted it *right now*. (*High* comes out of nineteenth-century street slang, first used around 1880.) But he never got his desire. Injecting drugs was not really possible until fifty years after Sertürner discovered morphine, when, in 1853, a Scottish doctor named Alexander Wood invented a crude hypodermic syringe, making it fairly simple for anyone to inject morphine directly into his or her own bloodstream.

By the time of the Civil War, American surgeons on both sides regularly dispensed morphine to soldiers on the battlefield. Farmers cultivated poppies in both Union and Confederate territories, with Virginia, Tennessee, South Carolina, and Georgia as the major producers. One particularly well-liked Union surgeon, Major Nathan Mayer, who found giving injections much too cumbersome, poured generous amounts of morphine onto his gloved hands. Riding past the troops, he invited them, like so many puppies, to take a lick. It mattered not at all that morphine left the battlefield littered with addicts: Immediate pleasure trumped long-range pain. Could such a potent drug count as the secret of life? It could, indeed, but could not, it seems, hold on to its top position.

For chemistry did not pause at the pure morphine stage for long. So intense was the search for more and cheaper ways to get hold of the spark of life that, in 1874, a pharmacist in London, searching for a nonaddictive alternative to morphine, boiled a batch of it with acetic anhydride, producing a substance with immensely powerful narcotic properties. (Though he did not know it, he had produced something highly addictive once more.)

By 1898, a worker at the Bayer company in Germany had noted the amazingly powerful properties of that solution as a painkiller and, again quite accidentally, a cough suppressant. The head of Bayer's pharmacological laboratory, Heinrich Dreser, tried the drug and called the experience absolutely *heroisch*, "heroic." Like De Quincey, he had been yanked up to heaven and dropped into hell. His laboratory assistant exclaimed, after injecting a dose of heroin, "I have kissed God!" Such a tremendous high, experience tells us, brings with it an equally horrific downer.

Beginning in November of 1898, Dreser marketed the new drug under the brand name Heroin. An anodyne of such heroic proportions, Dreser proclaimed, should go by no other name. By 1899 Bayer was producing over a ton of Heroin a year and exporting it to twenty-three countries. Nine years later, after learning of the terribly addictive qualities of his new product, Dreser tried to bolster Bayer's reputation by marketing a much safer albeit less potent anodyne. Dreser succeeded in developing a pain reliever from natural ingredients, extracting from the willow plant the chemical salicin, which he marketed as a powder under the trade name Aspirin.

In West Germany, meanwhile, another German chemist, Friedrich Gaedcke, was working to isolate the alkaloid of the coca leaf. His experiments proved successful around 1855, at which point he coined the name *cocaine*. The word appears for the first time in English in 1874. Here was another very powerful and very popular anodyne that physicians came to use as an anesthetic, in this case around 1860. The Coca-Cola Company used the coca leaves in its drink, which it advertised—in an understated way—as having great medicinal properties.

In 1884, Freud wrote a famous research paper on how the drug affected levels of awareness, entitled, simply, "Über Coca" ("About Cocaine"). In the essay, Freud talked of "the most gorgeous excitement of ingesting the drug," and goes on to sound out a testimonial for the drug's "exhilaration and lasting euphoria, which in no way differs from the normal euphoria of the healthy person . . . You receive an increase of self-control and possess more vitality and capacity for work . . . In other words, you are simply normal, and it is soon hard to believe you are under the influence of any drug." Freud recommended cocaine to cure morphine addiction and used it himself as an anodyne for about two years. Both of the drug's manufacturers, Merck and Parke-Davis, paid Freud to endorse their rival brands. Freud was a believer, and his use of the drug, some people believe, led directly to his work on dreams.

In that *annus mirabilis,* 1800, Sir Humphry Davy, a chemist, poet, and pioneer in electricity, came to the laboratory of a friend, Thomas Beddoes, in Bristol, England, called the Pneumatic Institute, to assume the role of supervisor. At his laboratory, Beddoes dedicated himself to exploring the healing effects on sick patients of inhaling various gases. The Pneumatic Institute was a popular place; the poets Robert Southey and Samuel Taylor Coleridge frequented it to take what they called "the airs," not for any particular illness, but for feelings of general well-being. In 1772, the English chemist Joseph Priestley had discovered an odorless, colorless gas that produced an insensitivity to pain. While working at the Institute, Davy purified that chemical compound and named it nitrous oxide. After his first inhalation, he quickly lauded its astonishing property of inducing feelings of euphoria.

Completely taken with his discovery, Davy immediately announced to his colleagues that he had stumbled upon the true philosopher's stone. He dazzled various assemblies of friends by inhaling his odorless gas and then sticking pins and needles into his body without any noticeable pain, giggling like a child through the entire experience. That proved, he declared, that he could control life, for he had located the seat of all feeling and sensation. Even the esteemed psychologist William James devoted an entire essay, which he published in the journal *Mind* in 1882, to the "fleeting brilliance of nitrous oxide inhalation." Titled "The Subjective Effects of Nitrous Oxide," James's article extols the virtues of finding insight by inhaling the gas: "With me, as with every other person of whom I have heard, the keynote of the experience is the tremendously exciting sense of an intense metaphysical illumination."

Robert Southey, one of the wilder poets of the period, on one of his trips to Beddoes's laboratory, tried the odorless gas and praised it as the highest order of religious experience: "I am sure the air in heaven must be this wonder working gas of delight."[6] That was enough for Davy to keep his research alive on what came to be called in the period the famous "factitious air." With James Watt, another wizard of the invisible—the inventor of the steam engine—Davy built a nitrous oxide chamber, in which people could absorb the wondrous gas through all the pores of their body. After one such session in his own chamber, Davy wrote the following paean to the power of the invisible, in his diary: "Nothing exists but thoughts. The universe is composed of impressions, ideas, pleasures and pain." Another session in the chamber prompted the following poem from Davy: "Yet are my eyes with sparkling luster fill'd/Yet is my mouth replete with murmuring sound/Yet are my limbs with inward transports fill'd/And clad with new-born mightiness around."[7]

In England, nitrous oxide became a popular plaything. One of the features of traveling carnivals through the countryside of England was something called "nitrous oxide capers," where for a few pence people could enter a tent, inhale the wonder gas, and giggle their hearts out. They staggered so dizzily that they, themselves, became part of the amusement. Inhaling intoxicants became a staple of British life. Traveling mountebanks, calling themselves professors, would extol the virtues of, say, nitrous oxide or ether, and then invite audience members to step forward and breathe deeply.

A group of amateur scientists, who called themselves the Askesian Society, fueled their curiosity with group inhalations of nitrous oxide. After serving some time with the Society, a young member named Luke Howard gave a lecture to the group, in 1802, on the most evanescent thing imaginable, clouds—one vapor seeming to be as good as any other. He had done something, he said, that no one else had ever done—a taxonomy of clouds. The names he chose—cirrus, stratus, cumulus, and nimbus—meteorologists still use today. Believing that nitrous oxide had provided him with his revelation about the new science he had launched, meteorology, Howard came back to the gas so many times he became addicted.

No intellectual groups formed around nitrous oxide in America, but nonetheless it had a following in this country, too. By the 1820s, students at Yale used laughing gas regularly at their weekend parties to break from their studies. Different from England, someone in America found out quickly how to make money off the giggling gas. A Hartford, Connecticut, dentist, Horace Wells, witnessed a volunteer inhale nitrous oxide in 1844, while someone else cut a long gash into the man's leg; the man looked down at his wound, wondered aloud about the long red line running down his thigh, and began laughing uncontrollably. The next day, Wells had a fellow dentist administer the "laughing gas" to him and extracted one of his teeth. Wells later commented: "It is the greatest discovery ever made. I didn't feel as much as the prick of a pin."[8] And so nitrous oxide gave birth to a new profession in America: painless dentistry.

Davy, meanwhile, turned his discovery to more serious medical uses, most notably to surgery: "As nitrous oxide, in its extensive operation, seems capable of destroying physical pain, it may profitably be used with advantage in surgical operations in which no great effusion of blood takes place."[9] While he made that statement in 1800, it took almost half a century more, all the way to 1844, for hospital officials to allow his laughing gas into the operating room in the form of *anesthesia*. The word first enters the English language (from Latin by way of Greek) in 1721, to describe those who, because of some major paralysis or other disabling injury, experience "a defect of sensation." In November 1846, Oliver Wendell Holmes suggested that the state created by nitrous oxide be named anesthesia, from Greek *an*, "without," and *aesthesia*, "sensibility." Just two years later, in 1848, *anesthesia* had already entered common parlance as a loss of all sensation induced by some chemical agent, which, at this early stage in its development, lasted for no more than two or three minutes.

Davy believed that anesthetized patients lay in a state of hibernation, lingering at the border separating life and death. The age had thus to confront this new creature, a breathing human frame that had been intentionally stripped of all feeling. It would do so over and over, in many permutations. Would anyone still call that seemingly inert lump of flesh on the operating table a human being? A truly sensate human being? Did that thing actually "have" a body? Or, more to the point, did it "have" a life? Though the patient felt no pain, he or she or it certainly seemed to lack consciousness. Or, on the other hand, was the patient pure consciousness, the state that everyone so vigorously pursued but that no one could ever name?

Michael Faraday, a chemist and physicist, towered over the Industrial Revolution as one of its chief inventors, producing an electric motor, dry-cell batteries, and a machine that powered a good deal of the revolution: a device he called a dynamo, a word from the Greek meaning "power and force." He began conducting laboratory experiments at the Royal Institution in London in 1808, transforming liquids and then reversing the action, a process he called phase changes. In 1818, Faraday, a decade into his intense experiments, concocted an odorless gas that, he claimed, could produce much longer-lasting anesthetic effects than nitrous oxide.

Because of the potency of the new gas, Faraday claimed that he, and he alone, had tapped deeply into the secret compartments of life. So assured was he that he even named his discovery after the element that only the gods had the privilege of breathing—the quintessential or fifth element: the ethereal, or simply *ether*. With his new success in the laboratory, Faraday bragged, all human beings could now breathe deeply of the very same stuff as the gods; but the question remained, could they feel godlike? Crawford Long, a young doctor in Jefferson, Georgia, threw a series of wild parties where he dispensed ether to his guests, which he called his "ether frolics." A protégé of the dentist Horace Wells, named William Thomas Green

Morton, administered ether to a patient at Massachusetts General Hospital on October 16, 1846. While the Boston Medical Association marked the success of Morton's operation by naming October 16 Ether Day, the first successful operation using ether as an anesthetic did not take place in England until a year later, in 1847.

• ❦ •

BUT SOME OTHER chemist or physicist always lurked in the wings, just waiting to announce the next potion that would throw that all-important switch, releasing the subject from pain and moving him or her into a fully altered state. Thus, in November of 1847, Sir James Simpson, a noted chemist, announced the anesthetic properties of yet another new substance, trichloromethane, that Simpson insisted would place patients in a much less troubled slumber than all the other chemicals combined. He shortened the technical name to *chloroform*. (A Frenchman named Jean Dumas had compounded the greenish liquid—*chloro*—in 1834.)

Linda Stratmann, in her book on the history of chloroform, aptly titled *Chloroform: The Quest for Oblivion,* points out that never had anyone devoted so much attention to the quest of deposing consciousness. These experiments, for lots of people, carried real dangers. She says:

> Sleep was believed to be a halfway house between consciousness and death, during which the brain, apart from maintaining basic functions, was inactive. The higher functions of the brain, the essence of what made an individual human, were therefore locked in the state of consciousness, and to remove, or suspend, these functions was to reduce man to little more than an animal. The creation of artificial unconsciousness therefore raised the specters of madness and idiocy. It was not only life, reason and intellect that were at risk, for the search was still in progress for the physical seat of the human soul, which might be in some part of the nervous system as yet not fully understood.

And then we have to think about the testimony of an expert, a doctor named James Parke, of Liverpool, who wrote his colleagues these words of warning in 1847: "I contend that we violate the boundaries of a most noble profession when, in our capacity as medical men, we urge or seduce our fellow creatures for the sake of avoiding pain alone—pain unconnected with danger—to pass into a state of existence the secrets of which we know so little at present." Parke believed the very profession itself was at stake, and he saw the field of medicine headed in the wrong direction. He may have been right, for medicine did begin to focus on two things after mid-century: the cessation of pain, and the prolongation of life.

Such warnings did not, however, go totally unheeded. Parke and others like him prompted a cadre of professionals who believed that they could explore the foundations of life much better and more efficiently, without the use of any chemicals or gases. The list includes mind readers, a great number of spiritualists, ghost talkers, experts on a new phenomenon called *paramnesia* or *déjà vu*, showmen, and even some scientists. James Braid, a highly respected Manchester surgeon, embodied all of those categories, along with a fairly large helping of daring and self-promotion. In 1841, reacting to the idea of anything so artificial as chloroform, Braid lectured about a much more powerful and organic fluid that coursed through the limbs of every man, woman, and child, uncovered earlier by the psychologist G. H. Schubert. Braid called this fluid "animal magnetism," and it did not just hold the key to the secret of life, he told audience after audience; it was life itself. A trained practitioner, Braid advised, could reinvigorate the élan vital in a sickly person, even in someone near death, and, like Paracelsus himself, miraculously return the person to a healthy and robust life. Or, that same practitioner could move a person to a state where feeling totally disappeared, allowing a physician to perform the most complicated operations on the subject using as an anesthetic only Braid's method.

Braid called his regimen *neuro-hypnotism*, which he shortened, in 1843, to *hypnotism*. The popular press called it "nervous sleep" or "magnetic sleep," a quasi-coma in which people found themselves unusually susceptible to suggestions. No matter the name, Braid, with his new field of hypnotism, or Braidism, as the press came to call it, declared that he had found the philosopher's stone—the pluck of life—the seat of liveliness itself. And, at the drop of a three-shilling ticket, Braid would most happily prove, through his onstage manipulations, that he could turn a fully animated, waking life off and on in even the most defensive, disbelieving person. Capitalizing on the period's emphasis on the gaze—in cinema, in the new museums, in photo galleries—Braid would begin each of his performances with the line, "Look into my eyes."

Braid's method migrated to America, in the late 1840s, through a flamboyant character named Andrew Jackson Davis, known during his lifetime as the John the Baptist of modern spiritualism. Davis had the ability, he claimed, to enter at will into a state of higher consciousness, what he called a "superior state," lifting him far beyond ordinary clairvoyance. From that rarefied position, he said, he could see the secrets that so many scientists were looking for and failing to find. For instance, the human body became transparent to him, allowing him to view each organ and, most dramatically, those organs with direct access to the source of life. That's why, without being told the illness beforehand, he could bring patients not just back to health, he wrote, but to extended life. Davis bore witness to the entire process of death and the soul's voyage to the hereafter, a place that, with the help of a bit of Braidism, he claimed, he had entered many times. And while he could not bring other people to his own superior state, he could, through the use of Braid's techniques, place them in a trance, allowing them to enjoy, even momentarily, a somewhat higher level of spiritual awareness, and a taste, brief though it was, of eternal life.

But some social philosophers in the period believed that if wakefulness could be disembedded from daily experience, enhanced through various opiate derivatives, muffled through anesthesia, or suspended through hypnotic power, then it did not serve well as the fundament of the human condition. It behaved more like an accessory to something else, something much more thoroughly basic and unshakable. With wakefulness as the defining element, people could easily go through life as transparencies—as ghosts. They might just as well feel that they did not exist, except in those moments of peak emotions—profound euphoria or deep depression. In short, drugs worked at just too ethereal a level for some professionals, the experience just too evanescent in the turbulence of the nineteenth century, to serve such a vital role. Scientists demanded something more perdurable, perhaps even tangible, by which to define human existence. They went off in different directions to find the bedrock, the fundamental.

As with many advances and inventions, this next one also came about quite by accident, but it fit perfectly into the period's desire to define human essence. A worker in a chemistry laboratory in England, J.E. Purkyne, thought he had found that foundational correlative when he picked up a glass slide one day in 1823 and noticed that he had left behind an indelible, precise impression of the patterns on the ends of his fingers. After some rather simple experimenting, he had to conclude, much to his own amazement, that everybody possessed a unique system of identification within easy reach—at the tips of their fingers. While a person might alter his or her behavior, or even personality traits, or fake being hypnotized, prints persisted absolutely unaltered, over a person's entire lifetime.

Even before the publication of Darwin's *On the Origin of Species,* Herbert Spencer, the English philosopher responsible for the phrase "survival of the fittest," posited a theory that the growing human sciences later tagged "social Darwinism." His idea fit tightly into the period's belief in the inferiority of those people with darker skin. Spencer argued that those with a decided lack of social and moral development—criminals—were nothing more than "savages," an inborn state, which included the poor, the laboring class, the Irish, women of lower class, and of course blacks. One could spot their internal deficiencies by distinctive outward signs. To ensure the smooth functioning of upper-crust white society, authorities needed to describe, type, classify, and, most important of all, keep these dangerous people under close supervision and observation. To keep its population safe, the state should have to produce a taxonomy of deviants.

Key social changes were underway to place great emphasis on the criminal. The revolution in production created a new bourgeois appreciation of property, bringing with it a wide range of new punishable offenses along with punishments of greater severity. Carlo Ginzburg, in a brilliant essay about crime and punishment in the nineteenth century, "Morelli, Freud and Sherlock Holmes: Clues and Scientific Method," makes the following observation:

> Class struggle was increasingly brought within the range of criminality, and at the same time a new prison system was built up, based on longer sentences of imprisonment. But prison produces criminals. In France the number of recidivists was rising steadily after 1870, and toward the end of the century was about half of all cases brought to trial. The problem of identifying old offenders, which developed in these years, was the bridgehead of a more or less conscious project to keep a complete and general check on the whole of society.

A novelist like Dickens could thus identify all kinds of brutes in his books strictly by their appearances. "Low brow" and "high brow" referred to people's foreheads—those who looked like Neanderthals or those who looked like intellectuals, as if such a thing were even possible—as they occupied either a lower or higher class. People came into the nineteenth-century world, then, born as criminals, an innate and irreversible fault of character and personality. Anthropologists, psychologists, sociologists, ethnographers—all the emerging sciences devoted their attention to identifying and categorizing the antisocial element in society.

We have not shaken ourselves free of such base and racist thinking; it operates for some unconsciously, for others more overtly. But it is, nonetheless, part of the essentialist thinking of the period; a good part of that thinking that tried to find the bedrock of, well, everything. Taxonomies ruled the day: Order and definition and category made the world come alive, and made it possible at the same time for those in authority to control it with ease. One of those most basic and wrongheaded essential nineteenth-century categories was race.

That narrowing of thinking continues through the twentieth century, and on through the twenty-first. The majority of men in prisons today in America are African Americans, the overwhelming majority of those for nonviolent drug offenses—inhaling or ingesting or imbibing some controlled substance. America incarcerates its black adult males at a higher rate per capita than did the South African government during the worst years of apartheid. Sentences turn out to be much harsher for young men of color than for whites who commit the very same crimes.

Francis Galton, the cousin of Charles Darwin, knew the problem only too well, and decided to do something about it. Galton had already expressed his deep-seated fear of the end of the "highly evolved" white race in his first major book, entitled *Hereditary Genius: An Inquiry into Its Laws and Consequences,* which he published in 1869. In that book, he made his case that the highest ideal for the white race could be found in the ancient Athenians. The closest to them in his day, he maintained, were the aristocratic British. And he named the enemy that threatened the established order and heredity as the darker, lower, and less moral races.

He relied on earlier work on fingerprints carried out by the founder of histology, J. E. Purkyne, who, in 1823, distinguished nine types of lines in the hand, with no two individuals possessed of the same exact combinations. Galton turned Purkyne's discovery into a practical project and began it by sorting fingerprints into eight discrete categories to use as a tool for mass identification. To make his taxonomy practical, Galton proposed that hospitals take the hand- and footprints of every newborn, thus creating an indispensable record of every citizen's identity. If someone committed a crime, the authorities could more easily track down the identity of the suspect.

Near the end of his life, in 1892, Galton finished his project of sorting fingerprints and published his results in a long and dull tome titled, very simply and directly, *Finger Prints*, in which he laid out, with graphic detail, the eight major patterns—swirls, whorls, curlicues, spirals, and so on—shared by every last person in the entire world. England quickly adopted his method, and other countries, including the United States, soon followed. Carlo Ginzburg, in "Morelli, Freud and Sherlock Holmes," says about Galton's project, "Thus every human being—as Galton boastfully observed . . . —acquired an identity, was once and for all and beyond all doubt constituted an individual."

We reach an incredible crossroad here: a semiotics of the individual based on patterns—or numbers—and not on anything so indeterminate or even as informative and telling as personality. Ginzburg points out that by the end of the nineteenth century, and specifically from 1870 to 1880, "this 'semiotic' approach, a paradigm or model based on the interpretation of clues, had become increasingly influential in the field of human sciences."

Fingerprints as a unique identifying tool had to compete with an already existing system of identification called *bertillonage*, named for a clerk at the prefecture of Paris, Alphonse Bertillon. His intense scrutiny of police files had convinced him that no two human beings—not even identical twins—carried the exact same physical features. He worked out a fairly crude classifying system—the base identity of the human being, or as he called it, anthropometry—and thus developed, around 1879, the world's first codified system for identifying human beings. Bertillon had such faith in his system that, on the basis of an oral description of a criminal, he had an artist sketch what the prefecture called "mug shots," and used them as wanted posters. Later, he had two photographs taken of the accused, one frontal and the other in profile—the template for booking photographs to this day. Bertillon called these shots *portraits parlés* ("speaking likenesses") and kept them filed by measurements of facial features.

Bertillon became well known in this country when his methods went on display at the World's Columbian Exposition in Chicago in 1893. This is the place that so many young women went missing without a trace: This is where they had disappeared in some numbers. Erik Larson opens his book *The Devil in the White City: Murder, Magic, and Madness at the Fair That Changed America* very calmly with an unsettling one-sentence paragraph: "How easy it was to disappear." And then the next paragraph: "A thousand trains a day entered and left Chicago. Many of these trains brought single young women who had never even seen a city but now hoped to make one of the biggest and toughest their home." "Vanishment," Larson goes on to explain, "seemed a huge pastime. There were too many disappearances, in all parts of the city, to investigate properly, and too many forces impeding the detection of patterns." The Chicago police grew more and more anxious and they adopted Bertillon wholesale the following year, and in 1898 Chicago established the National Bureau of Criminal Identification based on his methodology.

Two other schemes took a radically different approach to identification and worked at defining human beings at a much more fundamental, more essentialist level. Like Galton's and Bertillon's, they also aimed at identifying the most terrifying of the new and growing problems in the nineteenth century, the ultimate destroyer of existing categories, the criminal. In every country police hoped to identify criminals before they committed their antisocial acts. Given the theories of social Darwinism and racial inferiority, scientists had no doubt that they could satisfy the police. Here, social scientists plumbed the most essentialist level imaginable, trying to define what it meant to be not only a human being, but an aberrant human being, at that.

In the first, a German physician named Franz Joseph Gall, working in the first couple of decades of the nineteenth century, believed he could determine character, personality traits, and, most important, criminality, by reading the bumps on a person's head. As a medical man, Gall engaged in a kind of medical semiotics, making serious declarations about personality, for instance, based on certain telltale signs. Gall held to a fairly complicated theory about human essence. In principle, he argued, the brain functioned as an organ of the mind, and the mind possessed a variety of different mental faculties, each of which represented a different part, or organ, of the brain. The brain consisted of exactly twenty-six separate organs, including the dreaded "murder organ"—more precisely, the Organ of the Penchant for Murder and Carnivorousness. These organs, or areas, raised bumps on the skull in proportion to the strength of a person's particular mental faculty. Fortunately for society, he allowed, he knew how to find the murder bump, and could do so by the time the poor subject reached puberty. He named his new system *phrenology*.

Like Gall, an Italian physician named Cesare Lombroso, the person mentioned by Havelock Ellis earlier in the chapter, resorted to this same sort of medical semiotics. He stands as the first person, really, to articulate the biological foundations of crime. Lombroso, too, believed perhaps even more strongly, and certainly more ardently, than someone like Galton in social Darwinism and genetics to declare that criminals were born and not created out of conditions of poverty and class and color and so on. In 1876, Lombroso published a book titled *The Criminal Man*, in which he listed a range of physiognomic details that indicated a propensity toward both brutishness and criminality in men. These included large jaws, high cheekbones, handle-shaped ears, fleshy lips, shifty eyes, and, most telling of all, insensitivity to pain. He writes with a style that borders on the pathological:

> The problem of the nature of the criminal—an atavistic being who reproduces in his person the ferocious instinct of primitive humanity and the inferior animals. Thus were explained anatomically the enormous jaws, high cheek-bones, prominent superciliary arches, solitary lines in the palms, extreme size of the orbits, hand-shaped or sessile ears found in criminals, savages, and apes, insensibility to pain,

extremely acute sight, tattooing, excessive idleness, love of orgies, and the irresistible craving for evil for its own sake, the desire not to only to extinguish life in the victim, but to mutilate the corpse, tear its flesh, and drink its blood.

Fingerprinting and *bertillonage,* phrenology and physiognomy, all those systems of classification, led to moving medical forensics out of the hospital ward and into the offices of new nineteenth-century professionals, detectives. The man credited with that move, Sir Bernard Spilsbury, an Oxford graduate, went to work in October of 1899 for St. Mary's Hospital Medical School in Paddington, London. As his biographer bluntly says: "Single-handedly he transported forensic medicine from the mortuary to the front page with a series of stunning, real-world successes."[10] In the process, he also developed the role of the expert witness. The staff of St. Mary's quickly came under Spilsbury's spell, and saw him as a person possessed of supernatural powers of deduction; they talked about him as if he were Sherlock Holmes come to life. Spilsbury prided himself on solving crimes with the slightest of clues, and preferred working in the field, alone, sifting through the muck for the slightest shred of evidence: "While others preferred the comfort of the predictable laboratory, he clambered across muddy fields, stood knee-deep in icy water, bent his back into howling blizzards, wrinkled his nose over foul-smelling corpses, prepared to travel to any destination and endure any hardship in order to study the fractured detritus of death."

What made him perfect for the age is that he needed no body, no corpse, to solve, say, a murder case. At one point he concluded, for instance, that a pool of grey pulpy substance spread over a basement floor had once been a human being. In the way that he could construct the most complex of stories from the simplest of clues, Spilsbury stands as the forefather of the most celebrated of contemporary pathologists, like Michael Baden, Herbert MacDonell, and Doctor Henry Lee, notably of the O. J. Simpson trial.

More than anything, Spilsbury loved to work on the long forgotten and unsolvable—what we today know as cold cases. Ordinary citizens in the nineteenth century followed Spilsbury's magic in the newspapers the way contemporary audiences watch on evening television the wonders of *CSI* and *Cold Case*. As in the nineteenth century, we live in fear—there are crazies out there—and we must have our crimes solved, or at least we have to hear a good story about one, no matter how true, that ends in the resolution of the case. Then, we can breathe a bit easier, walk a little freer.

As comforting as Spilsbury may have been, it's hard to imagine besting the well-ordered and logical mind of that quintessential sleuth, Sherlock Holmes, of 221B Baker Street, London. In story after story, Holmes focuses his infallible reasoning abilities on a jumble of evidence in order, as he repeatedly says in solid nineteenth-century fashion, "to get to the bottom of the matter." Holmes continually amazes his friend, the naïve Doctor Watson, with his ability to solve crimes—*CSI* redux—and, like Spilsbury, he needs no corpse. Why Holmes, how did you ever come to that conclusion? the doctor asks over and over. To which Holmes answers, using the one word popular with nearly every scientist of the nineteenth century, *"Elementary,* my dear Watson, *elementary."* An essentialist to the core of his very being, Holmes processes all experience, including fingerprints, facial characteristics, and other bits of evidence, as elementary stuff. He cares not a whit about punishment or justice, desiring only to finger the culprit—to identify the perpetrator—and announce to an expectant audience the suddenly obvious truth.

Through his superhuman powers of deduction, Holmes plays the pure scientist, discarding everything superfluous to arrive at the rock-bottom, basic truth. At certain moments, when Holmes finds himself stumped by a crime, he reaches a heightened awareness—actually, just the sort of state that the chemists were after—by using his favorite seven-percent solution, cocaine. Under the influence, or high, Holmes, following the model of Andrew Jackson Davis, claims for himself the clarity of insight or the seer or the clairvoyant. (Recall, Freud recommends cocaine use for increasing levels of awareness.) In the middle of a welter of information and facts, Holmes sees an immediate pattern; or, rather, the cocaine, like an intellectual magnet, pulls all the particles into a pattern.

In a story titled "The Adventure of the Cardboard Box" (1892), some unidentified culprit has sent a box to an old lady, containing two severed ears. Who would do such a vile thing to a nice old lady? Such is Holmes's usual problem, and the reader's usual delight. Holmes solves the case using a version of Gall's "medical semiotics" (recall, Conan Doyle had been a doctor before he took up writing):

> 'As a medical man, you are aware, Watson, that there is no part of the human body which varies so much as the human ear. Each ear is as a rule quite distinctive, and differs from all other ones. . . . Imagine my surprise when, on looking at Miss Cushing, I perceived that her ear corresponded exactly with the female ear which I had just inspected. The matter was entirely beyond coincidence. There was the same shortening of the pinna, the same broad curve of the upper lobe, the same convolution of the inner cartilage. In all essentials it was the same ear.'
>
> Of course, I at once saw the enormous importance of the observation. It was evident that the victim was a blood relation, and probably a very close one.

Usually, when Holmes comes down from one of his highs to confront Watson, he assumes the intellectual strategy of Socrates, a seeming know-nothing—who of course knows everything—and more, allowing Watson to come to the solution as if through his own powers of induction. As the characters trade roles, Conan Doyle makes apparent to his readers that Holmes and Watson are really twin aspects of each other. In "The Adventure of the Cardboard Box," however, Holmes instructs: The details are too important, the lessons too crucial. He lectures the doctor on his own profession, about the most crucial topic, a way of seeing individuality.

In this example of semiotics at work, Holmes attempts to deduce the solution to a crime based on one small set of details, in this case the shape of the pinna and lobe and cartilage of one ear. Carlo Ginzburg, in "Morelli, Freud and Sherlock Holmes," connects the case to a nineteenth-century art historian named Giovanni Morelli who authenticated paintings in museums across Europe based not on stylistic features like color and strokes, but on such "inadvertent little gestures" as the shape of the ears of the artist's figures. Ginzburg points out that Freud had read and commented on Morelli's strategy, causing Ginzburg to realize "the considerable influence that Morelli had exercised on [Freud] long before his discovery of psychoanalysis." Detective, psychoanalyst, and art historian all share (or exhibit) the age's obsession for ordering and classifying: for the semiotics of seeing.

The task for all the practitioners of the so-called human sciences, then, was precisely Holmes's task—to find the pinna, the lobe, that one essential truth. Like Holmes, they were trying to solve a major crime, the theft of human essence, to find ultimate meaning in the marginal, the irrelevant—the detail, to quote Freud, that lay "beneath notice."[11] No one particularly cared who had pulled off this particular slick robbery. The idea was just to return the booty, to redefine the human being at the core level. The academic branch we now know as the social sciences, devoted to the study of human behavior, came into existence in the latter half of the nineteenth century. One of its first fields of study was something called *eugenics*, a word coined in 1883 by Francis Galton, the same man who eventually concluded his career, out of exasperation, with fingerprints.

Just as Holmes arranged seemingly random details into recognizable patterns, Galton applied statistical methods to myriad physical characteristics and arranged them into basic definitions and types. By so doing, he caused the century to face new, bizarre questions: What does it mean to be classified as a Negro (or Ethiopian, to use the nineteenth-century term), or a Mongoloid, or—of supreme importance for Galton—a person who occupied the most elevated of those categories, a Caucasian? In his 1869 study *Hereditary Genius,* Galton expressed his fear about the demise of superior breeding if the upper classes did not maintain their dominance. After all, they had the good fortune of occupying that premier category, the "highly evolved" white race, and that meant they had certain responsibilities; for instance, they were charged with keeping the race pure.

While Galton turns out to be a somewhat obscure but pivotal figure in the debate over heritable traits, his new science of eugenics supplied the necessary foundation for all the later discussions of the key essentialist idea of the late nineteenth century—race. Galton argued that people inherited all their behavior, and insisted that those traits could and should be measured. Moreover, he wanted to rank them so as to demonstrate the relative worth of one group of people over another: Bad behavior meant bad genes. So, for example, in a shocking display of racial hubris, Galton proposed to show the superiority of whites over blacks by examining the history of encounters of white travelers in Africa, their manners and deportment, with unruly, hostile black tribal chiefs.

In the most public display of quantification—in which he used statistical methods to reduce living human beings to numerical arrays—Galton set up a makeshift laboratory at the International Health Exhibition of 1884. For threepence, a man in a white smock would test and measure participants for all sorts of indices, including head size and its alleged concomitants, intelligence and beauty. People came in one end of the tent as personalities, and left the other end as averages, norms, and deviations. Each of these measurements, Galton believed, would take the world of science that much closer to the ultimate definition of the human being.

So convinced was Galton that he had found the way to define human essence, he wanted to use his theory to effect a social cleansing. In Galton's scheme, heredity governed not only physical characteristics but talent and character as well, so, he said, "it would be quite practical to produce a highly gifted race of men by judicious marriages during several consecutive generations."[12] In *Macmillan's Magazine,* a popular monthly, he proposed an idea that mimics Victor Frankenstein's—the creation of life. His plan involved state-sponsored competitions based on heredity, celebrating the winners in a public ceremony, culminating with their weddings at no less a location than Westminster Abbey. Then, through the use of postnatal grants, the government could encourage the birth of eugenically superior offspring. (Later, he would argue that the state should rank people by ability and authorize more births for the higher- than the lower-ranked unions.) Finally, he would have the state segregate and ship off to monasteries and convents the categorically unfit and unworthy, where society could be assured that they would not propagate their enfeebled kind.

Charles Darwin went beyond mere individual races. He believed that he had found the secret for the collective human species. Like the death of God, evolution was an eighteenth-century idea that took hold in the nineteenth century. No one in early Christian Europe took seriously the idea that the present emerged out of the past. Of course, people observed change, but they did not necessarily hold to the idea of continuity, for Christianity postulated a world of living things completed in six days, a creation that forever after remained unchanged. The Christian worldview could accommodate sudden change, even catastrophe, but not slow, small changes over long stretches of time. For Christians, today's natural world has existed this same way since its creation, except, as with Noah's flood, when God chose to alter it.

In titling his 1859 book *On the Origin of Species by Means of Natural Selection,* Darwin deliberately overreached, for the idea that the origin of anything could exist outside God, he knew, would smack of heretical thinking. Against every acceptable theory of the scientific community, Darwin set out to prove by himself the mechanism by which plants and animals—most notably humans—had achieved their present form. How could anyone get any more fundamental than Darwin, who was after all determined to plumb the very origin of every species on Earth, to trace our evolutionary ancestors back to the primordial muck from which they arose? With just one overarching mechanism, natural selection, Darwin could account for the endless variety of nature using only three related principles: one, all organisms reproduce; two, within a given species each organism differs slightly; and three, all organisms compete for survival. Not a divine plan, but changes in climate, weather, geology, food supply, and numbers and kinds of predators, created nature's incredible biodiversity. Darwin had no patience with the idea of creation through any supernatural force.

Ironically, despite the tremendous controversy surrounding *On the Origin of Species* in the nineteenth century, Darwin does not mention human beings until the next to the last page, and then only in a single sentence: "Much light will be thrown on the origin of man and his history." Twelve years later, in 1871, in *The Descent of Man, and Selection in Relation to Sex,* he quite explicitly places human beings at the forefront of evolutionary theory, depicting them, along with other animals, as totally shaped by natural selection, a conclusion he had reached much earlier, in his notebook, in 1838, with the following absolute certainty: "Origin of man now proved— Metaphysics must flourish—He who understand[s] baboon would do more toward metaphysics than [John] Locke." In the simplest terms, Darwin sought to wind back through time to uncover humankind's ancestral traces, using every prehistoric cache of bones as evidence of the origin of species— ancient fingerprints of the ur–human being. Science would never reach a definition of the human being, Darwin reasoned, until it could fully explain its origins. In fact, its definition lay in its origins. The popular press interpreted his ideas in a simple, incorrect, and, for the great majority of people, frightening way: Human beings were descended from apes. It gave Edgar Rice Burroughs great delight to parody such ideas in his Tarzan books.

Darwin subtitled *On the Origin of Species by Means of Natural Selection, "or The Preservation of the Favoured Races in the Struggle for Life."* Race was a convenient vessel into which scientists began to pour one of their major definitions of human essence. Here, as Darwin suggests, not all races compete as equals. Some, like Caucasians, are inherently more intelligent, stronger, craftier, and so on. Africans belonged to a much inferior race, a designation they could never shake. Caucasians could take heart that they enjoyed a superior existence. At the coaxing of many scientists, whites could at least define themselves by what they were not. And they definitely were not Africans. Testing would demonstrate the point—for instance, in cranial size. Centimeters mattered greatly.

Darwin and Galton—along with every other scientist in the nineteenth century—shared an almost religious fervor, as Stephen Jay Gould has observed, for the comfort of numbers: "rigorous measurement could guarantee irrefutable precision, and might mark the transition between subjective speculation and a true science as worthy as Newtonian physics."[13] Both Darwin and Galton constructed precise x-ray photographs of the roots of humanity, several decades before Wilhelm Roentgen discovered what many called the Roentgen Ray in his laboratory in 1895. Not knowing exactly what he had found, and refusing to name it after himself, Roentgen settled on the name x-rays. The x-ray camera functioned as the ultimate tool for revealing the blueprint—the basic skeletal structure—of a single human being. Just as the cosmos contained under its visible crust a compelling, invisible structure that held it together, so people carried bones under their flesh that functioned in the very same way. Roentgen's discomfiting magic camera—people complained of its invasive and insidious nature—allowed everyone to miraculously see the human substructure without killing the patient. Think, today, about the outrage against proposed airport screening machines that can x-ray the entire body at various depths. In Paris, near the turn of the century, x-ray "technicians" purported to show photographs of ghosts taken with the new invention.

Self-styled social philosophers, roughly around the same time as Roentgen—that is, in the last decades of the nineteenth century—held that the skeletal structure of human interaction lay in language and the stories that percolated out of language. The Grimm brothers, before they began their project of collecting and sorting fairy tales, had helped to construct, in an early philological undertaking, the Proto-Indo-European family of languages. In their drive to find that same elusive origin of the human species, the Grimms pushed the beginning of language back beyond historical record to a construct called Proto-Indo-European, or Hypothetical Indo-European. Some philologists argued that in studying Greek one could discover humanity's basic tongue. Others countered, No, one must tunnel farther back, to Hebrew, or even the older Aramaic, to hear pure utterance prior to the babble of the Tower of Babel. There, one could come into contact with speech uncorrupted by time and thus tune in to what provides human beings with their essential humanness. Whatever the language one settled on, the brothers Grimm launched the study called philology, arguing mightily for the philosopher's stone in the first primal grunt.

What makes the pedigree of languages visible is something called *cognates*—words common to several languages but with variant spellings. Similar sound patterns and slight sound changes across languages suggest family members—from distant cousins to brothers and sisters. Using the analogy of cognates, a concept promulgated around 1827, Carl Jung constructed his theory of the collective unconscious, whereby our stories, myths, and even our dreams find expression in similar symbolic patterns from one culture to the next. Why else would themes repeat themselves in stories and dreams, from disparate countries over vast spans of time? Surely, such cultural echoes must reveal yearnings deep within the DNA of human experience.

An English physician named Peter Mark Roget embodied the period's obsession for classification and ordering, coupled with a great love of the language. He was one of those remarkable people who knew a little about a vast range of things. He came to understand the way the retina made a series of stills into moving images, an observation that led to the discovery of an early version of the motion picture camera, the zoetrope. Roget also helped Humphry Davy with his experiments with nitrous oxide.

As a young man he made lists—of death dates, of remarkable events—but most of all he loved to collect words that had similar definitions. In 1852, he published one of his most extensive lists, of words with overlapping definitions, and gave it the title *Roget's Thesaurus of English Words and Phrases Classified and Arranged So as to Facilitate the Expression of Ideas and Assist in Literary Composition.*

The Grimms had dug through the culture at such a basic level that their work seemed in perfect harmony with the birth of both the idea of the "folk" and the idea of the "folk soul." We owe to the nineteenth century the fact that we can talk so freely about such a thing as the German people as distinct from the French or the Irish. The anthropologist Peter Burke sets this most radical discovery into its historical context: "It was in the late eighteenth and early nineteenth centuries, when traditional popular culture was just beginning to disappear, that the 'people' or the 'folk' became a subject of interest to European intellectuals."[14] German philologists, like the Grimms, first posited the idea of "the people," and introduced a cluster of new terms to help give shape to their discovery: *folk song, folktale,* and *folklore.* This idea had far-ranging implications, of course, for politics—just think about nascent nationalisms—but the idea also changed the face of education around the world.

A German educator, Friedrich Froebel, believed that the folk soul developed very early in children. And so, in 1840, to nurture that most basic quality, Froebel invented the idea of kindergarten. In those "children's gardens," where teachers planted their seeds of learning, Froebel hoped to bring out that very same thing that scientists and philosophers were also pursuing, "the divine essence of man." To that end, Froebel designed a series of blocks in various forms—the world reduced into its constituent shapes—and asked children to make out of them stars, fish, trees, and people. (Frank Lloyd Wright's mother bought her son a set of Froebel blocks with great results. Maybe the blocks helped shape his sense of space and form.) As an educator, Froebel was asking children to see everything in its basic, elemental parts. No wonder, for Froebel had a background in crystallography, and just as crystals grow from a molecular seed, he believed, children could create the world out of similar seeds—in this case, building blocks. His exercises further reduced the world to forms of nature (or life), forms of beauty (art), and forms of knowledge (science, mathematics, and especially geometry).

The British immediately delved deeply into their own country's folk soul and found a rather distinctive and powerful one. Francis James Child, Britain's first major folklorist—the British and American Folklore Societies have their beginnings in the nineteenth century—did for ballads what the Grimms, in their later careers, managed to do for fairy tales: He collected, described, and arranged them in the 1890s. And because he dated them as much earlier than most fairy tales, Child claimed ultimate cultural authority for his ballads, arguing, in fact, that he had caught more than English ballads in his net. He had far surpassed the Germans, he claimed, for he had found the folk soul of all the Anglo-Saxon peoples. Child lobbied all European countries to establish a national repository of their own earliest songs and tales.

In all these narrative expressions—language, myth, song, fairy tale, ballad, dream—social scientists tried to reduce the great and wild variety of creative production into its elemental parts. This kind of early anthropological study acquired the name, quite appropriately, of structuralism, since it attempted to disclose the scaffolding of society, the armature on which every artistic pursuit rested. As its name implies, structuralism purported to uncover essentials or elementals—the defining units of human interaction, across various cultures. The idea spread. Emerging scientists of human behavior, soon to be called social scientists, sifted every human activity and enterprise for its constituent parts, in the desire to reveal the blueprint of the human psyche.

Taking structuralism as a model, for instance, technological advances made it possible to shatter the illusion of activity itself by breaking movement into a series of stills. And one remarkable piece of nineteenth-century technology, cinematography, perfected by Auguste and Louis Lumière in 1895, exemplified what virtually every scientific invention and innovation attempted to accomplish during the period: to arrest the rush of history and analyze it in a single, understandable unit. Likewise, as experience tried to run away, the camera continually froze it in place. The *fin de siècle* knew this technological marvel initially in a machine called a stroboscope, part of the burgeoning science of chronophotography. (The Lumières had borrowed from the technology developed by Louis Daguerre in the 1830s for photo reproduction.)

What is myth, after all, but a series of events retold in a fabulous way? What is speaking but the uttering of discrete sounds, which the linguists of this period called *phones* and later *phonemes*—sounds that, in the right combination, the mind perceives as words? What is motion but a series of still frames? The century had prepared for such ideas, and the motion picture camera caught on quickly. In less than a year after its introduction, a number of dealers in various European cities began selling the Lumières' new invention. In Vienna, one of those dealers staged the first public performance of moving pictures on March 22, 1896. Writers began to refer to something called "the age of the cinema" and "the new cult of the cinema." The world now had something startlingly different—mass entertainment. The novelty not only refused to die out or disappear as nothing more than a fad, it increased in popularity and continues to this day, of course, to grab the imaginations of audiences.

At the end of the century, as philosophers and scientists exhausted their attempts to seize on essential definitions for a world that seemed to be fast slipping away, technology came to the rescue. The camera stanched the hemorrhaging of humanity by making at least one instant of experience permanent. But that technology had another, opposite side, for the photograph left its trace in nothing more substantial than ghostly images—the very same state, ironically, as the disappearing fleshy existence it hoped to record. With motion picture technology, perceiver and perceived came eerily together.

This new technique of reproducing amazingly exact, moving images of objects and people, as one historian of nineteenth-century Vienna puts it, "went hand in hand with a loss of the material, haptic and vital existence."[15] The haptic life—that is, a touching and feeling, fully alive existence—presented itself to people, for the very first time in history, as a choice. In an astonishing historical moment, screen images, only slightly fresher, brighter, and glossier than the original, began to compete with reality for people's attention. Marx adapted his writing style to counter this draining away of feeling. In 1856, he asks, "the atmosphere in which we live weighs upon everyone with a 20,000 pound force, but do you feel it?"[16] Are we really expected to? Is it possible for us to feel it? With enough wakefulness and awareness, can we really feel it? We are supposed to answer yes, I believe, for one of Marx's major concerns was to wake people up to their feelings. According to the scholar Marshall Berman, Marx even tailored his writing style to this goal, expressing his ideas "in such intense and extravagant images—abysses, earthquakes, volcanic eruptions, crushing gravitational force,"[17] forcing people to read from their nerve endings out.

Over time, as their experience included less and less of the fleshy original, people would do more than just accommodate themselves to ghostly emanations. They pushed aside the real thing and went for the image. After all, the simulacrum was neater and less messy than the real thing. The U.S. Army made life-sized cardboard cutouts of soldiers serving in Iraq—made from photographs of the real person—to pass out to families, to keep them company while their sons or husbands did battle ten thousand miles away. The Marines could not fashion these so-called Flat Daddies fast enough to keep up with the demand. People in the nineteenth century, just like these contemporary families, were being asked, more and more, to situate themselves within the new world of flattened images, to place their faith in a technology that robbed them of their senses.

Indeed, faith—in its base, religious sense—became an issue, in some ways one of the grandest issues, in the nineteenth century. It started early in the century; we continue to debate its influence today. In the late summer of 1801, some twenty thousand people—young and old, men and women, overwhelmingly white but with a few blacks as well—gathered for what was billed as the largest revival meeting in all history, in Bourbon County, Kentucky. The event became known as the Cane Ridge Revival. Its interest and influence developed over the course of the century, emerging as a politically powerful evangelical wing of Protestantism. The publication of Darwin's godless theories mid-century gave the movement just the boost it needed to ensure its success, causing it to spread throughout the South and West.

One can trace an almost uninterrupted history of religious fundamentalism from August 6, 1801, at Cane Ridge, Kentucky, to the present day. A reemergence of Darwin as a scapegoat for the alleged moral lassitude of the majority of Americans has helped recharge fundamentalism today. We still live, in large part, in a context shaped by the nineteenth century. School boards and legislators and clergy argue the case for evolution or creationism with great, if not greater, conviction and rancor than in the nineteenth century. And, repeating conditions in the nineteenth century, technology directs a larger and larger share of our lives, serving to intensify the debate. Intelligent design, creationism soft-pedaled, vies now with evolutionary theory for space in school curricula—a continuation, in other words and terms, of the old nineteenth-century struggle to understand how the world exactly works.

The Indo-European family of languages, the structural components of myths, the phonetic patterns of speech; other innovations of the period such as the Braille reading system, the gestures of sign language, and the symbols of the International Phonetic Alphabet; and, perhaps most important, the fundament of God's creation—all these undertakings and endeavors left their trace, a distinct and basic pattern that, like footprints in the sand, one could read. The family tree of languages also described a distinct outline, a particular shape of human communication. Architecture provided perhaps the clearest outline, the most salient blueprint of order and arrangement. It also provided something more, a bonus for this period.

In both England and America, architecture meant out and out solidity. The Victorian critic and man of letters John Ruskin reclaimed the Gothic as the *arke techne*—the highest artistic pursuit—of the nineteenth century. Architecture in general, Ruskin argued, was not about design but about something much more fundamental, pure, and basic. Buildings rose in the air through a strict adherence to mathematical relationships. Those relationships revealed God's imprint, His divine plan for the order of things, from the golden mean to the magic square.

If one wants to study the subject of education in the nineteenth century, or even in the Middle Ages, for that matter—when architecture predominated—one must look it up in any encyclopedia under the heading "edification." Germans called a nineteenth-century novel of a young man or woman moving toward maturity a *bildungsroman*—a foundation book in which a young person begins to construct his or her own life, hopefully on a solid foundation. Within this context, to raise a child is to build a building. To edify is to build buildings, but it also refers, in the nineteenth century, to moral education, to the building of character.

In Europe and in America, in the nineteenth century, schools for teaching teachers were called *normal* schools, named after the seventeenth-century template, the *norma,* used for drafting perfect right angles. Being normal is about assuming right angles to the ground, a perfect ninety degrees so that one stands true and tall. Posture reflects attitude, a particular kind of leaning or inclination. In the nineteenth century, the idea of the normal expands to refer for the first time to human behavior. Such language conflates architecture, building, posture, and growing up, as if there were no inherent stability and solidity to the idea of education itself, and it needed to borrow the vocabulary of the most seriously engineered activity—architecture.

In the nineteenth century, as buildings rose higher and higher, architecture more and more appeared to defy gravity. Just at the end of the century, America erected the first skyscrapers in concrete, made possible by a contemporary British invention, around 1824, cement, which gave the requisite strength to concrete so that buildings could reach far into the sky. People could mimic those buildings—standing tall and powerfully straight by gaining bulk and mass and, above all, strength. Many people achieved such stature through weight training, what devotees today call "pumping iron."

An American naturopath named Bernarr MacFadden developed a weight-training program during this period, employing a regimen of both nutrition and exercise for a population that he saw in desperate need of strength and solidity. Aiming his program at both the body and the mind—at physical as well as moral well-being—MacFadden redefined for the common person the idea of the normal. He took the metaphor of the body as edifice quite literally, and called his new movement, in an odd locution, as if everyone served as his or her own biological engineer, bodybuilding. His magazine, *Physical Culture,* carried the slogan "Weakness Is a Sin." MacFadden made the normal person synonymous with the strong person. In times of moral and psychic uncertainty like the nineteenth century, as well as ours, it appears, people need to keep up their strength. To do otherwise, for MacFadden, was to deviate from a path of absolute righteousness. As everyone else began to disappear, he gave his disciples a way to solidly stand their ground. He offered them a way to attain substance and strength. He fortified them—with words and with nutritional supplements.

Nineteenth-century architecture made the idea of solidity starkly visible. It is hard to argue with a building's presence. America, in particular, reached its architectural apogee in one particularly amazing structure. John A. Roebling, a structural engineer, completed the first successful suspension across any appreciable span—1,595 feet—in 1883, with the Brooklyn Bridge. The so-called stiffened suspension bridge—hovering high above the earth, levitating in midair—seemed to be fashioned out of solid metal, but poised in a powerful hypnotic trance. Seen from the side, it could even pass for a bony x-ray of a bridge. The suspension bridge, an image of architecture turned inside out—suspended, dependent—held aloft by . . . what? A few steel cables? Cement piers? Perhaps only faith.

If Gothic architecture characterizes the High Middle Ages, the suspension bridge characterizes the late nineteenth century. The master mason of medieval Britain, the architect, gave way to a new magus of the Industrial Revolution, the structural engineer. The suspension bridge shows itself off in underlying, basic elements—in tensile strength, coefficients of expansion, braided steel cables, the calculus. But what makes Roebling's bridge defy gravity lies in his refinement of a seventeenth-century invention for the building of cathedrals—the cantilever—or as a nineteenth-century book on bridge building more accurately refers to it, "the flying lever."[18] The architectural exuberance of the Brooklyn Bridge hangs in space as a monument to the underlying philosophy of the period—the drive to uncover the essential in virtually everything in the natural world, and in the created world, as well.

But there was another world, too. The bridge also served as a potent symbol for the idea of crossing—in particular, the idea of crossing over to the other side. To find the secret of life, some explorers ventured to that other world where the dead were thought to congregate, and brought back news of eternal life. Séances provided them a bridge. As we shall see, the nineteenth century found other such bridges—out-of-body travel, trances, hypnotic states, and so on. In this sense, we can count all bridges as suspension bridges—suspended between the land of the living and the land of . . . well, no one knew for sure.

TWO | When Death Died

EATH THREW ITS BLANKET of crepe over the country during the Civil War. America turned black—black with mourning, black with despair, black with the most ferocious slaughtering this country—or the world—had ever seen, and which went by that enticingly polite name, the Civil War. But the war proved to be anything but civil. As if the country were in the throes of some nuclear winter, unbelievable numbers of human beings and animals lost their lives. General Grant, not known for hyperbole, described the aftermath of one particular battle, at Shiloh, in an especially apocalyptic way: "I saw an open field . . . so covered with dead that it would have been possible to walk across the clearing, in any direction, stepping on dead bodies, without a foot touching the ground."[1] Grant struggles to get the scene across, but it's difficult given the enormity of what he has witnessed. In his description, Grant reveals that such a staggering amount of death has the power to render human life glaringly insignificant—turning real people into nothing more, in this case, than fleshy stepping stones.

So many men lost their lives that the subject of death overwhelmed most public conversations and news stories, not just during the height of the war but for decades after the war, as well, continuing well into our own times. I have been arguing in this book that attitudes toward death changed dramatically in the nineteenth century. People in the period began grappling with so much death that whatever meaning it had, whatever it fear it held, seemed to be fast fading away. This, just as they began grappling with its opposite, with the vibrancy of life losing its gusto.

James M. McPherson points out, in his review of books on the Civil War dead, that America of the mid-nineteenth century knew death well:

> "Life expectancy at birth was forty years, largely because of an infant and child mortality rate nearly ten times as great as today. Most parents had buried at least one child; few young people reached adulthood without the loss of siblings of cousins. Many husbands grieved for wives who had died in childbirth. . . . The scourge of 'consumption'—tuberculosis—blighted the existence of many in middle age as well as those who had managed to live beyond it."[2]

This country had already confronted an epidemic of death well before the Civil War, in 1832 to be specific, when cholera, with no known cause and no known cure, hit the city of New York. So terrifying had the invasion become that those with means fled the city entirely. Others, less well off, moved into Greenwich Village. Here's the *New York Evening Post*'s description of the mass exodus from the city, on one particular sunny Sunday, in July of that eerie year; keep in mind that the automobile did not yet exist, so this is an exodus by all available means necessary: "The roads, in all directions, were lined with well-filled stagecoaches, livery coaches, private vehicles and equestrians, all panic-struck, fleeing the city, as we may suppose the inhabitants of Pompeii fled when the red lava showered down upon their houses." The *Post* describes but one day, and yet it gives the event grand historic significance—an entire city of some twenty thousand buried under ten feet of ash. New Yorkers experienced real terror.

The cholera outbreak killed 3,515 people in New York City, which at that point had a population of 250,000 people (in 2008 figures, with a population of eight million, over one hundred thousand New Yorkers would have to die, a shocking number considering it is more than thirty times greater than the deaths in the Twin Towers). Like the Great Plague that arrived in London in 1665–1666, cholera hit the lower classes hardest, since they lived in the most crowded conditions, which only spread illnesses easier and faster. And that made the poor and the destitute more of a scourge than they already were. A contemporary civic leader and wealthy merchant named John Pintard, the founder of the New-York Historical Society and the American Bible Society, wrote to his daughter, Eliza, about the attitude of the upper to the lower classes. He told her that the epidemic "is almost exclusively confined to the lower classes of intemperate dissolute and filthy people huddled together like swine in their polluted habitations." In a second letter, Pintard seems to have grown even more angry, as if the poor had hatched the disease themselves as an insidious plot: "Those sickened must be cured or die off, and being chiefly of the very scum of the city, the quicker [their] dispatch the sooner the malady will cease."[3] Pintard saw these people as worthless before they took ill; he could care less if they died, or worse yet, if the authorities had to "dispatch" them.

Slowly, very slowly, the dying abated. But a second wave of cholera hit the city less than twenty years later, in 1849. The population of New York City had by then doubled to five hundred thousand, and the number of dead rose substantially, to over five thousand. The dying had slowed not because the cholera was any less virulent, but because so many poor people had died that crowding had eased a bit.

Across the ocean, cholera hit London hard in 1854. More than Manhattan, London was an amazingly overcrowded city. In fact, within its ninety square miles or so, according to the census of 1851, lived 2.4 million people, making it the most populated city in the entire world. As Steven Johnson points out in his book *The Ghost Map: The Story of London's Most Terrifying Epidemic—and How It Changed Science, Cities, and the Modern World*, "All of those human lives crowded together had an inevitable repercussion: a surge in corpses." He then cites the then-twenty-three-year-old Friedrich Engels, who surveyed the city for his father:

The corpses [of the poor] have no better fate than the carcasses of animals. The pauper burial ground at St Bride's is a piece of open marshland which has been used since Charles II's day and there are heaps of bones all over the place. Every Wednesday the remains of dead paupers are thrown in to a hole which is 14 feet deep. A clergyman gabbles through the burial service and then the grave is filled with loose soil. On the following Wednesday the ground is opened again and this goes on until it is completely full. The whole neighborhood is infected from the dreadful stench.

The stench: Not only did people have to contend with the dead, but they also believed that the smell of putrefying flesh, miasma, could make them seriously ill. That's why municipalities eventually moved graveyards to the outskirts of town, like the burial ground in Islington, which had been designed for three thousand but during the cholera outbreak held an astonishing eighty thousand corpses. An Islington gravedigger, sounding straight out of Shakespeare, describes being "up to my knees in human flesh, jumping on the bodies, so as to cram them in the least possible space at the bottom of the graves, in which fresh bodies were afterwards placed."[4]

The Ghost Map recounts the story of a London physician named John Snow, who finally made the connection between the bacterium *Vibrio cholera* and contaminated water, but not until 1854—not until, that is, tens of thousands of people had died of exposure to cholera. He made his discovery by plotting the outbreaks of cholera on a map of Soho and deducing that all the victims had drawn their water from the same public pump. By itself, that did not solve the mystery, but that a mother had tossed her infected baby's diaper down the well did clinch the case for him. He would have made Sherlock Holmes proud, for at that point it all seemed so elementary.

Categories are like prison beds: Once you have one, it must be filled. The nineteenth century had a category not called simply death, but a degraded death, a death out of all proportion that requires gravediggers to stomp on corpses to make room for more decaying flesh. It is a death that disparages the poor as the cause of all of civilization's ills and woes. In the nineteenth century, death, as a category, opened wide its huge maw and demanded more and more. And somehow the United States in particular willingly satisfied that voracious appetite.

Prisons can fill their beds most efficiently by creating more and more criminals. Filling the beds allows the public to see that everyone is doing his or her job, and thus making the average citizen feel safer. The category of death was so wide and so deep, it took a lot of dying to fill it. And America, as I've said, responded, as if it were just waiting for the right situation. If the world-famous magician and escape artist of the period, Harry Houdini, did not exist, the age would have created another, equally magnificent magician to entertain them. This is dangerous thinking, I know, to suggest that as a people, or as a nation, we could call into being a grand cause to satisfy such dying. It is dangerous to suggest that the age precipitated something like the Civil War because of its erasure of the deep meaning of death. But it almost seems that actually happened. I want to focus in this chapter on the Civil War, but first a peek beyond the war—just a few years—and then back to the war itself.

As the United States started to climb out of its Civil War, the country also began its slow and steady emergence as the world's major superpower. The country moved westward, acquired new blocks of land, and annexed new territories. Ideas and policies that the United States articulated had a remarkable effect in shaping much of the world; people looked to America to find what was in the leading edge, say, of technology and commerce, and now, politics. By century's end we would be at war in the Philippines. We had our eye on new shipping routes. We had to, for the great machinery of the Industrial Revolution hummed loudest in America. One startling result of the emergence of an America constantly on the make is that, in the twenty-first century, with only five percent of the world's population, this country manages to consume an astonishing twenty-five percent of the world's total resources.

Those numbers, so grossly out of proportion, reveal a particular atti-tude—one of absolute certitude if not downright arrogance. For a long time, what America argued politically and pulled off militarily carried enormous weight with a good deal of the world. For a very long time, much of the rest of the world read our policies as dicta, and took our acts as exempla. For roughly one hundred years, from the end of the Civil War to the end of the Vietnam War, America polished its reputation as the world's key imperial power—in both ideas and actions. We have the capacity for backing up what we claim, with money and military might. In every significant way, America invented the idea of the world superpower, just as we helped to demonize a good portion of the East and Middle East.

It's in this country, then, that we begin to see bold moves in the world of technology rolled out on a grand scale—early on with the railroad, and then with photography, cinema, industry, and in most dramatic fashion with warfare. America, in its wealth—in land and money and enterprise—meant change and progress. The technological revolution, to a great extent, occurred in this country. Although it took nearly a century, in the welter of that rapid change, both death and life assumed new meanings. Though not as noticeable at first as in other areas, technology exerted a tremendous effect in this country on those two very basic ideas—life and death.

It's in America that we first hear those fierce debates on "pulling the plug" on a dying patient, on the one hand, and "aborting a fetus" on the other. (The 1925 Scopes trial may represent the first modern attempt at de-veloping legal arguments for the beginning and end points of life, through trying to determine the nature of human essence.) And so in this chapter, I want to look at the radical change in attitude toward living and dying that coalesced in this country around the second greatest upheaval of the nine-teenth century after the Industrial Revolution, the Civil War.

In the nineteenth century, artists and philosophers and scientists all began to raise the same basic question: Who is alive and who is dead, or where do we find that line that separates the living from the dead? The

Civil War added to the blurring of the line: More than at any other time in the nation's history, life felt and looked more like life-in-death. Ordinary citizens turned zombie-like, killing the enemy at point-blank range and then robbing the corpses for loot. And in 1861, when the war began, only the most foolhardy thought it would end any time soon. Moreover, unlike war today, say, in Iraq or Afghanistan—that is, killing in a remote part of the world that we periodically hear about—the Civil War raged on in the American backyard and, in ways that we would find hard to fathom, death's long reach touched nearly every citizen.

In the most obvious way, the soldiers fighting that war came from households close by the battlefields where they suddenly found themselves holding rifles in their young hands. No man got "called up" and then left home for a period of training. Men—sons and husbands and fathers—lay down their hoes and plows on the farm one day, volunteered for military service, and the next morning woke up wearing boots and carrying a canteen and a rifle. They took up arms against folks from their very own country, but who happened to live on the wrong side of the Mason–Dixon line.

Aside from all the outright slaughter, the war also disrupted lives, interrupted marriages, and destroyed families. This war, a monstrous battle of state against state, was immediate; no one had to speechify about sacrificing for something abstract like "the war effort," or "to make the world safe for democracy." In its ability to devastate family and friend and neighbor, the war was close at hand. The president of the United States himself, Abraham Lincoln, instructed the nation that the stakes could not be higher: the continuation of the Republic, the integrity of an idea that had come to be called the United States.

Even if the battles did not take place on or near a family's own farm, any person could look at the war up close in the most grainy detail—in large part on account of the various kinds of fledgling technologies that made for the reproduction of reality: ambrotypes (aptly derived from the Greek word *ambrotos,* "immortal"), tintypes, collotypes, daguerreotypes, amphitypes, melainotypes, ferrotypes, albumen prints, camera obscuras, and those silver prints so familiar to us today. The age of mechanization—in which the machine began to inform virtually every aspect of daily life—had even wormed its way into war, and immediately proved the axiom that any technological change destroys both time and space. For even though many of the battlefields were at some remove from the great majority of Americans, some folks still made their visits to search for loved ones. They also went to spectate. The morgue drew its crowds in Paris, and the battlefields in America drew their own visitors. People in the nineteenth century loved to spectate, especially at death.

Those with the means needed to travel no further than a local gallery to see the war up close in one kind of photographic reproduction or another. And thus, more than collapsing space—take a trip down the road and view the war on a gallery wall—the photograph more effectively destroyed notions of time. By freezing the events of the Civil War, people could gawk at a single moment of violence over and over again. Other technological advances would help shape the conduct of the war, by making killing an act of efficiency, but more than any of those other innovations or inventions, the photograph deeply affected the popular imagination and helped to shape popular opinion, not so much about the war but about death. Most of the Civil War photographs recorded the grim aftermath of one battle or another. In the imaginations of some, the war never ended, just as it had never begun—it just *was*. That new and startling invention, the photograph, made it so.

The father of what we now call photojournalism, and the man who made the Civil War most vivid in the minds of Americans—then and now—is Mathew Brady, principally a portrait photographer, who opened his first studio, in New York, in 1844, followed by others in Washington, D.C. At his major gallery in New York City, he brought home the most graphic evidence of the decimation of war to thousands upon thousands of viewers. Everyday citizens, sometimes far removed from the field of battle, came to stand and stare at scenes of monumental death up close, thanks to Brady and his assistants, who took their equipment out onto the field of battle and captured unfiltered and directly the grisly details of killing.

He chose for his first show several hundred photographs of the war's most bloody battle, and titled it, appropriately and without embellishment, The Dead of Antietam. Mathew Brady opened the show in his Broadway gallery, in October 1862, knowing all too well the truth of things: War meant bloody and horrible death—plain and simple. With the Civil War in particular, the battlefield spilled over with an unimaginable and pervasive amount of the most gory and bloody images of death. People needed to bear witness to all that death; most of them wanted to see it. Like people fascinated with highway accidents, Americans liked to stare at death. They could not avert their eyes. They could not turn away from death.

Brady chose his subject deliberately, for the Battle of Antietam, which had been fought on September 17, 1862, already had, by October, when Brady opened his gallery show, the well-deserved reputation as the most gruesome, bloodiest single day of combat in all of American history. Twenty-three thousand men (and maybe as many horses and mules) lost their lives with even more soldiers suffering serious wounds on that one day, on the field of battle, in Washington County, Maryland. In the over-whelming enormity of its scope, Brady knew, the Battle of Antietam would do more than pique the curiosity of the average American. Antietam went far beyond the pull of any ordinary automobile accident. The sheer extent of the carnage fascinated people, making them realize that ordinary, virtually untrained human beings now had the power to eradicate tens of thousands of other human beings—in a confrontation that need last no more than a simple farmer's workday: sunup to sundown.

Up to that point, the majority of Americans had heard only reports of the war; they had seen only paintings and drawings of various battles. Many, though not all, had followed the course of the war by reading the news. And just as the French went to the morgue, in the heart of Paris, to stare into death's implacable face, so in this country scores upon scores of Americans managed to travel to the most well-known local battle sites to see the war for themselves. They were used to visiting death. Beginning in the 1830s America had undergone a remodeling of its cemeteries that contemporaries called "the cemetery movement." At places like Mount Auburn in Cambridge, Massachusetts, and Green-Wood in Brooklyn, traditional graveyards transformed into large parks, with trees, rolling mounds, and lakes filled with swans. From the 1830s on, photographers sold an enormous number of pictures of these parklike cemeteries, where visitors could come, picnic, and contemplate God. Americans knew their death.

And they knew it better once they visited Brady's gallery (and other local galleries). When they arrived he offered them something shocking: a panoramic and detailed look at the real thing—or more exactly, a picture of the real thing. Americans, who might in other ways have little direct experience of the war, found themselves lingering in Brady's gallery, and conversing with one another about that most fascinating and taboo of subjects, death itself. A *New York Times* reporter offered this eloquent description of Brady's Antietam show:

> We recognize the battlefield as a reality, but it stands as a remote one. It is like a funeral next door. . . . It attracts your attention, but it does not enlist your sympathy. But it is very different when the hearse stops at your own door, and the corpse is carried out over your own threshold . . .

> Mr. Brady has done something to bring home to us the terrible reality and earnestness of war. If he has not brought bodies and laid them in our door-yards and along [our] streets, he has done something very like it.[5]

So Brady gave the people death—but a kind of death they had never before experienced. The Civil War went beyond people's usual experience of the random and sometimes sudden occurrences of death—what the period referred to as "ordinary death"—and allowed them to see the lethality of human beings visiting death on other human beings with colossally devastating results. They got a view of the Civil War as a reprise of Armageddon—as the end of civilization. They witnessed death as something deliberate and calculated, as thoroughly planned and executed. Men literally held in their hands the lives of other men. And in the process, average Americans learned a simple and chilling truth about themselves: They were very good at both creating an enemy—in this case, other Americans—and perhaps even better at wiping that enemy off the face of the earth.

With so many dead in so many places, the idea of death lost a great deal of its menacing power. Photographs turned death into a fashionable subject, just like portraits and landscapes, for study and display. Even without the aid of photographs, however, a great many people in the nineteenth century saw this change in attitude toward death coming from a long ways off. And, as if the change over those years was heading toward one climactic event, the Civil War provided just that right historical moment. It brought together all the knotty issues in its great focusing of death and devastation in the American imagination and psyche. But placing that four-year battle in the category of *war* does not do justice to such a stupefying amount of devastation. Americans bore witness not just to an ordinary war—if such a thing ever does exist. Beginning in 1861, the conduct of war underwent an escalation in kind, an escalation that brought the art of killing into a new kind of modernity. Such marked changes gave a different meaning and shape to death.

Hatred on the battlefield seemed to unleash in the business world a rush of entrepreneurial know-how to find the best ways to totally and completely eradicate the enemy. As in Europe and England, the machine came to dominate American life in hundreds of disparate and unexpected areas—just as the computer has come to dominate our lives today. Instead of acting as an agent to improve the quality of people's day-to-day lives— such was the promise—technology now came to herald new efficiencies in killing. Civilization had turned topsy-turvy and seemingly evil. We had all fallen down Alice's hole in the ground, into a surreal world of our own making.

The war became a surprisingly rich place where mechanical innovation transformed the chaos of killing into a kind of smooth-running, efficient operation. For the first time, the military started holding hands with industry. Of course, at this point in the country's history, 1861, it is difficult to talk about something as specific and nefarious as the military-industrial complex. A much cozier relationship would certainly come to full flower later—but, nonetheless, one can see that partnership developing here.

Two mechanical innovations in particular helped turn the average, poorly trained soldier into an efficient and effective killing machine. The first involved a simple adaptation of machine tooling. Up until 1850, the military provided its soldiers with standard, smoothbore muskets. The soldier fired his musket and hoped to hit something with a ball that most often tracked through the air, for relatively short distances, in an erratic fashion. On top of inaccuracies, the smoothbore musket had a limited range of about one hundred yards. But with an innovation called rifling, which consisted of etching one continuous spiral groove inside the entire length of the barrel, soldiers could fire their muskets not just with remarkably more accuracy but at astonishingly greater distances—up to three hundred yards. Some military historians claim a one-thousand-yard range for those new rifles, the equivalent of ten football fields. But even if that claim falls short of the truth, the military historically has pursued a goal, through advances in technology, of continually increasing the range and firepower of its arsenal of weapons.

That goal begins here, with the Civil War, as soldiers began using a new kind of ammunition called the minié ball, a muzzle-loading bullet named after Claude-Etienne Minié, who had perfected his design in 1840. Which brings us to the second innovation in technology. Minié's initial change was to make the rifle easier to fire by using a ball slightly smaller than the rifle's bore. He next filled each ball with its own gunpowder, making it possible for the soldier to do something revolutionary—to load the rifle at the breech, instead of through the muzzle. Later, he added grooves to the ball and gave it a much more aerodynamic shape, both of which added to the accuracy and carrying power of the projectile and caused it to leave the muzzle of the rifle at much faster speeds than the old-fashioned ball. The percussion cap, invented in England, began appearing in the 1840s. It allowed rifles to be fired in all kinds of weather, even in the rain, something not possible with the older flint system.

Because a soldier no longer had to spend time tamping both the ball and its gunpowder down the muzzle, Minié's new method cut the time for loading and reloading to a fraction of the original, which helped turn the basic and undervalued rifle into an instrument of mass destruction. And because these rifles cost more than the old arms, the North (with more money) had a monopoly on them—much to the great disadvantage of the Confederacy. For the minié ball's speed and caliber, coupled with its rapid spinning motion through the air, shocked the South by ripping through flesh and causing the most jagged and gaping wounds, leaving field surgeons, many times, to amputate limbs rather than trying to close gaping wounds and stanch bleeding. The war turned into a horror show.

This new bullet that could fire great distances, a seemingly simple technological change, reverberated throughout the century. Innovations in the act of killing provided a new and powerful impetus to the great technological race. Consider the following example: Hiram Stevens Maxim, born in Sangerville, Maine, in 1840, loved to tinker, making various gadgets. For him, he said, invention and innovation meant only play and amusement; he had no bold ambitions. And although he had very little formal education, that did not seem to hold him back. By 1878, for example, he rose from journeyman assistant in the United States Electric Lighting Company, Edison's main rival, to become chief engineer. In 1881, the company sent him to Paris for an exhibition of new electrical products.

There, someone said to him, Maxim reports, "If you wanted to make a lot of money invent something that will enable these Europeans to cut each other's throats with greater facility."[6] Use your technological know-how, that is, for killing. An entrepreneur enticed Maxim to come to England to improve on the Gatling gun, which needed to be turned by hand. In 1883, Maxim received a patent for an automatic machine gun, water-cooled and fed, automatically, by its own belts of ammunition.

Technological change on the battlefield reverberated throughout the entirety of the next two centuries: Military people especially wanted to kill faster, more thoroughly, and always more efficiently. Total and complete eradication would be the best thing possible, and from greater and greater distances. Paul Virilio, in his book *Speed and Politics,* summarizes the change in a single sentence: "Territory has lost its significance in favor of the projectile." He adds: "In fact, *the strategic value of the non-place of speed has definitively supplanted that of place,* and the question of possession of Time has revived that of territorial appropriation."

Weapons systems since World War II, Virilio goes on to argue, "have created an aesthetics of disappearance, for the arms race is only 'the arming of the race' toward the end of the world as distance, in other words as a field of action." Cannons on battleships fire their missiles from distances of several miles. Fighter planes and bombers do not need to occupy territory; "shock and awe" is meant to destroy the enemy fast. Drones over Baghdad are operated by ghost pilots who move a mouse over seven thousand miles away, from inside a bunker in Las Vegas, Nevada.

As technology comes more and more to dominate warfare, that disappearance to which Virilio alludes has come to include human beings themselves. With the military deciding to use fewer and fewer pilots and relying more and more on drones, along with its increasing use of robots to perform tasks like dismantling improvised explosive devices and destroying bunkers, the military has already announced that it no longer needs (or wants) so many able bodies. Wounded and dead soldiers just bring bad press, and the military can ill afford that. This country went from a draft in Vietnam to a volunteer military in Iraq, and will perhaps proceed to a ghost military in the next war.

That one technological innovation, the new minié ball, greatly contributed to the astronomic numbers of wounded, near dead, and dead that littered the battlefields in the Civil War. Up to 1840 or 1850, say, the word *bullet* referred to a small round ball of lead. After that time, *bullet* referred to Minié's innovation, that conical slug with which even young children are all too familiar. But beyond the technological horror, beyond all the killing and the wholesale industry of killing, lay that one strange and fundamental fact, a fact that stood well outside the grasp of technology: This devastating war pitted American against American.

The killing ground went on for four long and trying years. During that time, the average American could quite easily get the feeling that nearly every man—young and old—in the country was fast passing away. Translated into today's figures, to match the two percent of the population that died in the Civil War, over six million Americans would have to lose their lives on the battlefield. In the South, alone, an astonishing twenty percent of white males—one out of every five—of military age lost their lives.

Six million represents a staggering number—three-fourths of the population of New York City, or over twice the population of Chicago. Imagine every person in Los Angeles dying in some protracted battle. It would be unimaginable, shocking, an absolute and utter disaster. The government would perhaps fall into chaos. Cries of the end of the world would be heard. Every person in the country would mobilize, emotionally and perhaps physically, behind one side or the other. No one does such a thing to us. We will not take it. But look, someone would eventually point out, we are delivering this horror to each other. In proportionate numbers, and in that scenario, that's exactly what happened in this country.

The young nation had such a huge number of heroic dead that the United States War Department created, for the first time, in 1863, a

Soldiers' National Cemetery, at Gettysburg, Pennsylvania. Gettysburg, a battle that lasted but three days, from July 1 to July 3, 1863, reached its climax on the third, when over twelve thousand Confederate soldiers attacked the Union lines. Even though the assault—named for its general, George Pickett—made the deepest incursion of the war into Northern territory, the eventual devastation surpasses the limits of the imagination. The historian Drew Gilpin Faust reflects on the killing in terms as gross as its subject: "By July 4, an estimated six million pounds of human and animal carcasses lay strewn across the field in the summer heat, and a town of 2,400 grappled with 22,000 wounded who remained alive but in desperate condition."[7] Claude-Etienne Minié had triumphed. Able bodies turned into bloated corpses, soldiers decayed into mere carcasses, and flesh got measured in pounds. Where had all the people gone?

All that putrefying flesh turned the town of Gettysburg, in the most bizarre fashion, into something of a tourist attraction—an open-air morgue— as people from neighboring communities and distant towns came to see and touch the ground where so much slaughter had taken place. They came to hold clods of hallowed dirt in their hands and to sit on the ground, hold their picnics, and just contemplate the enormity of death. The Gettysburg cemetery held 3,512 Union soldiers. Nearly half of the 303,536 Union soldiers buried in national cemeteries lie in graves marked UNKNOWN.[8]

On November 19, 1863, those who came to that plot of ground had the great privilege of hearing one of history's most memorable speeches from the president of the Republic, Abraham Lincoln, who that day commemorated the new cemetery. He delivered his address not so much to the assembled group but to every person alive in this young country—North and South alike. He spoke elegantly, and he spoke to make their hearts whole. He delivered one of the greatest political speeches we have.

Every schoolchild knows about the Gettysburg Address; some can even recite lines (beyond the famous opening, "Four score and seven years") from that short speech from memory. Few if any, however, can tell why

Lincoln delivered it. Drew Gilpin Faust observes about that roughly two-minute address, "The ceremony and the address that historian Gary Wills has argued 'reset America' signaled the beginning of a new significance for the dead in public life." The speech did, I believe, remake America, but it did not signal a new significance for the dead, unless one counts the loss of significance as something new. In my estimation, Lincoln uses the dead in the service of what he believed constituted a much larger issue—the preservation of the nation. Standing knee-deep in spilled blood, Lincoln really talked around the atrocity that was the Battle of Gettysburg.

In that 272-word speech, Lincoln used the word *dead* three times. He used the word *men* twice, the term *honored dead* once, the indirect reference *those* once, and the indirect referent *they* three times. By contrast, Lincoln used the very specific noun *nation* some five times. To this president, much more important than the valor of the men who died on the battlefield was the rebirth of the nation. The dead cannot rise; the nation can. And thus the Gettysburg Address uses as its structure the life cycle: Lincoln begins by invoking the fathers who brought forth this nation, and he ends with a new freedom born in this nation under God, only to be reborn on the battlefield under generals.

We should notice that Lincoln does not draw on the phrase "founding fathers," already in use, but uses, instead, the more broadly construed word, "fathers." Politicians and writers used the word *fathers* to refer to the founding fathers, but Lincoln uses it strategically here, for he needs to make a crucial point. Genealogy, continuity, responsibility—those become the key ingredients and actors on this piece of hallowed land, not some aristocratic and more abstracted notion of the founding fathers. Lincoln could be talking about *your* father, *my* father: We are all in this together. This is our nation. It will go on. It *must* go on. Death is not an impediment to progress. We can build cemeteries to house the dead. We can say our prayers, deliver our very short addresses, and then we must move on.

In between those two births—the nation and the freedom of the new nation—lies the death of hundreds of thousands of men; and Lincoln for the most part lets this fact go by without very much mention—certainly without focusing on the gritty details. Even though every soul present that day knew the terrible death toll, death took a holiday during the Gettysburg Address. It is fair to say that in order for Lincoln to talk about the rebirth of the nation, something had to die; and it seems clear to me that on that brisk fall afternoon, before a rapt audience, death died.

Senator Charles Sumner remarked that Lincoln's speech was more important than the battle; that history would remember the Gettysburg Address long after it had forgotten Gettysburg. And so Lincoln gave the world an important transitional speech. He gave his country a speech that accorded the idea of men dying in great numbers a secondary or tertiary place to the ultimate importance of the nation itself. Men would have to sacrifice themselves—and it did not matter much which ones they were—to the greater good, which in this case was freedom or democracy or republican values, or any number of other politically articulated and abstract goals. How ironic that the man who delivered that speech would himself soon die, but that the nation would of course continue. (The king is dead; long live the king.) In a chilling reversal, in a very short speech, Lincoln managed to turn death into an abstraction and the idea of the nation into something specific and tangible. It's as if his speech had become as streamlined as combat on the battlefield.

Death surrounded the president; it would not let him go. Death seeped into the life of every person, young and old, alive in the country at that time. But Lincoln contained all that death within a much larger issue, and he made it almost vanish. That was his rhetorical strategy. For in November 1863, the end of the war was still nowhere in sight, and he had to assure his audience that "government of the people, by the people, for the people, shall not perish from the earth." Both war and death extended far beyond the horizon of anyone's imagination. Lincoln may have "reset America," as Gary Wills suggests, but he did it, for better or worse, by sacrificing American deaths to the American republic. After nearly three years of an amazingly grueling war, Lincoln seemed to tire of death, to pass it by in favor of something much more sacred: the survival of a unified republic. He was, after all, the president of the United States.

Not everyone shared Lincoln's views about this country. William James, in a speech honoring the Civil War dead, spent time honoring individual people, including his own brothers. But he refused to praise the war itself. He simply did not believe in war. William James's brother, Wilkie, had died of battle wounds suffered during the war. Nations find their salvation in pursuing avenues other than war, James declared in a speech he delivered in 1864 (his third year at Harvard), through "acts without external picturesqueness; by speaking, writing, voting reasonably; by smiting corruption swiftly; by good temper between parties; by the people knowing true men when they see them, preferring them as leaders to rabid partisans and empty quacks."

We can see the values that Lincoln articulated in his speech reflected in the radical architectural changes of the cemetery he had come to dedicate. Beginning with Gettysburg, national cemeteries differed from all other military burial places by according to each and every grave the very same importance. Unlike at other military cemeteries, a visitor could discern no difference in rank in the individual plots; no grave stood out in importance from any other ones. Death had not only entered the national consciousness; it had now taken over as a great leveler, smoothing out those differences in rank and identity, background, and even hometown or state that loom so large on the field of battle. Death had thrown a true blanket of crepe not just over the country but over the collective imagination. Death was the ultimate unifying sacrifice: No one's passing, regardless of rank or background, should trump anyone else's.

But even with a capacity for holding over three thousand dead souls, Gettysburg proved insufficient for the countless number of soldiers who lost their lives during the more than four years of the Civil War. So many soldiers lost their lives that Lincoln found himself presiding over the inauguration of five separate national cemeteries. By 1871, death—elevated and consecrated death—had become so commonplace that Congress had authorized an astonishing seventy-four national cemeteries. (From 1872 to 2007—over the next 135 years, that is—the country consecrated only sixty-five more. One implication here: Death shifted away from our own military and, due to our continual technological advances—the snappy military-industrial complex—hit the enemy and civilians alike with much more force, resulting in a whole new vocabulary, including "friendly fire," "collateral damage," "surgical strikes," and the especially annoying "human error" or "command error.")

Union soldiers told of routinely tripping over bodies as they slogged their way across the battlefield. Thousands upon thousands of corpses lay bloated and decaying in the mud, their skin gradually giving up its fleshy tones and turning a strange shade of blue and then, perhaps even more disturbing and certainly shocking for the great majority of white people in the United States, ending up a frighteningly deep black. Witness this revealing testimony from a Northern soldier at Gettysburg: "The faces of the dead, as a general rule, had turned black—not a purplish discoloration, such as I had imagined in reading of the 'blackened corpses' so often mentioned in descriptions of battlegrounds, but a deep bluish *black*, giving to a corpse with black hair the appearance of a negro."[10]

If people did not get the point about the enormity of death on the battlefield of that one place, Gettysburg, the French artist Paul Philippoteaux let them have it up very close. Over twenty years after the battle, in 1884, he and a team of assistants painted four versions of Pickett's Charge, the Confederate general George Pickett's attack against Union troops, on a 360-degree cyclorama. Of massive size, the cyclorama paintings stretched longer than a football field and towered into the air fifty feet or more. These paintings, the largest ever done in America, enjoyed amazing popularity in this country and in England and were displaced only by a much more powerful and arresting screen, the one for motion pictures.

Typically, the artist painted the scene with oil on a canvas that totally encircled the viewer, and which curved inward to heighten the illusion of reality. Philippoteaux made some of the figures life-sized. Auditoriums held special showings of cycloramas, where the audience stood on a platform in the middle of the action. On such a scale, the observer can almost count each of the twenty thousand or so troopers, both North and South, standing toe to toe and killing each other. One can see in minute detail bodies and body parts lying strewn about; some soldiers are burying their compatriots, and still others lie on the ground bleeding and dying. It is a huge and ghastly scene of outright chaos and mayhem.

The total number of the dead on the battlefields of the Civil War absolutely staggers the imagination. As I said earlier, Americans would find it hard if not impossible, today, to cope with such wholesale and seemingly rampant devastation, particularly on the most familiar soil imaginable, in their own country. Recall the level of public outrage that followed the attack of the Twin Towers in New York City, on September 11, 2001, when nearly three thousand people perished. Beyond that, recall the Bush administration's preemptive retaliation, attacking both Afghanistan and Iraq. The numbers for the Civil War dead—over 620,000—total over two hundred times as many dead as those nearly three thousand Americans who lost their lives in Manhattan. As Faust points out:

> The number of soldiers who died between 1861 and 1865, an estimated 620,000, is approximately equal to the total American fatalities in the Revolution, the War of 1812, the Mexican War, the Spanish-American War, World War I, World War II, and the Korean War combined. The Civil War's rate of death, its incidence in comparison with the size of the American population, was six times that of World War II. A similar rate, about 2 percent, in the United States today would mean six million fatalities. As the new southern nation struggled for survival against a wealthier and more populous enemy,

its death toll reflected the disproportionate strains on its human capital. Confederate men died at a rate three times that of their Yankee counterparts; one in five white southern men of military age did not survive the Civil War.[11]

The rampage of death greatly affected the collective imagination; it changed attitudes toward the humanness of human beings. Men on the battlefield came to describe dead human beings as "putrefied meat, not so much killed as slaughtered." A soldier who stepped on a dead man's leg remembered it not as a person's leg, but as "a piece of pickled pork—hard and yet fleshy."[12] A Union soldier described Antietam a week after the killing stopped: "The dead were almost wholly unburied [and] stretched along, in one straight line, ready for interment, at least a thousand blackened bloated corpses with blood and gas protruding from every orifice, and maggots holding high carnival over their heads."[13]

The fact that there were almost as many dead bodies lying on battlefields as living soldiers standing on them reinforced such seemingly callous attitudes toward human beings. Bodies lay everywhere, and to prevent those hundreds of thousands of corpses from decaying beyond all recognition on the battlefield required new technologies of recovery. Undertakers went through professional training, and funeral homes, certified by various municipal agencies, sprang up all over the East Coast. Much of this new mobilization in the name of death came about because it took such an extremely long time for workers to collect, identify, and remove the hundreds of thousands of bodies from the scores of places where they had fallen.

As it had helped so much with creating the dead, so technology now stepped in on the other side of war, to aid in the removing of the fallen. Both sides of combat—the killing and the interring—underwent wholesale revision in the movement toward modern warfare. Here, as we come face to face with the technology of preserving the flesh, the professional serves to repeal, for the family, for loved ones, the awful and final sentence of death. Technological innovation attempted, in a bizarre way, to erase the gruesome realities of such methodical killing. Such a promise, for instance, lives at the heart of the newly improved and utterly necessary technology of embalming. Through artistic mastery, the embalmer seems to say that the man laid out on the slab, looking like just so much meat, is only peacefully asleep. I beg you, do not think of your son or husband as existing no more. He is merely resting, just waiting in peaceful repose to sally forth into heaven.

To get those hundreds of thousands of bodies back home in some reasonable state of wholeness meant returning them to their places of rest as fast as possible. At odds with that goal, however, to slow down the process of decay—once again, technology responsible for the collapsing of time—physicians tried all kinds of new embalming fluids that they could administer while still in the field. By themselves, however, all the fluids proved insufficient (formaldehyde did not come on the market until 1867), which prompted the reliance on further technological innovation. In this case, entrepreneurs borrowed the technology from the meatpacking industry, which used refrigerated boxcars to ship dressed cattle from, say, Chicago to places in Missouri and farther west. Driving cattle overland meant that the animals would shed precious weight and take even more precious time to get to the slaughterhouses. And so the Chicago meatpacker Gustavus Swift developed these new "reefer" cars, in the 1840s, to take his dressed cut meats to distant markets, where sides of meat arrived much faster and in much fresher condition. Through his adaptation of new refrigeration methods, Swift helped usher in the age of cheap beef. (Jacob Perkins, born in Massachusetts, and who eventually held some nineteen separate American patents, developed the first practical refrigeration machine in 1834.)

On the battlefield, the same technology that resulted in cold storage, modified for human beings, took hold fast. The new device went by the rather gory name of the icebox coffin, a refrigerated casket designed to keep corpses cold so they would remain intact and, much more important, recognizable as they made their sometimes long journeys back home.[14] Surely, some people must have noticed the comparison of dead bodies with dressed beef, one more instance in the slow draining away of human essence. And so, to soften that demeaning psychological blow, entrepreneurs began marketing those portable refrigerated coffins under a more palatable (and commercial) name, transportation cases. Advertisements boasted that the new transportation cases could "Preserve the Body in a natural and perfect condition . . . for any distance or length of time."[15]

Working outside the world of technology, philanthropic organizations inaugurated a series of "sanitary commissions," through whose auspices thousands of volunteers "in the field assumed care of hospital graveyards and registries of death [while] others worked to arrange for burials in the aftermath of battle; still others assisted families in locating lost loved ones and providing for their shipment home."[16] Civilians, too, roamed the battlefields, curious to see the great numbers of dead, but also to help in identifying loved ones lost in battle, and to help with burials as well. It is difficult to separate searching for loved ones on the battlefield from mere spectating about death, a pastime that we have seen taking place in other conditions, in other countries. Maybe the two activities—searching and spectating—can never be made discrete.

In the nineteenth century, death and dying quickly drift to that dividing line of dead *and* alive. In the rush to rid the battlefield of its dead, tales—or what we sometimes today call urban legends—circulated of soldiers finding themselves buried prematurely; and of desperate men suddenly and eerily screaming and clawing to get out of their suffocating prisons as their coffins were being shipped back home. Some of those stories were no doubt fueled by a genre of gothic literature made popular in the 1840s by that premier author of the maudlin and the macabre, Edgar Allan Poe. Poe had a morbid fascination with characters so evil and perverse, they routinely entombed their rivals while the latter were still alive, a calamity that occurred often enough in the period for it to have its own name, "living inhumation." Poe made those sinister killers into the heroes of several works, most graphically present in stories like "The Premature Burial," "The Fall of the House of Usher," and "The Cask of Amontillado."

The unnamed narrator of "The Premature Burial," to take just one story, believes he has been buried alive, and narrates the story from inside his coffin. Adopting the tone and demeanor of a university scholar, the narrator informs the reader that "to be buried while alive is, beyond question, the most terrific of these extremes which has ever fallen to the lot of mere mortality. That it has frequently, very frequently, so fallen will scarcely be denied by those who think." The narrator's own profound fear of being buried alive has been intensified, in great part, because of a malady from which he has greatly suffered his entire life, "attacks of the singular distraction which physicians have agreed to term catalepsy."

The malady causes the narrator to fall into unpredictable, deathlike trances—into what he terms a "hemi-syncope, or half swoon"—sometimes for days at a time, so that he resembles one who has died. He has a great fear that, during one of these spells, he might be mistaken for dead and so buried alive. As the narrator describes his strange and chilling condition, he seems at the same time to describe the spirit of the age:

> The boundaries which divide Life from Death, are at best shadowy and vague. Who shall say where the one ends, and where the other begins? We know that there are diseases in which occur total cessations of all the apparent functions of vitality, and yet in which these cessations are merely suspensions, properly so called. They are only temporary pauses in the incomprehensible mechanism. A certain period elapses, and some unseen mysterious principle again sets in motion the magic pinions and the wizard wheels. The silver cord was not forever loosed, nor the golden bowl irreparably broken.

And then Poe ends this line of reasoning with the key question for him, and a line that reverberates all through the nineteenth century: "But where, meantime, was the soul?"

Enough people took those stories of premature burial seriously enough for the period to coin a new word, *taphophobia,* which translates literally as "fear of the grave," but more figuratively as "fear of being buried alive." One well-known American funeral director, T. M. Montgomery, reported that "nearly two percent of those [bodies he had] exhumed were no doubt victims of suspended animation."[11] Families paid Montgomery, and funeral directors like him, to dig up bodies on the battlefield for reburial in family plots or in a national cemetery. The nineteenth century was a time of wholesale exhumation of bodies—either for the reasons I just mentioned, or for sale to medical students for experiments. Body snatching grew into a large and thriving business.

The New York Times also seems to have taken living inhumation quite seriously, for in 1899 the newspaper of record reported on a bill—introduced by the state assembly of New York—designed to prevent premature burial: "No body shall be received unless a statement on the part of the attending physician or Coroner, whether he has found the following signs of death or not, is with it." The bill then goes on to list the five undeniable signs of death, emphasizing the most obvious and fleshy of those signs, the decomposition of the body.

Prominent Europeans who found themselves stricken with severe cases of taphophobia joined the Society for the Prevention of People Being Buried Alive, in large numbers, in order to protect themselves. They wrote wills that contained fairly wild clauses as preventions against premature burial. Some members demanded that, upon their seeming death, some disinterested person must cut their heads off, or pierce their hearts with a stake, or dismember them, or drain all the blood from their bodies. Some wanted crowbars and axes placed inside their coffins; some wanted a pipe installed that would lead from inside their coffin aboveground, so that the one entombed could command the attention of those hanging around outside.

The United States Patent Office approved nineteenth-century inventions designed to make such a profoundly macabre mistake impossible.

They went by their commercial names "safety coffins" or "security coffins," and typically involved nothing more than a string that ran from the inside of the coffin to an aboveground bell, so that the not-so-deceased could signal his or her continuing connection to this world. Some linguists believe that the phrases "saved by the bell" and "dead ringer" come from these patented safety devices.

In Poe's "Premature Burial," the narrator rigs his family's tomb with one of those hell's bells for easy exit. He also remodels the family tomb with the most elaborate mechanisms, all with the aim of opening the vault with ease from inside:

> The slightest pressure upon a long lever that extended far into the tomb would cause the iron portals to fly back. There were arrangements for the free admission of air and light, and convenient receptacles for food and water, within immediate reach of the coffin intended for my reception. This coffin was warmly and softly padded, and was provided with a lid, fashioned upon the principle of the vault-door, with the addition of springs so contrived that the feeblest movement of the body would be sufficient to set it at liberty.

Nineteenth-century physicians evidently did not possess great skill at determining if a person had actually died. Pulses, they believed, were unreliable indicators; temperature offered no sure gauge. Many of them took as the safest sign of death the odor of decaying flesh—what we commonly refer to as putrefaction—which placed those physicians in opposition, of course, with the desire of families to receive their loved ones back home quickly. In Austria and Germany, physicians relied so extensively on putrefaction as a test of certain death that funeral homes built special places called *leichenhäuser,* or waiting rooms, which they kept at fairly warm temperatures. Funeral directors placed the recently deceased in those rooms until the corpses began to rot, and of course to smell—sometimes, of course, quite badly. When a body really began to stink, morticians knew they could then safely put the body in the ground.

One of the characters in Mark Twain's *Life on the Mississippi*, a book that he published in 1883, visits one of those *leichenhäuser* and gets a job there as a night watchman. (The great rise in body snatching necessitated the use of guards to watch over the corpses.) One night, after working the job for a year, with no interruptions in his routine, he receives a fright that nearly kills him:

> I was sitting all alone in the watch-room, one gusty winter's night, chilled, numb, comfortless; drowsing gradually into unconsciousness; the sobbing of the wind and the slamming of distant shutters falling fainter and fainter upon my dulling ear each moment, when sharp and suddenly that dead-bell rang out a bloody-curdling alarum over my head! The shock of it nearly paralyzed me; for it was the first time I had ever heard it.

> I gathered myself together and flew to the corpse-room. About midway down the outside rank, a shrouded figure was sitting upright, wagging its head slowly from one side to the other—a grisly spectacle! Its side was toward me. I hurried to it and peered into its face.

Notice how Twain sets up the reader: The guard character slowly loses consciousness—he is chilled and numb, almost paralyzed at one point in the narrative. He is still and lifeless, without sensation, as Twain nearly turns him into a corpse. The wind, on the other hand, comes alive: It sobs. As for the real corpse, someone, it turns out, whom the guard knows from several chapters earlier in the story—it suddenly rises from the dead, or not so dead, or never dead. One does not know what category in which to place him. Twain's point is that not very much, really, separates the two states, living and dead, and that we might do well to see them, as Poe surely did, more as states along a continuum, rather than as discrete categories. In this regard, Twain the trickster, acting as Twain the philosopher, very much captures the attitude of the period, which viewed living as a kind of suspended animation between birth and earth.

The stench of putrefying flesh announced the certainty of death, making the job of the undertaker so much easier, for a truly putrid smell eliminated all doubt about the end of life. While putrefaction took place over a period of time, family members, recall, wanted the return of their loved ones fast—now! Those two timetables played themselves out in stark opposition to each other. And so one reads descriptions from the battlefield like the following: "The dead and the dying actually stink upon the hills."[18] And a Union surgeon declares, "The stench arising from [the countless dead bodies was] such as to breed a pestilence."[19] Faust herself claims that "for a radius of miles, the 'mephitic effluvia' caused by rotting bodies ensured that even if the dead were out of sight, they could not be out of mind."[20]

And so it's possible to believe that amid all the other weirdness about death and near death and premature death, at least with some of the corpses, military officials deliberately allowed bodies to decay on the battlefield so as to preclude any mistakes. In a period marked by ghosts and specters and a movement called spiritualism, the invisible held great significance and meaning. Bear in mind Marx's dictum that "all that is solid melts into air." "All that is solid": Even death in this period ultimately turns invisible, ghostly—but nonetheless present, definitely present, powerfully present, even though the bodies have long since gone. That is, the smell of death—death's ghost, in a very real sense—lingers long after the bodies have been removed.

Mothers and fathers, wives and brothers, sisters and daughters—all the family members and relatives—wanted desperately to see their loved ones one more time. For them, removing the bodies from the battlefield with all due speed was of paramount importance. They needed to know that, yes, that unidentified body was once *my* living and breathing husband or son. This, in great part because nearly forty percent of Union and Confederate soldiers died anonymously and got buried by fellow soldiers in mass graves. Identifying the dead, as one might imagine, most often proved both a complicated and daunting task: Soldiers did not carry identification, except for the introduction in the Civil War of what in World War I would come to be called *dog tags*. But serial numbers oftentimes proved little help; soldiers typically lost them in the heat of battle, or passed them on to buddies to bring back home in the event they died. Reports from other soldiers on the field about the death of a loved one also proved not very useful and certainly not conclusive. For good reason, the notion of the Unknown Soldier dates from this time.

The open casket, the viewing, the visual inspection of the body, were all absolutely essential clues to making death final, but such steps accomplished much more. Family members needed to know in what state of mind—with what expression on the face, that is—their loved one left this earth. Such concentration on detail made up an important part of what the period called the "good death"—how the person died would determine how he or she would take up residence in the hereafter. The good death meant an easy death, one in which a person passed over without pain or much suffering—a true blessing from Providence. Religious leaders encouraged people to adopt a pattern of good behavior their entire lives if they desired a holy way of dying.

Dying as an art characterized the earliest years of the nineteenth century. As Shai J. Lavi points out in his book, *The Modern Art of Dying: A History of Euthanasia in the United States,* "Methodists, the largest organized religious community in early nineteenth-century America, taught Americans how to die. More than any other religious group, Methodists were concerned throughout life with forming the proper disposition regarding death. They would gather around the deathbeds of neighbors and relatives to view the final departure and to meticulously document the hour of death." Lavi goes on to point out that the Methodists expected the dying person to face the final hours "like a fearless soldier ready to die a triumphant death. It is precisely this way of dying that the most celebrated of all New England Puritans, Cotton Mather, termed 'euthanasia.'"

Christian leaders characterized the manner of one's dying as an art and, from the fifteenth century on, collected the precepts of the good death under the rubric of the *Ars Moriendi* ("the art of dying"). The *Ars Moriendi* became especially popular during the Black Death of the fifteenth century, and underwent a revival in the opening years of the nineteenth century. In just the way the Boy Scout manual, in the first decade of the twentieth century, would offer precepts to young people on how to live a moral life, so these little books on the art of dying acted as handbooks, as sourcebooks where one could find rules of decorum and behavior on facing the inevitability of one's final hours. By the time of the Civil War—that is, by mid-century—the *Ars Moriendi* had faded away, replaced by the autonomous and secular work of the embalmer and the other professionals associated with funereal services in general, and those who specialized not in the art of dying, but in the art of death—the morticians.

What a change this was, what a great handing over of one's autonomy and soul and character to the new cadre of technicians. The Methodists spent time recording deathbed experiences, which they published for the family of the departed and which they titled "biographies." For that's what they were, the *bios,* the authentic life of the person in his or her final hours. Friends and neighbors listened for last words, which revealed the state of the soul more truthfully and more forcefully than any other sentences the dying person had ever uttered in his or her lifetime. "People believed final words to be the truth," Faust writes, "both because they thought that a dying person could no longer have any earthly motivation to lie, and because those about to meet their maker would not want to expire bearing false witness. As sermonizers North and South reminded their congregations: 'A death-bed's a detector of the heart.'"[21]

By mid-century the practice had stopped—the stories gone, the telling of the tales over and done. The religious person at the side of the bed was replaced by the physician. This perhaps inevitable slide into the medicalization of death is a part of what the philosopher Heidegger means when he talks about the decline of art and the rise of technology in the modern world, or what Shai J. Lavi calls the "expanding technical search for mastery over death."

Some Christian theologians believed that the final expression on the face revealed the state of the person's conscience at that critical moment of death. And in the strong evangelical reach of the nineteenth century—forty percent claimed such affiliations—people entered heaven in the same way they exited life. Beyond any consideration of the *Ars Moriendi,* people achieved an everlasting life predicated on the kind of actual life they had pursued on Earth. And so facial expressions, attitudes, posture—a whole range of gestures and emotions—factored into a person's smooth transition into a blessed and eternal life. Thus the key question: How did the soldier—*my* soldier—actually die? For that final expression offered a clue to what kind of paradise the departed might expect. Such was the price of solace during those most torturous of times.

Embalmers, of course, knew that families desired a countenance of tranquil acceptance on the faces of their departed loved ones, and most decidedly not one of anguish or revenge. Expressions that smacked of rage or anger—or even what might be deemed discontent—did not ensure an easy entrance into heaven and, in fact, tended to foreclose on an eternal life in the hereafter. Families needed to see expressions of peace and repose, the kind of beatified countenance associated with a quiet and restful sleep.

Such expressions of ease had side benefits, as well. As Shakespeare put it, sleep was just death's second self—life and death collapsing onto each other. And thus, according to Gilpin Faust, "to contemplate one's husband, father, or son in a state of seemingly sleeplike repose was a means of resisting death's terror—and even, to a degree, its reality; it offered a way of blurring the boundary between life and death." As in life so in death, in the nineteenth century—no one quite able, no one quite willing, to point to that line that separated life from death.

The dead hardly ever come home from war. And when they do, they certainly have been drained of all humanness. This extends far beyond the Civil War. Witness the Vietnam War, where young men and women came home in what looked like large Hefty sacks, called body bags. In the first Gulf War, the military sent the dead home in the gruesome-sounding "human remains pouches." And in the Iraq and Afghanistan wars, the dead never came home. Well, the American public was never allowed to see them return because the Pentagon had adopted a new policy of forbidding news photographers to take pictures of flag-draped coffins. The president argued this policy out of respect for the families of the dead soldiers. Clearly, the Bush administration followed a consistent policy of disregarding actual deaths in battle. Unlike many other presidents during times of war, this president did not attend soldiers' funerals. Family members accused the administration of treating their dead sons and daughters, their husbands and wives, as if they were invisible.

So pervasive had death become during the Civil War that entrepreneurs could capitalize on its nervy presence. On the most fancy shopping boulevards of Manhattan and Philadelphia, and in other cities on the East Coast, as well, stores opened to meet the needs of the many widows that the war had produced. As with any sensible capitalistic scheme, stores catered to their clientele's needs, and in this case shop owners managed to design a lively business in death by offering smart costumes to match the level of grief of any woman, so long as she could afford it. On the racks of these mourning stores, a widow might find the blackest of clothes—as black as the corpses themselves—which high-society women in "heavy or deepest mourning" would deem appropriate for their parties or teas or social gatherings.

But those shops, eager to cover all needs, also carried an assortment of garments in mauve and pale lavender for those a step below "heavy mourning," what the period called "full mourning"; and a very few articles trimmed in white for those below that, in the mildest throes of only "half mourning." Store clerks served as elementary bereavement counselors, able to assess a widow's proper level of grief and to offer the proper costume for that emotional stage.

Imagine walking down Fifth Avenue today and seeing window displays devoted solely to death, including examples of the startling handiwork of the many embalmers who had opened thriving businesses after the start of the war. We would find such portals into death appalling, a publicity stunt, one of those cynical moves on the part of some hip young window dresser to pull the unsuspecting shopper up short. But that's just what a fancy shop like Lord and Taylor showed in 1863, yards and yards of black crepe, fashionably rendered into elegant costumes for mourning. We have all but forgotten the names of those outfits now, but they sold fantastically well in the years of the Civil War: black crepe grenadines, black balzarines, black bayadere *barèges,* black *barèges,* black *barège* hernani, summer bombazines, mourning silks, *barège* shawls, grenadine veils, English crepes and veils, collars, sleeves, and on and on.

One can only wonder, today, what wearing those costumes actually meant. Clearly, the clientele consisted solely of wealthy widows. (Men, too, in mourning wore black, but confined their expression of grief to a black armband or a ribbon of black crepe pinned to a suit jacket.) But even so, what did it mean to walk around society with such visible displays of grief? What were those costumes meant to convey to the rest of the public, including those widows too poor to afford such outward symbols of inner grief? Perhaps those costumes did the work of real grief; after all, churches and funeral parlors prescribed set times for mourning—one week for a child, one month for a loved one, and so on.

But, beyond matters of time, could it be that those mourning outfits actually rendered it unnecessary to pass through real and deeply felt grief, that the clothes signaled it all, and that these rituals of death actually provided another example of the falling away of the importance of immediate, lived experiences? Is a black getup the equivalent of a photograph of death, all color drained away to form a shadow of the real thing? Did these women parade the streets, unknowingly, as images? Such conditions would jibe perfectly with the changes we have seen in this period toward the human being. It was as if the country suddenly had been saddled with a department of grief, and had decided to place Coco Chanel in charge.

If the theology of the period dictated that soldiers had to face their final moment with dignity and calm—that is, with just the correct and appropriate expression—then what about the obligations of the living? If meaning had been drained from death, what meaning remained for those who lived? In certain ways, those mourning costumes dictated the proper attitude toward death: Anyone could tell by the widow's garb that she had fulfilled her obligation and addressed death in the correct, sufficient, and accepted manner. In just the way one could tell the rank of a military man, one could tell the rank of the mourner—from heavy grief to something absurdly called half grief. Mourning costumes served as uniforms. And uniforms eliminate doubt and confusion; they dispense with thinking. Uniforms offer immediate recognition and orientation and comfort; they define and categorize—just one more instance of deep and complicated meaning in the nineteenth century fading away.

So while one might think that, in the midst of such rampant carnage, in the midst of such a "harvest of death," death would imprint itself indelibly on the popular imagination and make it much more of a reality, just the opposite seemed to happen. The facticity, the finality, of death faded from consciousness, and the rituals of death, like some kind of after-image—not unlike Brady's photographs—persisted. Listen to William Dean Howells on the subject of James Garfield, the future president of the United States, when he was still a Union general. It typifies a general movement taking place during the nineteenth century: "At the sight of these dead men whom other men had killed, something went out of him, the habit of a lifetime, that never came back again: the sense of the sacredness of life and the impossibility of destroying it."[22]

Drew Gilpin Faust herself seems to believe much the same thing. "Human life diminished sharply in value," she points out, "and the living risked becoming as dehumanized as the dead. Soldiers perhaps found it a relief to think of themselves not as men but as machines—without moral compass or responsibility, simply the instruments of others' direction and will."[23] This was, after all, the machine age, and as the mechanical began to invade most of life, it also crowded in on death. The Civil War seemed to crystallize and congeal those attitudes about death that had been building since the outset of the century.

Inventors turned their mechanical skills on the emotion of hate and made out of young men in uniforms automatons that dispensed rage and death. Meanwhile, embalmers used preservation and makeup to erase those expressions of rage from the faces of the dead soldiers. In fact, they erased all emotions, including, if there is such a thing, the look and pallor—the black mask—of death. For those who did die, religion and the prayers of their loved ones carried them to a new and everlasting life in heaven. Families buried their soldiers in their uniforms and, to complete the cycle, the living, mainly the widows, donned their own uniforms, the black and somber clothes of grief.

This era outlined so many stages of death: passing away, ranging from a state called *coma* to suspended animation and on through hypnotic trances of one kind or another; people gradually losing substance and fading away into specters, ghosts, voices, and emanations from the other side. We can count nearly as many stages of death as we can of life. How would we enumerate them? Is there a taxonomy of death that the culture began delineating in the nineteenth century, and is it that taxonomy that allows us today to parse the beginnings of life?

To repeat: In this period, death began to vanish. Life, too, lost its once familiar parameters. To say that life and death vanished is to say, really, that the embodiment of those two states, the fleshy human being, somehow lost its importance, which occurred in all kinds of ways, even when people died in the most hideous, violent manner. Technology eviscerated the experience of death, cleaned it up, sanitized it, and made it palatable. The ultimate extreme of this continuum would be death with no body whatsoever. One sees glimpses of this in contemporary crime investigation programs on television, or with Doctor Henry Lee, the coroner on the O. J. Simpson murder case, who typically reconstructs crimes with the barest shreds of physical evidence, convicting criminals without a body present, and with only the smallest and seemingly most insignificant shred of evidence.

Is it possible, in the midst of such a continuous and all-pervasive pall, that death itself actually died? Is it possible that people can grow too familiar with death's devastating hand? Certainly, photographic reproductions of death and dying render the real thing more remote. Mechanical reproduction seems to drain the real thing of its essence, no matter the period in which it takes place. Which is to say that, once such an extraordinary percentage of the population passes away, death perhaps must inevitably lose its dominion. Death in the Civil War had a numbing effect. In addition to this, attitudes toward grief in the nineteenth century had momentum from the underlying scientific and philosophical and artistic theories of the loss of humanness. There are at least two significant reasons to suspect that just such a diminution of death happened in the period. The first is religious, and the second is that movement which extended beyond religion, spiritualism.

As I said earlier, in the context of a growing evangelical Christianity, people did not die. They merely filled out their days in this world in order to pass on to another, more pleasant and more ennobled one in heaven. Egged on by the idea of the good death, surviving soldiers would give testimony about the way their buddies went out—always valiantly, always with a light heart, always willing to help others. The dead soldier always dies accepting and not fighting his fate. As a result of such a system of belief, no one ever really died. Each person calmly and—by all surviving accounts from the Union battlefield, at least—eagerly passed into another state, into another place; there, in heaven, he or she would spend his or her life in everlasting bliss.

And those on this side, also, as we have seen in an earlier chapter, knew the state of their loved ones on the other side by making contact with them through spiritual exercises—Ouija board encounters, séances, channeling, and so on. Those spiritual strategies, along with the Protestant notion of everlasting life after death, provided assurance that no one ever really died. Life merely went on and on, although in a different form, in a different place. The period even entertained questions about soldiers who had been mutilated in battle. Would they ascend into heaven intact, or would they remain forever maimed? (The preponderance of opinion, by the way, seemed to suggest that the body rose into heaven with all the parts restored and in good working order.)

In one of the most alarming moves, especially for a person with such political acumen as Abraham Lincoln, the president of the United States, in the midst of the bloodiest war America had faced—or would ever face again—attempted to suspend one of the most fundamental and sacred precepts of jurisprudence, the writ of habeas corpus. The Latin writ *habeas corpus* loosely translates as "You have the body," and intends to act as a safeguard against unlawful detention of a person, demanding that the person, the body, be brought before a judge to face charges, so that a fair and speedy trial might ensue, or that the magistrate release the person. Lincoln recognized, it seemed, that the body was no longer that important—so many corpses, so many burials, so many men lost to the vagaries of war. Yes, families wanted to see the body, and yes, they needed to know that their loved one had actually died, but religious principles had annulled death, had blunted its power to snuff out life. The physical form of the person, particularly in America and particularly in the latter part of the nineteenth century, in the end meant very little.

Faced with unruly mobs bordering Maryland, the northernmost slave-holding state, Lincoln sought to suspend the writ of habeas corpus there, as

well as in some midwestern states, on April 27, 1861. In part, Lincoln hoped
to make it impossible for Maryland to secede from the Union, a move that,
if it happened, he felt would complicate and prolong an already seemingly
interminable war. To that end, he planned to detain for undisclosed periods
of time rioters and rebels and various militiamen—those whom Lincoln
singled out and designated troublemakers—in local jails until the war ended. But Lincoln's efforts to subvert one of the Constitution's basic rights
failed. The circuit court of Maryland argued that Lincoln had overstepped
his presidential powers and so struck down his proposed legislation.

How could he take such a bold step against a doctrine that had been
in place since the fourteenth century? Surely, the impossibly difficult times
dictated such a phenomenal political risk. But also the idea of the body,
the fleshy corpus of the person, had by 1861 undergone a radical leaven-
ing, making it much easier for even a person so committed to freedom as
Abraham Lincoln to hold the individual human being in such low regard.
He not only could but had to sacrifice the soldier to the war, the person to
the nation. We do not think of Lincoln as a failed dictator, striking out on
his own and rewriting the law to suit his own rules. History sees him in just
the opposite way. Lincoln stands in history as the great emancipator: interested less, perhaps, in individuals than in groups of individuals—slaves, for
instance, or freemen, or Negroes—but nonetheless an emancipator.

But he laid the groundwork for someone who stands so far from
Lincoln, President George W. Bush, who in the course of holding so-called
"enemy combatants" at the secret prison in Guantánamo, Cuba, dispensed
with the writ of habeas corpus in a de facto way. But if Lincoln seemed to
care more about something called "the nation" than the individuals who
made up that nation, then Bush shared a good deal of that same attitude.
Bush, too, seemed to care less about individuals, and much more passionately about classes of people: terrorists, enemy combatants, members of al-
Qaeda, Islamofascists, evangelicals, neocons, and on and on. In some significant ways, with no real direct connection, of course, Lincoln paved the

way for the behavior of that other war president, George W. Bush. Indeed, in several speeches about the alleged war on terror, Bush used Lincoln's impulsive move as a precedent for his own actions during the war.

Lincoln made it easier for Bush, because by attempting to suspend the writ, Lincoln just naturally acted on the assumption that the body, the flesh that constituted the person, no longer held the same kind of importance as it once did. And that gradual erosion has reached its peak, I believe, in our own period. While torture recognizes the existence of the body, at the same time it seriously denigrates its importance. Or at least it reduces the complexity of the person to one feeling—pain. Torture knows the human body only in that one intimate but singular way. And so the one who tortures—literally the one who "twists" or "torques"—turns the screws until he hears those magic sentences that will render his work worthwhile and, at the same time, grant the victim his or her freedom.

Lincoln had the overwhelming experience of the Civil War, which focused the country's collective attention on the human body—but on its utterly transitory nature. War simply cheapens life on both sides—enemy and ally. War, in general, rests on a fundamental irony—it requires able bodies but, at the same time, it must treat those bodies as utterly dispensable. The Army corps devolves into the Army corpse. People die, but the war must go on, to its ultimate conclusion—which in modern terms means something other than victory. This distorted logic usually goes by the name of sacrificing for one's country, or, more commonly, patriotism; it sometimes, more elegantly, gets expressed in lines like "I only regret that I have but one life to lose for my country." That's of course Nathan Hale, just before his execution by the British, in 1776. History knows him as the ur-patriot—the executed ur-patriot.

The Civil War in particular had at least as one of its goals the abolition of slavery. That is, in great part the states fought the war over a crucial issue: Would the country ever conceive of the Negro as a whole person? If we can see that human beings, their very beings, were fast fading in importance in this period, think then about blacks. For the most part, as we have seen, the country saw and treated them as something far less than human beings. Native Americans fared no better. By the time of the Civil War, the cavalry had either cleared out or wiped out a good majority of America's indigenous peoples.

The conclusion to the Civil War brought its own national—international—hero, a star who earned a fortune on the stage, William F. Cody. Cody became of course one of the most successful mass entertainers in history, with the stage name Buffalo Bill. Onstage, he re-created battles against the "Indians," with the white folks always in triumph, guns and rifles always besting bows and arrows. For those who thought about it, Buffalo Bill gave audiences a taste of technology over the vernacular. Such a lesson was not lost on the usually acerbic journalist Russell Baker, who asks: "Is there a more relevant historical figure for a nation that marches off to a televised war promising the audience a spectacle of shock and awe?"[24]

Again, Russell Baker, reviewing several books on Buffalo Bill, makes the point that some historians see "the Cody show as a metaphorical expression of the late-nineteenth-century American psyche, with its brutal urge to domesticate what white Americans saw as a hostile wilderness."[25] How can we talk about the disappearance of the human without talking about the absolute decimation of the American Indian? How can we talk about the disappearance of the human being without talking about the many ways that the country had for making the Negro disappear in the nineteenth century—as slaves, as so-called freemen, as runaways, as maroons? In the century before, remember, an African person got divided up, three-fifths of a Negro worth one whole white person.

The eighteenth-century Lockean idea that, as citizens, we possess inalienable rights acquired through negotiating the social contract, gets expressed in that key founding document of the Republic, the Constitution, which gets implemented in the nineteenth century through an articulation of civil and legal rights. On one level, the civil rights movement of the late 1950s and 60s represents a great failure of the imagination. If this nation had accepted Africans as human beings when we first brought them to this country in 1619, we would not have needed the civil rights movement. But now all of us—everyone, black and white—have been reduced to an articulation of a series of rights.

A recent issue of *The New York Review of Books* carried an essay about torture, which the paper printed with no author's name, but simply the byline Human Rights Watch.[26] In an odd configuration, a worldwide rights group is writing about the denigration of incarcerated Iraqi prisoners in a prison named Abu Ghraib, and other prisoners confined by the United States military in the foothills of Cuba. How international and how vulgar that conglomerate of nations and peoples sounds. The essay devolves into rights and obligations contained in the Geneva Accords. It focuses on humane treatment, and turns on whether this country ever resorts to torture. Without anybody, or any body, present, we have now moved to a place in the modern world where we can have reasoned and intelligent discussions about the methods and aims and results of torture.

Everything I have been arguing in this book about the waning of human essence, the draining away of the intrinsic meaning of the human being, came to the fore during those four agonizing years that Americans fought against each other in the backyards and on the farms and fields of what was then the discordant and not very tightly united collection of states.

In this regard, we should count every person in uniform as the Unknown Soldier, both during the time that person is alive and in that person's death. Serial numbers, standard haircuts, uniforms—all those things designed to erase a person's personality contribute not just to the leveling of life in the military, but to life's cheapening, as well. Notice that newspapers like *The New York Times* keep a daily tally of GI deaths in the war in Iraq. Americans took to the streets to protest the continuation of the war when the death toll reached three thousand. The country saw very few demonstrations when the number reached the next benchmark: four thousand United States military men and women dead. But why not a protest, even though it would take an inordinate amount of time, for each and every death? What if we did that for every Iraqi man, woman, and child who died in this years-long fiasco? The corpus easily settles into a corpse, and no one much notices anymore. Oh yes, there is grieving and mourning, but that has become so ritualized that the observing rules, the *Ars Moriendi*—the art of dying—are more significant than death itself.

As the machine invaded the medical world more and more aggressively over the years, it pushed death through a series of dizzying changes. By the time we reach the twentieth century, a person has great difficulty understanding death—or life, for that matter—at all. I want to end this chapter with two recent examples of that kind of strangeness. In the first, death occurs without the slightest trace of a body or a corpse. In this instance, death gets negotiated in a courthouse, and a judge must first establish the fact that the person actually lived. Once he establishes that fact, the judge must then immediately declare the living person legally and finally deceased: life and death in the same instant. Every bit of this is a figment of the legal imagination—and we not only believe in it all, but act on it, as well.

In the second example, surgeons remove the heart from a human being for the duration of an operation, while the person, of course, is still alive. During that recess from his major and vital organ, the person considers himself dead. The doctors operating on him, of course, can hold no such idea, and consider him, while in a totally altered state, also totally alive. Once again, we see life and death occurring at the very same instant. In the context of contemporary medicine, an out-of-body experience means something radically different from any such version of that experience in the nineteenth century.

I begin with the first example. In just one month's time, Steve Fossett, a billionaire adventurer, went from somebody to no body. In just thirty days, Fossett's sixty-three years of living got totally erased. Search parties could not find him; no one knew where (or how) he and the plane he was flying had so thoroughly disappeared without any trace whatsoever. This happens periodically: We read about someone lost in the woods. People search, but with no luck. And then the question arises: How long do we wait before we call off the search? That's a question that really means, of course, How long do we wait before we declare the person dead? But Fossett's disappearance—he was a man of some prominence and certainly of some wealth—added another level to the usual pattern.

The only obituary to appear in *The New York Times* for February 16, 2008, announced the death of billionaire adventurer Steve Fossett. It described how he disappeared in September 2007 on what he called a two-hour pleasure flight from the Flying M Ranch in Nevada, in a single-engine two-seater plane elegantly named the Citabria Super Decathlon. He took off by himself for just a quick look-see of the surrounding desert and mountains, he told his friends, but he never returned.

Fossett and his plane completely disappeared. Search parties, scouring the wild terrain around the California and Nevada border with both fixed-wing aircraft and helicopters, could find no trace of the wild man everyone knew as Steve Fossett. Family and friends finally had to conclude that the person they knew as buddy, as father, as husband, had met some untimely end. The search continued for weeks and weeks. No one could find him.

So, in November of that same year, Fossett's wife, Peggy, petitioned the court to have her husband declared dead. She needed to, for in order to settle their sizable estate, Peggy Fossett had to somehow establish her husband as officially and forever dead—as no more. And thus on February 15, 2008, Judge Jeffrey A. Malak of the Circuit Court of Cook County, Chicago, heard evidence from Peggy Fossett, as well as from the rescue workers, and reached a verdict. In a single sentence, Judge Malak killed off Steve Fossett forever by declaring him legally deceased, in the root sense of the word, meaning "to go away," "to depart," "to leave."

The judge asked no questions about Fossett's description—how tall he was, how much he weighed. He did not need to know where he lived, or how old he was, how he behaved, or how he laughed. Judge Malak may not have been even able to identify Fossett in a lineup. His physical appearance mattered not at all. Fossett had become a legal issue, a problem that had to be solved.

Even though no one had a corpse, even though everyone knew he could no longer possibly still be hanging on to life, the family needed to confront those two categories, *life* and *death*. And the only way they could do it was through legal dictum, in this case through a circuit court judge. That person, speaking through the office of the Illinois legal system, would have to make the crucial declaration. Notice that Judge Malak stands in a different relation to death. He, too, will of course someday die, but the office will continue: "The king is dead; long live the king." Government officials enter death differently from the ordinary citizen.

When there is no longer any person named Steve Fossett around— no embodiment of that personality, that is—when there is no longer any *body* around, the court provides the one officially sanctioned way to die in the twenty-first century. Reporters at the *Washington Post* debated about when to run the obituary, and also about where to run the notice. One reporter said that if the rescuers had in fact recovered the body, the *Post* could have run the news of Fossett's death on the front page. But without a body, the editorial staff decided to relegate Fossett to page thirteen, along with the other dead souls. Here is an example of *habeas corpus* taken in its most literal sense. For us moderns, we must have the body, but it remains many times out of our grasp.

In a logical but absurd extension of the professionalization of death as it first began to make itself felt during the Civil War, people undergo death today in such strange and outlandish ways that only writers, it seems, can capture their bizarre nuances. For instance, when Larry McMurtry underwent quadruple bypass surgery, he speculated on what had happened to his personality during the time the surgeon had removed his heart and placed him on a pump—a mechanical heart. He recounts his journey to the other side, or to the very edge of the other side, in a slim book titled *Walter Benjamin at the Dairy Queen: Reflections at Sixty and Beyond.*

Listen to McMurtry—not in his own words, really, but as you will see, *as* his own words. Notice, too, in this account, that surgeons can in great part perform their intricate, highly technical work on McMurtry because of a simple nineteenth-century invention, anesthesia:

> I was one person up until the morning of December 2, 1991, at which date I had quadruple bypass surgery. . . . When I woke up from the operation, after about twelve hours in deep anesthesia, I began—although I didn't realize it immediately—my life as a different person—my life as someone else. I am still struggling, more or less, to reconcile the two histories, to go back to being who I once was, rather than the seriously altered person that I became.

A mechanical contrivance, an H. G. Wells kind of contraption known as a heart-lung machine, interposes itself between McMurtry, the public persona, and that interiorized, tiny McMurtry—that quiet little recluse, the homunculus that is his "self"—responsible for guiding the entire sixty-year-old enterprise known as Larry McMurtry the Western writer. During the time the operation takes, there is no Larry McMurtry, only a facsimile, a shell on the operating table, ready to assume the personality of the old self. McMurtry reflects on such a condition in the most profound way: Does my personality after the operation exactly match my personality before the operation? Here is McMurtry again:

> In choosing the operation I did the correct, the intelligent thing, but it wasn't the passionate thing, and I did it without conviction. I came out of it with a sense that we are now, indeed . . . able to leave our basic functions, for quite long stretches, to machines. The question is how long we can hand over these functions without, at the same time, relinquishing our personalities, and our spirits, too. The personality might

slowly elide until it is no longer recognizable or regainable as itself; it may cease to be the personality that goes with a particular self.

What happens next may be even more extraordinary. McMurtry, historian of every mote that ever swirled in a Texas dust devil, goes horror on us, as he slides into the passive voice and the past tense: A huge succubus has sucked out his very soul. "I think of the heart surgery now mostly in metaphors of editing," he writes. A surgeon has revised his organs—appropriately, it seems, since McMurtry has constructed his sense of self out of an accumulation of texts. He has read his entire life, he has written his entire life, and in recent years he has bought, collected, and sold hundreds of thousands of books—rare and otherwise. Suddenly, he finds himself constitutionally unable to read and unable to write. He picks up books, even familiar ones, and tries to read them but the words hook up to no external reality. He picks up his 2H pencil, but it's just a dead stick—he can shake nothing out of it. Literacy has abandoned him, because his very being has been so much fabricated out of texts.

As McMurtry "lost sight of himself," as he puts it, literature, too, turned invisible. His self absconded with literature because, for him, they are one and the same. "The self that I had once been had lost its life"—a feeling that compels him to write, in a most ghoulish, walking-dead way, "The thing, more than any other, that convinced me I had in some sense died was that I couldn't read. I went to my bookshops but could not connect with the books. . . . Reading was the stablest of all pleasures, and now it was gone."

Somehow, somewhere, someone had punched McMurtry's delete button. For years and years, McMurtry, the man of letters, simply vanished. When he finally gets his love of books back, and it remains a mystery how it actually happens, the prod comes as a message from the other side. Practically four years to the day after his heart attack, McMurtry suddenly recalls a passage in *The Sun Also Rises*, the first edition, and he turns to that book on his shelf. It isn't that his love of literature miraculously returns, but rather that a reassurance returns, born of something strikingly human—quirky, sloppy fallibility. Oddly enough, a mistake reconstitutes his love of letters—the thumbprint of mortality—what Walter Benjamin calls the "aura" of a work of art: "In the fourth year I recovered my interest in the rare-book trade, something that has been a fascination for most of my life. My memory for bibliographic minutiae returned. Once again, I could open a copy of *The Sun Also Rises* and turn automatically to page 181, where in the first issue, 'stopped' is spelled 'stoppped.'"

The Nobel Committee awarded Ernest Hemingway the Nobel Prize in Literature in 1954. Hemingway was a blazingly important writer not just in this country, but also around the world. His publisher, Charles Scribner's Sons—after editing and reediting and vetting *The Sun Also Rises*—published it, in 1926, with a mistake. How refreshing! How wonderful! The printer's devil beat the printing press. It's not unlike the example of a Japanese pottery master, who makes the perfect vase and then at the end intentionally dings it to let the world know that the pot was crafted by a human being. Machines make perfect objects, perhaps, but not human beings. Human beings fall far short of perfection. Human essence made itself known and felt through the one thing that society and authority ask us to avoid at all costs—mistakes.

Incredible: What McMurtry chooses to remember—and I would argue here that *remember* must be taken in its literal sense of "membering," of putting limbs back together, the reassembling of his soul—is a significant word that does more than reflect his condition. It *is* his condition. He got *stopped;* he stopped himself; his heart stopped. However one phrases it, McMurtry had become, for a time, a mechanical creature of sorts. Off the machine, his heart back in his body—should we consider him dead here, or simply suspended? Newly resouled, as it were? He certainly had to settle back into himself, where only reading and writing—those two activities out of which he had fashioned his entire life—could project him back into the world. But he could not do it. He could not write anymore, or read anymore. The rhythm of his life had fallen out of sync with all those old sentences.

What makes Larry McMurtry remember? What stirs him to reach for *that* specific passage in Hemingway? Who knows? Maybe he never forgot it. Maybe he only lived *over* it—and went on with his life, which seems imminently reasonable. We might find a clue to his peculiar kind of return in another text, Raymond Williams's marvelous book *Keywords: A Vocabulary of Culture and Society.* In it, under the entry for *humanity,* Williams points out the need to add a note about the word *human*: "It is . . . commonly used to indicate warmth and congeniality ('a very human person'). But there is also a significant use to indicate what might be called condoned fallibility ('human error,' 'natural human error') and this is extended, in some uses, to indicate something more than this relatively neutral observation."

In the end, a misspelling, a keyword, *stoppped,* with an extra, terrifically upsetting letter, a single *p*—came to slap him on the shoulder. A mistake brought McMurtry back to his senses; a mistake brought home to him the nature of being human. For that's at least one good measure of being human, McMurtry realizes, the seemingly infinite capacity of the human being to make mistakes.

McMurtry is so much built out of books that death temporarily erases the pages of his interiorized texts—the pages on which his memories, his experiences, his lives, are written. When he returns to his craft, he comes back with his writing style—or reading style—severely altered. He craves different sentences and different rhythms. Having caught a second wind, he finds his breathing has drastically changed. The result of Larry McMurtry's return from death, or however we can describe the man who for a time had no heart, is a new and slow-paced, drawn-out series of sentences, to which he confesses by heaping praise on two writers who match his new sluglike style:

I'd rather read biographies of writers than read their works. Proust and Virginia Woolf are two exceptions, perhaps because their works are not only rivers of language, they're rivers of gossip, too. My time with these two masterpieces—[*Remembrance of Things Past* and Woolf's diaries]—I owe to the heart surgery because, without it, I might never have been open to them so profoundly. This is a bonus that goes far toward overshadowing the trauma. My self has more or less knitted itself together again, the trauma has faded, but the grandeur of those books, the White Nile of Proust, the Blue Nile of Virginia Woolf, will be with me all my life.

If we do not know where we can locate our dying, we do not know, then, how or where to locate our living. One can only wonder, now—and the phrasing does indeed sound weird—if it is even possible to die. When does that moment of death actually occur? Which is to say, when does the moment of life take place—if it ever does—or can we, with any intelligence, even phrase such a question anymore?

Since this chapter has settled into literature, I want to end it with a quotation from literature, from one of America's smartest contemporary authors, Don DeLillo, from his novel *White Noise*. DeLillo explores here the quality of living in a postmodern world, which is to say that he also explores the strange ways we have these days of having our life drain away. A key experience that people used to describe with some assurance has now turned into a murky and confused series of moments:

> You are said to be dying, and yet are separate from the dying, can ponder it at your leisure, literally see on an x-ray photograph or computer screen the horrible alien logic of it all. It is when death is rendered graphically, is televised so to speak, that you sense an eerie separation between your condition and yourself. A network of symbols has been introduced, an entire awesome technology wrested from the gods. It makes you feel like a stranger in your own dying.

We might even call this a virtual death, a simulacrum of the real thing. To watch one's own dying on a screen makes it seem as if some critic should review it as a performance of sorts, and give it one or two thumbs up.

How can we feel like a stranger in our own dying? Is such a condition even possible? Is that the one moment when we should feel totally engaged with our fate—or is it absolutely natural to feel like a stranger? Do we first have to feel tightly intimate with our living before we can eradicate the feeling of being a stranger in our dying? Ivan Illich, the radical social critic, says that "the ability to die one's own death depends on the depth of one's embodiment." He calls ours an "amortal society," and writes, "There are no dead around; only the memory of lives that are not there. The ordinary person suffers from the inability to die." DeLillo hints at that same terrifying state of affairs. To be a stranger to one's own dying certainly has to stand as one basic and crucial form of dissociation from life.

That feeling of confusion makes up a huge part of our legacy from the nineteenth century, and in that legacy death becomes a commodity, an engineered and ordered fact of our engineered lives. Disembodied, "unfleshed," disoriented—such words describe the human condition in the twenty-first century. We got here because of the sweep of the past, specifically of the nineteenth century—and in particular the way the Civil War congealed the many and various and contrary themes of death and life.

But matters will grow worse. People will move beyond a mere withdrawal or alienation from death. In the late twentieth century, as we shall see, they tire of death and come to see it as a failure of that key system known as our living and breathing selves. Some people will come to view death as a flaw in our design that can and must be corrected. Without that nasty interruption that goes by the name of death, we might just live forever, just as Count Dracula promised we might.

THREE | A Couple of Sarahs Later

MANY THEMES—self and naming; personality and monomania; stardom and fame; unveiling and the revelation of truth; the necessity, against a proliferating number of ghosts, for finding a definition of human essence; and a closely related issue, the belief in the inferiority of all African peoples—come together in the lives of two nineteenth-century women. They could not be more opposite from each other. One of them passed through the world totally devoid of a sense of herself; the other embodied a heightened sense of self-awareness. I choose women because they still represent "the other" in the nineteenth century. A good indication, for me, of the health of a society is how it treats its outsiders—its mavericks, minorities, and citizens who live out on the margins.

While one of the women I take up is Caucasian, and the other African, the difference in the way society treated them is a matter of kind, not of degree. They both dominated the news and commanded worldwide attention, but for radically different reasons. White people had a most certain means of ratifying their own identity, which they did, in a decidedly offensive way, by making themselves as distinct as possible from black people. We cannot in the nineteenth century separate white identity from black inferiority. White people may have been struggling to find the proper category for themselves in the nineteenth century, but social scientists had already consigned blacks to their own category, and it was not, in any stretch of the imagination, a winning or favorable one. In this period, at least, in a most bizarre way, whites desperately needed blacks to assure a sense of their own well-being.

The two women I have chosen narrate absolutely disparate stories about sex, about the relationship between sex and power, and perhaps about the thinnest of lines that separate being critically examined and judged (becoming an object) from being greatly admired and appreciated (becoming a subject). In an age of photographs and motion pictures, of people glancing out of a train window at the landscape rushing by or watching reality moving past on a screen, we can ask, What does it mean to gaze, to ponder, to observe? People in the nineteenth century grew accustomed to seeing the natural world for an instant only. They simply had less and less time to concentrate on detail. In great part, this emphasis on continuous movement caused people to lose a grip on their own lives.

The haptic, material life was fast coming to an end, the surface of things assuming importance over their depth, the image over the real. Such emphasis quite naturally reinforced the idea of racism, which gains its meaning and import from a surface reading, from a refusal to face the complications of reality in favor of delving only skin deep—to paraphrase Martin Luther King, it is cover over content, color over character. In the new century, substance fell away, reduced to something of secondary or tertiary importance.

More and more, people found themselves as members of one audience or another—spectators rather than actors at an event. They looked, they gaped, they stared, they gazed. But even more unsettling, technology came to define for them just what constituted an event. Newspapers, magazines, and motion pictures increasingly shaped their reality, dictating to them what to think and how to feel. Professionals replaced amateurs: Undertakers became morticians, doctors became physicians, midwives became nurses, cops became law enforcement, and teachers turned into professors. Extended, tedious, and repetitive acts marked the workweek, which could stretch from six to six and a half and even seven days. The randomness of life gave way to the regularity of the clock. For working stiffs, time did not fly; it crept at a petty pace. People desperately wanted, they needed, what the French call *divertissement*—entertainment, spectacle, events that were grouped under the apt name of "pastimes." Hordes of ordinary, working men and women made the cinema immediately and incredibly popular. Others traveled great distances to observe so-called rarities of the human race, or something akin to the human race, from around the world—oddities that rewarded the curious and the depraved.

One of the women I have chosen belongs in that most destructive category of rarities. At best a reluctant performer, she shied away from any notion of the limelight, but got thrown into its bright center nonetheless, and received a great deal of worldwide fame and notoriety. (Stage technicians invented a new concoction, "limelight," in the nineteenth century, by heating pieces of lime in an oxyhydrogen flame. Such intensity of illumination corresponded well with the new idea of heavenly stardom.) The object of hundreds of thousands of people's piercing gaze, she turned into a freakish kind of spectacle, a puzzling link in the Great Chain for men and women to ponder. She stood out as an example of self-abnegation, or worse yet, of a person denied any chance of developing a sense of self.

The other woman went after stardom with a vengeance, pursued it deliberately and passionately, and got exactly what she wanted, worldwide fame. She, too, became the object of fascination, but for altogether different reasons. For a great many people in this country, as well as in Europe, she served as an exemplar of self-reliance, or better yet, of self-cultivation. The press dubbed her "The Incomparable One." Historians associate both of these women with a strong, a terribly strong, sexual presence.

Both women carried the same biblically charged name, Sarah; and both shared the same initials, S. B. The first woman, Sarah Baartman, was born in South Africa's Eastern Cape in 1789. History does not record her tribal name. Her Dutch captors baptized her Saartjie Baartman, or "Little Sarah," in Afrikaans. Standing only four feet, six inches tall, she faced a

doomed, painful, and violently shortened life—but not because of the hard-
ships endured in her native country or out of her own doing. Just after
her twenty-first birthday, in 1810, a Dutch physician brought her life as a
member of the Khoikhoi tribe to an abrupt and brutal end.

In the early nineteenth century, Dutch farmers, greedy for more land,
launched a brutal campaign against the Khoikhoi, an ancient and essentially pacific nomadic, cattle-raising people, slaughtering thousands and
thousands of them. One of those Dutch farmers, a man named Peter Cezar,
captured Sarah during one of the raids and enslaved her on his farm. Peter's
brother, Henrik, a surgeon, examined Sarah during one of his visits from
England and prepared a detailed description of her, from her head to her
feet, in his diary, a level of description he could get only from the most
invasive and humiliating of inspections. In her enormous buttocks and en-
larged labia, he wrote, he found a confirmation of the world's general belief
in black female sexual depravity. (Anthropologists call the accumulation
of fat in the buttocks *steatopygia*). He decided that by removing her to
London and putting her on display, he could offer the world a living and
quite graphic answer to the question, as he put it in his diary, "Are African
people human?" According to some accounts, Henrik also promised Sarah
vast amounts of money.

Cezar was suggesting nothing new. The practice of exhibiting people
of color in the West had existed since the earliest encounters between
Europeans and indigenous populations in the New World and Africa. On
his return to Spain after his first voyage to the New World in 1492, for
instance, Columbus brought several Arawaks to Queen Isabella's court,
where one of them remained on display for two years. But the exhibition of
exotic people of color reached its height in the nineteenth century, in both
Europe and America, when freak shows and gunpowder entertainment became fairly common and incredibly popular family fare.

Promoters displayed so-called savages from what was then known as the
Dark Continent, along with the most vicious Native American aggressors,

in circuses, zoos, and museums, turning them into popular attractions in England and America. In America, in particular, millions of people came to see traveling extravaganzas like Buffalo Bill's Wild West, which began its run in 1883, and the Barnum and Bailey Circus, which threw up its big top five years later, in 1888. (Even Wild Bill Hickock took to the stage for a brief time.) Newspapers carried word of a breakthrough in good times, which went by the name "mass entertainment."

In a time of shifting personalities, of ordinary folks rising to super-stardom, people shed old names and took new ones, as easily as they changed their clothes—Friedrich Wilhelm Mueller became Eugen Sandow, Henriette-Rosine Bernard became Sarah Bernhardt, Erich Weiss turned into Harry Houdini—and, of course, William F. Cody, frontiersman, transformed himself into a huge fictional hero, Buffalo Bill, performing his Wild West taming of the Indians twice a day on the stage. As con men on the streets and mountebanks on the stage, the most ordinary of citizens also took on new identities. And it is in this context of personality shift-ing that we might want to place a work of literature like John William Polidori's short story "The Vampyre," published in 1819, about a person who, under the right conditions, changes from a civilized, titled man into a wild beast. Buffalo Bill has a touch of this, as he hoped his partly animal name might suggest.

In a review of Louis S. Warren's book on Cody, *Buffalo Bill's America: William Cody and the Wild West Show,* the reviewer Russell Baker, quot-ing from Warren, notes:

> It was an age when Americans believed that "progress, the rise of technology over nature and of settlement over the wild, seemed inevi-table." The Buffalo Bill show made Americans feel good about them-selves by encouraging them to believe "that western industrialized society was the apogee of human development, the beginnings of a more peaceful, humane world, and even to fantasize that one person could embody its promise."

In the midst of that euphoria about the world in general and about America in particular, a person could pay a penny to see various kinds of bush people on display, offering eager white audiences one more way of feeling more assured, in a most bizarre and inhumane way, about their world. In 1835 one of the greatest showmen of the period, P. T. Barnum, brought to Manhattan an elderly, infirm African American named Joice Heth, and billed her as the 160-year-old nurse of "Little George" Washington. Barnum exhibited her in a makeshift location near Broadway and Prince Streets, promoting her appearance with handbills, posters, and newspaper articles, all of which he wrote himself. When she died the following year, knowing the period's fascination with death and decay, he sold tickets to her autopsy, at which the coroner estimated her age at sixty-five or seventy years of age, considerably less than what Barnum advertised.

Barnum puffed up so many mediocre attractions into headline events that the popular press came to call that kind of showmanship "Barnumizing." Everyone knew that P. T. Barnum had no particular love for the facts; the newspapers often quoted him as saying, "the people like to be humbugged."[1] In 1841, Barnum opened his American Museum at Broadway and Ann Street and, according to John Strausbaugh, filled the five stories with

a stupefying surfeit of exhibits and activities: dioramas, panoramas, "cosmoramas," scientific instruments, modern appliances, a flea circus, a loom run by a dog, the trunk of a tree under which Jesus' disciples sat, a hat worn by Ulysses S. Grant, an oyster bar, a rifle range, waxworks, glass blowers, taxidermists, phrenologists, pretty-baby contests, Ned the learned seal, the Feejee Mermaid (a mummified monkey's torso with a fish's tail), a menagerie of exotic animals that included beluga whales in an aquarium, giants, midgets, Chang and Eng the Siamese twins, Grizzly Adams's trained bears and performances ranging from magicians, ventriloquists and blackface minstrels to adaptations of biblical tales and "Uncle Tom's Cabin." Some 38 million customers paid the 25 cents admission to attend the museum between 1841 and 1865. The total population of the United States in 1860 was under 32 million.[2]

People traveled from other countries to visit the museum. Barnum hit it big. People wanted oddity, and they wanted the bizarre. A good deal of life in the nineteenth century seemed to take place under a big top. After 1865, for instance, Barnum did not close down, he ratcheted up. By the 1870s, he had created a new and bigger and better attraction, the Greatest Show on Earth, and in 1874 he opened Barnum's Great Roman Hippodrome, a ten-thousand-seat arena between 26th and 27th Streets, and Madison and Fourth Avenues, succeeded by the first incarnation of Madison Square Garden. There, Barnum introduced the world to his famous three-ring circus. And always, at the sideshows, P. T. Barnum reserved space for his African "specimens."

"Hottentots" became a particularly favorite attraction, both in America and in England, for they seemed to many social scientists of the period the most degraded and malformed freaks in all of nature. The renowned anthropologist Samuel Morton had a particular fascination for these people, whom he described, with the assured tone of a scientist, as "the nearest approximation to the lower animals . . . Their complexion is a yellowish brown, compared by travelers to the peculiar hue of Europeans in the last stage of jaundice. . . . The women are represented as even more repulsive in appearance than the men."[3]

Morton is just one of scores of social scientists in the nineteenth century who grounded his belief in black inferiority in the prevailing racist theories of the period, in Morton's particular case in social Darwinism. The geologist Joseph Le Conte also condemned blacks in America to the cellar of humanity: "Laws determining the effects of contact of species, races, varieties, etc. among animals" also applied to "the races of men." As a race, Negroes persisted as creatures "still in childhood that had not yet learned to walk alone in the paths of civilisation" and were destined, Le Conte went on, either to "extinction . . . [or] relegation to a subordinate place in the economy of nature."[4]

White people viewed Negroes, then, as just another sport of nature, freaks that helped satisfy their shaky belief in their own white correctness and, at the same time, helped to reinforce their own desire to appear totally normal. The more I can cast the other as aberrant and abnormal, the theory of exclusion goes, the more normal I look. England led the way in staging elaborate sideshows and freak shows. Colorful handbills, posters, and broadsheets advertised with great fanfare an assortment of human anomalies, like the pig-faced woman, or the sixty-pound fully grown man, or the giant Hungarian schoolboy. But, again, what really drew the crowds were the exhibits of bushmen and Zulus.

For over sixty or seventy years, from the middle of the nineteenth century well into the twentieth century, crowds of people went to gawk at collections of African peoples, from the smallest Pygmies to the tallest Watusis. An 1847 newspaper account of a bushman display at the Egyptian Hall in Piccadilly reflected the public's prevailing attitude toward almost every person of dark skin, from Filipinos to Africans: "In appearance they are little above the monkey tribe. They are continually crouching, warming themselves by the fire, chatting or growling. . . . They are sullen, silent and savage—mere animals in propensity, and worse than animals in appearance." Samuel Morton, called Hottentots "the nearest approximation to the lower animals. . . . Their complexion is a yellowish brown, compared by travellers to the peculiar hue of Europeans in the last stage of jaundice. . . . The women are represented as even more repulsive in appearance than the men."[5] Decades after Morton's comments, a Canadian entrepreneur named William Leonard Hunt, who adopted the exotic theatrical name Farini, made a fortune by exhibiting a family of Zulus in England and America from 1879 to the middle of the 1890s.

Farini cashed in on the spirit expressed in the Wild West shows, of taming the savage—Indians, in the case of the Cody shows, but also savages no matter where we might encounter them, even in Africa. All sorts of people, from scientists to businesspeople, were intent on making white destiny very manifest indeed. If ordinary people could concoct their own personal myths—making themselves anew, adopting fabulous identities like Buffalo Bill or Annie Oakley—why not a national myth?

People of all classes and levels of education came to gawk and marvel. The bush people exhibits constituted popular entertainment at its most grotesque: Come see the exotic and the marvelous for only one shilling admission, children under twelve half price. Although they look human, don't fret; they belong in some other, related but not equal category. At one point, even the great reformer Charles Dickens confessed his repulsion at seeing a bunch of Zulus, at the Egyptian Hall in London. In 1853, in a magazine he had started himself called *Household Words,* he wrote an essay ironically titled "The Noble Savage," a reference to the so-called primitive man uncontaminated by civilization. Without compunction or seeming embarrassment, Dickens confesses in his opening sentences, "I have not the least belief in the Noble Savage. I consider him a prodigious nuisance, and an enormous superstition." A progressive and an activist when it came to the plight of the poor and the exploitation of children in the workforce, Dickens, it appears, reserved his compassion for whites only. For on the subject of Africans, he went out of his way to find the most absolutely monstrous and vicious things to say, including his definition of a savage as "something highly desirable to be civilised off the face of the earth." Plain and simple, he would have preferred to see all people of Africa eradicated.

In the rest of the essay, Dickens turns his attention to an exhibition of Zulu Kaffirs at St. George's Gallery, in Hyde Park. Those warriors, in particular, he found "extremely ugly"; and when he tried to understand their behavior, he could only conclude:

> What a visitor left to his own interpretings and imaginings might suppose these noblemen to be about, when they give vent to that pantomimic expression which is quite settled to be the natural gift of the noble savage, I cannot possibly conceive; for it is so much too luminous for my personal civilisation that it conveys no idea to my

mind beyond a general stamping, ramping, and raving, remarkable (as everything in savage life is) for its dire uniformity.

Poor, benighted Charles Dickens, the man who could go on for pages about the smallest nuance of human behavior in novels like *David Copperfield* and *Bleak House* and *Hard Times* and *A Tale of Two Cities*, just cannot figure out why those unschooled, frightened, and disoriented creatures, locked inside their six-by-nine-foot cages, act the way they do.

His repulsion took him only so far: Dickens went to see every African at every display in London, many times over. Why did he keep going? Did he want to make certain that those savages truly repulsed him? Or was the fascination something entirely else? Perhaps those Africans were possessed of a power and strength that also fascinated him, or perhaps they made him realize what the world was actually losing—or, worse yet, had already lost.

Perhaps the same kind of attraction and repulsion worked its way through the population at large, for England and America both offered plenty of exhibitions. Historians count as one of the most controversial of those exhibitions, however, not one of the minor events but the Africans on full display at one of the largest but temporary sites, the 1893 World's Columbian Exposition, in the city of Chicago. There, prompted by the likes of Barnum, promoters outdid themselves by building an entire village, and peopled it exclusively with women from Dahomey, now called Benin. Through them, we can get a glimpse, perhaps, of the desperate situation of all those people, everywhere—in small venues and in large—who were forced to parade themselves before hordes of curious and largely unsympathetic onlookers.

During the performance of one of their chants, rather than praising America as they were supposed to do, the women from Dahomey were said, by one man who claimed to know a bit of the language, to utter something along the lines of the following: "We have come from a far country to a land where all men are white. If you will come to our country we will take pleasure in cutting your white throats."[6] Local newspapers carried the story, whereupon key civic leaders in Chicago demanded the show's immediate closure. But the public uproar for its continuation grew too loud and large. The public's desire for spectacle won out over its demand for punishment. The show remained open and continued to draw large crowds of men, women, and children from around the country. Such was the drawing power of nineteenth-century entertainment, and the crushing virulence of nineteenth-century racism.

Sarah Baartman arrived at Piccadilly Circus in London, in the latter part of the year 1810. Advertised in full-color drawings as the "Hottentot Venus," she became an immediate success, appearing nude before sold-out audiences at the Egyptian Hall. Sharing top billing at various times with another favorite, the "African Hermaphrodite," she paced in small circles inside her cage like some deranged animal. But no matter who appeared alongside her, Sarah took over, in the most perverse sense possible, as the star. According to one observer: "[O]n being ordered by her keeper, she came out. . . . The Hottentot was produced like a wild beast, and ordered to move backwards and forwards, and come out and go into her cage, more like a bear on a chain than a human being."[7]

After a degrading year in London of people gawking at her and prodding her, Peter Cezar took her, perhaps out of a sense of guilt, to Manchester and there, on December 7, 1811, had her undergo ritual baptism. During that time, members of the English Anti-Slavery Society sought to free Sarah Baartman by bringing her case to court. By this time, as evidence of her keen intelligence, Sarah had learned a bit of Dutch (as well as achieving fluency in both English and French) and told the judge that she was not telling her story under restraint. To no one's surprise, Henrik Cezar testified that Sarah was nothing but a willing participant and was receiving her fair and handsome share of the profits of the sideshow. The court proceedings lasted only three hours. The judge dismissed the case. Sarah returned to work.

No record of her surfaces until three years later, on December 12, 1814, when Cezar sells Sarah to an animal trainer in France. The *Journal of Paris* announced her arrival with great fanfare. She even attracted the famous French anatomist Georges Cuvier, who visited her often. She posed in the nude for scientific paintings at the Jardin du Roi. Cuvier observed her there, as well. A French journalist, who tried to render an accurate description of Sarah, must have been totally baffled by her presence, because he could only offer up a string of unrelated details: "Tears come from her eyes, complexion light green, she jumps, she sings and plays drums. Someone gives her sweets, around her neck she wore a tiny piece of turtle shell."[8] Barkers touted her as one of nature's supreme oddities; popular writers dwelled on her bizarre habits and proclivities; spectators, including little kids, gawked and jeered, yelled obscenities, and tossed scraps of food at her through the bars of her cage. Doctors paid a premium for the privilege of probing and examining her in private.

We get a glimpse of her true feelings, as we may have with the dancers from Dahomey, on only one reported occasion. At a ball one evening in Paris, where her keeper had taken her as part of the evening's entertainment—what would the Hottentot Venus look like in a silk gown? How would high society handle a black person in their bright white midst?—she allegedly described herself to a Frenchman with a line so poignant we must seriously reconsider her testimony in court that she felt no constraint in her captivity: "My name is Sarah, very unhappy Sarah."[9]

And truly unhappy she must have been. For one day, not long after that ball, Sarah collapsed into the deepest depression. She lay on the floor of her cage in a fetal coil. Slowly, but with great determination, she ate and drank less and less. No one and nothing could force her to resume life again. She began to waste away and, finally, fell desperately ill with an undiagnosable inflammatory illness. On December 16, 1815, less than one year after being exiled to France, Sarah Baartman died. She was twenty-six years old. She lived only five years out of her native Africa, separated from her family and friends, to suffer the worst indignities—all for the entertainment of white audiences. But those five years, for all the pain and humiliation, must have seemed to her an eternity. She had no life out of Africa. From the vastness of the bush, she spent her days and nights in a six-by-nine-foot cell, a prisoner to Western fantasies of that faraway place called Africa, of black inferiority, of black women, and of depraved sexuality. We can safely count as her death date the moment that Henrik Cezar declared her, in the African veldt, an oddity with great commercial promise.

The Academy conferred on Georges Cuvier the distinct honor of dissecting Sarah Baartman upon her death and, according to Stephen Jay Gould, "he went right to the genitals."[10] Cuvier published his findings in the *Mémoires du Musée d'Histoire Naturelle* in 1817. He might just as well have been dissecting any old primate: "I have never seen a human head more like an ape than that of this woman." He next commented on Sarah's tiny head—recall she was a small person, standing only four and a half feet tall—and dismissed any suggestion of intelligence because of "that cruel law, which seems to have condemned to an eternal inferiority those races with small and compressed skulls." And then in case anyone should miss his true feelings about her, Cuvier made clear that Sarah Baartman, and all those like her, occupied only the lowest rung on what people mistook as the evolutionary ladder: "Her movements had something brusque and capricious about them, which recall those of monkeys. She had, above all, a way of pouting her lips, in the same manner as we have observed in orangutans."

Her death did not put an end to her humiliation. Cuvier presented Sarah's dissected genitalia before the Académie Royale de Médecine, in order to allow his colleagues to observe, as Cuvier insisted, "the nature of the labia."[11] Cuvier and his contemporaries concluded that Baartman's oversized and primitive genitalia offered physical proof of African women's "primitive sexual appetite." Cuvier preserved Baartman's genitalia and brain in alcohol and placed them on display at the Musée de l'Homme, in

Paris, the institution where he held an appointment. They remained prominently displayed on a shelf long after her death, until 1985, when a group of South African medical students demanded that the museum return them to her native country. Some medical historians insist that scientific racism was born on her body.

•❦•

THE OTHER SARAH, Sarah Bernhardt, became in the nineteenth century a symbol of sensual, even sexual presence and exotic allure. Newspapers dismissed Sarah Baartman as one of the true monstrosities of the world; they embraced Sarah Bernhardt as the Eighth Wonder of the World. Like Sarah Baartman, Sarah Bernhardt went on display in London and Paris, but on her own terms, performing roles as the leading lady before mostly upper-crust audiences in the grandest, most opulent theaters of England and Europe. Like some Renaissance aristocrat, she adopted a motto, *quand même,* "even though," or "in spite of everything." She cast herself as success and perseverance incarnate.

Born to a Jewish mother (we know little about her father, who abandoned the family fairly early) on October 22, 1844, in Paris, as Henriette-Rosine Bernard, she was decidedly white, precocious, an inveterate liar, and somewhat privileged. Like the other Sarah, sexual provocation and even at times total nakedness also marked her life. But, again, those events took place through her own choosing: Clothing fell from her body of her own free will, when she wanted, and where she wanted. She, and not some anonymous collection of Dutch traders, deliberately changed the spelling of her name. ("Bernhardt," for her, echoed the more mysterious and exotic-sounding "burning heart.") She decided precisely when she would take the stage, and exactly when she would take her leave. She tantalized and titillated sold-out audiences in England, on the Continent, and in America, with her acting, dancing, and outrageous and opulent style of living.

Contemporary writers enthroned her as the white, Western standard of nineteenth-century beauty. Even Freud, not given to outbursts of emotion in public, managed a most passionate description of Sarah Bernhardt. In 1885, Freud came to Paris to study hypnotism and, with the founder of neurology, the Frenchman Jean-Martin Charcot, to investigate both neuropathology and hysteria. One evening Charcot took Freud to see Bernhardt in the lead role in the most sumptuously produced *Théodora,* by the playwright Victorien Sardou. Freud immediately and thoroughly fell under her spell. Freud had just turned twenty-nine, a young man setting out in the intellectual world of Vienna; Sarah Bernhardt was a woman of forty-one, and a fully accomplished actress. No doubt the elaborate production contributed greatly to the mood of seduction. Set in sixteenth-century Istanbul, *Théodora* explored the themes of sadism, lust, and revenge against the backdrop of lavishly painted sets. Playgoers were treated to a depiction of the Orient in its most romanticized, dreamlike form.

For these and perhaps a score of other reasons, Freud fell hard:

How that Sarah plays! After the first words of her lovely, vibrant voice I felt I had known her for years. Nothing she could have said would have surprised me; I believed at once everything she said. . . . I have never seen a more comical figure than Sarah in the second act, where she appears in a simple dress, and yet one soon stops laughing, for every inch of that little figure lives and bewitches. Then her flattering and imploring and embracing; it is incredible what postures she can assume and how every limb and joint acts with her. A curious being: I can imagine that she needn't be any different in life than on the stage.[12]

He begged to have an audience with her after the performance, and she most willingly agreed. He confessed: "My head is reeling."[13] As a token of her sincerity, she presented Freud with an autographed picture of herself, which he displayed on his office desk—one of the first things, if not *the* first thing, that his clients encountered on entering the doctor's own little theater of wonders and marvels. He of course expected his patients to "believe at once everything [he] said." Perhaps the photograph helped.

Sigmund Freud did not stand alone in his admiration of Sarah Bernhardt's seductive personality. As a young man, another expert on the subject of love, D. H. Lawrence, saw Sarah Bernhardt perform the lead in Alexandre Dumas's *La Dame aux Camélias* at the Theatre Royal in Nottingham, England. As Camille, she loved the consumptive fits; critics wrote about her knack at dying. After seeing that play, Lawrence recounted his experience with that language of lust-driven primitive sexuality that became so familiar to readers of *Lady Chatterley's Lover.*

If Sarah Bernhardt were not white, if she were not a commanding actor, if her dramatic performance were drained of all of its high culture, we might easily believe that Lawrence had the other Sarah, Baartman, in mind: "There she is, the incarnation of wild emotion which we share with all live things, but which is gathered in us in all complexity and inscrutable fury. She represents the primeval passions of woman, and she is fascinating to an extraordinary degree. I could love such a woman myself, love her to madness; all for the pure passion of it."

Unlike the more fortunate Sigmund Freud, Lawrence never actually met Bernhardt. While Bernhardt's fleshy and very real being prompted Lawrence's description, he makes her sound so much like a cliché, offering his readers a glimpse at the ur-passionate woman as nothing more than mere image. "A gazelle," he said, "with a beautiful panther's fascination and fury."

Then, in what seems like an uncharacteristic move, Lawrence issued a warning. Bernhardt's beauty had hit him in a physical and quite fundamental—dare one say savage—way: "Take care about going to see Bernhardt. Unless you are very sound, do not go. When I think of her now I can still feel the weight hanging in my chest as it hung there for days after I saw her. Her winsome, sweet playful ways; her sad, plaintive little murmurs; her terrible panther cries; and then the awful, inarticulate sounds, the little sobs that fairly sear one, and the despair and death; it is too much in one evening."[14]

That's fairly heady company, Sigmund Freud and D. H. Lawrence, but they did not especially capture her attention. It took someone who lived a life at the edges of socially acceptable behavior, as Bernhardt lived hers, to fully appreciate her true nature and what she was capable of accomplishing. The most notorious playwright of the period, Oscar Wilde, demanded more than mere contemplation of Sarah Bernhardt's beauty. He wanted to exploit it, to secure it for his own—if at all possible to possess it for himself. Like Freud, he too had been bowled over by her wonderful outspokenness, her life of slips and surprises, her eagerness to toss aside the expected and the conventional. Bernhardt promoted herself as a figure of mystery, at selected moments revealing only the smallest bits of herself. The critic Jules Lemaître wrote of Sarah Bernhardt as if she were unfettered consciousness itself, a continual unveiling of selves: "She could enter a convent, discover the North Pole, kill an emperor or marry a Negro king and it would not surprise me. She is not an individual but a complex of individuals."[15]

The great nineteenth-century photographer Nadar (Gaspard-Félix Tournachon) took languorous photographs of her reclining on a fainting couch just when she turned twenty—the diva on the divan. The famous artist Alphonse Mucha, the man who defined the Art Nouveau style, designed her theater posters. She played Cleopatra and Joan of Arc; she sculpted statues. In 1890, *Le Figaro* newspaper noted that visitors came to Paris to see two profiles: that of the Eiffel Tower and that of Sarah Bernhardt. Sixty years later, in another century, when the equally famous and notorious Marilyn Monroe chose to talk about her own fame, she said, apropos of a toothpaste that Madison Avenue had asked her to publicize: "People don't realize that every time I show my teeth on television I'm appearing before more people than Sarah Bernhardt appeared before in her whole career."[16] So Marilyn Monroe, the ultimate star of the twentieth century, calibrated her own fame by the standard of Sarah Bernhardt. (Like Marilyn

Monroe, Bernhardt signed a fairly lucrative contract to endorse a brand of toothpaste, that one called Sozodont, "the only dentifrice of international reputation." One wonders about the connection between raving beauties and teeth. Perhaps only Sigmund Freud could reveal the mystery; I am certain that, had he been asked, he would have propounded some theory that would hold our interest.)

Such a complicated, anarchic human being—a woman, at that—appealed to the devilish Oscar Wilde. He loved to exploit the idea of a gradually unfolding personality or, rather, personalities, in his own fiction, most dramatically in *The Importance of Being Earnest* and most mysteriously in his several stories about ghosts. His new play would provide for him the major opportunity to push the possibilities of the twin themes he loved so much—concealment and revelation.

The coming together of Sarah Bernhardt and Oscar Wilde has to stand as one of the great artistic collaborations of the nineteenth century. Born to a socially prominent Anglo-Irish family in 1854, Wilde was well-known in London society as a dandy, a sharp wit, and an enormously talented writer—but also as an underground figure, the dubious star of the demimonde and, as we saw earlier, of the aesthetic movement known as the decadents. While he would achieve great success in the theater, he would also suffer condemnation, as a homosexual, from no less a personage than the Marquess of Queensbury. Most of Wilde's biographers interpret that scorn as a way for the Marquess to put an end to the romance between his son, Lord Alfred Douglas, and Wilde. Seemingly unflappable, Wilde turned the disapproval to his own purposes, answering the Marquess in the form of a letter of bitter reproach entitled *De Profundis* (1905). He continually searched for the right subject into which he could pour his nontraditional ideas about power, attraction, revelation, and sexual freedom. He found what he wanted in the Bible's second example of seduction, the young and beautiful Salomé.

Salomé was a first-century Palestinian princess, daughter of Herod's son Philip and Herodias, who was responsible for the death of John the Baptist. By the time Wilde took hold of the Salomé story, almost every writer in the last few decades of the nineteenth century—English, Swiss, Russian, Portuguese, Spanish, Lithuanian, American, German, Polish, Irish, but mostly French—had tried to capture her in print. Salomé had become by that time a symbol of decadence, a coming together of love and death in a single person. According to one literary historian, by 1912 close to three thousand French poets had written about her. Flaubert actually traveled to the Middle East in 1850 to research "the harem dance" for his own rendering of Salomé, who entranced every other character in his novel, *Salammbô*. The previous year, Gustave Moreau had shown his two paintings of Salomé, which created such a sensation in the local press and in Parisian society that over half a million people traveled great distances just to see the canvases for themselves.

Wilde drew his immediate source for the story of Salomé from two passages in the Bible, the Gospels of Mark (6:17–29) and Matthew (14:3–6). But the biblical version did not serve either his dramatic or his political purposes. The Bible gave readers an innocent, young Salomé bullied by her mother to make off with the head of John the Baptist. She agrees to the dance as an act of redemption to rid herself of the taint of her mother. Wilde, on the other hand, saw the story as a parable of woman's outsized sexual power. He transformed Salomé into a young woman keenly power-ful, independent, and in total control. In Wilde's revolutionary version, the young Salomé takes great delight in dancing naked before the king; she revels in her newfound power; she delights in both confronting and controlling the gaze of the court. A brief outline of the play reveals Wilde's intentions.

King Herod has recently married his sister-in-law, Herodias, after im-prisoning and then executing her husband, Herod Philip, who was also his half brother. In celebration of his birthday, Herod plays host to a grand banquet. In a situation that Wilde absolutely loved, Herod has married his own sister-in-law, and thus become stepfather to his own niece, Salomé, a strikingly beautiful young woman.

The king has several times cast his eye on young Salomé, making Herodias more than a bit jealous. While that provides grist for the mill of jealousy, the drama does not get going, however, until Wilde introduces another conflict, John the Baptist, who has been traveling up and down the land announcing the coming of the Messiah. He has also condemned the marriage of Herod and Herodias. Herodias has insisted that her husband imprison him and has further demanded his execution. But Herod has balked at the idea, afraid that John might indeed be carrying the news directly from God.

At that moment, Wilde shifts the action back to Herod, who, in his wine-soaked state, decrees that the young Salomé must dance for him to enliven his celebration. To everyone's horror, Salomé refuses. Her mother, standing by her side, supports her brazen daughter. In fact, she openly chides her new husband for his lascivious eye. Herod then decides to offer Salomé whatever she chooses, including elevation to high priestess, if she will only dance for him. Again, he hears only staunch refusal. But he's Herod, after all, a man not to be spurned. And so Herod raises the ante and offers half his kingdom as payment. Finally, Salomé agrees but declines the offer of the kingdom. She has something else in mind, which she will only disclose, she teases, at the conclusion of her dance.

Salomé leaves for a brief moment and reappears, to everyone's surprise, wearing only seven diaphanous veils of seven different colors. Then she gracefully begins to dance, slowly removing each of the veils—first from her face and shoulders, then her waist, hips, legs, breasts, and finally, spinning slowly round and round, she pulls off the final veil and stands before the king absolutely naked.

Salomé pleases Herod beyond his wildest expectations. He asks her what she now desires as a reward. Without hesitating, she asks, in a very straightforward manner, for the head of John the Baptist on a silver charger.

Herod receives the news with shock. He pleads with her to ask for anything else—"He is a holy man. He is a man who has seen God." But, with her mother by her side urging her on, she stands her ground before the mightiest of kings and repeats her solitary demand in the same emotionless way: Bring the head of John the Baptist before me on a silver charger.

Salomé remains insistent, in part, because earlier in the evening she has seen John the Baptist in his cell and hopelessly and passionately fallen in love with him. When she declares her love to him, John the Baptist scolds her and turns her aside in a most rough and rude manner. She persists, confessing her love, she announces, for a trinity of reasons—for his body, for his magnificent hair, but most of all for his mouth. "Suffer me to kiss thy mouth," she urges as she pushes herself on him. But he, as stubborn as she, will have none of it: "Never! . . . Daughter of Sodom! Never." He rebukes her and he is done. The matter is closed.

A bargain is a bargain and Herod reluctantly agrees to Salomé's demand. And, when Herod has the head brought out to her, in a scene that startles all the birthday guests, Salomé walks calmly and deliberately over to it and, by slowly planting a kiss on the mouth of the severed head, finally succeeds in getting her earlier demand. A bitter taste lingers on her lips, she tells the startled assembly, but adds that, in the end, bitterness may be the true and only taste of love. Revolted by her behavior, Herod scolds Herodias. "She is monstrous, thy daughter. . . . In truth, what she has done is a great crime. I am sure that it is. A crime against some unknown God." In the last line of the play, the audience can hear Herod screaming, somewhere offstage, "Kill that woman!" Herod's guards move swiftly, with swords raised, ready to slay the young Salomé.

Wilde planned to stage *Salomé* at the Palace Theater. According to notes that he sent to his friends, Wilde had written the play with Sarah Bernhardt in mind. Why not? By the 1890s, Sarah Bernhardt was the richest, most flamboyant, and most publicized actress of her time. Only

Houdini, and at times the strongman Eugen Sandow, performed before larger audiences than the divine Sarah Bernhardt.

Both Bernhardt and Houdini were masters of illusion—their stock in trade, utter and absolute power over appearance, which is to say power over disappearance. Both were shape-shifters: two Jews born in Europe who changed their names to take on more exotic and intriguing characters. Both of them worked hard at not fitting in, at defying all categories. They acted like vamps, in that late-nineteenth-century sense of sensually enticing vampires—creatures who changed identities (names), who lived on that thin line separating life from death, reality from irreality, and who threatened to suck the life out of respectable society. Death defying, convention defying, they wrapped themselves in mystery and intrigue. On the stage, however, in full view of the public, they wrapped themselves in very little, preferring to perform near naked, or even totally naked. Sandow, Bernhardt, Houdini: Audiences knew and respected all three, first and foremost, as strongly in possession of something that they themselves found missing: bodies.

As with Oscar Wilde, fans simply could not get their fill of gossip about the private life of Sarah Bernhardt, her torrid love affairs, her more perverse sexual adventures, her penchant for posing nude for well-known artists, and her general extravagant style of life. For Wilde, the biblical Salomé merged with the mythical Sarah Bernhardt. She hired the modern equivalent of the premier public relations firm, Downey of London, to create an image for her and to spin it, like a giant coin, around the world. (Keep in mind this is the period when a new professional appears on the scene, the literary agent.) She commissioned the famous photographer Nadar to concoct the most daring poses of her—with various exotic animals, in the most whimsical and far-out locations, such as African backdrops, pyramids, and the deepest jungles. In some ways, Bernhardt needed no agent, for, like Salomé, with just her presence she mesmerized audiences all over the world. Again, like Salomé, she could also extract from theater owners whatever ransom she secretly or openly desired. She could, as the saying goes, name her own price. After all, she repeatedly sold out the largest theaters in Europe. Audiences lined up well in advance of her performance date to make sure they had tickets.

In love her entire life with characters out of the Bible, Bernhardt went into rehearsal for the Wilde play with great enthusiasm. She adored Salomé, she confessed to reporters. In May 1892, she even transported her entire acting troupe from Paris to London for one express purpose, which we learn from a letter written by Oscar Wilde to the French poet Pierre Louÿs: "You've heard the news, haven't you? Sarah is going to play Salomé!!! We rehearse today." That turned out to be an historic moment in the history of theater.

After all, Wilde was promising audiences that they would soon see the incomparable and elusive Sarah Bernhardt up close and dancing before King Herod. Every aspect of her being that audiences mooned over—her exotic movements, her sensuality, her desire to titillate and shock—they might behold in that one dance. Newspapers talked of it; theater lovers dreamed of it. What does Salomé's dance look like? I do not know. No one does. Except for the veils, I can only imagine its shape. Wilde invited theatergoers and readers not just to imagine, but to imagine the far reaches, the outer limits, of something as commonplace as a dance.

"Too much was just enough" could stand as Wilde's motto. For this play, he insisted that the actors all dress in yellow, against a deep violet sky. He demanded a stage filled with huge braziers blazing with fire during the entire performance. Not content with just any fire, Wilde wanted the flames to fill the auditorium with a variety of exotic perfumes, wafting into the audience and intoxicating each person.

Just before working on the play, Wilde had been reading Richard von Krafft-Ebing's *Psychopathia Sexualis*, an anthology of graphic and aberrant sexual case histories based on medical testimonies. (Recall, this is a period that created the idea of deviance, the outsider, and the freak.) In particular,

Wilde had been deeply fascinated by Case VII in Krafft-Ebing, an account of a woman who, from the age of thirteen, found herself addicted to lust and an all-consuming desire for sexual intercourse. He took detailed notes about her behavior, holding up for praise her refusal, even at such a young age, to recognize norms and boundaries. He found in this young woman the living example of Salomé. I will return to the dance in a moment, but to appreciate Wilde's fractured conceptualization of something as familiar as a dance we must keep in mind the fact that Wilde derived enormous pleasure and power from his own penchant for breaking the rules of decorum.

In that regard, Wilde shared a great deal with Nietzsche. More than anything else, both yearned for freedom from the constraints of normal or even so-called avant-garde behavior. Wilde's behavior was of a piece, refusing, even in his writing, to respect the standards of recognizable, understandable prose. His obsessive patterns of repetition and the hallucinatory quality of his descriptions remind one of Edgar Allan Poe on some psychotropic drug. Consider, for example, his brief description, in *Salomé*, of the moon. The moon is no longer a planet but has become humanized. No more man in the moon—it is now an evocative and seductive woman:

> The moon has a strange look tonight. Has she not a strange look? She is like a mad woman, a mad woman who is seeking everywhere for lovers. She is naked, too. She is quite naked. The clouds are seeking to clothe her nakedness, but she will not let them. She shows herself naked in the sky. She reels through the clouds like a drunken woman . . . I am sure she is looking for lovers. Does she not reel like a drunken woman? She is like a mad woman, is she not?

Nietzsche loved the dance, the naked, intoxicated dance; and he loved laughter. For him, a true life could be lived only when it had rid itself of all constraints. Only the brave, the heroic, could risk something so magnificent. Wilde imagined precisely the same kind of world; and he saw his own superior self reflected in his double, Miss Sarah Bernhardt. For both Wilde and Bernhardt lived like *Übermenschen*—supermen—beyond good and evil, beyond the slightest thought of recrimination from those critics who continually took aim at their extravagances. To what end? Wilde and Bernhardt had no shame; they felt no guilt. They experienced no remorse or regret. If ever there were a celebration of the unrestrained, unfettered self onstage—the free expression of individual spirit—*Salomé* was that play. And Sarah Bernhardt would take the stage as its embodiment, the polar opposite of that other Sarah, the one from South Africa. Wilde gave birth to the entire dramatic undertaking: He was playwright, director, and entrepreneur. He, too, was a star, a person of total self-reliance and total self-absorption. Wilde apologized to no one, and responded to everyone.

It may seem strange, then, that Wilde barely referred to that crucial and climactic moment of the play, the famous dance, and offered no details and gave no stage directions for its execution. He merely mentioned on one page of the script, in mostly lowercase letters sandwiched between brackets, that "[Salomé dances the dance of the seven veils.]" Wilde confided to friends, however, that he saw the dance as the key to unlocking the central meaning of the play. That he gave no specific directions, however, attested in part to Oscar Wilde's faith in Sarah Bernhardt's talent, attraction, and, more important, her keen intellect coupled with her wild spirit. Wilde knew that Bernhardt could turn a simple dance performance into a protracted episode of sheer exotic fantasy. He would, it appeared, allow her to improvise and see how her instincts played out in front of a live audience.

In 1900, he wrote to a friend about what he saw as Sarah Bernhardt's truest, deepest nature, an inexplicable quality born of the most mysterious imaginings of the Orient. In the note, Wilde says, "The only person in the world who could act Salomé is Sarah Bernhardt, that 'serpent of old Nile,' older than the Pyramids."[17] Wilde doesn't say she could merely act the part of Salomé. Instead, he says she can "act Salomé." The word *act*—Bernhardt's chosen profession, after all—in its broadest sense refers to a confluence, of sorts, between deep emotion and its expression through the whole body. The word *actor* is cognate with *author*: A good actor creates his or her own new, fabricated self on the stage by paying strict attention to narration. The actor dies into the role. And so, in Wilde's mind, Sarah Bernhardt had surpassed mere acting. She had become something greater, something more, certainly, than a mere character in a play. Playacting was all right for the run-of-the-mill. Sarah Bernhardt had *become* Salomé. Again, in Wilde's scheme of things, she had prepared for this moment her entire life.

Sarah Bernhardt may have felt the exact same way, as we witness in the following two incidents. In the midst of rehearsal one day, some skeptical theater critic asked Bernhardt, then forty-eight years old, whom she would choose to perform the dance in her place. She snapped back, saying that as long as she could manage a single step, she and no one else would dance Salomé. And when another critic asked what she had in mind for the choreography of Salomé's dance, she yelled in the poor man's face: "Never you mind."[18]

Wilde was less cryptic. In fact, he spoke rather bluntly, telling a friend that Salomé must end up on the stage no other way but naked. But Wilde had a different take even on the idea of nakedness. He intended a stylized version of nakedness, one that smacked of the exotic: "Yes, totally naked, but draped with heavy and ringing necklaces made of jewels of every colour, warm with the fervour of her amber flesh."[19] Wilde indirectly opened the door to the craze for the Salomé dance, as well as for other versions of so-called Oriental dancing, that marked the last decades of the end of the nineteenth century. If Africa represented nineteenth-century white fantasies of savagery and racial inferiority, the Orient symbolized the exotic, the amorous, the highly charged sexual life. Baartman and Africa, Bernhardt and the Orient: One could not hope to find in this period more extravagantly opposed pairs—of countries, of styles, of Western perceptions of humanity, of stardom and fame, of sexuality, and, finally, of women.

To refer to something called the Orient and something called Africa is, of course, to refer to not very much, if anything at all. Africa is vast, made up of many nations, and the same holds for that highly romanticized abstraction, the Orient. Both terms refer to fantasies, constructions generated by the colonizing, imperial mind and imagination of the British Empire in the nineteenth century. Both concepts reduce enormous complexity to a single, easily digestible concept.

Bernhardt and Wilde tried their whole lives to break out of that kind of colonizing grip. Indeed, they pursued the exact opposite—an uncircumscribed life, free of constraint or definition of any kind. And that is why those in authority worked at putting them into that new, nineteenth-century category where they put homosexuals and thieves and, evidently, some divas, the *deviant*. Here was a category they could understand and deal with; the category made sense out of loose and undignified behavior. Once they placed Wilde inside that definition, then of course they could refuse Wilde the opportunity to mount his play. And they could further prevent his sultry compatriot Sarah Bernhardt, no matter the role, from stepping foot on the English stage.

The examiner of plays for the Lord Chamberlain, Mr. Edward Pigott, banned *Salomé*, he said, because it dealt with a biblical subject. Very few people believed his explanation. And, indeed, in a letter to a friend—kept secret for many years—he made his real reasons for canceling *Salomé* quite clear, referring to Wilde's play, among other insulting descriptions, as "a miracle of impudence."[20] Both playwright and actress expressed their disappointment in the local newspapers, Wilde fuming to reporters that he could no longer live in a country like England that would stoop so low as to condemn a biblical play: "I shall leave England and settle in France, where I will take out letters of naturalization. I will not consent to call myself a citizen of a country that shows such narrowness of artistic judgement."[21]

Wilde may have announced his intention to move to France, but he did not immediately flee England; and of course he faced all kinds of indignities, including a protracted trial, imprisonment, and later forced exile for his unapologetic homosexuality. Sarah Bernhardt immediately returned to

France. Wilde's *Salomé* finally reached the stage in 1896 at Aurélien Lugné-Poë's Théâtre de l'Oeuvre with Lina Munte as Salomé. Her dance followed closely my own imagined choreography of seven colored veils falling about her as she spun slowly around and around in the muted light.

While Oscar Wilde may not have actually been the first person to promote disrobing onstage, professional stripping—a most sensual disappearing act—did have its birth in the nineteenth century, and Wilde certainly hurried its evolution along. The famous nightclub the Folies Bergère had opened in 1869, shocking Parisian society with a chorus line of women who, for that time, wore quite revealing costumes. With the opening of that club came a new performance art, perhaps more popular today than in the nineteenth century, the striptease. In time with orchestras playing schmaltzy renditions of Oriental-sounding music, women, in carefully choreographed movements, would slowly remove their lavish costumes onstage.

At the 1893 Chicago World's Fair, a young Algerian woman named Ashea Wabe performed what the fair billed as the ultimate Oriental dance, the "hootchy-kootchy." Part of the allure came from her stage name, Little Egypt. She fanned her own flames by selling her petit provocations to clients on the Upper East Side of Manhattan. Arrested one evening at the apartment of the son of one of her backers, the wealthy circus promoter Phineas T. Barnum, she defended herself in court by cooing to the magistrate, "Oh, Monsieur, just a little pose in the altogether, a little Egyptian slave girl, comprenez-vous? . . . I do what is proper for a-r-r-r-r-t."[22]

Newspaper accounts of Little Egypt's performance described her shedding her garments one at a time until she stood before the audience in the absolute altogether—that is, totally naked. But the climax of the dance had a hook, and the Salomé dance no doubt reached its finale in the same way. Given the various exotic dancers at the time, like Little Egypt, and dozens of others including the equally famous Maud Allan, we can only assume the same conclusion for all of them. I turn again to the master, Oscar Wilde, to reveal the unusual conclusion to the striptease. In an inscription on a copy of the French edition of *Salomé,* dated March 1893, addressed to his equally outrageous friend, the artist Aubrey Beardsley, Wilde wrote: "[F]or Aubrey: for the only artist who, besides myself, knows what the dance of the seven veils is, and can see that invisible dance."[23]

Wilde called the dance of the seven veils an invisible one not so much, I believe, because he withheld all stage directions, but because the dancer ended up, in a sense, on the stage unseen and without location. After removing her seventh and final veil, Little Egypt, say, stood motionless for an instant totally naked, but only for an instant. For immediately the lights went out, the house went dark, and the audience at one and the same time saw everything and nothing. The dancer disappeared, vanished. And the audience was left with only an afterimage—a ghostly presence—the entire performance devolving into nothing more than the definition of titillation, of provocation—a living symbol of the ghostly nature of the times. Just as disappearance marked the age itself, so disappearance—of the dancer, of what the dance promised, of the artistic climax—really stood as the theme of Salomé's remarkable act.

Peel away the layers of meaning from reality, from any subject, including—or perhaps especially—the unending layers of human sensibility, and you find . . . nothing. Or, a person might for an instant believe that he or she had indeed seen something, but the belief lasted but an instant—once again, leaving the person with only a ghostly image, the specter of evidence. You have it, or you think you do, and then it vanishes. It's over in the blink of an eye. We have heard this same lament from fictional characters like Sherlock Holmes and from serious authors like Nathaniel Hawthorne. Scientist after scientist thought he or she had found the philosopher's stone, the basic, core meaning of human existence—the structure of experience— only to have it, *poof,* disappear out of hand. The answer turned out to lie somewhere else, to be something else. Another, more appealing theory came along to supplant the earlier one.

Edmund Gurney is a good case in point. A Cambridge scholar and one of the founders of Britain's Society for Psychical Research, Gurney had the most profound experience of his life, he wrote, while sitting in a dentist's chair. Under the influence of heavy drafts of nitrous oxide—a gift, you may recall, from Joseph Priestley and Humphry Davy—he saw with utmost clarity the secret to eternal life and could not wait to tell the dentist, and then the entire world. Alas, when he shook off his dreaminess, he could remember no details of that most compelling secret. Nothing remained, he lamented, but the feeling—and even that slowly drifted to nothingness, as well.

Poor Gurney, left with only the fading memory of the event. And for everyone else, too, nothing remained but performance, the art of looking: the search itself. We can regard the incipient striptease, the dance of Salomé and her magical veils of seven different colors, which had its magical birth in the latter part of the nineteenth century, as a dramatic representation of the investigative method titillatingly at work as scientists tried to lift the layers of illusion and peer into reality itself. And maybe that was the lesson in the end, that nothing mattered (and, at the same time, had no matter), really, but the dance itself. Living, itself, is finally all that we have. Perhaps that is the only truth. Which leads to Wilde's second source for his character of Salomé.

Wilde found his other, more ancient source for his dance of the seven veils in the goddess Ishtar, who dates from some four thousand years before the birth of Christ, in Babylon. In a journey reminiscent of Orpheus, Ishtar descends to the underworld to retrieve her son (and sometime husband) Tammuz. (Tammuz is also an ancient Hebrew month that follows the summer solstice and marks the retreat of the sun and the shortening of the days. It is a time of mourning, of fasting even—an appropriate moment to begin a descent into the underworld.) Before each of the seven portals to the underworld, Ishtar has to remove some article of clothing or adornment until, in the "land of no return," she stands absolutely naked, divested of all illusion—the naked truth embodied. (Here, she resembles literature's other great embodiment of the naked truth, King Lear.) According to Carl Jung,[24] Ishtar descends not into some nondescript underworld, but into the unconscious itself. There, she must confront her shadow self, her double—in this case, Tammuz. In Ishtar, Wilde found perhaps a perfect symbol, for he always concerned himself with the deep psychological underpinnings of behavior. In this reading, Salomé engages in the ultimate unveiling. (It is important, in this regard, to keep in mind that Sarah Bernhardt titled her memoir *My Double Life.)*

Imagine the entirety of a complicated century devolving into nothing more than a veil, that small and diaphanous piece of material that occludes the object from the gaze of the viewer. The veil is a film, through which one sees objects and events in a most ghostly way. Historians first used the word *film* for the new technology of photography in the 1840s, giving precise recognition to film as a thin veil on which the camera imprinted a picture of reality. This principal substance, film, came to stand for the art form itself. Moviegoers in the late nineteenth century went to theaters to watch films, a series of ghostlike, evanescent images projected onto a screen. Unlike their visits to brightly lit museums, people got used to seeing more and more of their images in darkness or half darkness, as shadows in the twilight play between light and dark.

They entered the theater, many of them reported, as if into a cave—or, perhaps, like little Alice, into the underworld of imagination and fantasy. Once inside, once underground, anything could happen, and usually did. For the theater offered a brand new, reordered world, one characterized not by logic or reason but by magic, or, more accurately, the strange and shifting logic of dreams. The old rules fell away. It was mythmaking, shape-shifting, elusive and marvelous: the mundane world, heightened and attenuated. The movie theater had its projector, the live theater its phantasmagoria, a machine for creating ghosts that seemed to flutter and glide in midair. Theater images suggested rather than shouted; they insinuated rather than commanded. They moved at a fairly rapid clip. The glimpse replaced the stare. Victorians increasingly viewed the world as through a glass darkly: Meaning moved closer to metaphor, fertile ground for aesthetic movements like impressionism and pointillism, and fertile ground, too, for the desire for entertainment that dominated the end of the period, and which took over in the following centuries.

Liminality works its power by promising so much and delivering so little; it vibrates with an erotic charge. It titillates. Like impressionistic paintings, veiled and suggestive images leave much to the imagination. The observer has to work, providing many of the fine details and, in the process of interpretation, revealing just a bit of himself or herself. (The words *veil* and *reveal* come from the same Middle English root, *veile*, "a sail." To reveal literally means "to pull back the curtain," hence "to disclose," so that every intellectual revelation resembles a stage entrance—a surprise.) The veil is the translucent shower door through which we catch the barest outlines of a naked, lathered body; or it is the oiled rice paper door in the traditional Japanese house through which family members observe, as a blur, various intimacies.

But of course the veil also serves as a mask. Muslim women hide a good bit of their faces behind the *hijab* or *purdah*. Even in the East, the veil sends mixed messages: Some say it liberates the woman, some say it oppresses. And we also know the veil as another, more pointed kind of religious symbol: To "take the veil" means that a nun has chosen God as her bridegroom. Salomé and Little Egypt, along with the other nascent stripteasers, incorporated all the various meanings of the veil and used them in just those ways—Salomé, oh so exotic, so religious, so liberated, and yet so sensual. Or, perhaps dancing in front of the male gaze, Salomé collapses into nothing more than a sexual object. She reveals, she occludes. She gives, and she steals reality back again.

The veil also characterizes that incredibly popular genre born in the nineteenth century, the detective story, which gains its literary life from the twin themes of concealment and disclosure. (The word *detective* appears in England in 1843 for the first time, in the phrase "detective policeman," what today we would call the plainclothes detective.) The heart of those stories, from Poe to Conan Doyle, always moves to an unveiling of the truth. Anyone with a keen mind can pierce through the veil "to discover matters artfully concealed" (per the *Oxford English Dictionary*). "Beyond the veil" was not just a nineteenth-century stock term for referring to the world of the departed, but for seeing through the profusion of details to the root meaning of reality. And thus Marshall Berman points out that "for Marx, writing in the aftermath of bourgeois revolutions and reactions, and looking forward to a new wave, the symbols of nakedness and unveiling regain the dialectical depth that Shakespeare gave them two centuries before. The bourgeois revolutions, in tearing away veils of 'religious and political illusion,' have left naked power and exploitation, cruelty and misery, exposed like open wounds."[25] But the veil also connects Salomé with Sarah Baartman in yet one more way.

Along with her huge buttocks, Sarah Baartman's vagina also fascinated scientists. Georges Cuvier had hoped to study the unusually large piece of skin that supposedly covered the vaginas of African bushwomen, what scientists called the *sinus pudoris,* or "curtain of shame," or, as others in the period called it, more crudely, the Hottentot apron. Sarah Baartman kept that part of her anatomy hidden during her lifetime, however, even refusing to reveal her genitals when she posed in the nude at the Jardin du Roi. Unlike Sarah Bernhardt, Sarah Baartman was not trying to be coy or seductive. She was merely trying to hide her shame. Her anatomical veil was all she had left to hide behind. (Ironically, I find that scientists sometimes mistranslated *sinus pudoris*—even Linnaeus himself—as "women are without shame.") Her reluctance explains in part Cuvier's great delight at being able, finally, not just to observe her private parts, but to dissect them as well. Scientific certainty lay at the end of his scalpel.

So Cuvier went right to the genitals, explaining to his assembled colleagues at the Académie Royale de Médecine, in the most shocking of terms, that "there is nothing more famous in natural history than the *tablier* [the French rendering of *sinus pudoris*] of Hottentots, and, at the same time, no feature has been the object of so many arguments."[26] The arguments to which Cuvier referred revolved around the true nature of the veil. Did it really exist? Was it actually outsized, as Western scientists had claimed? Could one actually see through it? Cuvier asked fundamental questions about Sarah Baartman that no other scientist would ever conceive of asking about white women. When Cuvier presented Sarah's genitalia to the Académie, he held them aloft as a kind of trophy, declaring: "I have the honor to present to the Académie the genital organs of this woman prepared in a manner that leaves no doubt about the nature of her *tablier.*" His distinguished audience now had the scientific evidence—a thin membrane, a veil—that they claimed they so badly needed to convince the world of the bestial sexuality of African women.

In the end, in fact, nothing was left of Sarah Baartman but that kind of degraded sexuality that Cuvier and others had constructed around her. She was taken apart, bit by bit, by lurid spectators while she lived, and dissected afterward by Cuvier's clan. In the end, no real person, no Sarah Baartman of South Africa, no vibrant Khoisan tribal member, existed. She lived out her days as a cipher, silent and unheard, in the strangest sort of intimacy with those who exploited her. No one in that white world, it appeared, ever heard her continual cry of anguish. She resembled the horrific quiet—pain as no more than a ghostly presence—that Edvard Munch rendered in his painting *The Scream* in 1893. White men in white smocks measured and described in elaborate detail every part of her anatomy, even, as we have seen, the most private of those parts.

At the conclusion of Sarah Bernhardt's dance of the seven veils, also, nothing remained. The stage went dark, leaving the audience on their own to wonder and imagine. No magnificent, larger-than-life superstar stared down at them from that most elevated stage. And while she may have vanished, she momentarily gave audience members back their feelings, for, as with a thrill ride at an amusement park, what lingered were titillation, excitement, and the magic of the moment. Most important, Sarah Bernhardt gave the audience a chance to think about what they had just seen. After a brief pause, gaffers would bring the lights back up on a stage empty save for an array of seven veils of seven different colors. For all anybody knew, Sarah Bernhardt might have died. (She in fact loved to feign her own death. Photographs of her asleep in an open coffin sold by the thousands around the world. Early on, her publicists offered the photographs as proof of her sudden demise. Then she would suddenly appear in some out-of-the-way city, with great fanfare, having bounced back, mysteriously, to life: the actress playing the role of the queen of the undead.) But of course the audience knew better. Every last one of them had been thoroughly entertained—taken in—by the mistress of illusion. She had not died; she had disappeared. And audiences ate it up.

For those who observed the other Sarah, Sarah Baartman, all that remained were repulsion and repugnance—and, of utmost importance, the knowledge that they, the white audience, inhabited different and more elegantly designed bodies. Which is to say that they belonged to a separate and superior species. In a key sense, white people were bearing witness, they had come to believe, to a graphic representation of the awful but all too evident truths of polygenesis, two races forever separated, one inferior to the other and, in some strange ways, each defining its existence by the other. Racism and beauty share at least one salient point—they are both only skin deep.

And so, before the very startled eyes of thousands of onlookers, both Sarahs vanished on the stage: The audience found nothing more to observe but a congeries of thoughts and expectations, a swirling of desires. The dance of the seven veils and the striptease—the "hootchy-kootchy"—represented in quite dramatic fashion one of the major struggles in the period: the attempt by scientists and philosophers to find the essence, the ground, of human existence by dissecting reality into its constituent parts. Science provided but a glimpse at some truth, offering a theory that quickly got supplanted by yet another, more reasonable-sounding theory. And still the period persisted in trying to find that one essential answer to existence. Ironically, it may have been there all along, right before their very eyes. The essential ingredient may have been the paradoxical nature of their own act of looking: the grand expectations and the inevitable letdown. The process and not the product provided the actual meaning. The searching, the curiosity, kept them going. The secret of life lay in the living itself, the lesson seemed to be, not in the outcome, and certainly not in the allure of fame or fortune.

Social and political conditions in the nineteenth century made the times ripe for the emergence of the striptease and its wholesale embrace by bourgeois French society. It appealed for obvious sensual and sexual reasons. It made nightlife exciting, provocative, and allowed clubgoers to feel safely like outlaws. For a brief few hours, Oscar Wilde and his crew had nothing on them. But deeper social reasons also contributed to its spectacular popularity. Though very few people stopped to think about it, the striptease carried powerful metaphoric meaning in its ritual of removing layer upon layer, revealing—maybe something, but most often absolutely nothing. To paraphrase *King Lear*'s fool, "Nothing will come of nothing, my lord." The fool reveals the shape of reality. For he describes precisely how people do in fact negotiate reality—we all construct meaning out of our own perceptions. We typically make something out of nothing.

The fool, one of the most wickedly intelligent persons in the kingdom—speaking his enigmatic sentences that point to nothingness—strips Lear of his rhetorical excesses and reduces him to his most basic human essence. At the climax of the play, he stands beside his lord in the middle of a raging storm, as Lear peels off his robes, divesting himself of royal authority: He stands stark naked before raw nature, a Renaissance embodiment of Ishtar. Still holding on to the title of king, Lear gives himself over to the elements, declaring that he is nothing more than a "poor, bare, forked animal." The howling storm, the howling Lear—it is a moment of overwhelming terror for the battered old man. Shakespeare's vision is dark here, as dark as the storm. But, as so often happens in nature (and tragedy), a bolt of lightning punctuates the dark with a momentary brilliance.

In one of those brief flashes, Lear turns to the fool and, for the first time in his rather long and painful life, offers another person refuge inside his meager cave. As the play suggests and the nineteenth century makes apparent, in the end one has only the basics: faith and friendship and love—the highly invisible, bedrock ideas on which we try so hard to build our lives. The king, the man whose rank suggests worldly wisdom, is only just learning this simple but profound lesson. A fool is his teacher; nature provides the classroom. And we, the audience members, are learning that basic lesson along with him.

Such basic truths come to us thinly veiled. To hear it from Nietzsche, truth can *only* come to us opaque. We see as through a glass darkly. Indeed, once the light shines brightly, truth falls away: "One should not," Nietzsche says, "believe that truth remains truth when you remove its veil."[27] Truth comes, then, as an approximation, in that liminal space as we cross the threshold from darkened theater and move slowly into the fading, outside light. In that transition, like Lear, we get thrown back on ourselves. We turn elemental, basic, essential. In a sense, the move into daylight from the theater is a move into a radically different light—hopefully, into insight. We change from spectator to seer. That radical shift can happen when we leave Sarah Baartman's cage, or Sarah Bernhardt's stage.

We must remember, there is always the chance that the sunlight will blind. Thus Plato cautions us in the parable of the cave. Maybe shadow puppets should suffice. In the end, we are the projectors—projecting light onto the shadows, and projecting meaning onto those puppets. We make them move. When is it that we actually see into the deepest heart of things? Does it ever really happen? Perhaps not. But we persist. We doggedly persist. That's what it means in great part to be alive.

Shakespeare equates nakedness with the unadorned truth. As I have argued in this chapter, the two Sarahs participate in different kinds of nakedness that posit different sorts of truths. We can seize on nakedness ourselves, like Lear; or have it imposed on us, like Sarah Baartman; or manipulate others with it, like Sarah Bernhardt. Lear learns from his experience, and comes to see that his very own kingdom is filled with scores of people, just like him at the moment, who face the elements without protection. They live their lives as "poor naked wretches." With that insight, he heads back into the cave; but first he asks the fool to enter before him—a small gesture that reveals a change in Lear's attitude toward the world around him.

So that's what Lear ultimately sees—and that's what, in the end, redeems him. But, like the sun, lightning can also blind. Keep Plato in mind here: It's possible to learn not a single thing—nothing may indeed come of nothing. To guard against coming up morally short, we just need to lean a little closer to Lear: We need to pay more attention to the suffering. Wilde and his crowd may be right—the fools and the outliers do bring us the news. Those are real people in the kingdom. They need shelter from the storm. We just need to heed their existence. We must pay attention to their needs.

Lear is a play. People paid admission to see it. Two hundred years later, they also paid to see the two Sarahs. As far as audiences were concerned, they viewed both women as theatrical attractions. We certainly need the recreation of the world through art and entertainment, but diversions intrigue us more when we carry their lessons back into the harsh realities of life. To use an example from the most popular form of mass entertainment in the period: An early, obscure piece of film footage from the turn of the century shows Sigmund Freud, the avatar of high seriousness, making his dignified way through Steeplechase Park at Coney Island. At some point, although the film does not record the transaction, the great Sigmund Freud will have to say "so long" to Coney, hop on the subway, and walk the streets of Brooklyn once again.

What would the tenement buildings look like to him then? What would the plain speech of the butchers and waiters and fishmongers sound like to him then? Would new theories, of pleasure and pain, work their way into his consciousness that summer Sunday afternoon? Did he welcome the fear growing in the pit of his stomach as the Loop-the-Loop, an early roller coaster at Coney built in the form of several graceful ovals, turned Doctor Freud upside down as it made its circuits high in the air? Or did he just put the damper on his emotions?

FOUR | No One's Dead

O, that this too too solid flesh would melt.

—HAMLET

"WE WILL EACH of us write a ghost story."[1] That's the challenge Lord Byron gave to his friends the evening of June 16, 1816, as they huddled around his fireplace at the Villa Diodati. In past years, standing on his balcony, Byron could see to the far side of Lake Geneva. But that particular summer was strangely and wildly different, as if some preternatural force had descended over the Swiss Alps. Each day passed without relief, unbearably hot and humid with overcast skies. When evening came, the temperature dropped dramatically, bringing severe rainstorms and electrical shows in a night sky so clouded over that for weeks no one had seen even a trace of the moon. The weather drove tourists indoors both day and night. So strange were those three months that newspapers took to calling 1816 "The Year Without a Summer."

That night Byron offered refuge to the poet Percy Bysshe Shelley, Shelley's soon-to-be wife, Mary Wollstonecraft Godwin, and Mary's stepsister, Jane (Claire) Clairmont, at the Villa Diodati. Shelley was twenty-four years old, Mary eighteen. George Gordon, Lord Byron, twenty-eight and a full-fledged hypochondriac, traveled nowhere without his personal physician, John William Polidori, twenty years old and a loner of a man with a knack for alienating virtually every person he met. After some cajoling, Polidori consented to join the others that night.

Before his friends arrived in Switzerland, Byron had been spending his leisure time reading contemporary ghost stories translated from the German, in a volume eerily titled *Tales of the Dead,* stories truly ghostwritten. From childhood on, Byron had had a fascination with ghosts. And so, on that evening of June 16, he decided on a little parlor competition to further his own interest: Each of his friends would make up a ghost story and tell it to the group. Byron permitted none of his guests to retire until they had come up with the general outline of some enticing, wildly imaginative haunting. They did not disappoint their host.

What started out as a lark ended as a landmark event. Those four friends had transformed the ghost story, or the spectral story, for English audiences—tales that mined the extraordinary in everyday life. Byron's friends coaxed the horrific and the terrible out into the open, and turned the evening into a literary success beyond anyone's wildest expectations. The young Mary Godwin launched her serious literary career with the opening gambit for the gothic romance *Frankenstein; or, The Modern Prometheus,* which she published in 1818. Shelley started work on "Mont Blanc," a poem about the pursuit of power in a world bereft of God. And Doctor Polidori, having recently read the French version of *Tales of the Dead,* titled *Fantasmagoriana,* found to his own surprise that he, too, had inside of him the germ of a story. Polidori's tale eventuated in the enormously successful piece "The Vampyre," which he published in 1819.

Only Byron, the master of ceremonies himself, claimed to have trouble conjuring a ghost story, and decided instead to continue writing his tragedy *Manfred.* To be fair, Byron had already turned his attention to Jane Clairmont, who had just turned eighteen, and who fell in line, under the beguiling and oftentimes crushing charm of Lord Byron, as the next of his many mistresses.

Of course, Byron's small coterie of friends had enormous talent, but a good deal of their success came from tapping into a deeper, more general and more widespread interest in ghosts and spirits. While Byron's guests had all made up stories about ghosts, about the supernatural, their tales also mirrored that important cultural change: the disappearance of human beings. More and more, ordinary people in the nineteenth century had come to feel an undertow, an erosion of their sensibilities. On this deeper, more metaphysical level, ghost stories revealed basic truths about their own lives, and the general public simply could not get their fill. Following the publication of *Frankenstein* and "The Vampyre," both British and American readers devoured all kinds of literature about ghosts, and their appetite for the spectral continued to grow throughout the nineteenth century.

This interest in ghosts reached a literary climax, of sorts, in England with the publication, in 1848, of a book titled *The Night Side of Nature*. Written by an author of children's books, the rather slim volume turned its creator, Catherine Crowe, into an immediate celebrity. Borrowing her strategy from Byron and his friends, Crowe gathered hundreds of ghost stories from friends and relatives. Not only could Crowe tell a story well— after all, she had been successful with youngsters for many years—she also invented new words, like *poltergeist,* that entered the popular vocabulary and imagination. But beyond merely wanting to entertain with her anthology of ghost stories, she demanded action: "I wish to engage the attention of my readers, because I am satisfied that the opinions I am about to advocate, seriously entertained, would produce very beneficial results." She never reveals, however, just what those beautiful results might include. *The Night Side,* as it came to be affectionately called, stayed in print for more than fifty years and helped to fuel the movement for serious psychic investigations.

After Crowe, almost every well-established and sophisticated writer, from H. G. Wells to Oscar Wilde, from Robert Louis Stevenson to Henry James, conjured ghosts on the page. Even Harriet Beecher Stowe, the author of *Uncle Tom's Cabin*, wrote several tales about ghosts: "The Ghost in the Mill" and "The Ghost in the Cap'n Brown House." The Cyclopaedia of Ghost Story Writers, an online inventory for the Georgian, Victorian, and Edwardian periods, lists over one hundred writers of ghost stories.

Oscar Wilde was well steeped in the supernatural and he embraced it wholeheartedly, having his chart done and his palm read with regularity by a well-known clairvoyant who went by the name of Mrs. Robinson. And he certainly took a lighthearted and comic attitude toward the spiritual world. In "Lord Arthur Savile's Crime," people mistake chiromancers for chiropodists and have their palms read to discover, much to their chagrin, that they have been involved in some undisclosed murder. It's all great drawing-room fun and disruption of high-society manners.

In his second story, "The Canterville Ghost," which he calls "A Hylo-Idealistic Romance"—which is to say an unclassified tale—he sets about to parody the Gothic world. The story takes place in a haunted house and features an upper-crust spirit named Sir Simon. Along the way, no less a dignitary than the United States ambassador to the Court of Saint James learns to take seriously the power of ghosts and specters. Jules Dassin turned the story into a film, in 1944, starring Charles Laughton—the heavy, substantial Charles Laughton—as Sir Simon the ghost of the House of Canterville.

H. G. Wells figures more prominently in the Cyclopaedia, perhaps because he took his haunting more seriously. He published one of his most famous and well-known stories, "The Invisible Man," in 1897. As with so many other narratives in the nineteenth century, this story turns on a scientific experiment gone completely and tragically wrong. In "The Invisible Man," the main character, Doctor Griffin, of University College, develops a potion to turn himself invisible—but, to his horror, he cannot, even with all his scientific knowledge and academic training, reverse course to attain fleshiness again. This, even though he thought he would prefer total invisibility to his normal state. Doomed to his strange new life, Griffin moves from one place to the next as an unwilling and slightly confused specter.

Like Victor Frankenstein, he has uncovered one of the secrets to life, and, again as with Victor, the experiment turns nasty.

The master of the genre was Henry James, who published three ghost stories over a thirty-year period: "The Romance of Certain Old Clothes" (1868), "Sir Edmund Orme" (1892), and his most popular ghost tale (and one of the most well-known ghost stories of all time), the amazingly enigmatic novella *The Turn of the Screw* (1898). Henry James's fascination with ghosts and the unanswerable would slowly rub off on his younger brother, the renowned psychologist William James, who became one of the staunchest, most vocal, and most respected advocates of the paranormal.

Henry James drew the title for his last ghost story from Shakespeare's *Macbeth*, in which Lady Macbeth, demanding nothing less from her husband than the murder of King Duncan, throws a shocking command at her frightened and cowering partner in crime: "But screw your courage to the sticking-place." Have courage, take heart, particularly in the face of terror and the unknown. A person cannot tighten the screws and still feel feeble and ghostly; murder requires strength and deliberateness—an act of will. Or so Lady Macbeth hopes. How appropriate for the nineteenth century, how mechanical, to "screw" one's courage until it sticks tightly. I can only wonder if James meant that stiff industrial meaning and was thereby sending a sly warning to his Victorian audience: We are not machines; we possess powerful souls and spirit. It would have been an absolutely appropriate message, as the machine exerted more and more control over people's lives, and human beings lost more and more of their humanity, until they began to feel invisible.

As with the ghost-telling sessions sponsored by Lord Byron at the Villa Diodati, James got the idea for *The Turn of the Screw* from a storytelling session. But this one had an odd source: no one other than Edward White Benson, the Archbishop of Canterbury. While a student at Cambridge, Benson had started what he called a "ghost society" and made no secret of visiting local mediums and attending séances. On the coldest of the London winter evenings—and one encountered many such evenings—Benson would host what he called "ghost evenings" at his home. He and his friends would gather in his library, around a hearty fire and even heartier brandy, and try to top each other with tales of some local character who had recently encountered a friendly or, better yet, unruly and demanding specter. To the query, Did that really happen?, the storyteller always responded, My informant swears to it! An odd pursuit, his critics charged, for a man of the cloth. But Benson strongly disagreed. The invisible world held a variety of spirits. Wasn't the Holy Ghost invisible to us all, and did not that specter exert great influence on our daily lives? Did not Christ live in this world and in the invisible one, as well? Won't we all at some point turn spectral?

We should not think of the archbishop as an oddball. The idea of invisibility attracted a huge portion of the population. The theme of disappearance infected everything—science, literature, technology, and virtually all forms of popular entertainment. Even children became conjurers. Victorian boys and girls took great delight in popular toys designed to project pictures of ghosts against a wall, smaller and simpler versions of the more sophisticated ghost-producing machines that would eventually dominate the London stage. Inventors received general patents for the first of these machines, called phantasmagoria, early on in the century, in 1802. Very quickly, they became enormously popular. By the 1830s, ghosts not only took their place on the London stage but, thanks to the more complicated phantasmagoria, also began to assume major roles.

One director in particular, Dion Boucicault, used a phantasmagoria in combination with an elaborate series of trapdoors in an 1852 production of *The Corsican Brothers,* which he adapted from the Alexandre Dumas novel of the same name. Boucicault's gliding trapdoors for the conveyance of ghosts became known in the history of drama as the Corsican traps and enjoyed widespread use for many years in London theaters. By all contemporary accounts, the traps produced the most frighteningly real effects. In the Dumas play, for example, a ghost suddenly appeared "moving in an indistinct, surreal manner: standing still, gliding silently across the stage, and ascending at the same time."[2] Not only was the play an incredible success, but historians of the stage still refer to the appearance of Boucicault's ghost as one of the most fabulous and startling entrances in all of British theater. That same year, 1852, in homage to John Polidori, Dion Boucicault staged an adaptation of "The Vampyre" and played the leading vampire role himself.

Where did the ghost come from? Only Boucicault knew the secret, and he refused to reveal anything. The Victorian toy, he allowed, along with the phantasmagoria, had served as crude models. But he couldn't keep his secret long. Soon enough, inventors figured out Boucicault's mechanical marvel and rushed to create even more realistic specters. A civil engineer and ardent playgoer named Henry Dircks made a few complicated improvements to the phantasmagoria and conjured his own eerie ghosts on Christmas Eve—the traditional start of the English theater season—in 1862, at the well-respected Royal Polytechnic Institution, home of a continuing science fair in the heart of London. There, Dircks knew, he would encounter a most skeptical audience of highbrow scientists. If he could win them over, he reasoned, he could find wild success and universal acceptance anywhere he desired.

At the Institution, Dircks manufactured the ghosts for one of Charles Dickens's most popular holiday stories, *The Haunted Man and the Ghost's Bargain*, and, to the astonishment of a good many critics, managed to wow the skeptics. Contemporary descriptions of Dircks's handiwork make the stage sound truly haunted. In one climactic scene, the audience watched as "a student rose from his chair and seemed to leave his own glowing, transparent soul behind, still seated and watching the action." As if that were not thrilling enough, at the play's conclusion, having vanquished a second ghost that had threatened him, the actor eluded the specter "by seeming to walk through the walls and disappearing." The audience went totally wild.[3]

When the newspapers printed their reviews of that evening's performance, Londoners wanted to see Dircks's ghosts firsthand. The demand grew so insistent, so quickly, that the Polytechnic Institution decided to put on *The Haunted Man* every night for an unheard-of fifteen months in a row. Dircks packed the house every evening. An estimated total of over 250,000 people came not so much to see the play, for audiences knew the story only too well, but to observe the Dircksian phantasmagoria producing its ghostly effects and to try to figure out how the director managed to fool them. Producers everywhere clamored for Dircks the impresario and his fabulous machine. Drury Lane appropriated Dircks's phantasmagoria to produce an array of ghosts for a production of the three-act choral tragedy *Manfred,* the very play that Lord Byron had been working on that haunted evening of June 16, 1816, at the Villa Diodati.

In other countries, audiences demanded their own ghosts. Responding to overseas producers, Dircks brought his magic machine to the American stage in 1863, first to Wallack's Theater in Manhattan and then to other venues. In Paris, a magician named Henri Robin raised families of ghosts at the Theatre Chatelet, adding excitement to his ghost performances by giving his machine a more provocative name, the Living Phantasmagoria. By projecting his lantern images onto diaphanous curtains or onto smoke, Robin could now produce even more startling effects. Reviews described the images as not just dramatic but also strikingly magical: "One terrifying scene portrayed a cemetery. As a man walked among the gravestones, a vision of his fiancée, as a spirit bride, materialized. He reached to embrace the glowing bride, but his arms passed through her. Slowly, she disappeared, leaving him desolate."[4]

Some newspaper articles called Dircks a genius; others described him as nothing more than a trickster, a low-level magician, or, worse yet, a crude technician. What did his critics want—"real" ghosts? One can only suppose so. But every magician harbors the not-so-secret desire to create the wildest, most fabulous illusions ever witnessed. And Dircks was no exception. He thought of himself as a master illusionist, except that he knew how to take his tricks to a remarkably higher level by exploiting the very thing responsible for turning people into ghosts in the first place—technology itself.

But he had his limits. Dircks could astound audiences by making ghosts float and hover, but he could not figure out how to project a believable image of an animated human being and in particular the illusion of the human gait. That was the truly great trick. And while it baffled many inventors, the breakthrough happened sooner than one might have expected—and it happened, like the illusion of movement itself, in discrete stages.

Just about this same time, in the early 1870s, the English-born photographer Eadweard Muybridge refined the technology for photographing motion in general. In San Francisco, while working for the city's most prominent photographer, Muybridge hit on the idea of making still photographs move. He accomplished this by running in rapid succession his photos of horses in a machine he called the Zoopraxiscope, creating the illusion of actual movement, though not in any fluid way. He transformed one meaning of *still*, "quiet and without movement," into its other meaning, "continuous movement." Rather than the feel of contemporary movies, the result resembled the herky-jerky look of early Disney cartoons. Though the technology remained fairly crude, the invention assumed monumental proportions, for Muybridge had taken the first step in turning people's attention away from the real to the *image* of the real.

In 1877, Leland Stanford, who owned some fifty thousand acres in northern California, also owned thoroughbred racehorses and his own racetrack. One question continually plagued him: Does a horse galloping at full speed ever leave the ground with all four hooves at the same moment? If he knew the answer, he believed, he could then train his horses accordingly. And so he hired one of the most experimental photographers of the period, Muybridge, to photograph his favorite horse, Occident, in full stride. The historian of photography Rebecca Solnit points out that "understanding the gaits of a horse in a mechanical way enhanced the possibility of tinkering with it, through breeding, training, and other forms of management. For Stanford, the experiment would allow him to further shift the essence of the horse from the mysteries of nature to the manageable mechanics of industrialism."[5] On top of his love of horses, as president of the Central Pacific Railroad, Stanford had the railroad magnate's maniacal desire to stop time, a topic that I take up in the last chapter.

Muybridge managed to find the answer for Stanford, but only with great effort. First, he developed an incredibly fast shutter, which aligned the speed of the camera almost exactly with the speed of a galloping horse. The next year, 1878, he placed a series of twenty-four cameras around the racetrack, each shutter triggered by a tripwire and set off by the hooves of the running horse or the wheels of a sulky. The series of photographs, which Stanford later published—without acknowledging Muybridge—as The Horse in Motion, indeed show Occident with all four hooves off the ground at once.

Having stopped Occident dead in his tracks, Muybridge then proceeded to revive the horse and make him move once again in 1879, when he unveiled his invention, the Zoopraxiscope, a round metal container fitted with a rotating glass cylinder inside its circumference. On that glass Muybridge painted a series of pictures of the horse and sulky in incremental positions of movement. When a viewer looked through a slit in the side of the machine, the revolving cylinder created the illusion of motion. So impressive was the Zoopraxiscope that it prompted Edison to pursue his own development of a motion picture system, which he first discussed in 1888, and which he called the kinetoscope.

People's current fascination with the simulacrum begins here, with moving images. No one, of course, has to comment on the consuming appeal of motion pictures on both young and old people across the globe. Movement on the screen fascinated viewers then; movement on the big screen with big stars quite obviously fascinates hordes of people today.

In nature, people in the nineteenth century accepted motion as something expected and natural and normal. On the screen, those same people viewed images in motion as spectacular and miraculous. We still do, even sometimes preferring the reproduction over the real thing. In the late nineteenth century, people's attention slowly turned from nature to the nature of the machine; from how things looked to how things worked. It led people to a series of questions in the period about themselves: How do we work? Who are we? What does it mean to be alive? What is the soul, and where does it reside?

Muybridge straddled the line between science and entertainment, winning bets, for instance, with animal trainers about the way horses actually ran. But his appeal extended far beyond the scientists who might have found satisfaction in his experiments because of the physics of motion. Hordes of ordinary people crowded into small spaces, taking turns to peer through his revolving magic machine. They traveled great distances to watch, say, Muybridge's array of photographs of a nude man in various still positions turn into a strangely accurate, and quite magical, rendering of a nude man running, continually running, like the lovers on Keats's Grecian Urn.

Muybridge based his own viewing device on an earlier and simpler machine called the zoetrope, fabricated, in 1834, by an English inventor named William George Horner. While both men created the semblance of actual movement, we owe that cliché phrase "the magic of the theater" to those two French brothers, Auguste and Louis Lumière. Without doubt, the Lumières developed the most sophisticated ghost-making machine. All modern projection machines follow closely on their initial design. By 1890, just two short decades after Muybridge, the Lumières had pushed technology to the point that people moved on the screen with a convincing human grace, and in 1895, they received a patent for their new projection machine, which they called the Cinématographe, which projected still photographs at the rate of twenty-four frames a second. The following year Thomas Edison patented a similar projecting machine, which he named, ironically, the Vitascope. Using the technology he had developed in his phonograph, Edison had managed to outdo the Lumières by producing a crude soundtrack, but he still could not beat them for veracity of images.

Motion pictures caught on so fast, particularly with the masses, that moviegoing went well beyond making graphic the growing, shadowy nature of human essence. Ghost stories could accomplish that. Cinema did that and much more: Cinema helped shape perception itself. Pictures in motion influenced the way people experienced reality, and, without their being conscious of it, encouraged them to prefer the image over the actual—to derive pleasure from the miraculous way technology replicated reality. One simply cannot overestimate the importance of that one invention, the motion picture camera. A great many young people today can talk with more sophistication about film than they can about their own experiences. They know literature, understand history, and encounter psychology, all mainly through movies. Film is firsthand these days; experience takes place at two or three removes.

Those two French brothers rose to the top of the world of legerdemain, reigning supreme as the century's ultimate magicians. As conjurers, they had, in an odd way, tapped into what the scientists could not, the secret of life—into that dark corner that Victor Frankenstein so frantically and so desperately explored; into animation itself. (How curious that that word *animation,* in film, came to refer to something so robotlike, so herky-jerky.) Yes, the cinema did make stills move, but it did not actually animate life—it did just the opposite.

The motion picture camera sucked the life out of what were once fleshy human beings, and the projector filled the screen with their ghostlike images. The playwright Kevin Kerr gave his recent play about Muybridge the title *Studies in Motion: The Hauntings of Eadweard Muybridge* as a way of capturing the photographer's close connection with ghosts. Some critics argue that film offers more than hauntings; after all, we can run a movie as many times as we like and the same images keep reappearing. Such an experience sounds closer to permanence than evanescence.

As a rebuttal, we have Maxim Gorky's famous comment on first seeing the Lumières' film *The Arrival of a Train at the Station* in St. Petersburg in the late nineteenth century. The experience terrified Gorky, who remarked that by stepping into the theater he had entered "a kingdom of shadows": "This is not life but the shadow of life and this is not movement but the soundless shadow of movement."[6] Gorky found himself less struck with the medium's power to create magical images that pretended to approximate and fix life, and more taken with its ability to generate in viewers the feeling of substantial loss, to leave them with the general sense of death in life, or, more poignantly, with their own death in life. In the theater, audiences surrendered the majority of their senses—smell, touch, taste—making film a great disappearing act. In a curious way, both actors and audience members undergo the same operation: They both turn evanescent. If anything, theater is all sight and sound: *son et lumière.*

For thousands and thousands of fans in the nineteenth century, no one, and of course no machine, could surpass the king of the conjurers, Harry Houdini. What they did not know is that he, too, exploited the new technologies to make his act even more impressive and spectacular. Born Erich Weiss in Hungary, a Jewish immigrant, he named himself after the great French magician Jean Eugène Robert-Houdin. Houdini rose in prominence as the highest paid popular entertainer in the nineteenth century, and amassed an enormous fortune by performing his illusions in almost every country around the world, before kings and queens and presidents. In the same way nineteenth-century social conditions made the twin pursuits of the ghost story and motion pictures possible, so those same conditions helped create the phenomenon called Houdini.

Contemporary audiences made Houdini enormously successful. Just as audiences demanded more spectacular special effects from the Lumières, they demanded from Houdini more and bigger ghosts, and wilder and more miraculous illusions. Fool us, stupefy us, fill us back up with wonder once again, they seemed to be saying. Snatch us out of this dull, mechanical world and show us what reality might look like if the world were re-enchanted and if we truly believed. If Harry Houdini had not appeared on the scene when he did, in the late nineteenth century, audiences would certainly have called forth some other master magician, someone like Georges Méliès, and guaranteed his success, as well.

Over one hundred years have passed since Houdini's debut, and still not a single illusionist—not even David Blaine or David Copperfield, with all the state-of-the-art technological support imaginable—has been able to top Houdini as the supreme master of the art. Nineteenth-century audiences crowded into the most elegant theaters, in this country as well as in Britain and all across Europe, to sit spellbound as Harry Houdini made the world disappear. Illusion simply represented the age in a most spectacular way, and Houdini, in fine-tuning his most familiar and formidable tricks, placed the idea of disappearance into everyone's imagination. Better: He showed it to them in action. His name, like Sarah Bernhardt or P. T. Barnum, became part of common speech. "He's a regular Houdini," people would say about someone who seemed to have superhuman powers, or who could slither out of tight situations. He performed high up on that ghostlike structure, the Brooklyn Bridge; deep down underwater; in the cramped space of a jail cell; in the vast expanse of an Indian desert; in the Underground in London; and on the Jungfrau in Switzerland. People were primed, both psychologically and emotionally, for Harry Houdini, or any other master illusionist, to take the most solid objects and have them melt into thin air before their very startled eyes. The nineteenth-century audience was a prime enabler, an accomplice in every staged illusion.

Houdini holds the title as the most astounding escape artist of all time, but early in his career he performed as a "spirit medium," raising the dead and making their presence noisily apparent. (It certainly did not hurt his reputation as a conjurer of ghosts that he died on Halloween.) Houdini could cause the departed to rap out Morse code messages from inside the walls of a theater, ring bells, overturn tables, knock off the caps of audience members, and just generally create havoc. Houdini had fun, and audiences had even more fun. And they thanked the maestro by paying him huge amounts of money to make them believe in the invisible and the impossible.

Houdini never gave up his dedication to ghosts, working almost his entire professional life at perfecting what was for him the ultimate ethereal illusion. For years and years he broadcast his desire to perform what he called the Great Feat. He wrote essays describing its details; he generated a stir in the press about his lifelong theatrical desire. Here's what he wanted: As he declared over and over again—the consummate showman generating excitement—Harry Houdini would turn one of the largest mammals into a ghost. Or, to put it more directly, he would cause an elephant to disappear.

Anyone, Houdini believed, could make people disappear. That was no big deal, since they already shared such close associations with the ghostly. And besides, people could willingly collude with the illusionist. But not an elephant. An elephant, as Houdini so carefully pointed out, had a mind of its own. Although he worked on it for almost fifty years, only once, at the height of his career, did he successfully pull off that illusion. Perhaps he could have done it whenever he wanted, but he milked the trick for all it was worth.

To negotiate his consummate trick, Houdini, ever the showman, demanded the immensity of the Hippodrome and the enormity of its stage, the largest, at that moment, in North America. The elephant he chose stood over eight feet tall and weighed more than three tons, weighing out at 6,100 pounds. In that Moorish-inspired palace on Sixth Avenue, in downtown Manhattan, before a capacity crowd of over 5,200 astonished people, Houdini made a full-grown Asian elephant, Jennie, and its trainer totally vanish. The audience literally fell silent, struck dumb and amazed by the enormity of what Houdini had pulled off. Other illusionists tried, desperately, to repeat the illusion—with absolutely no success.

• ❦ •

A PROMISING STAGE MAGICIAN named Georges Méliès owned the Théâtre Robert-Houdin, in Paris, but when he came across the new cinema, he found a more powerful kind of magic. He very quickly manipulated the mechanics of filmmaking toward what we today would call special effects. Méliès attended the Lumières' screening of their *actualités* on December 28, 1895, and the following month bought his own camera, determined to get on film the great magic acts of the period. The connections between magic and film, however, immediately struck him, which led him to exploit in particular the dreamlike quality of motion pictures by using certain techniques like double exposure to create the illusion of people appearing and then quickly disappearing. Born in 1861, Méliès made some five hundred short movies up to 1912, on average almost ten movies a year. He died in 1938. Historians of film rank him as possibly the greatest filmmaker of fantasy and the surreal in all of cinema.

One reviewer credited his films with exploring "transformations and collisions: among humans, objects, animals and various creatures with unearthly powers; between mechanical and natural forces, and, of course (and so pleasurably), between visual styles. Méliès moves in an instant from stage-set realism to storybook phantasm or mechanical animation." Speed was essential to his technique. To see a Méliès film is to see stage magic miraculously and wonderfully transposed to the screen. More than virtually any other artist, Méliès saw the potential in the medium he had chosen—in the initial senses of "movies" (those which move) and "films" (those which inhabit the ghostly). The innovation of special effects belongs to Georges Méliès.

The public's interest in disappearance—onstage or in film—reflected a general questioning about the nature of life itself. Literature began to explore reality in its own, ghostly way, cracking life wide open to reveal its wide range of unexpected possibilities. Readers responded. They favored stories in which the central character seemed neither alive nor dead, or sometimes acted like a live human being but then transmogrified into an eerily foreign and frightening creature. Did death really exist as a finality? Or, like the beginnings of life, did it hold its own secrets? The word *narcolepsy* appears in the English medical journal *Lancet,* in 1888, to refer to a disease in which an otherwise normal person falls into "short and frequently recurring attacks of somnolence." *Catalepsy,* too, appears at the same time, as Poe points out, to mean much the same thing. In a time when all definitions of humanity were up for grabs, neither the beginning nor the end of life had a hard and fast meaning. Victor Frankenstein creates life; Dracula beats death. Dorian Gray thinks he may be dead; Roderick Usher thinks his house may be alive. Life had turned into one grand question.

Mary Shelley, for example, leaves readers in doubt about the exact nature of Doctor Frankenstein's creation: He resembles a person, although a much larger and much more powerful being than most; but now and again he slips beyond the boundaries of recognizable human behavior. The first lines of her short story "The Mortal Immortal" read this way: "July 16, 1883.—This is a memorable anniversary for me; on it I complete my three hundred and twenty-third year!" Is the main character immortal? Even though the narrator has downed a magic potion concocted by the sixteenth-century Kabbalist Cornelius Agrippa, he still does not know the answer: "This is a question which I have asked myself, by day and night, for now three hundred and three years, and yet cannot answer it." When the invisible man, Doctor Griffin, first steps foot into the story after having drunk his own potion, Wells describes him as "more dead than alive." Polidori, too, introduces his vampyre as living in torment beyond life and death, and relegates him to a category that no writer had visited since the fifteenth century, the "undead," which in the late Middle Ages meant, quite simply, "to be alive." He, too, must drink a magic liquid—blood.

To be undead in the nineteenth century, however, implied something entirely different. To be undead in Doctor Polidori's world, for example, meant that Count Dracula enjoyed a fiendish kind of immortality, one that bypassed Christianity or any hint of the afterlife, and certainly any hint of a representation of Christ himself. A broad range of contemporary authors exploited the idea of the undead and modified it for their own purposes. Sir Arthur Conan Doyle stands out as a prime example. Doyle met with enormous success, producing a total of four short novels and fifty-six stories, after he first appeared in *Beeton's Christmas Annual* for 1887 with *A Study in Scarlet.*

In 1893, out of fatigue, or to provoke a reaction, Doyle decided to put an end to his famous detective. To pull off the caper, Doyle enlisted the help of Holmes's arch-nemesis, Professor Moriarity, whom, some critics insist, Conan Doyle modeled after Friedrich Nietzsche. In a startling episode titled "The Final Problem," Holmes plunges headlong into the roiling waters of Reichenbach Falls in Switzerland, wrapped in the arms of Moriarity. Sherlock Holmes's literary demise had such a devastating affect on the reading public that, for the first time, a local newspaper carried the obituary of a literary character. In a piece nearly a full page long, the *Geneva Journal* announced the death of that ace detective, Mr. Sherlock Holmes, on May 6, 1891.

But Doyle wrote in that fantastic world of the nineteenth century, where death turns out on closer inspection not to be death at all. And so, because of the enormous and sustained outcry of Holmes's loyal fans (including Doyle's mother) and the insistence of his publisher, Conan Doyle felt no compunction about simply raising his hero from the dead—no, from the realm of the nearly, almost, damned-near dead. Sarah Bernhardt for a time returned from her death, it seemed, every other week. In a volume titled *The Adventure of the Empty House,* Doyle brought Holmes back to life. Rather than his readers crying foul, they rejoiced in having their hero enchant them once again in the pages of yet another Conan Doyle story. As Watson explains, on first seeing the resurrected Holmes: "I gripped him by the sleeve, and felt the thin, sinewy arm beneath it. 'Well, you're not a spirit, anyhow,' said I." Holmes had not gone over the falls, it turns out, but sidestepped Moriarity's lunge at the last minute, through the ancient Japanese art of baritsu, and survived—his demise a mere illusion. At the end of the tale, Holmes taps into a deep truth of the period when he laments, "We reach. We grasp. And what is left in our hands in the end? A shadow."

Not just a popular writer like Sir Arthur Conan Doyle but serious novelists like Nathaniel Hawthorne played with people's desire to conquer death. An age that placed so much importance on awareness and the nature of human sensibilities might be expected to produce such seemingly outlandish ideas. Hawthorne had already toyed with the idea of magic potions for extending life in a short story titled "Dr. Heidegger's Experiment." Near the end of his life, he became intrigued by the idea once again. In 1863, in failing health, he took up residence in a grand house in Concord named the Wayside, where he began work on a short story prompted by a remark made to him by Thoreau. Thoreau had heard about a man who in the distant past had taken up residence in the Wayside and who desired to live forever. Hawthorne transformed the remark into a story about a seminary student named Septimus Norton who kills a British soldier and discovers on his body the secret formula for eternal life. Ironically, Hawthorne found himself too sick to finish the story. He died a short time later, in 1864.

Hawthorne's comments in his journal shortly before he died sound much like the frustration of the scientists of the period, who also desired to find that magic potion that might enable humankind to beat death, and amazingly similar to Holmes's just after Conan Doyle brought him back to life. In *The Adventure of the Empty House,* we hear for the first time a lament from that indefatigable character, Sherlock Holmes, about the nature of perception, about the futility of trying to know anything at all: "There seems to be things that I can almost get hold of, and think about; but when I am just on the point of seizing them, they start away, like slippery things."

On a trip in London in 1897, Mark Twain received two telegrams from the editor of the *New York Journal*. The first read: "IF MARK TWAIN DYING IN POVERTY IN LONDON SEND 500 WORDS." Then the follow-up: "IF MARK TWAIN HAS DIED IN POVERTY SEND 1000 WORDS." Those two missives prompted from Twain one of his most well-known retorts: "THE REPORTS OF MY DEATH ARE GREATLY EXAGGERATED."[7] Twain, a writer seemingly far removed in style, substance, and geography from Conan Doyle, wrote a comedic play late in his career, 1898, about murder, filling each act with death, fake death, and funerals without corpses. Twain titled the play, with a twist on the theme of being undead, *Is He Dead?* Twain loved such absurdities about the supposed finality of death, most especially about his own. Twain did not shy away from the paranormal. In the December 1891 issue of *Harper's*, for instance, Twain published his own ringing endorsement of Britain's Society for Psychical Research.

Even Lewis Carroll's little Alice lives underground in a place characterized neither by life—certainly not by normal life—nor by out-and-out death. The underground is a wondrous land, but Alice continually wonders just where in the world she possibly could have landed, in a place where all the familiar categories have come crashing down around her. Carroll's fantastical book appeared just when the great American carnage, the Civil War, was coming to a conclusion, in 1865. Which was stranger, audiences had every right to wonder, the fantastical underground or the grim overground?

Finally, Henrik Ibsen created characters more dead than alive, in one of his most intriguing plays, which he titled *When We Dead Awaken*. His suggestion seemed to be that most people passed their days as dead men walking, but with some great effort they could come wide awake. A caveat:

Like the heroes of medieval romances, the walking dead must ask the right questions, discover the right path, and then summon the courage to forge ahead. The path never presents itself as obvious, the idea of an invigorated life never as apparent or clear as we might prefer. Murkiness and even outright darkness characterize the landscape of the knight of faith. A veil hangs in front of everything.

That's the lesson of a good deal of nineteenth-century fiction. As with Ibsen, Shelley, and Polidori, authors chose to explore liminality, in this case the opaque or invisible seam separating life and death, this world from the world beyond. The title of master of the genre must go to Edgar Allan Poe. Everything that can be written about Poe seems to have been written. He is for those with even a passing interest in the macabre a cult figure; people still sit by his grave in Baltimore, guarding his headstone and watching out for the unknown soul who comes each year, unseen and unheard, to place a snifter of brandy on his grave. Poe is scary and he is smart and he nailed the age in tale after tale. Every one of his stories seems to probe another basic interest of the age. I provide a glimpse of only two of them here.

The first is one of his more obscure stories, titled "The Domain of Arnheim," which he published in 1847. It is an important tale for it lays bare the almost obsessive intense fascination the age had with the invisible world. In this tale, Poe goes beyond mere ghosts—the most common of the revenants—to fantasize about the invisible creatures that hold the visible world together and infuse it with logic, order, and meaning. There is indeed a divine plan, but it does not emanate from God. And whatever we interpret down here as disorder and pain and suffering, the invisible creatures, with their commanding vision, see as exactly the opposite. We are deluded because we do not have the higher powers necessary to truly perceive the world. The narrator, a Mister Ellison, puts it this way: "There *may* be a class of beings, human once, but now invisible to humanity, to whom, from afar, our disorder may seem order—our unpicturesqueness picturesque; in a word, the earth-angels, for whose scrutiny more especially than our own, and for whose death-refined appreciation of the beautiful, may have been set in array by God the wide landscape-gardens of the hemispheres."

In the second tale, a truly macabre one, "The Cask of Amontillado," Poe places the main character of his story quite literally in that space between life and death. The story tells of a master mason who walls up his rival, while he is still alive, in the basement of the mason's house. In an unforgivable act of inverted hospitality, the host turns hostile and attacks his unsuspecting guest. Trapped in a living death, the guest's cries of terror slowly fade at story's end into nothing but a terrifying silence, Poe deliberately turning his guest into a ghost.

With "Cask," Poe continued a series of stories involving the deliberate burial of a living person, or the mistaken burial of a person presumed dead. Both kinds of stories explored that oh-so-mysterious and thin line where breathing grows faint but does not cease altogether. Where did death begin? That is, when did breathing actually stop? Equally beguiling: When did breathing actually begin? As astounding as it may seem, we must remember that only near the end of the century, in 1875, in the search for that millisecond when life actually blossoms into being, did a German biologist named Oscar Hertwig stumble on the idea of conception. Only in that year, by observing sea urchins mating, did the scientific community understand the way a sperm fertilizes an egg in order for life to begin.

Ghosts and the various other versions of the undead provided fairly graphic ways of representing the disappeared human being in the nineteenth century. The age, however, found other, equally effective ways of exploiting the idea of the disappeared—of the body deprived of its essence. In the growing visual and commercial culture of the nineteenth century, at a time when ordinary people became both more aware of and more fascinated with their own radically changing condition, entrepreneurs exploited an eerily lifelike representation of the undead. Municipalities made major renovations to city museums to accommodate a new interest in public displays of the disembodied body. In England and in the Scandinavian countries, curators moved from straightforward taxonomic displays, early in the century, to the *tableau vivant,* living scenes projected onto walls by yet another ghost-producing machine, invented by Daguerre and patented in 1824, called the diorama.

While the movie theater certainly had an influence on the creation of new resting places for the disembodied body, two very different kinds of venues appeared during the period to capitalize on the feeling of loss that had so terrified Gorky. One was a new phenomenon called the wax museum, the most famous of which Madame Marie Tussaud opened in her first permanent location in London in 1835. In a cavernous space, she exhibited effigies of historical figures. Alongside those figures, to capitalize on the century's attraction to and repulsion for criminals, she opened what she called the "Separate Room," which the press dismissed as "that ghastly apartment into which ladies are not advised to enter."[8] Such a pointed and gendered dismissal, of course, only boosted attendance by ladies desperate to see up close the wax models of history's most depraved and dangerous.

So popular had that exhibition of the gruesome become that, by 1846, the Madame had indeed opened a separate room, this time without the scare quotes, and this time consigned to its proper psychological place, the basement. She dedicated the space entirely to the effigies of criminals in the act of, say, bloody murder. This new room, which drew more people than the upstairs ever did, she named, with all the great entrepreneurial flair she loved to employ, the Chamber of Horrors. To walk down the staircase into the deep recesses of the chamber was to descend into the subconscious of the general London population.

The 1880s and 1890s were a boom time for wax museums all over Europe as popular bourgeois entertainment, particularly in the Scandinavian countries and in Germany and Italy. Each featured its own version of the Chamber of Horrors; it was inevitable, for the wax effigy, as other historians have pointed out, carries an automatic association with the dead, or the seemingly dead, body. (By the mid-nineteenth century, the press had begun to use the word *effigy* as a verb, "to body forth.") Wax effigies are psycho-logically confusing mannequins. (The word *mannequin*—spelled *manikin* beginning in the sixteenth century—refers initially to a dwarf or pygmy; and, in 1837, for the first time, to a highly lifelike model of the human be-ing.) While they offer to an audience a model of the departed, these waxy mannequins are still and forever with us; they seem prepared, forever, to leave for the other side, but never really take off and make the journey.

Wax figures occupy an odd and unsettling category, odd enough to unhinge even Sigmund Freud. They upset him so much that viewing them prompted from him a famous essay, first published in 1925, titled "The Uncanny" (literally, "The Unhomely"). Struggling to find what makes wax effigies and automata so unsettling to us, Freud finally decides that effigies unnerve because they appear as indefinable creatures hovering so indefi-nitely (and so contentedly) between life and death. From a distance they look very much alive, but on closer inspection we declare them decidedly dead. We even say about people who look very ill that their skin has turned waxlike. In titling his essay, Freud borrows the word *uncanny* from the previous century, when it referred to people strangely possessed of super-natural powers.

During those same years, in the 1880s and 1890s, people included various kinds of animals, too, in their growing fascination with the un-dead. This came about because of the rise of a related new art, taxidermy. People had been tanning animal skins for a very long time. But in this pe-riod, professionals began stuffing the animals with cotton and other batting material, lending to a lion or tiger all the aliveness of, well, a wax effigy. Taxidermy shops opened in both small towns and large cities. The revival of ventriloquism, too, helped foster a general feeling of undeadness—dum-mies, made of wood and wax, grew more lifelike and eerie, and helped, as some critics said, to separate the voice from its source, a necessary feature of the telephone and the radio and motion pictures. Ventriloquism came in handy at séances, as well.

Which leads to the second venue for viewing the undead. From its inception, the morgue, a French institution, served as a depository not just for any dead person, but for those who had died anonymously. In 1800, the Paris police had issued a decree that argued strongly for establishing the exact identity of those who died, as essential to preserving "the social order." That desire for closure gets reflected in the word *morgue* itself, which derives from the Old French *morguer*: "to have a haughty demeanor"—or, more to the point, "to stare, to have a fixed and questioning gaze." While no one seems to know the word's exact origin—much the same fate as the orphaned corpses themselves—the choice of that word for a place to house the dead perhaps tries to capture the look of frozen desire on the faces of the corpses, the hope of reclaiming an exact identity.

Whatever prompted the word into existence, by 1840, the morgue, now newly relocated to the Ile de la Cité, had opened with a large viewing room, enabling crowds of people to gaze upon row upon row of neatly lined-up corpses. One contemporary observer, Léon Gozlan, called the morgue "a central neighborhood spot": "The morgue is the Luxembourg, the Place Royale of the Cité. One goes there to see the latest fashions, orange trees blooming, chestnut trees that rustle in the autumn winds, in spring, and in winter." By 1864, city officials had relocated the morgue to yet another new location, this one elaborately designed as a Greek temple, with the words *Liberté, Égalité, Fraternité*, the slogan of the French Revolution, cut deeply into the marble across its imposing front entrance. The revolution may have prompted, to some extent, the horrors of both the wax museum and the morgue. Madame Tussaud kept models of the guillotine and other instruments of torture as permanent parts of the exhibits in her Chamber of Horrors.

According to the newspaper *L'Eclair*, the new morgue attracted an astonishing number of visitors—over one million a year. A very scant few of them came to identify a missing loved one. The great majority of them came to stare, to gaze, to sip a glass of wine and, as the French do better than most, toss about this idea and that; surely a good many of those discussions must have touched on the topic of death, and in particular anonymous death. The morgue provided a gruesome twist on the old philosophical question: If no one is there to claim the body, did anyone actually die? Or, if the body has no name, did anyone really die? On both counts, I say not really, for here was death, it seems, not as a mournful gathering, but as occasion for intimate social interactions. Here was death as a museum event, a gallery opening. By 1867, the curious could even linger over the bodies for extended periods of time, for in that year a German chemist, August Wilhelm von Hoffman, had discovered formaldehyde, the chemical that became the foundation of modern embalming, enabling the morgue to hold bodies with no cold storage for weeks on end.

Physicians contributed to the period's fierce obsession with corpses. In the first decades of the century, scientists tried to understand the nature of life and death by cutting up human bodies. Under the Murder Act of 1752, when London authorities hanged murderers, they transferred the bodies to the city's Royal College of Surgeons for their experiments in dissection. Such cuttings constituted additional punishment for the heinous crime of murder; the practice lasted until 1832, when legislation outlawed cruel and unusual punishment. Even in this legal way, anatomists could not satisfy their needs and they demanded more—many more—bodies. So, in 1829, when John Abernethy, a surgeon, addressed his students at St. Bartholomew's Hospital with the line, "There is but one way to obtain knowledge . . . we must be companions with the dead,"[10] he was sending a message: Get the bodies any way you can. And that meant buying corpses from a nefarious group of entrepreneurs, the grave robbers, or the body snatchers, or, as the newspapers called them, in a creepy religious echo, the resurrectionists. These were the undesirables who went out in the dark of night burking, named after the chief grave robber in Scotland at the time and a hero to the medical profession, William Burke. With his accomplice, William Hare, Burke not only robbed graves but obtained other bodies by strangling to death unsuspecting victims. Burke's crimes gave rise to another, even more insidious meaning of *burking:* "murdering, as by suffocation, so as to leave no or few marks of violence." Helen MacDonald, in a book about the history of autopsy in London, *Human Remains: Dissection and Its Histories,* places the gruesome practice of body snatching in the context of the century's continuing search for that Frankensteinian secret of life:

> The social anxieties about the precise boundary between life and death that were common in Europe at this time were expressed in novels and poems, and also circulated in dark tales about people who had been buried alive. Certain people who had been executed had even later revived on the College's own dissecting table.
>
> Some experiments performed at the College aimed to determine the time of death with certainty. They were so violently crude that Clift [William Clift, conservator of the College's Hunterian Museum] clearly found his job distressing. In an uncharacteristically stumbling hand, he recorded what he was instructed to do to the body of Martin Hogan as it lay on the dissecting table in 1814, which was to thrust a needle into each eye to see if that produced an effect. Other investigations were undertaken in a more systematic way as College men sought to understand whether an absence of obvious animation was a sign that the life force had merely been suspended or was irretrievably extinguished. And although this was never stated in the context of the College's work on murderers, they were also wondering whether it was in the power of medical men to return people to life.

Fascination with disembodied death continues into our own time. Starting his work in the 1970s, a German anatomist named Gunther von Hagens raised the embalming procedure to the level of performance art. Instead of injecting corpses with formaldehyde or some other chemical, Hagens, billing himself as a sculptor of dead people, pumped them full of a plastic compound. He took as his medium human flesh, flaying open the skin and emphasizing the organs, creating strange perversions of classical Greek statues. In 1997, Hagens launched an exhibition of his work, Body Worlds, at Mannheim's Museum of Technology and Work. Close to eight hundred thousand visitors came to see over two hundred corpses offered by Hagens as individual works of art, each with its own explanatory label, including a brief history of the subject along with the kinds of materials used.

In November 2005, the South Street Seaport Exhibition Centre in New York featured a show, titled Bodies . . . The Exhibition, promising "real human bodies, preserved through an innovative process and then respectfully presented." Soon afterward, in October 2006, the National Museum of Health and Medicine, founded in 1862 in Washington, D.C., as the Army Medical Museum, launched an art exhibit of prints made from the scars of people who had suffered horrendous traumas—automobile accidents, third-degree burns, gunshot wounds, mutilations, and so on. The art pieces carry titles like *Splenectomy Scar, Lung Removal After Suicide Attempt,* and *Broken Eye Socket Repair Using Bone from the Skull After Car Accident.* The artist, Ted Meyer, lays onto the scars and the surrounding area block-print ink, and then presses paper to the skin to make an image, which he further enhances with gouache and pencil. The National Museum of Health and Medicine owns a collection of over one thousand objects, including the preserved leg of a man afflicted with elephantiasis. The museum is the city's principal museum of fleshy art; the Army, while using young men and women as so much cannon fodder, may be the organization that makes mothers and fathers and wives and husbands and children most aware that what suffers heavy-duty wounds and even death are actually *bodies*—fleshy, breathing human beings. We ought to refer to those sons and daughters as something other than "collateral damage" or "body counts."

Even though no one referred to them as such, the corpses that arrived at the Paris morgue constitute the first official missing persons. In the 1880s, the Chicago Police Department did issue the world's first missing persons list. It had to, for the reality of people vanishing from sight, without a trace, had already taken hold of the popular imagination. Newspapers in

England and in this country carried banner headlines, in the seventies and early eighties, screaming about young women, lost forever, in the bustling cities of Chicago, London, and New York. For most of the nineteenth century, the disappearance of people had been a theoretical idea, discussed at a rather abstract level by philosophers and explored by artists and writers and a good number of scientists. But the police took the idea out of the realm of fiction and art, yanked it off the stage, and turned it into a grim reality: Image became instance, theory became fact. Day by day, it seemed, common citizens vanished from sight without a trace. Reports started to appear in great numbers during the Chicago World's Fair of 1893, where young English and European women had come to find jobs in one of the many booths.

As if simple murder were not gruesome enough, another, new and perverse form of vanishing began to haunt both England and America—serial killing. Much like the frames on a filmstrip, the serial killer committed the same act—in this case, the slashing and disemboweling of young women—over and over again. A corner had been turned, a moment had been reached, where art had foretold or forecast life itself. The serial killer firmly links the nineteenth century in England, the birthplace of serial killing, with our own times, in this country. A new kind of mayhem haunted nineteenth-century England. Not only was the world's first serial killer, known initially as the Whitechapel Murderer and later as Jack the Ripper, invisible, but his invisibility made him all the more dangerous. No one knew what he looked like, what he believed, how he walked, or where he worked. He started his spree of ripping prostitutes apart in the winter of 1888 in the East End of London, and committed his horrors always between the hours of midnight and dawn.[11] The milieu of the decadents had truly turned decadent. The Ripper killed at least five women, and left not a single significant clue. Newspapers described him as "the unseen killer." The police never found their man, but had their suspicions about an American doctor who had taken up residence in London. They could find no fingerprints.

Serial killers continue not just to fascinate us as historical oddities, but to raise serious questions for our own age, as well. Several dozen books in the last decade or two plumb the psyche of such monsters. Are these creatures human or subhuman? Can we even call them people? What creates and shapes them? Can society ever avoid such aberrations? The questions go on and on. In many ways, the serial killer more than the simple murderer exposes those places where the Chain of Being threatens to break apart. Serial killers not only make the night unsafe but because they come from the community itself—I knew that person at one time!—they make even the daytime frightening and charged. Can we really know for certain who will turn killer? As our paranoia and fear increase, we begin to see every custodian as a killer, every guard as a ghoul.

The nineteenth-century serial killer became an object of fascination for the twentieth. In 1988, the novelist Thomas Harris made Hannibal Lecter the fright of the year in his novel *The Silence of the Lambs*. It quickly became a blockbuster movie. (Who could ever look at Anthony Hopkins the same way again?) Alfred Hitchcock's *Psycho* used the perversions of the midwestern serial killer Ed Gein as a model for its understated whacko lead character, Norman Bates. Several films—including a documentary and a drama—trace the journey of an even stranger anomaly, Aileen Wuornos, the most well-known female serial killer.

In reviewing a shocking ten books on serial killing, in *The New York Review of Books* (1994), the novelist Joyce Carol Oates offers her own insights into the nature of such an aberration—murder—laid on top of a more perverse aberration—serial murder:

> Somehow it has happened that the "serial killer" has become our debased, condemned, yet eerily glorified Noble Savage, the vestiges of the frontier spirit, the American *isolato* cruising interstate highways in van or pickup truck which will yield, should police have the opportunity to investigate, a shotgun, a semiautomatic rifle, quantities of ammunition and six-packs and junk food, possibly a decomposing female corpse in the rear.[12]

What could Oates mean—six-packs, ammo, a semiautomatic, and junk food: Is serial killing all about consumption? Or is it a low-level fantasy excursion into a military commando impersonation? In the serial killer's demented mind, is he keeping us safe from the really bad people? Who knows? But the following statistic should give us pause: While the United States has only roughly five percent of the world's population, it produces an astonishing seventy-five percent of the world's serial killers.[13] Do these numbers reveal human nature at its most elemental, consumptive, and depraved state—a human being reduced to total and mechanistic voraciousness, without any moral constraint? What do we have here, Blackwater USA gone totally and literally ballistic? One critic must have that kind of greed and power in mind when he refers to the serial killer, in the most mechanical of terms, as "simply a biological engine driven by a primal instinct to satisfy a compelling lust."[14]

In that sense, we must consider deviants like Jeffrey Dahmer or Ed Gein as the other side of Victor Frankenstein, interested not so much in the power that comes from knowing the secret of life, but in the delight that comes from knowing the intimacies of death. There is terrific power in snuffing out life, as there is in igniting life into being. Nonetheless, serial killers blow apart all categories of human being. They prowl the night like vampires. Some nineteenth-century newspaper accounts threw them in with the living dead. Certainly, they do not deserve to participate with the fully alive.

•❧•

THROUGH TWO MAJOR conceptual shifts, the medical profession played its own inadvertent role in promoting the cult of the undead. In the first, British physicians adopted a remarkably different and modern attitude toward disease. To understand the meaning of life, physicians must know what brings people to the edge of death. The eighteenth century viewed the body as a hydraulic instrument, maintaining health through a balance of the four humors, which eventuated in four separate and distinct temperaments. From the time of Hippocrates, dis-ease involved an unbalance inside the body—an excess, say, of the liquid called black bile, which led to a malady known as melancholia. The melancholic was unbalanced or uncentered (eccentric)—not at ease. He or she had lost his or her "temper." Through the right combination of prayer, astrological prognostication, and chemical concoction, the physician could help set the body back into balance, into a renewed sense of harmony. In severe cases, the patient might need more serious medical intervention. At those moments, the surgeon would make an incision in an arm or a leg—or anywhere the patient felt pressure—and release some of the excess liquid. An enema or a powerful purgative could release even more of the offending fluid. Of course, to the untrained eye, all that liquid gushing out of the body looked like ordinary blood.

Beginning in 1803, physicians posited the idea of very small units, called germs—"the seed of disease"—that invaded the body, resulting not in dis-ease but in disease. This evolved into Louis Pasteur's "germ theory of disease" in 1863. The medical profession had thus reduced the idea of disease, and thus the essence of the healthy human being, to its most basic unit. Practitioners now viewed the body as a mechanism, capable of warding off illness through the internal warning beacon called the immune system. And the immune system became the basic mechanism by which a person sustained life itself. Like so many other innovations and ideas of the period, germs, too, constituted a eureka moment, a breakthrough in the path toward defining life. Only here, the definition started not with the beginnings but more with the finales, with life's nemesis, illness.

In that same year, 1803, the word *vaccinate* first appears, to refer to an inoculation of the virus cowpox as a protection against smallpox. With the new body, disease came, like William Blake's "invisible worm" in the night, to suck the life out of unsuspecting people, no matter their class or age or color, in a brand new way. Germs remained invisible to the naked eye, and so physicians sometimes implanted in the patient's body an all-seeing "eye"—prompting the use of a new word, *inoculation,* from *ocular,* to describe the procedure—to help ward off invading germs, such as those that resulted in the scourge of the century, syphilis. Hence the *Medical and Physical Journal* entry for 1803: "The vaccine virus must act in one or other of these two ways: either it must destroy the germ of the small-pox . . . or it must neutralize the germ." Vaccine is the body's Sherlock Holmes, helping to solve the mystery of disease.

If the doctors did not vaccinate, they had to find the right medicine to combat the invading germ. They even began using something they called placebos, what the period called "ghost pills," to coax the patient back into good health with medicine no stronger than an old-fashioned dose of goodwill. In the context of the new illnesses, we can view Dracula as a harbinger of the rampant diseases of the blood, the embodiment—or disembodiment—of infection. He enjoys a truly parasitic relationship with the living, feeding off of their blood. No wonder that the most popular play in the nineteenth century, in terms of audience attendance, was Ibsen's *Ghosts,* about the spread of syphilis, which killed thousands of people and transfigured thousands more into cadres of the living dead.

How the immune system worked, for the overwhelming majority of people, was not unlike the way most of us know the innards of our own computers—as an invisible and incomprehensible control center, a phantom program directing the entire operation. While we rely heavily on the computer's program, few of us, even with the box splayed wide open, can actually locate that program. Likewise, no physician or patient could locate the immune system. Not so with the four humors. Bloodlet a patient in the Middle Ages and, as the humors left the body, one could inspect them up close. But the immune system existed only as a relationship between parts. In and of itself, the immune system—a system in which we still believe wholeheartedly—did not exist, just one more theft in the great robbery of the solid human being, contributing to its ultimate ghostliness.

In the second and perhaps more important conceptual shift, the medical profession relocated the seat of feeling and perception, moving it from its earlier sites, in the Renaissance, in the heart or kidneys or liver, to the organ of current critical importance, the brain. This changed the way physicians configured morbidity. Patients died from the brain first, before they made their gradual slide into lethargy and bouts of deep sleep, descending finally into a coma. Nietzsche's own father began his demise in 1849, for example, with what the attending physician termed a "softening of the brain." His protracted death took eleven months of the most excruciating pain.

Beyond disease, of course, lay death itself. And very few scientists in search of the basic matrix of life wanted to acknowledge the finality of death. As patients made their passage to the beyond, they dwelled for protracted periods of time at the threshold. No one knew quite how long, and so physicians advised that friends and relatives could—or maybe even should—continue holding conversations with them, even though they got no response. They deemed those patients neither dead nor alive, but more accurately undead. The comatose could still hear, physicians counseled, and they comforted loved ones by insisting that they, the physicians, could measure the levels of understanding of the near dead with one of a variety of electrical appliances that had been developed in the nineteenth century. The most popular, the galvanometer, recorded the electrical activity that the body continued to release, in its aliveness and all through its stages of decay, through the skin.

Surgeons preferred to experiment on those who had very recently died, arguing that they held on more vigorously to that ultimate source of life, their so-called "vital powers." At London's Royal College of Surgeons, Professor Giovanni Aldini performed galvanic experiments on the recently drowned, believing that powerful electric shock could provide the "means of excitement" to bring the deceased back to life. He left a record of his many and involved experiments in an 1803 book, *An Account of the Late*

Improvements in Galvanism, detailing the scores of instances when he truly believed he had restored life in a dead person.

These so-called operating rooms, like the viewing rooms at the morgue, filled up every day with curious onlookers. Some came to witness the cutting up of cadavers. Many more came to see magic. They came specifically to gawk at the handiwork of Giovanni Aldini, scientist as showman, who played to that expectant and near-worshipping crowd. On one particular afternoon in that very charged year, 1803, he placed the heads of two decapitated criminals on two tables and jolted them with an electrical impulse to make them grimace. The crowd loved it, quieting down only when Aldini shouted out to them—Tell me, if you are able, are these criminals alive or dead? Moments later, he first made the hand of one of the headless corpses clutch a coin, and then made the other hand toss a coin into the by now frightened and astonished audience.

But by far the greatest experiment on the dead, and the one that attracted the largest crowds, involved shocking not just the hand or head of a dead person but the heart itself. Fifteen years before the publication of *Frankenstein,* Professor Aldini announced to the assembled crowd that he would reanimate the heart of a corpse. By contemporary accounts, Aldini's performance lasted several hours; not a single person left the room. With electrical stimulation, he first made the dead man's jaw quiver, his left eye open, and his face convulse. He then applied conductors to the ear and rectum, which muscular contractions, according to Aldini himself, "almost [gave] an appearance of re-animation," the operative words being *almost* and *appearance.* And then the climax of the reanimation show: The right hand clenched and the right auricle of the heart contracted. At any rate, that's what Aldini told the audience. They believed. The applause went on and on.[15]

The scrim separating the living from the dead became more and more transparent. While writers scrambled to find new words to capture that emerging world of otherness, scientists tried to find ways of entering that forbidden territory. In either case, the idea was to make that stubborn and ineffable world give up its secrets. If there is a need, some entrepreneur will always arrive to profit from it. By the 1870s, more and more people had suddenly found themselves with the uncanny ability to journey to the other side and make the dead communicate with the living. The list included magicians, mediums, illusionists, sensitives, ghost talkers, slate writers, hucksters, and average citizens with newly discovered and rare gifts.

A new vocabulary emerged to categorize these supernatural experiences. The English adopted the already existing French word *clairvoyance,* "a keenness of insight," and used it for their supernatural needs: "a mental perception of objects at a distance or concealed from sight." By the 1880s, the word was in common use. H. G. Wells, one of the most potent writers of a new kind of spectral fiction, used the word very early on. A short time later, Percy Bysshe Shelley coined a word to describe those semi-living patients who languished in hospital beds, and those semi-dead corpses on autopsy tables, and those other half-alive creatures that stalked the pages of short stories and novels. Shelley pronounced them hovering in a state of *suspended animation.*

The Grimm brothers, who collected European fairy tales in the nineteenth century, found one in particular emblematic of the period, "Briar Rose," or more commonly, "Sleeping Beauty," one of the tales that Freud may have included in his category of the uncanny. The era worked out gradations of those who hovered between categories. If they could still walk around, *Science* magazine had yet another word to describe people in that specialized state, sleepwalkers or *somnambulants.* And for those people who, under the influence of the full moon, sleepwalked, the period had coined yet another word, *lunambulants.*

The public's interest in scientific and medical anomalies such as sleepwalkers, hibernators, and those in hypnotic trances or in states of suspended animation culminated in a movement, beginning in the late 1840s, called spiritualism. As with the ghost gathering at the Villa Diodati in 1816, we can date the advent of spiritualism to a particular evening, May 31, 1848, in Hydesville, New York, when two young sisters, Catherine and Margaret Fox, astonished their guests by supposedly successfully communicating with departed celebrities. The two young women heard their "rappings" from the other side in a session they called a séance. I can find no instance of the word *séance,* as an occasion for making contact with the departed, before 1845.

From that first evening in Hydesville, the craze for talking to the dead—for what the locals called the "spiritual telegraph"—thoroughly and completely seized the popular imagination. P. T. Barnum helped the Fox sisters achieve worldwide fame by having them perform before large audiences in his American Museum, located in lower Manhattan, from 1841 to 1865. Thomas Edison, the man who loved all forms of "talking machines," worked on a device that would capture and amplify the voices of the spiritual world; he had much more success with a tool that closely resembled his design for listening in on the spirit world, the telephone. The most normal, solid citizens in America and England, however, did not really need Barnum or even Edison; thousands of the most ordinary men and women followed the lead of the Fox sisters and held séances in their own living rooms in hopes of making contact with friends and family who had passed, in the jargon of the day, into Summerland, or the borderland, the spirit world, the seventh heaven, or the misted realm. So numerous and varied were the séances that several newspapers came into being during this time covering the weekly news, exclusively, of the spiritualism movement.

By 1888, contemporary accounts put the number of spiritualists in America alone at an astonishing eight million. Towering spiritual authorities like Annie Besant and Madame Blavatsky lectured on the benefits of competing psychic movements, like anthroposophy and theosophy. Elizabeth Barrett Browning, according to her husband, attended way too many séances for her own good. Her favorite spiritual guide was a Scotsman named Daniel Dunglas Home. Sir Arthur Conan Doyle practically went through his entire family fortune trying to get the word out about the spirit world and the existence of fairies. He wrote lengthy and detailed explanations of the possibilities beyond the world of the visible, in his monumental study *The History of Spiritualism*. With its many and diverse sects, the spiritual movement had spread by the 1880s to most parts of the world. Byron's intimate gathering at the Villa Diodati, which resembled in its own way a kind of séance, had mushroomed, seventy years later, into an industry of colossal proportions—all in the service of rounding up and making contact with every available ghost. And the world held untold numbers of them.

Illusionists quickly saw the potential in the séance and took it, as they said, on the road. In England the great illusionist was Daniel Dunglas Home, a friend of William James and the favorite, as we have seen, of Elizabeth Barrett Browning. A Scotsman by birth, he moved to Connecticut as a young man, and worked his magic, in the early 1850s, out of a brownstone on the Upper East Side of Manhattan. Browning reported, in the summer of 1855, that at one of Home's séances, "we were touched by the invisible."[16] His great fame derived from talking to the dead and his purported feats of levitation, contemporary accounts of which have him at times hovering six or seven feet off the floor. A caricature of Home during the period shows him, like Mary Poppins, bouncing off the ceiling of a drawing room, three or four people standing around, their mouths wide open in shock and amazement. Not surprisingly, many people denounced him as an utter fraud.

No such charges were ever leveled at the great Italian spiritualist, a woman named Eusapia Palladino. She traveled all through Europe, Spain, Poland, and Russia producing, by all accounts, the most extraordinary effects, including "simple" levitations, elongating her body at will, physically materializing from the dead, producing the impression of spirit hands and faces in wet clay, and so on.

In America the leading spiritualists were the Davenport brothers, Ira and William, two established illusionists from Buffalo, New York, who typically raised the dead through spiritual rappings and made contact with them through slate writings and talking boards (the Ouija board). They began their careers in 1855 and very quickly began traveling the world and becoming incredibly famous. The brothers mightily disavowed any hocus-pocus or trickery and claimed a true "spirit connection" with the other world. Near the end of Ira's checkered career and life, in 1910, however, he revealed his secrets for tapping into the spectral world to his greatest admirer and often principal doubter, Harry Houdini. Ira Davenport died just one year later, a short distance from Lily Dale, a spiritualist camp in upstate New York.

In Britain, Alfred Russel Wallace, Darwin's coauthor of the theory of natural selection, attended his first séance in 1865, which he undertook, he said, in the hope of disabusing science of its total devotion to the mechanical. For Wallace, scientists needed to find the secret of life on the other side. And he came to wonder if evolutionary theory had really missed the essential point—it could explain physical evolution with great clarity but left no place for the soul and thus diminished the meaning of human life. He could find evidence for his theory, he conjectured, in no other place than psychic research. So fascinated was he with exploring the spectral world that he helped launch, in 1882, along with a few other colleagues, Britain's Society for Psychical Research. One of the colleagues he would eventually entice into the group was no less a figure than the author of *The Varieties of Religious Experience,* the younger brother of Henry James, William James. The American Society for Psychical Research opened three years later, in 1885. To give the group more legitimacy, basically in deference to William James, Wallace asked Cambridge University to consider psychical research as just one more branch of anthropology. They refused. Nonetheless, the BSPR grew rapidly, and counted as members medical doctors, barristers, scientists, clergy, business executives, writers, artists, and poets, all involved in sorting verifiable ghost stories from the fraudulent.

Change the conditions slightly, from the mechanical to the technological, and substitute the spiritual movement for New Age religion, and we arrive at the twenty-first century. The 2005–2006 television season opened with *Ghost Whisperer*. We should not forget the past success of the television programs *Crossing Over with John Edward* and *Medium*. The International Ghost Hunters Society, according to Mary Roach's book *Spook: Science Tackles the Afterlife,* boasts a membership of fourteen thousand, located in seventy-eight different countries. Roach details the furious and scientific search for proof of the existence of the soul going on today. She points to an abundance of amateur groups around the world investigating the paranormal.

In the 1840s and 1850s, amateurs and professionals took photographs of ghosts and fairies and other elementals, and brought hundreds of collections of such photographs to market. Since some of the general public believed the camera had the power to catch images of the invisible and the ephemeral, photographers were able to doctor their photographs and sell them to Civil War widows as final and ghostly glimpses of their departed loved ones. The general public bought them in astonishing numbers.

Again, the fascination continues. The Metropolitan Museum of Art, in September 2005, mounted a show titled The Perfect Medium: Photography and the Occult, a collection of spirit photographs from the nineteenth century. *The New York Times* retitled the show The Ghost in the Darkroom. In one image, "The Ghost of Bernadette Soubirous," made around 1890, the subject slowly discorporates as she moves right to left, finally walking through one of those very thick British brick buildings. The star of the show is the very first known spirit photographer, William H. Mumler. Mumler, of New York and Boston, created a photograph for Mary Todd Lincoln of herself sitting next to the ghost image of her husband. The mayor of New York, a staunch disbeliever, ordered an investigation of Mumler's practices, and in 1869 he went on trial for defrauding the public with his photographs. P. T. Barnum, the man who knew hokum better than anyone else in America, testified for the prosecution—not a good sign. But, with Mary Lincoln's testimony—after all, he had photographed her dead husband—the jury acquitted Mumler.

Spirit photography slowly captured the imagination of the public in France and in England. Groups formed to pursue ways of capturing on film the world of spirits. They went by the most wonderful-sounding names: the Society for the Study of Supernormal Pictures; the British College of Psychic Science; and the Occult Committee of the Magic Circle.

The museum show also features what the nineteenth century called "fluid photographs." Inspired by James Braid's theories of animal magnetism, the invisible power that he believed coursed through the body, photographers placed people's hands on sensitized photograph plates that recorded the body's essential and basic source of energy, its "effluvia." Without such basic energy, many adepts believed, the person dies, marking effluvia as one more candidate for the true secret of life.

In the more modern portion of the show, to prove that spirits still haunt us and can still be captured on a photograph, MoMA presented work done by a Chicago elevator operator, Ted Serios. Under hypnosis, Serios projected images from his mind directly onto Polaroid film. Serios calls his images "thought photographs." They resemble small clouds of swirling gas. Punch "ghost hunter" into Google and you get scores of entries, many showing contemporary images that purport to document the presence of life from the other side.

The principal issues in the nineteenth and twenty-first centuries remain the same. In an age overwhelmed by one machine or another, we struggle to maintain our faith, to hang on to our essence—no, to *find* our essence. We write today on computers with light, a version of the ghost writing that began in the nineteenth century. We walk down the street, earpieces in place, seeming to talk to nobody. People on the Internet, on MySpace, or on YouTube take on whatever identity they choose at the moment. Conspiracy theories abound, about rigged elections in Florida or bombed towers in New York City. One website dedicates itself to the hoax of the first walk on the moon.

We yearn for answers, or even contact, from the beyond—extended, in our own time, to include other planets, or other solar systems. The truth is exhausted on this planet; we have to look elsewhere. Books on astrology, television programs about talking to the departed, highly flamboyant magicians, the proliferation of screens (including those tiny ones on our handheld telephones): All of these, really, are our legacy from the nineteenth century. Doctor Phil holds the hands of millions of Americans each day as they tune in with their sometimes painful search to find their bedrock, essential natures. And again, as in the nineteenth century, so many of us feel so very ghostlike. Just look at the screen; no one is really there—neither beneficent Oprah nor Doctor Feel-Good. It's a world of pixels, a dance of light. Even my gas pump talks to me these days. With a delete button, the smallest child can be the king of the disappeared, a pint-sized generator of ghosts.

Every intellectual in the nineteenth century felt compelled to comment on ghosts, or to pursue them outright. Even Karl Marx had the idea of fading human essence in mind when he penned his famous and haunting statement, "All that is solid melts into air." That short, enigmatic, grammatically awkward assertion, which sounds like Hamlet's "too too solid flesh" brought up to date, stands as the philosophical equivalent of Byron's invitation to his guests to write their own ghost stories. Marx's line, from *The Communist Manifesto*, makes more sense in the context of what he called the new bourgeois epoch, dominated by a continuing revolution that capitalism itself demanded:

> Constant revolutionizing of production, uninterrupted disturbance of all social relations, everlasting uncertainty and agitation, distinguish the bourgeois epoch from all earlier times. All fixed, fast-frozen relationships, with their train of venerable ideas and opinions, are swept away, all new-formed ones become obsolete before they can ossify. All that is solid melts into air, all that is holy is profaned, and men at last are forced to face with sober senses the real conditions of their lives and their relations with their fellow men.

Yes, everything melted: toys and cars and machines, but the most disturbing meltdown came with flesh and blood. The established and solid way that people conceived of their flesh and blood selves had vanished into thin air. Which raises a most compelling question: What made people feel like they were fast disappearing, that they were becoming so insubstantial as to resemble nothing more than ghosts?

Here, we must think past the usual explanation of the way people's everyday lives radically changed in the midst of the Industrial Revolution. That argument says that by performing an unending series of repetitive tasks, people more and more resembled disposable parts. Machines degraded people into cogs. I would be foolhardy to dispute such a claim, especially given the deadening routine of assembly-line work even in its most rudimentary stage in the first decades of the nineteenth century. Besides, we have early and shocking evidence to prove the point.

People who had enjoyed a centuries-long tradition of working with their hands—weavers, spinners, carpenters, and blacksmiths—reacted quickly against wholesale industrialization, and made their feelings known in the most unruly, riotous ways. In the first decades of the nineteenth century, large numbers of them broke into factories all over London and took axes and hammers to the new motorized looms and lathes. Some of them even set off small bombs. The break-ins reached such proportions and turned so violent that factory owners implored Parliament to find a solution to the problem. In their discussions, members of Parliament equated the mayhem with the most heinous of capital crimes, namely murder. After all, the nation's economy was at stake; a way of life was seriously threatened. And so, in 1812, the legislature took the bold step of extending the death penalty to cover anyone convicted of destroying one of the new industrial machines.

Technology played its role as a major and obvious snatcher of bodies; people reacted, sometimes violently. But people would have difficulty seeing or describing the most corrosive effects. How does a person protest feelings of malaise or nervousness? No doubt about it, the new world of the nineteenth century—what Thomas Carlyle in 1829 termed for the first time the Mechanical Age—forever altered people's cognitive realities. A beautifully shocking phrase popular during the period argued that the new technologies, and in particular the train and the motion picture camera, had effected "the annihilation of time and space."[17] While no one knows who first uttered it, that phrase has achieved status as one of the most brilliantly illuminating declarations of the time. Railroad travel and motion pictures led the way in reshaping daily experience; the annihilation of time and space rested on the simultaneous eradication of the human body. Like Dracula and Houdini, the train and the camera were the perfect expressions of an age that became more and more peopled with countless numbers of ghosts.

•❦•

THE BODY HAS a history, and it took a radical turn in this period. A steam locomotive, hurtling through space, across time, eliminated any need for a body. The train did all the work. The passenger merely sat back, insulated from the outside, in his or her seat. Looking out the window of a railroad car that sped along at thirty miles an hour, a person saw what might have once been a familiar landscape turn into a rapidly changing, continual series of images. Railroad travel thus reduced the passenger, who perhaps only moments before stepping on the train had participated intimately in the mix of buildings, trees, rocks, animals, and so forth, primarily to a pair of eyes—without the need (or, stranger still, without the capacity) to smell, or taste, or hear.

Likewise, a person sitting in a movie theater could watch action take place across great chunks of time and space, with no physical effort on his or her part. As the house lights lowered, people's bodies disappeared, their sense of smell and touch and taste shut down. Of course, it was important for audience members to feel and respond, but only while sitting still, remaining fairly quiet, and gazing at the screen. Motion picture technology, the ultimate succubus, had the uncanny capacity to take human flesh and transform it into a ghostly, ethereal presence—or rather, absence. Gigantic images flickered into incandescent life on the screen every time some-one threw the switch on the projector to start its reels spinning around and around.

In either case, in the train or in the theater, bodies—people's own fleshy, well-evolved bodies—suddenly mattered little, if at all. Such dis-embodied experiences represented a radical departure from the farm-ing, laboring body of physical exertion, the one usually associated with the country as opposed to the city. In the ancient world, ecstatic religions claimed responsibility for out-of-body experiences. But here was something quite different. As one historian so pointedly put it, "'annihilating time and space' is what most new technologies aspire to do: technology regards the very terms of our bodily existence as burdensome."[18]

Karl Marx took up the concept of time and space's annihilation, but he indicted the exigencies of capitalism, rather than the intricacies of tech-nology, as the chief executioner. The more quickly entrepreneurs could get their products to market, the more profit they stood to make. Economists preferred to call this stepped-up pace a matter of efficiency. Marx saw it as thoroughly detrimental to living, as the erasure of haptic, touching, in-timate, sensual interaction with other human beings: "Capital must on the one side strive to tear down every spatial barrier to intercourse, i.e., to ex-change, and conquer the whole earth for its market. It strives on the other hand to annihilate this space with time, i.e., to reduce to a minimum the time spent in motion from one place to another."[19]

No wonder, then, that with such fantastical imaginings about the world of commerce, we get the first modern corporations. These were noth-ing more than collections of disparate people abstracted into a single fictive body, an imagined corpus, one that in the past owned material goods—called stock, sometimes livestock—but which goods now had been ab-stracted into certificates—called shares of stock, numerous and never live.

The earliest corporations, like Standard Oil, United States Steel, General Electric, and the Pennsylvania Railroad, quickly became known as titans or giants—larger-than-life Greek demigods—and acquired their substance through capital and power. They gobbled up land and devoured resources with voraciously hearty appetites: By the end of the nineteenth century, roughly three hundred industrial corporations controlled more than forty percent of all manufacturing in the United States. Unlike real people, corporations could not be jailed for wrongdoing. (Of course, as we now know, executives can indeed do time for certain crimes, like fraud or outright theft.) They could only be punished with stiff fines. Corporations followed the logic of money with a vengeance. They avoided the social contract in favor of the bottom line of the business contract. Feelings of discorporation led, in the nineteenth century, quite naturally to the creation of the first huge incorporations.

Most people only felt the effect of technology, but could not, of course, exert any control over it. By the beginning of the twentieth century, people could talk on telephones, listen to radio broadcasts, and watch motion pictures. One invention in particular, however, allowed people not only to exert great control over its use, but even made them feel a bit artistic, to boot. A great many middle-class people could afford to purchase a handheld camera. And thousands upon thousands of middle-class citizens bought a camera and used it, not only to ground themselves by documenting reality but also to counter feelings of disorientation and displacement by documenting their own existence. The photograph offered proof that things in the world—especially people, and most especially their very own selves—really existed.

In certain ways, it feels like the nineteenth century invented the eye—not just the actual eye but the mind's eye, as well. Think of the impressionists and their desire to break reality into constituent colors. Outside of the canvas, at least a dozen different inventions, from the phantasmagoria to the zoetrope, precede the invention of the camera. The period also provides a dozen or more ways to reproduce those photographs, from glass prints and wet prints to tintypes and silver prints. Such attention to picturing reality really came out of a desire to discover how the eye actually functions.

This was the goal of James McNeill Whistler, who describes having an insight into the way that proper drawing should be done—with the most detail at the center of interest, fading off into less and less detail out at the edges. Hermann von Helmholtz, the German scientist, wrote a treatise on the eye, which he published in English in 1873, titled "The Eye as an Optical Instrument." He fairly well corroborates Whistler's intuitions about drawing: "The image we receive with the eye is like a picture, minutely and elaborately finished in the center, but only roughly sketched in at the border." The camera lens works in the same way.

In a book about media and spectral visions in the twenty-first century, titled *Phantasmagoria*, its author, Marina Warner, points to what she calls *photographic looking:*

"Photographic looking" existed before the appearance of the camera, as several critics have pointed out, and the new medium responded to desires which were articulated in other ways—to order, analyse, and store data, to measure and inventory phenomena, to make memorials of the past. . . . At the same time, it responded to, and amplified, a growing realization that human vision was limited, discriminating, and linked to the vagaries of memory, and that a machine might be able to see more, more clearly.

The story of the invention of the camera takes up almost the entire century. It takes some time to tell.

To begin with, in 1826, a Frenchman named Joseph Nicéphore Niépce produced the first photographic image, using a camera obscura. The image required a continuous eight-hour exposure to sunlight, prompting Niépce to call his process heliography. But even then, even with all that intense light, the image gradually faded. Niépce died in 1833, but his partner, a chemist and artist named Louis Daguerre, continued his work, and in

1839, Daguerre succeeded in creating the first image that did not fade. But, true to the inherent power of technology, Daguerre did more than create a sense of permanency for his images. He cut the exposure time for making lasting images from eight hours to just around thirty minutes.

Daguerre printed his images on highly polished silver-coated copper sheets, so that to see anything at all the viewer had to tilt the sheet up and down until the image came into view—actually the image seemed to appear only by being coaxed, as if it were a ghost hovering into focus. Marina Warner says about such a particularly ghostly image that "[t]his spectral effect, intrinsic to the medium, provoked *frissons* from its first appearance, so much so that many early examples are hand-tinted to give bloom to the sitter's cheeks and lips, or gilded to enliven a cushion, a fob, a pair of earrings." The daguerreotype made a ghost of the person photographed and then the photographer helped bring that person back to life by adding color and highlights to the print.

The magic of photographic reproduction, this idea of literally writing with light, caught on fast. By 1840, one year after Daguerre's invention, an American named Alexander S. Wolcott had received the first patent for a portable camera. The following year, 1841, William Henry Fox Talbot, a native of London, received a patent for something he called a collotype, the first negative/positive process, making possible something truly revolutionary, the production of multiple images from a single exposure. By the time we get to pop art, Andy Warhol exploits this kind of cheapening of the original through its repetition as the subject of his silkscreen prints of Elizabeth Taylor, Mao, and other celebrities.

Following Talbot's innovation, it then took some forty years of technological change to allow people to own their very own cameras, each change, just as today, lowering the price a bit more and widening the audience even more. In 1880, George Eastman, a New York businessman, received an American patent for his film on a roll, and in 1888 he made his relatively inexpensive camera, the Kodak, available in greengroceries, apothecaries, and general stores. The camera, more commonly known by its brand name, the Kodak—compare Kleenex and the Frigidaire—immediately caught the imagination of the general public. Eastman's advertising motto enjoyed an enormous popularity because it tapped into the power of technology's ability to take life into the future and to made it so much simpler; with a slick marketing two-step, it also make the consumer feel that he or she was in total control: "You press the button, we do the rest."

The first Kodak sold for fifteen dollars and came with enough film to take one hundred pictures. Eastman made it small enough, light enough, and simple enough to use, so that the average person—he did not want to sell to professionals—could take a picture of almost anything he or she wished. After people took their one hundred exposures, they sent their cameras back to Eastman Kodak, in Rochester, New York, where the factory would develop the prints, fill the camera again with film, and send the finished prints to the customer. A person could buy into this elaborate process all for a processing fee of fifteen dollars.

Keep in mind that Eastman may not have captured the audience he had hoped for, since in 1880 the average U.S. worker—who toiled away some twelve hours a day, six or seven days a week—made a mere sixteen dollars a week. Remember, too, that the first Labor Day, celebrating the heroic factory worker, comes around this time, in 1882. With the help of the socialist organizer and politician Eugene Debs, workers were beginning to agitate for better wages and better working conditions. Only those with a bit of money could afford the camera in the first place, or afford to have the film developed later.

Eastman the entrepreneur knew that to make his camera a real success, he would have to lower the price a good deal. He also knew he would make up the difference in sales volume. And so in 1900 he put on the market his new Brownie camera, which sold for only one dollar—still nearly a half day's wages for most workers, but incredibly more affordable than the older Kodak. By calling his camera a Brownie, Eastman harked back to the intimate connection between the camera and the spirit world, for a brownie is one of the fairies and spirits that populated the Scottish woods in the nineteenth century.

Like almost every technological invention, however, photographs had their dark side, a fact that became much more apparent in the decades after Daguerre extended the camera's reach into family life. As the price of portraits declined, more and more families had their pictures taken in the hundreds of studios that opened in major cities and towns. In one year alone, 1851, studios churned out over three million daguerreotypes, most of them family or group portraits. While Daguerre's camera called people together as a fleshy group, it handed them back nothing but a cold, lifeless, odorless image of themselves. For that reason, it offered both a record of, say, a family's existence, at the same time that it reinforced its feelings of ghostliness. The literary and cultural critic Susan Sontag captured both characteristics in her description, in the book *On Photography,* of the photograph as "a transparent account of reality."

Photographers instructed family members to smile as they shot their images. We know this phenomenon today as the "Say cheese" factor. Family portraits introduced into the culture families draped with smiles. One can imagine a person in nineteenth-century America seeing one of these smiling daguerreotypes and wondering about his or her own family: Was it as happy as that family in the photograph? The family portrait thus brought a new (and unobtainable) sensibility into popular culture. Can the camera have prompted Lewis Carroll to create the Cheshire Cat grin in *Alice's Adventures in Wonderland?* Recall it's the cat that turns invisible at one point, in a tree, leaving behind nothing but a broad smile that hovers, ghostlike, in the air. Perhaps the cat stands for those ghostlike smiling photographs of invisible and nameless families.

By 1852, the camera was ubiquitous enough that the word *photograph,* based on its primary quality of consorting with the ethereal, took on a new connotation, referring to a mental or verbal image with such exactness of detail that it resembled an actual photograph. What an enormous turn of events: people beginning to use technology as the standard for trying to capture the quality of their own inner lives. No wonder we can talk so easily these days about the wonderful capacities of the memory of our computers without thinking anything wrong with that analogy, as technology outpaces, we think, our own capacities.

Almost every contemporary critic acknowledges that ordinary people found this triumph of technology—the photograph—as both liberating and frightening, miraculous and murderous, flat-out reassuring and absolutely terrifying. While that same dichotomy holds true for every so-called technological advance, innovation, or invention, the camera exposes the dichotomy very clearly and quite vividly.

People began taking photographs of the entire world. Some of them shot more and more landscape photographs as a way of situating themselves back into their immediate surroundings. The professionals turned to other subjects. One of the earliest of them, Nadar, produced magnificent portraits of French celebrities in the 1860s, like Victor Hugo, and the elusive Sarah Bernhardt at the beginning of her career. In fact, he helped make Bernhardt into a celebrity, as thousands of people saw his photographs of her in newspapers and on postcards and in advertisements in the back of magazines around the world. Other photographers, like Julia Margaret Cameron and Eadweard Muybridge, quickly turned their attention to the most important and problematic and elusive of all subjects, the human body. Cameron devoted herself to taking photographs of already established celebrities like Alfred Lord Tennyson, Robert Browning, and Ellen Terry.

Muybridge, as we have seen earlier in this chapter, took a radically different path. Historian Rebecca Solnit describes Muybridge's work in the mid-1870s, when he started photographing horses and people in motion, as "an avalanche of images of bodies, the bodies of horses, then men, then women, children . . . " Solnit does not mean to disparage his work.

On the contrary, she describes his photographs as liberating, as welcomed breaks from the quotidian: "[I]t was as though he were returning bodies themselves to those who craved them—not bodies as they might daily be experienced, bodies as sensations of gravity, fatigue, strength, pleasure, but bodies become weightless images, bodies dissected and reconstructed by light and machine and fantasy."[20]

Such reconstructed bodies, fabricated anew out of light and fantasy, no longer count as bodies. We greet them for what they are—nothing more than images. As with still photographs, motion photography constituted for many people another piece of evidence, like ghost stories, of their own eradication, but this time in a more accurate way. These images showed that they existed over dozens or hundreds or even several hundreds of moments in the flux of time, but the string of photographs gave them that proof, once again, only as abstracted, ghostly evidence. Muybridge himself, in a tacit acknowledgment of the nature of photography, felt impelled, in 1870, to photograph the Modoc ghost dance, an American Indian festival performed in the West. The Modocs celebrated Native American spirits on the day they left their graves and returned to join forces with the living, in this case to help battle the white man. Of course, given Muybridge's medium, ghosts appealed to him, though he refused to become part of the movement that exploited spectral photography.

No less a figure than Oliver Wendell Holmes commented on this powerful drift toward disembodiment that photography made so painfully and at times so artistically apparent: "Form is henceforth divorced from matter. In fact, matter as a visible object is of no great use any longer . . . "[21] And later, on the subject of stereographic photography, a close relative of modern motion pictures, Holmes expressed an even more critical urgency about the dissolution of the corporeal. His comments yoked together, in a weird metaphysical image, the seemingly disparate ways that photography and trains take us to far-off places: "[T]he shutting out of surrounding objects, and the concentration of the whole attention, which is a consequence of this, produce a dream-like exaltation . . . in which we seem to leave the body behind us and sail away into one strange scene after another, like disembodied spirits."[22]

A more contemporary critic of photography, Alison Hennegan, in her essay "Personalities and Principles: Aspects of Literature and Life in Fin-de-Siècle England," provides an important link between nineteenth-century images and our own period's fascination with what semioticians call the simulacra, images that make up a good deal of our experience projected onto one screen or another:

> There was, of course, nothing new about portraiture itself. But the ability to reproduce the same image thousands of times over, the means of distributing it swiftly across enormous geographical areas, the capacity to "capture" the human model and then offer it for sale to another human being who thereafter "had" the sitter in permanent, possible form—all these were different indeed. With them begins that curious and often frightening process whereby, over the years, the "image" of public people has become almost more important, because more "real" and available than the person.

What is the effect, we must ask here, on the staged and posed subject, neatly captured by the photographer in his or her studio? What can we trust the photographer to really tell us through photographs? How did the "photo" affect the representation of the truth? This is an especially potent question once we recognize that many photographers manipulated the negatives and played with the final image. Photography belonged to the world of technology, but it also had immediate connections with art and artifice.

Beyond that, we need to ask, how did people react to these new feelings of disembodiment and strange powers of ownership without really owning anything more substantial than print paper? How did they respond to the increases in speed in their lives? What did they do? What, in effect, *could* they do? Whatever the outcomes, reactions were not confined to the educated and the elite. General feelings of discorporation reached down into the general public, as well. George Miller Beard, an American physician and neurologist, developed a practice in this country in a medical specialty he called electrotherapy, in which he used electrical stimulation for curing disorders of the nervous system. In 1881, after seeing thousands of patients, he decided to publish a study on the psychological health of the average citizen, giving away his diagnosis in the title: *American Nervousness, with Its Causes and Consequences*. He could have just as easily saddled England and parts of Western Europe with that same diagnosis.

Beard concluded that railroad travel, telegraphy, and photography, along with severe competition and excessive brain work, compounded by the general speed of what he termed "modern civilization," led to a new phenomenon that he termed "nervous collapse," or what doctors would later call "nervous breakdown." He introduced a new word into the medical vocabulary, *neurasthenia*, which tried to capture people's "lack of nerve power" wrought by what he saw as "modern civilization." He listed symptoms including dyspepsia, inability to concentrate, impotence, and full-on depression. In an amazing insight into the way machines get under the skin, Beard pointed out that "today a nervous man cannot take out his watch and look at it when the time for an appointment or train is near without affecting his pulse."

The medical profession embraced his findings so enthusiastically that they began diagnosing a new malady called Beard's disease, which doctors defined as "unexplained exhaustion with abnormal fatigability."[23] In its initial use, in the fifteenth century, the word *nervous* denoted a certain strength or courage. By 1813, the word had totally reversed itself and came to mean a weakness of resolve, a condition of severe lassitude. Wherever we might want to locate the idea of "will," we can no longer find it, in this period, in the idea of "nerve."

The decade before the publication of Beard's book, the 1870s, the years of refinement in both the nature and quality of motion photography, also saw the invention of the telephone and the phonograph—two more lethal accomplices just poised to further do in both time and space. Clocks also began to appear with a third hand to measure the passing of every second. All these inventions and innovations added to the public's quickening descent into nervousness. Beard decried not just the speed at which people's lives suddenly seemed to be moving, but also the swiftness with which life could be calibrated. That is, he took note of the fact that punctuality had suddenly become not just a virtue but also a measure of one's character. Factory bosses, priests, and friends suddenly all demanded that people arrive at this job, or that prayer service, or even some seemingly casual office party, at five o'clock sharp, "on the dot," or "on the tick," or "on the clicker." The new watchwords of the age: "Be on time." "Do not be late." Workers got "docked" for showing up to work late, or for returning from lunch break beyond the prescribed time.

In a delightful book entitled *Keeping Watch: A History of American Time*, its author, Michael O'Malley, says that in the 1850s Americans observed eighty different local times. Joining the period's fervor for reducing the disorder of reality to numbers and essential units, Britain's Royal Society used the Greenwich Observatory, in 1848, to indicate an imaginary line called zero longitude, which passed through Greenwich, a borough of London, and which terminated at the north and south poles. We all know this line as "the prime meridian," the baseline for measuring time, one of the most ideal innovations of the nineteenth century. An international conference held in 1884 in Washington, D.C., adopted the Greenwich meridian, which promulgated the use of standardized times in longitudinal zones around the world.

The year before the Greenwich date of 1884, the railroad owners campaigned to eliminate those eighty local zones and to standardize time within longitudinal sections. As Jack Beatty puts it in his *Age of Betrayal: The Triumph of Money in America, 1865–1900*, "The sun told time from Genesis to 12:01 A.M. on November 18, 1883," the date when the railroads assumed dominion over time. "Basically," Beatty goes on to say,

"Americans took nature's word for time: Noon arrived when the sun looked nearest to being overhead, at times that differed with locations. . . . Town clocks, to be sure, were set not by sundials but by almanacs that averaged the sun's variations over months and years. A scattering of localities rented astronomically precise time from observatories, which wired them through Western Union." On November 18, 1883, America's railroads imposed standard time on the United States, dividing the country into four broad bands of longitude, each fifteen degrees apart. The railroads accomplished an amazing thing: They now could lay claim to owning time in this country. Michael O'Malley summarizes this monumental change: "Once individuals experienced time as a relationship between God and nature. Henceforth, under the railroad standards, men and women would measure themselves in relation to a publicly defined time based on synchronized clocks."

A much more seemingly minor refinement to time had come, in the last years of the eighteenth century, with the invention of the stopwatch and, in the nineteenth century, with the time clock. In reality, though, what happened here was no less monumental, for what we witness is the segmenting of time, its division into smaller and smaller units. It really starts with an American born in 1856, Frederick Winslow Taylor, who co-opted the technique of temporal segmentation from the earliest motion picture technology and applied it to the workplace to create a new field, which he called "time and motion studies"; when he decided to sell his ideas to industry, he called it by its more highfalutin-sounding name, "scientific management."

In order to increase production and efficiency in the office and factory— and thus to increase profit margins—Taylor broke down each worker's tasks into fundamental and discrete movements. Then he measured and timed those movements, down to the hundredth of the minute. In the end, Taylor dictated to workers the precise amount of time they should spend performing each and every routine operation. He made them further account for their time by requiring them to punch in to work in the morning and to punch out in the evening, using a new, nineteenth-century device called the time clock. In the language of the day, he had workers "clock in" and "clock out"; they got paid only for the time that they were "on the clock." He later made every worker account for his or her lunch and coffee break. Taylor's biographer, Robert Kanigel, says that Taylor "helped instill in us the fierce, unholy obsession of time, order, productivity, and efficiency that marks our age." His doctrine pervades so much of American culture, Kanigel stresses, and at such a deep level, that "we no longer realize it's there." And that is a most dangerous state of affairs.

Beard feared that, in a generation or two, people would no longer be able to cope with such temporal restrictions and constraints on the freedom of their lives: "The perfection of clocks and the invention of watches have something to do with modern nervousness, since they compel us to be on time, and excite the habit of looking to see the exact moment, so as not to be late for trains or appointments. . . . We are under constant strain, mostly unconscious, to get somewhere or do something at some definite moment." His predictions proved true. By the end of the century, according to some contemporary accounts, neurasthenia had reached epidemic proportions.

The Irish statesman James Beresford wrote a book early in the century to which he gave the most portentous title, *The Miseries of Human Life, or The Groans of Samuel Sensitive, and Timothy Testy; with a Few Supplementary Sighs from Mrs. Testy* (1806). In Beresford's world, the stopwatch dominates every aspect, virtually, of people's experience. He even gave a name to the new people of the new century: "Automata—people who regulate all their thoughts, words, and actions, by the stopwatch." The word *robots* might come to mind here, machines that in this period would carry out their tasks as no more than mechanical ghosts, programmed by some outside authority or force.

Mechanization—industrialization in general—was not the main enemy threatening to strip people of all of their humanity. The rock-solid definition of human beings began to fall apart the moment the nineteenth century opened, as I have said, when the idea of the human being radically shifted, both philosophically and scientifically. Without trying to overstate the case, we might equate such a monumental rupture with the unsettling caused by the Scientific Revolution of the sixteenth and seventeenth centuries. Novelists and poets served as one guide to the problems attendant on this epistemological crisis.

Some of the era's literature we can read as warnings about the psychological and social dangers of such a critical dislocation, especially in a world bereft of God. It is revealing that many contemporary critics viewed Dracula, the notorious Count Dracul, as the most seriously religious character in Bram Stoker's novel. Other literature, like *Frankenstein,* "The Invisible Man," and Goethe's *Faust,* impeached science for its relentless and distorted search for the command of all nature and the source of human life. Doctor Frankenstein may find the key to life, but in the process he loses his own soul, his creation merely a reflection of his own monstrous, disfigured urge toward power and absolute control. In trying to find the secret of life, of course, he wants to rival the power of God.

Given the blows to the core of human sensibilities, both literature and science in the nineteenth century had taken on an enormous task—not just to criticize and analyze, but also to reconstitute what it meant to be wholly alive. That meant starting over from scratch. "Scratch" may in fact be the wrong word. Reconstruction had to be accomplished out of thin air. That's what the phantasmagoria, the photograph, ghost stories, plays like Ibsen's *Ghosts* and August Strindberg's *Ghost Sonata,* Henry James's series of ghost stories, Robert Louis Stevenson's short story "The Body-Snatcher," Vincenzo Bellini's opera *La Sonnambula,* the investigations of the Society for Psychical Research, motion picture technology, and the continual reports of various sorts of visitants by one clairvoyant or another were all really in the business of doing—trying to tap into the zeitgeist of the times, and trying, oh so desperately, to arrive at some answers.

Such a monumental undertaking demanded that every profession, from science to art to popular entertainment—from Humphry Davy to Harry

Houdini—set out to find the essence of human life as a starting point for that key project of incorporation. Some public figures, like Davy, were more deliberate and conscious of their task than others. Can we say that Houdini knew he was engaged in discovering the bedrock of anything so highfalutin as human essence? Probably not. But his tricks and illusions were of a piece with the times. Certain ideas, as we often say, are "in the air." The age exerts its own unspoken, sometimes hidden, but decided influence.

Another key question: Did it actually happen? Did any scientist really find the answer, or did any novel really manage to capture that elusive essence, or was the course of history just a record of more and more anxiety as the nineteenth century moved into the twentieth, the twentieth wearily into the twenty-first? We will see. But it is important to think about the possible endings to this story.

What does it mean to be alive? is a key question that haunted the twentieth century. It haunts us today. Periodically, that question moved powerfully and often times noisily to the foreground, for instance with existential philosophy, the beats, the civil rights movement, the hippies, the yippies, and the liberation movements of the eighties and nineties. In the new twenty-first century, people still ask the very same question, only now in the midst of vastly increased technological advances, like DNA and genome research, along with a proliferation of screens and a resurgence of Protestant evangelical movements. It may in fact be harder to find an answer today, since we are in the thrall of more and more simulacra and more and more ideologies.

In 1869, William James published a famous essay, "The Perception of Reality." While the piece first appeared in the journal *Mind*, James added it as a separate chapter in his famous and influential *Principles of Psychology*. In that essay he posed the following question, which he required the publisher to set in italics: *"Under what circumstances do we think things real?"* Why do some things in the world seem more real to us, he asked, than other things? James asked the question in the context of his deep and committed

231

interest in the spiritual world, in his desire to show that our refusal to believe in the invisible world led to our own feelings of ghostliness. Part of the answer to why we believe in certain forms of reality and not others, James asserts, requires that a person take his or her sensory world seriously. That is, the observer must first feel fully alive before he or she can project that quality out into the world. By mid-century the philosophical and psychological discussions about the "realness" (James's term) of things and people were in full swing. James turned to the pursuit of ghosts to fill out his own scope of the realness of the real.

Interest in ghosts continues today, even in someone whom the academy takes so terribly seriously as the French social critic Jacques Derrida, the man who brought deconstruction to American universities. Derrida in fact coined a term specifically for the study of ghosts, *hauntology*, with a fairly obvious pun on *ontology*. Hauntology refers to the peculiarly paradoxical state of the specter, which is neither being nor nonbeing, neither dead nor alive, neither corporal presences nor absent spaces. Such an ambiguous state intrigues Derrida because it so deliberately blows apart the binary system that contains so much of our lives today. Derrida refuses to talk about presence and absence, past and present, body and spirit, life and death. Every one of those elements for Derrida contains in its nature a trace of its opposite. And so, in his work *Spectres of Marx: The State of the Debt, the Work of Mourning, and the New International,* Derrida laments the fact that "there has never been a scholar that really, and as a scholar, deals with ghosts." For Derrida, ghosts get at the very nature of aliveness itself. Ironically, it is ghosts and not flesh that force us to ask the right questions about the nature of existence.

The most basic of those questions must be, especially against the continual erosion of our own solidity and substance, How do we know we are alive? We have fallen under the sway of the medical profession, media conglomerates, the food industry, and the political machine: Some professional constantly tells us who we are, what we need, and how we should feel. In addition, this has become a much harder question to answer in a world where the image, more and more, asserts authority over the actual. It makes it harder to answer the question: What is it that constitutes the bedrock of human existence? People find all kinds of ways to show that they really are made of flesh and blood, from participating in extreme sports to finding validation in so-called reality television shows, from getting tattooed to having various parts of their bodies pierced. Those last two, tattoos and piercings, so tremendously popular in the early twenty-first century, had their resurgence in the nineteenth century, when the search really got under way.

Captain James Cook brought news of tattoos back from the South Seas Islands, and first mentioned them in his journals in 1769. He emphasized one aspect of the art, an important component for establishing the substantive reality of the body, and that was the level of pain exacted by tattooing certain parts of the body: "This method of tattooing I shall now describe. As this is a painful operation, especially the tattooing of their buttocks. It is performed but once in their lifetimes." If the procedure elicited pain, it must mean that the person truly existed, that he or she had feelings, and finally that he or she stood out as a human being who was fully alive—an important point for anyone suffering from feelings of dissolution. Ghosts do not feel pain. Tattooing became a popular art form in the last part of the nineteenth century, in England and in America. At the Chicago World's Fair, one of the best-attended displays consisted of a group of South Sea Islanders, their bodies almost entirely covered with needle art.

The same life-affirming qualities that characterized tattooing also marked the various forms of body piercing that became essential viewing at sideshows. One of the most popular and graphic sideshow attractions featured a man who drove a nail into the side of his nose with a large hammer, or sometimes deep into the side of his head. Feelings of insubstantiality may also account for the huge following that Eugen Sandow, the father of modern bodybuilding and a pioneer in the field of physical culture, enjoyed. While he began life in Prussia, as Friedrich Wilhelm Mueller, he made his debut in America on June 12, 1893, at the Casino Roof Garden in New York City, billed as nothing less than "The Perfect Man." He had just turned twenty-six. Touted as the strongest man in the world, Sandow captivated audiences with his enormous feats of strength and his public displays of muscular development. If only every one of you would pay the same strict attention to becoming solid and assured, he seemed to be saying, your body might look like just like mine.

In one dramatic climax to his act, Sandow made his body into an bridge, his chest upraised, his feet flat, and his hands arched back over his head, they, too, flat on the stage. Assistants placed a wooden platform on his shoulders, legs and chest. At that moment, the music grew louder, the house lights dimmed, the excitement rose. Three horses, which, according to the publicity posters, weighed a total of 2,600 pounds, stepped onto the platform and remained stock still for roughly five seconds. But that feat paled in comparison with his most outlandish display of the limits of human strength: lifting a full-grown elephant—perhaps using Houdini's own Jennie, and perhaps borrowing the master's own illusion—from the stage floor to high over his head with just his bare hands. In a certain way, Sandow presented to his audiences an astonishing example of the anti-ghost, the man who refused to fade away. Like Houdini, he derived a good deal of his substance from his status as a celebrity and a star.

Again, like Houdini, Sandow made a fortune just from performing prodigious acts of strength and showing off his well-developed physique. For a time, Sandow's was the most famous and recognizable naked body—male or female—in the world. Ninety-seven-pound weaklings had Sandow's poster pinned up on their bedroom walls. He paved the way for other strongmen—like Charles Atlas, whose advertisements would appear at the back of mid-twentieth-century comic books—and for the cult of bodybuilding. Nineteenth-century naturopaths, like Bernarr MacFadden, owe their popularity to Sandow. Recall that MacFadden introduced to America the idea of bodybuilding.

From ghost to solid muscle: The move may sound like a shift from one extreme to the other, but in a sense because all three characters—Mac-Fadden, Sandow, and Houdini—developed that one dimension, strength, they in effect lost their substance. The complicated, quirky, elusive side of people that we know as their personalities had, in each of their cases, completely vanished. All three men, in their passion for being solidly there, had ironically managed to turn themselves into phantoms. Some people use the same ploys today—living large and in charge, building bulk and giving notice of colossal strength through working out, taking steroids, driving huge SUVs, playing car radios at full volume, wearing oversize clothes, and sometimes carrying and even using guns. They get covered with tattoos and have their flesh pierced. A clothing company named Metal Mulisha sponsors a crew of hard-edged, tough, tattooed motorcycle riders and eager fighters. They want to give the appearance that their too too solid flesh will not melt. They need to feel that way. But of course, and sadly so, it's just not true. The thug life is life at a most essentialist level, at the level of power and strength and fear—of offering to the world an image of total intimidation.

It is impossible to think about the social contract without that crucial agent called the human being. The elimination of such a basic and complicated entity, *the human being,* makes all sorts of inhuman treatment that we encounter with great frequency today absolutely possible—and even probable. Once people come to feel that they have lost their essence, their sense of being, they fall to the level of immediate victims. Life loses its value. Whoever has power feels free to subject those others to the most violent and inhuman assaults—murder, or perhaps even worse, prolonged and painful methods of torture that eventually lead to death.

Extreme forms of torture do not constitute an exercise of the imagination. Such manipulations reveal a mind that refuses to see the other as a sentient human being. Once people begin to move around like ghosts, it is an easy step—or no step at all—for those in authority to eliminate them.

For in a sense that kind of deep-seated disappearance creates the feeling that they—or, more accurately, *we*—no longer exist. No one can blame people for wanting to recapture that feeling of being fully alive. There's no other feeling quite like it. But tattoos and studs will not do. There must be more.

FIVE | There Is Only Life

And yet, the ways we miss our lives are life.

—RANDALL JARRELL, "A GIRL IN A LIBRARY"

G OD DID NOT CREATE LIFE—not on the sixth, or seventh, or any other day. Science created life. Slowly and deliberately, over the course of the nineteenth century, a collection of professionals—philosophers, scientists, and those in the natural sciences—in their failure to find the essence of humanness, helped to pave the way for an artificially created entity called "life," or the even more alien, "a life." Beginning in the 1870s, in this country—during what has come to be called the Gilded Age—the barons of wealth managed to crush in the lower classes whatever little bit of living still remained.

Textile workers, for instance, spent fourteen hours a day in the factory, six days a week, and got paid $5 for the week. Workers included women, boys, and girls. And the numbers were getting worse: In 1875 twice as many children under twelve worked in Rhode Island as they did twenty years before, most of them in the mills. The New York *Sun* summarized the plight of workers thus: "There is, however, little danger of an outbreak among them. They live, as a rule, in tenements owned by the company employing them; and when they strike they are at once thrown out in the street. Then they are clubbed by policemen, arrested as vagrants, and sent to the county jail, to be released to take their choice of going to work at the old wages or starving."[1]

Politics, or what went by the name of politics, in the Gilded Age sounds grim indeed, and intent on destroying all life. Here is one historian's quick summary of the situation:

> Representative government gave way to bought government. Politicians betrayed the public trust. Citizens sold their votes. Dreams faded. Ideals died of their impossibility. Cynicism poisoned hope. The United States in these years took on the lineaments of a Latin American party-state, an oligarchy ratified in rigged elections, girded by bayonets, and given a genial historical gloss by its raffish casting.

> Jay Gould was president. He never ran for office, he never lost office—he *ruled*. He wrote the laws. He interpreted the Constitution. He commanded the army. He staffed the government. He rented politicians, fattening his purse off their favor. He was John D. Rockefeller, James J. Hill, Andrew Carnegie, Tom Scott, and George Pullman; and this was his time—this was his country.[2]

This description does not allow for very much living. Huge and over-reaching corporate wealth had taken charge in this country. Of the seventy-three men who held cabinet posts between 1868 and 1896, forty-eight of them either served railroad clients, lobbied for the railroad, sat on railroad boards, or had railroad-connected relatives. They passed the baton of power to the coal and oil moguls of our day, to the Cheneys and the Bushes. What choices did people have in the nineteenth century to grab back their sense of being, their autonomy? If one were a Boston Brahmin like Henry David Thoreau the idea of civil disobedience might come to mind. On the absolute other end of the scale, a worker might *strike* (a word, by the way, that appears first in America, in the report of a strike from 1810; a "strike" is a blow against control and for freedom), but historically such actions resulted in small payoffs and huge recriminations. (Between 1870 and 1903, in this country, authorities called in the state militia, the National Guard, or federal troops more than five hundred times to put down labor strikes.)

In the Great Railroad Strike of 1877, *The New York Times* referred on July 26 to those who refused to work, in a list of insults worthy of Falstaff, as

> roughs, hoodlums, rioters, a mob, suspicious-looking individuals, bad characters, thieves, blacklegs, looters, communists, rabble, labor-reform agitators, a dangerous class of people, gangs, tramps, drunken section-men, law-breakers, threatening crowd, bummers, ruffians, loafers, bullies, vagabonds, cowardly mob, bands of worthless fellows, incendiaries, enemies of society, reckless crowd, malcontents, wretched people, loud-mouthed orators, rapscallions, brigands, robbers, riffraff, terrible fellows, felons, and idiots.

Such overreactions, both verbal and physical, might explain the appeal in nineteenth-century America of one strategy for confronting the expanding oppressive authority, and that is anarchy—the opportunity to govern one's own living without a leader and through one's own actions. Anarchy may stand at the exact opposite pole from the artificially fashioned and thoroughly controlled entity called "life."

We refer with ease to this new entity "life" as if it had always existed, as if it were a solid, a historical phenomenon, and as if any group of people would consider such an idea normal and acceptable. Today, we accept life without question; it seems absurd to question the notion. *Life* now occupies such a firm and familiar place in our imagination that we talk freely about pursuing various "lifestyles," and making certain "life choices," and even about hiring one of the newest professionals known as "life coaches" to help navigate the rough waters of, yes, an overextended and overly stressed "life."

After graduating from college, say, young people now suddenly discover that they have "a life"; and with that life the world expects them to make something of themselves—at least "to earn a living"—otherwise their friends will tell them to stop sponging off their parents and "get a life."

When murderers "take" someone's life, the state feels justified, in turn, in taking theirs. To stay on the straight and narrow and lead a respectable and reasonable life may require one to occasionally enroll in a course in "anger management" and, when confronted with loss or death, perhaps even hand oneself over to the expertise of a professional "grief manager." This continual attention to detail I call the managed life. Several universities offer advanced degrees in the science of life management.

The managed life reveals its true nature most clearly in commerce, where every major corporation, to remain in compliance with the law, must have an office of human resources, along with a director, who carries the clinical-sounding title "HR Administrator." The director instructs the company on what it can and cannot do to employees—the "workforce"—without violating their rights. Many colleges and universities offer programs for older, returning adults, many with similar-sounding names, like New Resources, as if the school were mining an aging cadre of students for some rare metal or precious petroleum. Such is the state of affairs when the human being has passed out of existence—people presenting themselves, unwittingly, as a fleshy kind of resource, "productive" until around age sixty-five or, if things go well, maybe seventy. We have no reason to think of such resources as necessarily alive—but rather that they have a life. (The New England Mutual Life Insurance Company began issuing policies in the 1840s. A person could actually begin to think of his or her life in terms of worth, in terms, certainly, of lost income.)

It took one hundred years, the entire nineteenth century, in fact, for that feisty creature, the human being, to finally give up its ghost and pass out of existence. By the time of the first edition of the complete *Oxford English Dictionary,* published in 1933, that supreme arbiter of the English language contains no separate entry for *human being.* The idea of such a vibrant creature had already long passed into semantic obsolescence. The dictionary comments on just that circumstance in a number of ways. It provides, first, an entry on the use of the word *human* coupled with a series of adjectives that together denote a unique combination of qualities. As examples, it offers its readers strange-sounding compounds, such as *human-angelic* ("of the nature of a human 'angel'"), *human-hearted, human-headed, human-sized,* and *human-bounded* ("No human-bounded mind can comprehend love unconfined"—a use which dates from the year 1711). Then, at the end of the entry, as if an afterthought, the dictionary mentions the possible but admittedly far-fetched combination *human being,* without a hyphen, and defines the phrase, in words of one syllable, as simply "a man."

Finally, the dictionary offers the kicker, the real surprise. Mustering all the high seriousness they possibly can, the editors warn, in a parenthetical but amazingly shocking sentence, that the phrase *human being* "was formerly much used; now chiefly humorous or affected." In the list of citations that follows the entry, the *Oxford English Dictionary* offers not a single occurrence, over the entire course of the written language, of the phrase *human being.* The dictionary clearly holds a terrifically strong bias against the use of that phrase, and has no hesitation in revealing that bizarre stance to its readers: Do not use "human being," it says in so many words, and certainly never in polite company.

The warning, in its insistence, makes one wonder just exactly what anyone could find funny or even amusing about the use of "human being"; why would someone smile at that phrase? The editors imply, with an obvious earnest tone, that people who insist on employing the locution "human being" should know that they could be engaging in improper grammar, and most certainly in violating the protocols of received standard English. The *Oxford English Dictionary* implies that uttering that utterly anachronistic phrase, "human being," will turn an otherwise serious speaker of the English language into an object of ridicule and outright laughter. Therefore, the editors advise their readers, in their less than subtle manner, to settle on a different phrase, to replace such an outdated locution with a modern one, without pointing out, however, exactly what word the reader should choose.

In the revised edition of the *Oxford English Dictionary*, published more than fifty years later, in 1989, the editors seem to have relented a bit. While they continue to avoid listing historical citations of the phrase *human being*, the editors do seem to have buffed off their hard edge just a bit by eliminating the reference to obsolescence and laughter. They capitulate even more by deigning to expand their definition, even though it seems truly laughable, for *human being*: "a member of the human race"—a definition so broad (and so nearly redundant) as to hardly serve as a definition at all.

What word would be appropriate in place of *human being?* The *Oxford English Dictionary* seems to think that just the simple *human* would do. So what does it mean to remove that verb masquerading as a noun, *being?* The *being* part of the phrase conveys the idea of liveliness, of spirit, of ongoing activity and attention.

The nineteenth century seems to have had no problem with using it. Henry Adams and Henry David Thoreau both use *human being* with great frequency. Twain uses *human being* in almost every one of his books and short stories. I count some sixty occurrences in Ralph Waldo Emerson's essays of the word *human being*, which makes absolute sense, for that's precisely his main subject—the sentient, spiritual, and vibrant human being. One can locate his passion for the sheer power and deep divinity of human beings in almost every prose piece and poem. In an essay entitled "Power," for example, Emerson asks about creation's most transcendent creature, "Who shall set a limit to the influence of a human being?" And in "Idealism," a section from a long essay entitled "Nature," Emerson explores how human beings, so small in the grand scheme of things, have managed to exert such a powerful and pervasive influence: "[A] spiritual life has been imparted to nature; . . . the seeming block of matter has been pervaded and dissolved by a thought; . . . this feeble human being has penetrated the vast masses of nature with an informing soul, and recognized itself in their harmony, that is, seized their law." Yes, of course, he says, human beings have the capacity for doing what every other creature finds impossible: divining the divine.

About the century's erosion of humanness, Emerson would have none of it. To the contrary, he aimed to rescue human beings at the level of feeling. He faced an almost impossible task. In 1828, the year before Emerson's ordination into the Second Church, in Boston, Noah Webster published his new and definitive *American Dictionary of the English Language*. Read it and you feel as if human beings never existed. For instance, the dictionary contains no entry for one of Emerson's pet themes, a favorite of the twentieth century, *individualism*. For the far less controversial *individual*, the dictionary offers the most desultory definition: "[a] single person or human being." And it defines *individuality* as "separate or distinct existence; a state of oneness." Emerson's favorite phrase, *self-reliance*, had not yet made it into the dictionary. The *Oxford English Dictionary* lists as the first instance of *self-reliance* 1837, in a work from Harriet Martineau, during her visit to America.

Some deep cultural shift must have occurred for "human being," the phrase that people use with such frequency in both written and spoken English, to not only fall so mightily into disfavor. How could such an authority as the editors of the *Oxford English Dictionary* argue that by using that outmoded and archaic phrase, a person would evoke laughter and ridicule? The editors go out of their way to make their point about that basic phrase. But more than all the linguistic speculation, we must ask what happened to the reality that the phrase pointed to—the flesh and blood creatures that went by the name *human beings*. Did the phrase disappear because it no longer pointed to a flesh and blood reality?

The phrase "human being" does show up on a Google search, on the website Wikipedia, for instance, offering only the most abstracted and pseudoscientific of definitions: "a bipedal primate belonging to the mammalian species." That definition borders on the ludicrous and laughable, not unlike Plato's tongue-in-cheek definition of human beings as "featherless bipeds." In the very conservative scheme of the *Oxford English Dictionary*—the linguistic authority on which I have relied in this chapter—the word *human* situates itself merely as an adjective modifying the noun *being* (*being* is actually a verb functioning as a noun—an ongoing action rendered totally static). *Human being* thus refers only to a certain kind of being, distinct from, say, a nonbeing—an inanimate rock or block of wood. The human being passed out of existence as the social construction of "a life" came to the fore.

The idea of "life" or of "*a* life" has a short history. It simply does not exist, for instance, in the ancient world. Some words come close: *Bios,* as in biology, means a range of things in Greek, including a "mode of life," "a manner of living," a "livelihood," or "means of living"; and *zoe,* as in words like "zoo" and "zoological," refers to something that we try to capture in English with the word "aliveness." In the Hebraic tradition, *hai,* which usually translates as "life," along with *ruach* and *neshama,* really refers to "breath" or "soul," which gets passed on to us humans through God's own breath. This idea of something called "life" or "a life" is a fabrication, a social construct, the beginnings of this idea one can start to see immediately at the beginning of the nineteenth century, at about the same time that Charles White delivered his *Account,* which predicted the demise of the Great Chain of Being and pointed to the subsequent dislocation of the human being in the created order of the natural world.

Around the year 1802 or 1803, a Frenchman named Jean-Baptiste Lamarck published a work in which he used the word *biology,* and in so doing helped to bring into being a new field of study, biology, or "the science of life." Lamarck posited the existence of life as a way of distinguishing all living beings from all inorganic matter. He meant the new field of study to subsume the work of the prevailing botanists and zoologists, whose purely descriptive work reduced observable nature to a taxonomy, a series of more and more narrowly defining classifications. Lamarck argued for something more, something deeper and more complex than description, choosing to distinguish living beings from inorganic matter not through their visible structure, but through their underlying principles of organization.

Lamarck also wanted his science of life to lead the new biologists beyond the competing descriptive studies of those essentialists who insisted
on reducing the complexity of the human down to a single, defining characteristic, as the mechanists, vitalists, and materialists hoped to do. Digging
beneath the skin of things, the implications raised by this new discipline of
biology have reverberated down to our own time. As Ivan Illich points out,
what followed from the emergence of biology was that "as morphological,
physiological and genetic studies became more precise toward the middle
of the nineteenth century, life and its evolution become the hazy and unin-
tended by-products reflecting in ordinary discourse an increasingly abstract
and formal kind of scientific terminology."[3]

Biology now searches for its organizing principles in tissues, cells,
and the enormously complex and highly individualized genetic code. Illich
points out that the reigning question, "What is life?" is not a probing question that philosophers have asked from, say, the ancient world down to
ours, but arises as "the pop-science counterfoil to scientific research reports
on a mixed bag of phenomena such as reproduction, physiology, heredity,
organization, evolution and, more recently, feedback and morphogenesis."[4]
Today, we have to understand just what those "pop scientists" mean when
they raise the question, "What is life?" That deep-seated and broad question actually engenders very narrow and limited responses.

The major idea that makes up the concept of "a life" is that people are
born with myriad needs, and that everything they require to satisfy those
needs exists in the world as scarce commodities, which take great skill and
knowledge to get hold of. As human beings gradually lost their sense of humanness, they also lost the feeling that they were autonomous beings who
could make free and unencumbered decisions. Economists in the late nineteenth century, in reaction in part to John Stuart Mill, began to reinscribe
these new creatures—creatures who now *possessed* their lives; who now
owned their lives—as *homo economicus,* "economic man": rational beings
operating out of self-interest in a most singleminded way—to maximize

their own satisfaction and wealth. The market economy set the priorities, and offered full-blown descriptions of what the satisfied and successful life should look like.

Such desperate creatures, out of necessity, placed themselves at the mercy of a whole raft of professionals, who stood ready to provide just the right kind of management and control, and who could satisfy their needs by dint of commanding key places in the marketplace. And so life under these new conditions depicted human existence as a struggle against one's neighbors, and even friends, for limited and scarce goods. Which meant that, in order to stay alive—actually, to thrive—people had to engage in a nasty and daily Darwinian scramble for those limited goods and services. The driving force behind the entire human enterprise was one thing only—competition. Under these redrawn conditions, any sense of a communitarian spirit splinters and falls apart. It's all for one, and one for oneself. Those already marginalized—the poor, the people of color—must remain at the edges forever.

Bioethicists insist that a vast difference separates "being alive"—what the law has recognized up to now—from the more familiar and possessive "having a life." "The proven ability to exercise this act of possession or appropriation," to quote Illich again, "is turned into the criterion for personhood and for the existence of a legal subject."[5] What we watch, then, is the slow and steady progress of the sacralizing of this new possession called "a life" as it replaces the notion of the human being or the more familiar term, "a person." The end result is a newly crafted creature who comes into the world trailing a long list of rights—a legal and social construction.[6]

This new idea of possessing a life makes for odd locutions like "What do you plan to do with your life?" or "I hate my life," or even "He received life in prison." All of which gives the feeling of life existing as something external to and slightly remote from our very own selves—as if we were not alive but rather making our lives by standing outside all the activity and observing the passing parade as a process, an activity seeming to take place at a slight distance from our own beings.

This redefinition of the human being has resulted in terrible and sometimes horrifying fallout. Having a life, for one thing, can at times turn the
act of living into a dangerous and frightening undertaking. For, as Illich
has pointed out in various essays and books, the entity called "a life" falls
easy prey to management and improvement, and, perhaps most frightening, "to evaluation [that] is unthinkable when we speak of 'a person.' The
transmogrification of a person into 'a life' is a lethal operation, as dangerous as reaching out for the tree of life in the time of Adam and Eve."[1] The
move is a dangerous one because once scientists and social scientists have
completely emptied out those creatures we once knew as human beings, a
band of professionals stands ready to fill those empty vessels back up, not
just with goods and services but with new desires that, in turn, can only be
satisfied by yet another band of even more specialized professionals.

In the end, these new creatures are left feeling that they know virtually
nothing about their own needs, and thus throw themselves on the mercy
of a huge range of trained professionals who determine, for a price—sometimes a fairly steep price—what they need and then promise to deliver it
all. Thus, with the assistance of various kinds of self-help, the new human
being survives. And thus, as Thoreau so eloquently puts it in *Walden,* "the
mass of men lead lives of quiet desperation."

Once we understand the notion that we have been accorded "a life,"
we then have to recognize what follows from that oddity—which is that
almost every aspect of our lives comes under the direction, control, and
management of some agency or professional or of some corporation. A
key example is the regime of what politicians call managed care. While
we all want to feel healthy and well, most of us have been made to feel
totally inadequate in judging the state of our own well-being, and totally
incompetent in assessing and addressing our own illnesses. At the slightest
sign of disease, we turn ourselves over to medical professionals without
thinking, without questioning: After all, those doctors know so much more
than we.

Such a lopsided, mostly commercial transaction many times turns the healing process into a counterproductive experience, with nothing but disastrous results. People visit a physician for a specific illness, receive myriad medications, and find themselves worse off than before their medical intervention. Critics of the medical profession have coined a word for such blowback—*iatrogenesis*. *Iatros* is the Greek word for doctor, and *genesis* refers to something's origin, and so the word refers to illnesses that have been generated by physicians themselves. The American Iatrogenic Association reported, in 2008, that in-hospital deaths from medical errors occur at the rate of almost 195,000 a year.

Let me return for a moment to the question "What is life?" While that seems like a fairly weird question now, in the context of the redefining that *human being* underwent in the nineteenth century, a variation on that question that we ask in our own times seems even stranger, and that is "*When* is life?" Opponents of abortion argue over the exact nanosecond when the embryo or fetus acquires—possesses—that special something called "life." At no other time in our history could we ask such a question, as if, in some scene out of *Frankenstein*, we could point to a split second when sentience actually commenced, as if such a thing suddenly came into being with the flip of some central switch.

Again, this idea has little if any history. One cannot find a trace of this kind of thinking in the ancient world. Instead, the ancients recognize a quickening in the womb signaling the onset of life, and an eventual ending underground signaled by the onset of agony, "the personal struggle to die."[8] But the ancient world never mentions that mysterious state, or rather status, we call "life," or the even more bizarre "a life."

So then what does it mean to ask, "When does life actually begin?" The Twentieth Ecumenical Council, convened in 1869 by Pope Pius IX just to rule on such contemporary and knotty issues, declared that life begins at conception. The Roman Catholics have maintained that position ever since. Pre-Reformation Christian consensus placed the onset of life at the embryo's fortieth day. In a more secular sense, the question asks, "When, in the course of *pregnancy*, does life actually begin?" Anthony Kenny, in an essay entitled "The Beginning of Individual Human Life," reframes the "crucial moment" this way: "Is it the point of formation (when the foetus has acquired distinct organs), or is it the point of quickening (when the movements of the foetus are perceptible to the mother)? Can we identify the moment by specifying a number of days from the beginning of pregnancy?" Such an accounting, one day more or less, does on its face make a mockery of human life. The calendar does not seem to be the appropriate place to find an answer to the beginning of life.

Perhaps some other answer makes more sense, which is that life does not *begin;* it simply *is*—at every stage, during every moment of the gestation process, life unfolds. In a sense, this is a rendering of God's response to Moses, when Moses asks God's name and the Lord responds: "I am that I am," or "I am who I am." *Am*: first-person singular indicative of the verb "be"—the most concise and accurate rendering of my existence: "I am." I cannot enter into the now of the present moment with any more potency than to utter those two words, pronoun and verb: "I am." Emerson wrote in his journal for 1827, "It is said to be the age of the first person singular." It may be more accurate to say that the age struggled to find the first-person singular—and that the great grinding power of the age made it difficult for the majority of people to say, "I am," and have it carry meaning.

It does no good to ask our basic question another way, such as "When does *human* life begin?" because of course the newly formed conceptus is indeed a human, as distinct from a walrus or a dog. To ask about ensoulment takes us even farther afield. Thus, the task of trying to locate the moment of life, in the twenty-first century, brings us quite quickly to an intellectual and moral impasse. And yet, the contemporary realization that we "have a life" has brought us to a place where people on both sides of the argument—pro-life and pro-choice—need such a declaration.

If we resort to asking about when an individualized life actually begins, we find ourselves thrown back on John Locke's formulation that only persons possess rights. But, for Locke, not every human is a person, only one "who has reason and reflection, and considers itself as itself, the same thinking thing, in different times and different places." The logical conclusion here is that young infants lack that kind of self-awareness, and so the state cannot guarantee that creature any human rights.[9]

Finally, some theologians find it more informative to talk about potentiality. The fetus, or even the young infant, while lacking a personality, has the potential to become, in the near future, a fully realized individual. But that formulation raises even more problems. For any agency to carry out research on stem cells, say, someone, or some official body, must make the determination about the beginning of a life. That is why in England, for example, a group of scientists, ethicists, and educators, naming itself after one of its members, Lady Warnock, made such a declaration, in 1985. The Warnock Committee believed that if a date could be determined when "personhood" began, then researchers themselves could legally experiment on embryos. After a great deal of deliberation and testifying, the committee decided that experiments on embryos—extracting stem cells, for instance— could proceed up to the fourteenth day of the embryo's growth, one day before the appearance of the so-called primitive streak (the spine).

The secretary of health in Britain, Kenneth Clarke, elaborated on the committee's selection of a life-date this way: "A cell that will become a human being—an embryo or conceptus—will do so within fourteen days. If it is not implanted within fourteen days it will never have a birth. . . . The basis for the fourteen day limit was that it related to the stage of implantation which I have just described, and to the stage at which it is still uncertain whether an embryo will divide into one or more individuals, and thus up to the stage before true individual development has begun. Up to fourteen days that embryo could become one person, two people, or even more." We cannot, it seems, escape the calendar.

We can see what has happened to "life" by looking at it not just from its starting point but from its endpoint, as well. When we think of death, most of us immediately think of pain and suffering. The image of a hospital, tubes, and feeding lines comes immediately to mind; we've all seen it too many times. But people did not always die under such clinical conditions; death in the first part of the nineteenth century offers a radically different picture. I can best describe the change in death over the course of the century by looking at the changes to one particular word, *euthanasia*. I rely here primarily on the work of Shai J. Lavi and his book, *The Modern Art of Dying: A History of Euthanasia in the United States*.

In the simplest of terms, in the early years of the nineteenth century, Lavi points out, *euthanasia* "signified a pious death blessed by the grace of God." This is what I called earlier the good death or the easy death, a bounteous gift from God, who saw fit to make the dying person's last hours on Earth ones free of pain. Usually, the person has earned this gift by leading a life filled with God's grace. This is the earliest meaning, in the fifteenth century, of *euthanasia* (literally, *eu* meaning "good,' and *thanatos*, "death"), and it characterizes the first decades of the nineteenth century. This one word, *euthanasia*, changes its meaning over the course of the century, which reflects the changes toward both the human being and death. By the middle part of the century, the word takes a remarkable turn. The priest has left the deathbed and has been replaced by the physician, who now administers analgesics to the dying person to make his or her passage an easier and hastier one.

At that moment, no one faces death with anything but dread. Death involves nothing beyond acute pain and suffering; it comes to every person in exactly the same way, no matter how one has lived one's life. *Euthanasia* meant that, with the aid of the physician, the patient could then face a fairly painless and speedy death: The physician brought into being a chemical version of the good or easy death. A key question underlies this new attitude toward death: "Why should the person suffer so?"

Lavi wants to know how this new idea of euthanasia as "the medical hastening of death" came to occupy its place as "a characteristically modern way of dying." Asking this question raises several related and key nineteenth-century issues. First of all, in order to experience pain, one must believe in and possess a sensate body; and, as we have seen, bodies were fast disappearing. Second, with the loss of the body came the concomitant and logical need to eradicate pain. By mid-century, a person could purchase an analgesic for any minor or major pain. And finally, and perhaps the most important issue, death itself had begun to disappear. The old-fashioned Christian notion of experiencing death through protracted pain, to know of suffering at its base in imitation of the suffering of Jesus Christ on the cross, had lost its hold on the imagination—religious and secular.

A new philosophy, then, permeates the middle years of the nineteenth century: Let's get this ordeal over with so that the family can move on to grieving and gathering their old lives together once again. What has been eliminated from the picture is anything that the dying person might learn or even just experience, up until the very last second of his or her breathing, through confronting the suffering and pain that is death. Death no longer exists as an integral part of life, but as something distinct and separate. This represents a change of the greatest order. For as the physician intercedes, takes over, and administers his many painkillers to the dying person, the heart of the Christian life comes to mean very little.

The physician has assumed total control. Death will wrap its arms around the dying person at the pace that the medical person dictates and which he then very deliberately puts into practice. The patient's passing will occur at the physician's chosen speed, on his chosen schedule. The physician now assumes the role of God. But, in the process, the dying person loses an enormous amount, or I should say, the physician deprives the dying person of so much that is crucial to his very being—the person's will, drive, determination, the reflective time to ponder the meaning of living and the significance of passing. Instead of a strong-willed person, the patient turns into a doped-up, drugged-out victim, believing that the one sensation that defines his or her essence at that moment—intense and searing pain—is awful, bad, something to avoid at all costs. It's that attitude toward death that prompted Ivan Illich to call our contemporary world an "amortal society." He believed that most people find it impossible to die their deaths. The medical industry has robbed them of that opportunity. People have called in the medical profession to save them from the frightful suffering of death.

Finally, the definition of euthanasia toward the end of the century takes on a legal status: By 1869, the *Oxford English Dictionary* makes clear, people used the word "especially as a reference to a proposal that the law should sanction the putting painlessly to death of those suffering from incurable and extremely painful diseases." Unfortunately, one of those incurable diseases turned out to be death. Beyond that, as physicians diagnosed more and more diseases, it created more and more opportunities to put euthanasia into practice.

The look on the face of the dying person must be one of peace and calm and of the most somber resolve, not much different from the stoic expression on the faces of family members in early studio photographs. A new ethic begins to emerge in the nineteenth century: Expression is all. Surface carries all the meaning. The gesture, the look, the image—these all constitute the archetype of the new dying person. What lies beneath the skin—in the heart and soul—the life and the character, mean much less by comparison. The physician, in very real terms, works his alchemy in collusion with that other artist of the world of chemicals, the embalmer.

Historians like to describe society as slowly getting medicalized. Turn on virtually any evening television program, or listen to any sports broadcast, and every commercial tells the audience what medicines they should demand from their physicians. The phrases linger in the mind: Ask your doctor if Cialis or Viagra or Clarinex is right for you. A good many Americans now diagnose themselves, believing they have contracted the latest illness, whose etiology has been broadcast to them on the screen. They find out what is ailing them by checking their symptoms online. Side effects seem not to matter at all: One must pay a price for a pain-free existence. *The New York Times Magazine* investigates some bizarre and rare illness almost every week, in thrilling imitation of the most seductive detective story. And a popular author like Oliver Sacks, well, he has made a good living out of people who seem to mistake their hats for their wives. The analgesics that the nineteenth century developed came tumbling into the twentieth century with myriad variations and types; they fill the aisles in drug stores today. One of the most ubiquitous hyphenated "self" words today is "self-diagnosis," followed closely by "self-help."

In the nineteenth century, in a prelude to our current medicalized and narcotized state, medicine literally enters the home. That now standard piece of furniture in the modern house, the medicine cabinet, first appears around 1828, in England, as a "medicine chest." Medicine had reached equality with the refrigerator and the stove and the sink: all necessities for healthy and hygienic living. Medicine had so much taken over the house-hold that on the door of the chest, to tell them how much of a certain drug to take, family members pasted a chart, called a posological table, every family member with his or her name and drug and dosage. *Posological* derives from a word that enters the vocabulary at this time, *posology* (from the Greek *posos,* "how much?" and *ology,* "the knowledge of"). Inside their cabinets, people mostly stored a range of analgesics, or more commonly, anesthetics.

Anesthetics—ether, chloroform, nitrous oxide, laudanum; agents to numb every sensate feeling—came to the rescue for what everyone had come to believe was the bleakest moment in the life of a person in the nineteenth century: his or her own inevitable (and sometimes protracted) death. In the nineteenth century, then, while people began to own a life—such as it was—they at the same time began to surrender all control over their own deaths, to disown their own deaths. Many writers and poets and life scientists believed that people truly moved through the world, up to their very last inhalations, in the state that Percy Bysshe Shelley had recognized and named "suspended animation."

At a certain moment, the physician, like the man of the cloth, left the side of the patient's bed, allowing technology to take over completely. By the end of the nineteenth century, *euthanasia* carried the meaning familiar to most of us now: "The use of anesthetics to guarantee a swift and painless death." This was followed by attempts to make euthanasia legal. We have now gone beyond modern euthanasia, according to the American Medical Association, to the "intentional termination of the life of a human being by another," or what has come to be called "mercy killing"—wherein one person takes the life of another absent that other person's consent.

Witness the arguments and confusion surrounding the case of Terri Schiavo, who survived in a persistent vegetative state for fifteen years, until her husband obtained permission from the state, in 2005, to "pull the plug"—that is, to remove her feeding tube. Her parents objected, arguing that their daughter still retained a degree of consciousness. In a bizarre encounter with virtual reality, Senator Bill Frist, a medical doctor, diagnosed Terri Schiavo on a television monitor and declared that she "was not somebody in a persistent vegetative state." Such an absurdity cost him a run for the presidency of the United States. Jack Kevorkian ("Doctor Death"), recently released from jail, understands the nature of death in the twenty-first century perhaps better than most. And still, only two states in the nation, Oregon and Washington, have passed legislation for something called physician-assisted suicide, or what the states refer to as death with dignity laws.

The Dutch had legalized euthanasia, with the patient's consent, in 2002. In 2004, Dutch health offices considered guidelines that doctors could follow for "euthanizing terminally ill people 'with no free will,' including children, the severely mentally retarded and patients in irreversible comas."[10] After lengthy discussions, the Netherlands became the first country to legalize euthanasia—including ending the life of someone suffering from a terminal illness or an incurable condition, *without his or her approval.*

Debates about legalizing euthanasia, which we think of as so modern, first took place in this country in 1870, which makes sense, since the idea of the body was losing its significance, the idea of death was fast coming to an end, and life itself was being reformulated into some kind of very clearly definable entity. Deciding for oneself the exact moment when one will die may offer the last chance for one to regain one's will, or to know that one does indeed possess a will. One of the most insightful poets of the modern condition, T. S. Eliot, uses anesthesia—the nineteenth-century form, ether—for the opening image of his poem "The Love Song of J. Alfred Prufrock": "Let us go then you and I,/When the evening is spread out against the sky/ Like a patient etherized on a table." For Eliot, the poet who laments the disappearance of Christian ritual in modern lives, anesthesia does not mean freedom from pain, but mere languor and dissipation, the slow dissolving of all meaning. For Eliot, all of us need to wake up.

With both death and life gone, the possibilities seem endless. The idea of having a life has become, in the twenty-first century, only a transitional idea, a momentary resting place in the history of the human being. We are not only creatures in need of management and control and direction. We have now laid ourselves wide open to much more than a range of professionals. We now face an army of very serious and very determined biotechnical engineers determined to take over and guide our lives. I "have" a body that can now be harvested for its resources, for my organs, tissues, joints. My growing up turns out to be an investment in what goes by the name these days of biocapital. One historian of medicine, Catherine Waldby, figures my living tissues and organs into something she calls "biovalue," for the medical profession can, as she says, "redeploy" them for those who need transplants in order that those people can return to the workplace—hence the "value"—and hence add more value to the capital economy.[11]

Nikolas S. Rose, a sociologist, goes on to define the new bioeconomy, in almost the same terms as imperialism, as "a space to be mapped, managed, and understood; it needs to be conceptualized as a set of processes and relations that can be known and theorized, that can become the target of programs that seek to increase the power of nations or corporations by acting within and upon that economy." Within the parameters of biocapitalism, no one asks, "When does life begin?" The biotech future has moved us all well beyond such petty concerns. The new, enriched world forces each of us to ask, instead, "Just what is my life worth?"[12]

Robbed of every ounce of our essence, we move through the world as new forms of ghosts. Some people are now wandering through the world as robots or cyborgs—and choosing it on their own. In the 1860s and 1870s, the women who operated the new writing machine called the typewriter in business offices across America were themselves referred to as typewriters. In 1893, a woman named Henrietta Swan Leavitt went to work for the Harvard College Observatory to measure the brightness of individual stars. Astronomers referred to her, according to her biography, as "one of several 'computers,' the term for women who did the grunt work of astronomy for 25 cents an hour" (the minimum wage).[13] I have the chilling sensation that the same sort of dehumanizing conflation of machine and flesh is taking place today, only this time it is not some simple machine like a typewriter that directs things, but various kinds of highly sophisticated technological devices. And because we love our computers so much these days, we do not recognize the ways they have shaped our lives.

By coming up against computer programs in nearly every task we carry out during the day—on word processing and sending mail, of course, but also in playing games, running appliances, driving cars, talking to friends, buying tickets, paying bills, heating meals, washing clothes, performing the most mundane of office tasks—one begins to act, without really being conscious of the change right away, in imitation of the computer—that is, in a rather rigid and programmatic way. People give their inputs to other people, interface with friends, and impact social situations, to say nothing of carrying on relationships online, including a bizarre configuration called cybersex.

On the other hand, and in the other direction, the computer has a memory—which most people consider more powerful and accurate than their own—and has a command of language far wider than our own. Under the command of the machine, we slowly begin to feel powerless. Young people in particular push the on button and instantly know the power resides not with them but inside that mysterious box. People conceive of themselves as fabricated, like machines, out of replaceable parts. I can trade in my worn-out hardware—knees, hips, rotator cuffs, even retinas. Our software, our memory and consciousness, is harder to fix.

Recall the way the dead entered heaven during those years of the Civil War: Christians did not really die, but instead sailed over an invisible divide to enter into a blissful and eternal hereafter. In the new technologically driven regime of the twenty-first century, a group of brave new worlders have come to believe that they can control their inevitable destiny by eradicating it. This new breed laughs at the idea of euthanasia, because there is no more Thanatos. For them, death is only a lingering nuisance. In that new scheme, people will live forever on this plane, free of debilitating illness. Through genomic assaying, engineers can determine not only who we are but also who we want to become. Which means that human beings can finally dispense with those ultimately disabling professions of medicine and psychiatry—under this scheme rendered totally obsolete—since we can now pursue our lives free of any illnesses—including that most dreaded of all illnesses, our own mortality—that might await us. Insurance companies rest easy, for the new person will know that his or her life will proceed without medical trauma from the moment of birth to an end that continually approaches the horizon but that never arrives.

A disembodied life—a state in which people do not live and refuse to die—makes us today into a modern perversion of a nineteenth-century vampire. We find ourselves confronting the strangest kind of issues and ideas, like gene splicing, stem cell research, in vitro fertilization, cloning, abortion rights, right-to-life laws, pro-choice laws, mercy killing, euthanasia, do-not-resuscitate orders, the saving of premature infants, "partial birth" abortions, snowflake babies, embryo research, and organ transplants and donations. Just discussing the possibility of the prolongation of life automatically makes the sentence of life in prison a harsher punishment. It should cause us to rethink the death penalty itself, and in particular the death penalty for minors. With bioengineering, we could extend the sentence of a "lifer" nearly forever, taking punishment to a most bizarre level. This may constitute torture under the posthuman conditions of bioengineering.

The new life is also not necessarily directed by technology, but one in which leading-edge technology has thoroughly incorporated itself into life's every fiber. I offer as example the strange case of Doctor Dan Stoicescu, a multimillionaire, and only the second person in the world to purchase the full sequence of his own genetic code. For that picture of his deeply inner dimension, Stoicescu paid a private research laboratory the fairly hefty price of $350,000. He is not alone in his quest for individual identity. In fact, so many wealthy individuals now desire to carry their personal genome sequences in their wallets, like another ID card, that two private companies, Knome (pronounced in a revealing way as "know-me"), of Cambridge, Massachusetts, and Illumina (perhaps an echo of the Bavarian Illuminati of the Enlightenment), in San Diego, specialize in genetic cartography.

Illumina, which boasts of its ability to provide whole genome sequencing "to the rich and famous," has a goal of "applying innovative technologies and revolutionary assays to the analysis of genetic variation and function." An individual can then have the freedom to indulge in what the company calls "personalized medicine," utilizing the dimensions of what Illumina refers to as "genomics" and "proteometics." These two companies have gone well beyond the rather gruesome-sounding practice of "organ harvesting," providing seriously ill people with, say, a new liver or heart. Within the regime of this advanced personalized medicine, the genome laboratory can implant a chip under a person's skin that will regulate the variations in his or her particular gene sequencing over the years: human being as processor?[14]

Notice that I use the phrase "over the years." I cannot use the usual phrase here, "over the course of his or her life," for life may simply continue for as long as the client desires. Say goodbye to aberrations from birth, irregularities of this or that organ, incidence of various kinds of cancer, the onset of adult diabetes, or the most invasive restriction of human design—life expectancy. Say farewell forever, that is, to the human being, to everything you thought about the human being. Under the influence of the genome project, people will become living programs—pure and simple. Jean Baudrillard, the French philosopher and cultural critic, points to an essential irony in the current fascination with longevity: "By warding off death at all costs (burdensome medical treatment, genetics, cloning), we're being turned, through security, into living dead. On the pretext of immortality, we're moving towards slow extermination."[15]

Without actually referring to it, Baudrillard sees the transhuman transformation, in which social engineers use technology to improve human mental and physical capacities, as the logical conclusion to the nineteenth-century idea of vampirism. But while he says we are "being turned into," I see instead that we are *allowing* ourselves to be turned into. We are the actors, responsible for our own demise. And that means we can do something about it. But first we need to have some idea of just what is happening to us and who is doing it.

Baudrillard envisions, correctly, a system that goes well beyond managing life from the beginning, say, by monitoring the career of the fetus *in utero* by way of ultrasound pictures, diet, and exercise regimens. With gene sequencing, a laboratory like Illumina will reshape the resulting project of sperm fertilizing ovum, which, as we well know, never turns out perfectly. After all, people fall ill early in life, or die midlife because of some unexpected and unseen disease. To hell, then, with the rather sloppy work of creation or even of evolution. Intelligent design is dumb. Prayer is for dupes; faith for fools.

Illumina offers a new, bold, and technologically enhanced alternative to the old entity called life. Illumina presents itself as all seeing and all knowing—a much better producer (and marketer) of created human life than anything religion might envision. Again, I feel compelled to quote Baudrillard here, for he gets under the surface of change with such wisdom and clarity: "It's we who've undertaken to inflict the worst on ourselves, and to engineer our disappearance in an extremely complex and sophisticated way, in order to restore the world to the pure state it was in before we were in it."[16] And here I think Baudrillard speaks closer to the truth than in his previous comment, for he finally says we are responsible for engineering our own disappearance. We are doing it to ourselves. We should keep Baudrillard's comments in mind, for at the end of the book we will need some solutions for a way out of our fix; we will have to have some way to recapture our humanness. And "that way"—the transhuman way—to appropriate a line from *King Lear*, "madness lies; let me shun that; No more of that."

As mad as he may seem, Doctor Stoicescu knows all this only too well. That's why he chooses to place himself in a category that already lies beyond the human being, for only the old order of human being could care about such drivel as vitality, or potency, or agency. He calls himself a transhumanist, someone who believes that life (there is that commodity again, "life") can be extended for a forbiddingly long time, not just through diet and something Stoicescu calls "lifestyle adaptations," but through the more advanced and enlightened pursuits of nanotechnology and artificial intelligence.

Stoicescu's genome sequencing will permit him to know what illnesses he can be expected to contract and what adaptations at the level of genes he needs to undergo to rid his system of those potential illnesses.

Transhumanists, and there are thousands like Stoicescu, walk about on this planet, like Kierkegaard's knights of faith, unnoticed and unrecognized—not with the aim of enlightenment, however, but with the goal of beating death. They believe that such a move is absolutely possible, for they consider death merely an accident of faulty engineering, and consider suffering just the price we pay for imperfection.

Stoicescu, a Romanian, sounds frighteningly like that other pale Romanian, Count Dracula. Recall that in Bram Stoker's novel, Dracula has already beaten death at its own game; now he lives forever, condemned to a diet of that one rare delicacy, human blood. For Stoker, the count is a fantasy creation, a parody of the period's search for eternal life, a search that drains it of the very lifeblood it so badly needs. Stoicescu holds onto no such fantasy. He believes that his investment has guaranteed him a terrifically good shot at eternal life. It's all a matter of faith—in technology and gene manipulation. It's all a matter of moving beyond even that socially constructed idea of life, to a day-by-day regime fully determined and regulated by leading-edge technology. The transhuman credo: Human beings have been created as weak and vulnerable subjects in the universe, thoroughly in need of support and vetting, which only technology can provide. We now have the technology. Why not use it? That's what real evolution is all about. And that's what true integration involves: machines merging with humans. Thus, another transhumanist, Ray Kurzweil, has plans to upgrade the "'suboptimal software' in your brain."[17] He describes something called "Singularity," in which humans and machines evolve into immortal creatures with software that continually upgrades itself.

For transhumanists, the future exists as a continually expanding present moment. While such a belief may sound like a description from Saint Augustine, it is not—it is anything but Augustinian. Under the aegis of the new bioethicists, life constitutes a product of engineering at the highest levels, like an Apple G5, or a Boeing 757, or perhaps, better yet, like some intergalactic spacecraft. In the grasp of the transhumanists, individuals or persons or human beings have become walking CAT scan machines who have their "systems" continually monitored for irregularities, and who also have those systems continually corrected for every fault and irregularity.

Stoicescu describes himself as a prominent member of the World Transhumanist Association, a group that explores the full range of possibilities for what its members call the "posthuman future." With this group, we arrive at a place monumental and gigantic leaps beyond the simple elimination of the idea of the human being. We have also gone well beyond what looks like a very tame concept called "life" or "a life." The association proudly crows about having advanced in its thinking beyond the fragile and vulnerable human being to the new and improved, indomitable "posthuman." We come face to face here with a new world of life drained of all of its essence in order for people to entertain the possibility of eternal life—even if such a dream turns out to be a remote possibility. Like Dracula, these new vampires also must continually feed. But it is not blood they crave. They derive their strength from the latest advance or innovation in the world of biotechnology.

What does all this say about the already wounded and crippled and forgotten members of the population? What about the poor and those of color? Are we witnessing here the pseudoscience of racial inferiority and superiority so scarily popular in the nineteenth century, reinscribed in society as a nightmare of the technological revolution? After all, Stoicescu talks easily about a higher and more powerful breed of humans. It can only be a short step from that conception to talk about that most frightening Nazi phrase, *the superior race*. Technology applied to genetics may take us not into the future, as Stoicescu so optimistically promises, but all the way back to nineteenth-century eugenics and the perverse racial theories of Darwin's cousin, Francis Galton.

To be full and active members of society, transhumans, like the old humans, must have rights and must have them protected by the law. Even in the depths of the technological revolution, the law must define rights and provide safeguards. And so, in May 2008, Congress passed a bill prohibiting discrimination by employers and health insurers on the basis of genetic tests. Which means that whatever people find out about their genetic markers, they can feel free to reveal that information to a boss or fellow worker without being punished for those disclosures about possible disabilities. "This bill removes a significant obstacle to the advancement of personalized medicine," said Edward Abrahams, executive director of a group called the Personalized Medicine Coalition, a group devoted to fostering preventive medicine tailored for each person's *known* condition.[18]

Posthumans come into their own by an intensified merging of their own beings with the highest levels of technology, through the power of bioengineering, cybernetics, and nanotechnology. The World Transhumanist Association derived its power from the imagination of someone who went by the name of FM-2030 (né F. M. Esfandiary), so called because he was born in 1930 and believed he would live one hundred years. Upon his death, in 2000, Esfandiary had his body cryogenically frozen, with the hope that doctors would find a cure for pancreatic cancer, the disease that eventually killed him. His body rests today in a vat of liquid nitrogen in Arizona—a high-tech embalming technique—awaiting its eventual but, according to the central transhumanist creed, inevitable awakening to eternal life.

Esfandiary taught a class at the New School for Social Research, in New York City, in 1966, titled "New Concepts of the Human," in which he formulated his ideas about the future of the human being. Transhumanism, Esfandiary explains, is shorthand for "transitory human," in which transhumans provide living proof of the "earliest manifestations of the new evolutionary beings." Transhumans are on their way to forging a new, twenty-first-century definition of *human being*. They hope to leave their mark in the *Oxford English Dictionary.* We have been witnessing signs of the coming of these revolutionary transhumans, Esfandiary argued, through developments in physical and mental augmentations, including prostheses, reconstructive surgery, intensive use of telecommunications, a cosmopolitan lifestyle, androgyny, mediated reproduction (such as in vitro fertilization and cloning), the absence of religious beliefs and faith in general, and a rejection of traditional family values.

I ended an earlier chapter with the story of Steve Fossett, whom a judge declared dead without ever having seen him alive, and without ever having known anything about him, either physically or emotionally or psychologically. A judge had to declare Fossett legally dead since no one could recover his remains. He died without a body. In this chapter, people move beyond that circumstance: No one will have bodies, in the traditional sense. We will walk around with technologically enhanced somas, straight out of Aldous Huxley's *Brave New World*. And this will match perfectly the transhuman idea of conception—without much or any intervention of the parents. The real and true transhumans begin in glass—in vitro, or in test tubes, or on glass slides, free of much traditional medical meddling, and ready for manipulation by a team of bioengineers and bioethicists.

One of the heroes of the transhumanist movement is a person named Louise Brown, born on July 25, 1978, in Manchester, England, the world's first so-called test tube baby. Some two million babies have now been born, around the world, in the same way as Louise Brown, without sexual intercourse, fertilized in a solution at the bottom of a petri dish, inside the sterile corridors of a laboratory. Dolly the sheep came into the world, in 1997, using the same techniques of artificial fertilization—inside a laboratory, in Scotland, without copulation between animals. Since the year 2000, the world has witnessed the cloning of five generations of mice; several calves in both Japan and in the United States; Tetra the monkey, cloned in Oregon; and five piglets cloned in Japan and the United States. An American and a South Korean scientist both admit to having created a human embryo, but both also confess to having immediately destroyed it.

What would it mean to have exact copies of ourselves walking about, as if we were those photographic reproductions that Mathew Brady displayed? Certainly, such copies put the lie to the words *unique* or *individual*, and make problematic the concept of a personality. We might justifiably think of cloning as the exact opposite of reproduction: The cloned person finds himself or herself totally eliminated in the process of manufacture. Baudrillard thinks of laboratory duplication in exactly this way: "[C]loning can be said to be something like a slow-motion suicide. By that I mean not a sudden disappearance, but an innovative form of extinction of the species by . . . automatic doubling."[19] Notice that Baudrillard does not refer to the nineteenth-century double, or doppelgänger, the shadow self, but to an exact photographic copy, a *cliché,* in its original nineteenth-century sense of a "stereotyped reproduction."

The chant "pro-life" should sound a bit odd to us now, against the backdrop of all these posthuman genetic permutations. To be pro-life, in the context of this book, means to stand in support of the trumped-up, constructed entity that surfaces in the course of the nineteenth century. To adopt a pro-life stance, a person, or better yet the pro-life movement itself, has to decide on the exact nanosecond when life actually begins. That is, the entity "life" must have a discernable beginning and a recognizable end. The ancient idea of a "quickening in the womb" will simply not suffice. And the idea of agony, a confrontation with death, certainly will not serve as a signal of the end of things. And so, the struggle to find answers to such questions reveals the truly artificial nature of that construct called "life" or, as I have often repeated, "a life."

The transhumanists have employed a new phrase to refer to the new construction of life—"biocapital" or "genetic capital," both a part of something that goes these days by the name of the new bioeconomy. These terms refer to the use of genetic engineering (nineteenth-century eugenics, as I have said, made technologically appealing) to raise the level of genetic capital of the entire country, ideas made popular first in stockbreeding. In terms of the transhuman, bioethical movement, "in advanced liberal ethics, each individual is urged to live his life as a kind of enterprise to maximize lifestyle or potential, to become a kind of entrepreneur of oneself and one's family."[20] Companies like Genentech spend their time and money "patenting, sequencing, mapping, purifying, branding, marketing, and publicizing new life forms."[21]

And so life never has to officially end—or at least the thought these days is to prolong death's arrival beyond when it might be expected to come, a goal that can be achieved only by the medical profession devoting a good deal of its time and attention not to healing the patient, but to extending the person's life. Up to the point of death, the new transhuman desires a life as free of pain as possible; death itself, the source of so much suffering, must be rendered as an experience free of all pain. That is a transhuman imperative, and oddly enough, one that mirrors the pain-free form of death that develops during the course of the nineteenth century. And certainly we have the technology now to make the transition into death—if the person or the family wants it—an absolutely painless one. Life can end the nanosecond that suffering begins.

If all this sounds too far-fetched and expensive, a new generation of genetic marketers has come to the rescue. Navigenics, a California web-based company, launched a personalized DNA test in April 2008. According to *Newsweek,* the test is an easy one: "spit into a test tube and we'll tell you your risk for heart attack and other conditions—at a storefront in New York's trendy SoHo neighborhood." In January of 2008, another genetics company called 23andMe dispensed one thousand free tests at a strategic place, the World Economic Forum in Davos, Switzerland. The *Newsweek* article contained this strange line: "Featured photos: Naomi Campbell showing off her test kit, *New York Times* columnist Thomas Friedman spitting into his."

We might ask, When do those moments arise today when we find ourselves exercising our will when it means so much; when do we feel powerfully and totally alive? Perhaps there are not so many of those moments available to us these days. Maybe they come, in our post-everything world, at the strangest of times, in the most bizarre and outlandish of circumstances. I am thinking especially of so-called Islamic fundamentalists wrapping themselves in explosives and blowing themselves up. Do they lead their quiet and fairly unknown lives, only to come totally alive at the instant they explode—that is, the instant they die and achieve martyrdom? It's odd to think of a living human being exploding into total meaning and significance.

I am thinking also of those who tortured prisoners at Guantánamo prison in Cuba, and at Abu Ghraib in Iraq, for the armed forces. Did those drawn-out moments make the torturers feel exhilarated and totally alive? Did the torturer take the part of the nineteenth-century physician at the side of the deathbed, but with the roles totally reversed—the torturer intending not to alleviate pain but to inflict it, with increasing or decreasing intensity over time; to bring the subject to the very brink of death (indeed, to simulate it in something like waterboarding, or simulated drowning) only to yank the person back into life, the torturer thus playing a perverse kind of God?

The first time the United States used the torture we now so glibly call "waterboarding" occurred during the Philippine-American War, which started in February 1899. America revived that torture in the Vietnam War. (One of the costs a country pays for imperialism may be its willingness to inflict excruciating pain on the enemy through torture.) In the Philippines, the Army called this particular kind of torture, in the way only the military can employ its euphemisms, the "water cure," making pain sound like a detox treatment or a health fast. The report of the Philippine torture first appeared in a letter to the editor in the *Omaha World-Herald,* in May 1900, by an infantryman named A. F. Miller. He ratted on his unit by offering detailed instructions for the water treatment: "Lay them [the so-called insurgents] on their backs, a man standing on each hand and each foot, then put a round stick in the mouth, and pour a pail of water in the mouth and nose, and if they don't give up pour in another pail. They swell up like toads. I'll tell you it is a terrible torture."

As if that were not cruel enough, when the torture victim's stomach swelled sufficiently, a soldier would then jam his foot into his stomach, making him vomit up all the water; then the torturers would start the routine all over again, pouring water down the victim's mouth. This rather vicious cycle would not stop, of course, until the victim, at the point of suffocation and near death, had decided to give up the answers that the superior officers so desperately wanted.

The efficacy of torture rests on at least two premises, both of them well suited to the underlying philosophy of the nineteenth century. The first is that the torturer must see his victim as less than human, a task made easier if the victims are people of color. The nineteenth century already had experience with eliminating peoples of color from the Chain of Being, excising them from civilization altogether. And here was a war, in a remote island called the Philippines, against brown-skinned people. And so, to match the philosophy of the period, the military made certain to continually refer to the Filipino people as Flips—as far less than civilized.

General Robert Hughes, testifying before a Senate investigative committee on torture in 1902, said of the Filipino people that "these people are not civilized." Senator Henry Cabot Lodge, a noted Republican from Massachusetts, threw the horror of torture back at the Filipino people. If they were more civilized, he implied, America would not have to stoop to such tactics. Before that same Senate investigative committee, Lodge insisted that this country's reliance on the water cure had "grown out of the conditions of warfare, of the war that was waged by the Filipinos themselves, a semicivilized people, with all the tendencies and characteristics of Asiatics, with the Asiatic indifference to life, with the Asiatic treachery and the Asiatic cruelty, all tinctured and increased by three hundred years of subjection to Spain." What Cabot wanted to say was that "Asiatics" just do not value life in the same way we white Westerners do. Why should we then treat them with dignity or respect? It simply makes no sense. Let us treat them the way they deserve to be treated—with utter disgust and disregard.[22]

The military physician Henry Rowland defended the "water cure" in an even more offensive way, by arguing that the American soldiers' "lust of slaughter" was "reflected from the faces of those around them." Which is to say that those barbarians got exactly what they deserved. It's their fault. President Theodore Roosevelt, using the newspeak common to the Oval Office, allowed as how, by using torture, "[n]obody was seriously damaged." (One wonders if he included the Americans in that statement.) On the other hand, using the biblical mandate of an eye for an eye, Roosevelt opined, "[T]he Filipinos had inflicted incredible tortures upon our own people." Again, they got just what they deserved, or what they had been asking for all along.[23]

Whether in Abu Ghraib, in Guantánamo, or in Sual, in the Philippines, degradation rules the day. Filipinos must become "Flips," and Iraqis must become "ragheads." After that, the physical torture merely completes the work started by the verbal degradation. But there is another factor operating that makes torture acceptable. To work really well, those carrying out the torture—in this case, the military—must acknowledge, albeit unconsciously, the absence of the human being. The fact that most GIs at Abu Ghraib did not know the prisoners' names—knew them only by their serial numbers (five-digit numbers that made no logical sense)—and could not pronounce them if they did, helped make the prisoners disappear. Hoods also promoted that same kind of anonymity or invisibility, that same kind of ghostly hovering.

Communities create their own sense of normalcy by defining their deviants—by defining, that is, those who do not belong. The more the military sees those prisoners as bad guys—"the worst of the worst," as Donald Rumsfeld said of them—the more thoroughly and squarely the military defines itself as normal and right and beyond reproach. But there is more than just an expression of righteousness in what the guards were doing in the deserts of Iraq and the hills of Cuba. We need to bear in mind that the torturer comes to feel totally alive in the act of inflicting excruciating pain. Inflicting pain, in these incidences, incites pleasure. Think of the enormous and calibrated sense of power! If I go just a little past the edges of my imagination, I can kill. But do not worry: This is sport, and the victims merely, well, *victims.*

At the Abu Ghraib compound, the behavior of the guards took on a playful, sporting attitude. Recall the newspaper photographs of the guards at the Abu Ghraib compound taking pictures of their tableaux of degradation to send back home, souvenirs of "being there" and of "protecting us from the terrorists." Remember those same guards and military police playing the most sadistic and juvenile practical jokes on their victims, and in general acting like clowns and fools and school bullies in the midst of their victims' horrific pain and suffering, piling more humiliation onto the already humiliated and degraded. How clever to slip a pair of women's underpants over the heads of the Muslim prisoners, or to have them pose as homosexual lovers.

In this context, the torturer sees the body perhaps in one dimension only—as a voice box (give us what we want to hear) connected to nerve endings (let us see how much pain you can endure). The so-called "water cure" posits the human body as a most basic mechanical, hydraulic system: Fill the vessel up with water, and then force the liquid back out through the most extreme violent act imaginable—jumping on the person's stomach. Death—oh well, that might happen, but, again, so what? Death is only the result of some accident. And besides, no one knows the person's name, or background, or even the barest outlines of his "story." The killing of a suspected al-Qaeda member should only be considered a victory for our side—one less terrorist to worry about. And besides, those ragheads are not very alive, are they?

What are we to say about our lives today? For those of us who do not want the future that the transhumanists offer, what do we do about our lives? Must we become a new kind of Luddite to make it out of this mess? Another election, a new regime, a change of address, will not do it. That much we know. To back away from this abyss, we need to know what has happened to us. And that is the story that this book has tried to tell. For without all the preparation from the nineteenth century, all the erasure of our essence, we would not find ourselves in this horrible predicament at this moment. Contrary to every declaration made by George W. Bush, this country, the United States of America—this so-called democratic bastion in the free world—engages in torture. The fact is clear and obvious. And this says a lot about our attitude toward human life in the world.

As I write this, the United States marks its fifth anniversary in Iraq, which is to say, though few people put it this way, we enter our sixth year of the war in Iraq. We have been bombing for an even longer time in Afghanistan. The president of the United States said, on that fifth anniversary, that we would be fighting the war against terror for a very long time—perhaps forever. Americans are afraid, and they have been particularly afraid every day and every hour and every second since those two airplanes flew into the Twin Towers, in downtown Manhattan, on September 11, 2001. We know how to feel afraid very well, we Americans, and not only in movie theaters or in amusement parks. Many Americans also know it in airports and in dark alleys and in strange neighborhoods. And many Americans know it when talk turns to immigrants and African Americans, to jobs taken and daughters wooed by "those other people."

White racist politicians used fear to grab votes in the sixties and seventies and they use it today, in the twenty-first century, as well. We are docile, in our managed lives, and we demand more and more cops on the beat, just as every police chief of every major city tells us we should want them. We may live in fear, but, damn it, we will feel safe—no matter the cost. So be prepared to remove your shoes at the airport.

Fear is an emotion that makes us feel totally alive. Along with anger, perhaps, it's surefire, it's bodily; fear grabs us in the muscles and throat and joints. We come alive in the great rush of adrenaline. We even cultivate it, in driving fast, ingesting super drugs, participating in extreme sports like cage fighting, and going for broke in Las Vegas. We need to feel fear. Fear got us to Afghanistan and it got us to Iraq. It appears that fear will also keep us in those places for a very long time to come. And, by God, the rest of the world had better fear us.

SIX | Coney Island and the Mind

A S THE NINETEENTH CENTURY ENDED, one hundred years of the most unsettling scientific and technological activity came to rest in two seemingly unrelated events. In the year 1900, a couple of businessmen broke ground on the third and last park to open at Coney Island, in Brooklyn, New York. They called it Dreamland. (Steeplechase and Luna had opened several years earlier.) That same year, 1900, Virginia and Leonard Woolf published the first English translation of Sigmund Freud's *Interpretation of Dreams* at their Hogarth Press, in London. Historical coincidence—a mere accident of time; that's all we can legitimately call that confluence.

Those two events, however, reveal the true nature of the nineteenth century. It may seem odd to mention a couple of crass businessmen and one of the great couples of English literature in the same paragraph. But that's the very quirky nature of the period: Remember, we've seen famous philosophers talking to ghosts and well-respected scientists inhaling nitrous oxide. Contradictions, in an odd way, gave the century its coherence. Take only one subject, cocaine. While that drug seems frivolous and even dangerous to us today, and certainly illegal, scientists conducted serious research about the nature of human essence while under its influence. One of the most popular literary characters of the nineteenth century, Sherlock Holmes, could not have solved crimes, he claimed, without his cocaine.

As the twentieth century opened, we get to see the classes diverge in a most obvious way. The people who frequented Coney for its seemingly unbounded fun came mostly from the middle and lower classes, and those few who went to visit Freud for the "talking cure" came from the upper class. Coney offered mass entertainment, most of it outdoors, in the clear sunlight of day, which made it hard to hide anything, or to hide from anyone at the park. Even the postcard, Coney's favorite literary form, which had recently dropped in price to one penny, made it difficult to keep secrets. Freud, on the other hand, offered the most exclusive kind of privacy, behind his closed doors, to one patient at a time. Few people knew the names of his clients. Sigmund Freud had built his considerable reputation on secrets—secrets of childhood, secrets of the bedroom, secrets in general of the privileged class. Freud made people see just what secrets they did hold.

Coney and Freud represent the two threads that will tie the conclusion up. On one hand, Coney Island offered people the chance to forget the deep blues of the big city through fun and cheap thrills, and on the other, psychoanalysis offered people the opportunity to remember the events in their lives, no matter how painful or dangerous, and to finally pay them their strictest attention. Adam Phillips, the child psychoanalyst, points out that "people come for psychoanalytic treatment because they are remembering in a way that does not free them to forget." Americans and Europeans had been handed a choice—forgetting and remembering—and they went, overwhelmingly, for the former, for fun and good times—especially in this country. In a way, that drive toward fun builds and builds until it explodes in the singing and dancing and drinking that we know, in this country, as the roaring twenties.

Again, as disparate as they seem, both George C. Tilyou, the financier of fun at Coney, and Sigmund Freud, the doctor of the soul in Vienna, delighted in some of the same things: dreams—daydreams, nighttime dreams, and even, perhaps especially, those frighteningly dark and heavy dreams that go by the name of nightmares—and amusement. Freud believed that the work of uncovering repressed memories should and could be interesting and even amusing. He seized on jokes as a way into understanding the unconscious mind.

It's appropriate that the century should come down to essentially one motif, however, for dreams provide the appropriate prism through which to best observe the age. To begin with, the entire century, day by day, seemed to be unfolding as one large and collective dream: experience reduced to a gauzy reflection, living reduced to feelings of suspended animation. Dreams took over the age. One of the great poets of the period, Walt Whitman, used the word *dream* some seventy-five times in the last version of *Leaves of Grass,* four of those times in a single line of the poem: "I dream in my dream all the dreams of the other dreamers."

Every once in a while, in the nineteenth century, one comes upon a few outspoken and bold souls, like Nietzsche, Marx, Emerson, Darwin, or Freud, who began to stretch and groan awake and coax and cajole the great masses of people to wake up; they kept at it even if only a few people listened. Thus Nietzsche on the rage for life: "Death. One must convert the dumb psychological fact into a moral necessity. So to live, that one keeps hold also at the right time on one's will to death!"[1]

Those five original thinkers came alive in the manner of Rip Van Winkle, the hero of Washington Irving's eponymous short story (1819), who runs away from his wife, cavorts with ghosts, and falls asleep under a tree for twenty years—his first name, Rip, a pun perhaps on "Rest In Peace"; his last name perhaps a pun on "forty winks"—only to wake up to a world so totally changed he believes that he may be living inside a long, drawn-out dream. Rip finds, for instance, that he is no longer a subject of England, but a citizen of the United States. In 1865, the American actor Joseph Jefferson starred in a production titled *Rip Van Winkle* at the Adelphi Theatre in London, under the direction of the master of ghost production Dion Boucicault. By the 1880s, Jefferson had played Rip onstage more than 4,500 times.

That's just what the Industrial Revolution promised—a miraculous dream. Do not snooze, for the revolution will surely pass you by—just as it did then, and just as it does today. The new machinery of capitalism seemed capable of making almost anything that anyone could imagine a palpable reality—it would bring to every American "undreamed"-of things. And it had made good on exactly that promise on a vast range of things: fast-moving trains and slow-moving films, startling photographs and talking machines, telephones and telegraph, anesthesia and aspirin. A great portion of reality had turned dreamlike.

But then there are those other dreams, the nightly hallucinations—when we tell ourselves, one more time, that anything's possible, that anything's probable—*in our own lives.* Those are the moments when *we* are in control, and that's why, in part, Freud decided that dreams offered the "royal road to the understanding of unconscious mental processes."[2] The Lumière brothers—so aptly named—along with Georges Méliès, the magician turned filmmaker, created, in a very immediate way, a mechanically induced and collectively enjoyed nighttime dream with their motion picture cameras. Under no other circumstances do masses of people enter an auditorium where they know they will see no live actors, where they do not expect a single live person to ever take the stage. When the theater went dark—moonless dark—the moviegoing audience got a shock. It was not something furtive that caught the corner of their eyes, but something right there, smack in front of them, a congeries of ghosts. And when they left the theater, not much changed. Ghosts and specters floated everywhere and seemed, at one time or another, to visit everyone, in the daytime and most certainly in the dead of night.

Reviewing the history of the period, one might think that every last person was high on some kind of powder or smoke or gas or liquid, a good many of them, in their elevated states, dreaming up the latest outlandish invention. That's another definition of a dream, a style of thinking that has shaken itself free of nagging restraint. Imbibe with me, inhale with me, snort with me, invent with me—that's what the age sounded like it was saying to a whole host of expectant people. So much beckoning—art beckoned, drugs beckoned, psychology beckoned, the weirdly interesting and dangerous avant-garde beckoned—but most forcefully and most provocatively, in the end it was entertainment that got the attention of the great masses. And they came, the great American unwashed in droves and droves to the shore of New York, and specifically to that place that neither was an island nor had many conies—Coney Island.

Freud wrote a book about the meaning of those nighttime dreams, but he plucked his subject out of a time filled with almost nothing but dreams and ghostliness and the hallucinations of opium or heroin or morphine. Freud himself found that he liked cocaine very much, offered testimonials for its continued use, and then wrote his book about dreams. He made a guidebook for the period, a manual, if anyone cared, about how to understand the strange workings of the mind. But it was hard work getting through the book's five hundred or more pages; it took a long time for its initial edition, in German, to sell out its rather small run of six hundred copies. But, then, Freud did not intend his *Interpretation of Dreams* for the masses but rather for the genteel class, for the intellectual, and for those with the time and the inclination to read through its closely argued pages.

Freud describes his method of getting at the truth of dreams in the opening sentences of the first chapter:

> In the following pages I shall prove that there exists a psychological technique by which dreams may be interpreted, and that upon the application of this method every dream will show itself to be a psychological structure, filled with significance, and one which may be assigned a specific place in the psychic activities of the waking state. I shall further endeavor to explain the processes that give rise to the strangeness and obscurity of dreams, and to discover through them the nature of the psychic forces whose conflict or co-operation is responsible for producing our dreams.

Freud called what happens in the space between our recognition and our forgetting "dream work." That strangeness of our dreams comes from the way we repress memories so painful to us by transforming them—in a sense, keeping them by disposing of them. We turn them into disguised memories, as messages of desire; and for Freud desire, "the instinctual life," could never be repressed. We repress those memories but they leave their scars; they cause us pain; they leave us with symptoms—which are nothing but defense mechanisms. They protect us from ourselves. "In symptoms, in dreams, in slips of the tongue, in free-association and, of course, in memories themselves," to quote from Adam Phillips, "we are reminded of our disowned counterparts." And thus the psychoanalytic encounter enables the patient to reach those memories that he or she has hidden away because they were too unacceptable, too unbearable, or just too painful to process. Adam Phillips again: " . . . psychoanalysis is a cure by means of the kind of remembering that makes forgetting possible." Or as the French psychoanalyst Jacques Lacan put it, "The patient is not cured because he remembers. He remembers because he is cured."[3]

The patient's first blush with those painful memories Freud called "falsified memories," which do not further the cure for they aid the patient in the continued process of forgetting. Freud coined a name for this phenomenon in an essay he published in 1899; he called them "screen-memories." Such memories occur in childhood and act as a screen against later memories from adolescence. But they represent a first step toward the goal of remembering in order to forget. So important were these memories that Freud made the following blanket statement about them: "It may indeed be questioned whether we have any memories at all from our childhood; memories relating to our childhood may be all that we possess."[4]

We cover up our painful, repressed, cast-aside memories by narrating a consistent life to others. To get his patients unstuck, oddly enough—and reversals and counterintuition characterize a lot of the psychoanalytic enterprise—Freud had to interrupt the consistency of his patients' stories, or listen for their own interruptions, where they typically "revealed" (lifted the veil on) themselves. Puns and pauses, errors and jokes, provided breaks in the narrative flow. As Phillips points out, "our unspoken lives press for recognition . . . in our pauses . . . through free-association the patient's story loses its composition and becomes more like collage in which our favorite words unwittingly find alternative contexts."[5]

In an understandable way, because the unconscious is so filled with the craziest of images, Freud could more profitably mine those who had broken the rules—the odd and the marginal and the surreal. He cared a great deal about those who got paid attention only by, say, law enforcement. Since he took his cues from the bizarre and unexpected nature of the unconscious, it follows that he could learn more about the nature of human nature from those characters who lurk in the underbelly, from those who inhabit the demimonde of society, than from those who felt comfortably in control.

In Freud's scheme, characters like Oscar Wilde and Georges Méliès, those who made a profession out of shocking the sensibilities, had more to teach him than those who lived narrow lives—even though most of his clients came from the upper classes. Freud merges with Coney, then, at the level of the fantastical, in the sideshow glimpses of the freaky and the feared, like Jolly Trixie ("Queen of Fatland: She's so fat that it takes seven men to hug her"; six hundred and eighty-five pounds; five feet, two inches tall) and Princess Wee Wee (height, thirty-four inches).[6]

Coney and the unconscious intersect at that border between land and sea—the thin line of here and there—where those characters who are hard to define always seem to hang out, like Coney's spooky midget clown armed with an electric prod, always ready to pounce. Such a feisty clown is shocking to the sensibilities, but then so was Freud. But then everyone, it seemed, needed to be shocked.

Maybe dreams represent that elusive seat of consciousness the period so eagerly wanted to find. After all, dreams so wonderfully and easily seemed to partake of the miraculous. If only we could understand them. And so Freud devoted an entire chapter to "The Method of Dream Interpretation," Freud tells us what to look for in dreams and what the clues might mean and, in the process, gives us a much broader lesson in how to understand the period. As we have seen, Freud believed that every gesture and every object in a dream gave up strict and significant meaning. Nothing was lost on him. Even the way his clients constructed their sentences, the grammar they used, the phrases they chose, the stumbles and mistakes of words, revealed to him a great deal about their personalities. In his "dream work" with patients, he attempted to fill out a narrative of that person's life, to pick up their dropped threads and to help them reweave their own yarns. Metaphors provided a most potent way into meaning for Freud.

And so in that seemingly disparate-looking nineteenth century, marked by morphine and machinery, by opium and opulence, spiritualism and science, Freud, in his method of detecting the truth, would dig beneath the surface and excavate the salient connections. And he would uncover those connections by looking at the century as if it were a collective dream, and by acknowledging that he considered nothing—not a single event or idea— as trivial or insignificant. That is, after all, the way social and cultural history gets written, the scholar or researcher connecting one detail with another until a theme begins to reveal itself.

I end this book with entertainment because that's the culmination of the one-hundred-year-long dream. As people found themselves losing essence, all that they had left was fun and the most basic ways of feeling alive. One of those very basic ways involved receiving a blast of adrenaline, and that's what a good deal of thrill rides delivered—an unadulterated rush. Dreams come to an end, usually, when the sleeping person wakes up. And in America the sleepers woke up only in the most basic way they could, by pursuing various forms of fun: They felt alive for at least brief moments, quite ironically, in their bodies—in their viscera, in their nerve endings, in the way that the latest thrill ride toyed with their equilibrium.

In Freud's scheme, as well as in popular psychology, dreams announce our deepest wishes and desires; they reveal to us our close-held secrets and can make us feel through the course of an ordinary day like the most powerful and gifted person. Perhaps in dreams we find the truest, most naked expression of that internal creature we call the self. No one can stand in the way of that one short line, all monosyllables, "I have a dream!" I have a dream, but it is substantial as hell, and I aim to make it real. Stand aside, or stand up with me. In this calculation, dreams announce our aspirations—quite literally, our *spirit*—a signal of part of us as breathy and evanescent as our nighttime dreams. In America, at the turn of the century, while most people experienced both daydreams and their nighttime counterparts, they felt cut out of anything that the early twentieth century would call the American dream.

The great majority of people did not feel refreshed and powerful. Most people—"working stiffs"—felt out of control, and that's why they went to Coney, to feel out of control at America's major amusement parks—with two added ingredients, safety and exhilaration. They wanted to feel out of control—after all, that's what it means in part to be high—but only in the most controlled, most guarded way they could. They wanted bigger and faster and scarier, but they also wanted the assurance of a safety net. At Coney, the average man or woman could jump from a 250-foot tower, but the parachute was tethered to a steel rig; they could speed down a steep ramp into a pond of water, but the boat ran on a track. City dwellers went to Coney for thrills, for higher and faster and scarier, and Coney obliged by giving it to them: a huge Ferris wheel, the Wonder Wheel; the world's highest and fastest roller coaster, the Thunderbolt; and the world's longest steeplechase ride.[7] But all the rides had been designed by safety engineers and sanctioned by city inspectors.

In their entertainment, as in their consumption, Americans wanted more and more. And businesspeople were only too happy to give it to them. Think for a moment about amusement spots in this country, how they have expanded into larger and larger venues, expanded just like capitalism or the military—from Coney *Island* to Six Flags Magic *Mountain,* to this or that theme *park,* to Disney*land,* to Disney *World.* All that's missing is Disney Universe, or Disney Galaxy. We Americans take over land so that we can spread out and colonize—that's one of the underlying and repeating stories of the nineteenth century—and we annex land for the pursuit of our own personal enjoyment: It's only in America that one finds the imperialism of flat-out fun. America, in 1910, had a population of ninety-two million people, and an astonishing 1,500 amusement parks. Fans of amusement parks gauge the credibility of the park by its key ride, the roller coaster. In 1920, the country boasted 1,520 roller coasters, in small towns and big cities, in virtually every state of the union.

Wheeee!: so much fun, so much damned fun. Americans could not, would not, get their fill. Still, today, they cannot seem to get their fill—witness the monumental makeover of Las Vegas, now the premier destination for much of the world to grab hold of supercharged, barely legal fun for the parents and tame fun for the rest of the family. Mama and Papa hang out at the craps tables and the nightly bawdy shows while Junior splashes in the wading pool and watches television. Las Vegas makes Coney seem like a park for those in need of assisted living.

Throughout the nineteenth century, people—the heart of the people— kept slipping away. How to put the brakes on, how to stop the fading away—that was the problem and that was the plague. Perhaps the only safeguard people have against such erosion is that elusive creature, the self. And maybe *self* is just a highfalutin way of talking about will. At any rate, the self receives special attention in the nineteenth century from a range of public figures, from historians to poets, from the human scientists to those in the hard sciences.

Ralph Waldo Emerson was possessed of self-reliance. He would not let the new revolution in technology drain him of a single damned thing. Emerson seems like one of those persons today—we call them

Luddites—who turns his back on technology and the machine and who refuses to have his voice reduced to a series of electrical impulses that run along a telephone wire or a transatlantic cable. For Ralph Waldo Emerson is transcendental, which means that all that really matters to him already resides in the universe; it is just not visible to the naked eye. And it cannot be counted or quantified. He needs to buy or own nothing more. He is already in possession of everything he desires. He merely wants to reveal, say, the all-seeing eye; it has nothing at all to do with the cinema or motion pictures or a camera of any kind. It has to do with the self and what he calls the over-soul; it is, for him, the transcendence of this realm for a higher one—a spiritual one.

Emerson was self-reliance, and he was self-confidence, and above all, he was self-assurance. He needed nothing more than a hyphen to hold things together; that's because he had stepped outside the regular order of language. Emerson forged a new language. Like Freud, he is difficult to read; he takes time. Like Freud, he writes but he does not communicate. Communication is for Samuel Morse or Thomas Alva Edison. Ralph Waldo Emerson will stand fast; he sees the signs of a higher power everywhere. People did not go on weekends to amusement parks to hear Emerson; they went to the Unitarian Church on Sundays to listen to his sermons. And when they did, they felt themselves back in control—those who went and those who listened and especially those who paid attention to his words and sentences and his spectacular images.

The 1933 *Oxford English Dictionary* contains over seventy instances of the word *self,* dating from the middle to the late nineteenth century. Words like *self-reliance, self-assurance, self-confidence,* and so on appear for the first time during that period. (The overwhelming majority of *self-*words, in fact, appear in the nineteenth century.) Ralph Waldo Emerson, the poet, the essayist, the minister of hope, coined many of those compounds. No matter the source, the idea of the self moves center stage in the nineteenth century.

Here is one of his paragraphs from a key essay on the subject, "Man the Reformer," arguing for the fortitude of self:

> I will not dissemble my hope, that each person whom I address has felt his own call to cast aside all evil customs, timidities, and limitations, and to be in his place a free and helpful man, a reformer, a benefactor, not content to slip along through the world like a footman or a spy, escaping by his nimbleness and apologies as many knocks as he can, but a brave and upright man, who must find or cut a straight road to everything excellent in the earth, and not only go honorably himself, but make it easier for all who follow him, to go in honor and with benefit.[8]

But one must ask the following question: "Is there still an autonomous self capable of the act of living?" This is but a variation on the question that Ivan Illich asks, in an essay titled "Death Undefeated": "Is there still an autonomous self capable of the act of dying?"

If the self does stand as the ultimate barrier against total invisibility, then the question becomes how to hang on to it. That was the trick. It certainly did not happen at Coney—just the opposite. A visit to Coney Island overwhelmed one's senses—from rides and food to noise and the sea; from alcohol to fright to sexual titillation. Every ride and attraction, along with all of the odors of cooking food, was designed to make one forget the nagging and dragging self. To hell with that effort to stay fully human and totally alert, let's just have fun. Coney sold illusion, and the root of *illusion* is the Latin *ludere,* "to play." It's work all week long—hard and gritty work—until the moment of that brief respite, the weekend. But Coney offered fun in its own unique mode, as a way to "feel" totally alive—through the most intense and unambiguous of bodily reactions, including nausea, suffocation, unbalance, disorientation, and dizziness, and the ultimate reaction, the rush and whiff of death itself. The person feels totally out of control and can do nothing more than freeze up, and then give up.

But look, we're in a park, and it's all about the great cogs and wheels of the Industrial Revolution turning over and over in the service of our pleasure. It's technology from the workplace usurped and transplanted to the fun zone, to the palace of pleasure. Here, at Coney, no one has to fear the machine, for here the machine is your friend. Mister Ferris's wheel goes round and round, and at its top it looks as if one could see forever but, unfortunately, the wheel ends up, well, back where it started, which is to say, absolutely nowhere. So goes the merry carousel, the Shoot-The-Chutes, the parachute drop—all of it just like the daily grind: machines moving fast and faster and ending up exactly where they began. There's a lesson here, but who the hell cares—it's Coney, and it's time for a five-cent frankfurter and an ice-cold soda or even a beer.

Tilyou and the string of businesspeople who came after him made Coney out of reach to all competitors. No one could touch their state-of-the-art amusement park. Nevertheless, even though it represented the highest standard of fun at the end of the nineteenth century, we should not forget that amusement parks—what a glorious Americanism!—pitched their tents and erected their buildings and thrill rides all across the country. In Boston, it was Paragon Park and Revere Beach; in Philadelphia, Willow Grove Park and nearby Atlantic City; in Atlanta, Ponce de Leon Park; in Cleveland, Euclid Beach; in Chicago, Cheltenham Beach, Riverview Park, and White City; in St. Louis, Forest Park Highlands; in Denver, Manhattan Beach Park; in San Francisco, the Chutes. None of them as wild and as large and as popular as that place that was not an island and that had few conies (rabbits), that went by the name of Coney Island. But those other places threw open their doors and in rushed families in great numbers. Was anyone working? Was anyone feeling pain? Did anyone take anything—from poverty to immigration to war—seriously? It certainly did not seem so.

Certainly, the numbers say no: On a single day at Coney two hundred thousand people came to swim and splash and get prodded by a midget clown and soaked by a fast dash down a slide in a boat. At Luna Park, one of the three separate parks at Coney, five million people paid admission to get inside in a single season. They all came to get humiliated and to feel small and oh so out of control. They paid for their pleasure; they walked and ate and smiled and felt so damned good. How can anyone knock such good-natured entertainment? It was here to stay. It *is* here to stay. It has, today, taken over our lives with a thoroughness that few if any people could have imagined in the nineteenth century. Entertainment expanded into an industry in the nineteenth century. It enjoys a monopoly in the twenty-first century. American entrepreneurs knew how to take technology and turn it toward fun. Americans responded. They were waiting for such an opportunity. They learned quickly how to have fun.

In that kind of world of unlimited fun, Coney Island, America's first entertainment park, offered the ideal. "A dream world," one advertising brochure said of Luna Park. "Abandon your cares here," beckoned another flyer, "at Steeplechase Park." "Come to Coney and forget yourself" (or more accurately, "forget your self"). Coney Island lay where the land ran out and the sea took over wave by wave. It was a place to go where few if any people might know you; it was a safe haven, a resort where you could re-create yourself. At Coney, you found yourself at the edge of the world; you had been pushed and could not be pushed any further. In a very real sense, to go to Coney was to undertake a pilgrimage to the border, to the liminal edge of experience. Once there, anything could happen; anything was possible. And, because of the invention of the postcard, in 1869, for a penny people could tell their friends, "Having a great time. Wish you were here!" (A person could buy the first postcards in America in 1873, and find ample supplies of them at the Chicago World's Fair in 1893. Which makes utter sense, for the fair, or the World's Columbian Exposition, was certainly something to write home about.)

It's as if the entrepreneurs of Coney Island had read their Freud dili-gently, but most likely they did not. In *The Interpretation of Dreams,* Freud points out three or four recurring, or what he calls "typical" dreams: falling from great heights, finding oneself disoriented, experiencing the great exhilaration of leaving the ground and flying, and showing up in front of strangers nearly or totally naked. At Coney, some amusement ride would provide a person a living example of each of those dreams. One could fall from a great height on the parachute drop, feel oneself disoriented in the house with the tilted floors and walls, and get the feeling of defying gravity on the roller coaster. In the Blowhole Theater, people walked through a funhouse only at the end to find that the floor had fallen away. They then slid down a chute and landed in front of an audience, and then walked across a brightly lit stage, where a blast of air would blow women's dresses over their heads, much to the delight of the audience, who had gone through the funhouse themselves. The people who had paid admission to go through the house found themselves now as the entertainment, in full display before a battery of strangers, a confused and jumbled-up reality that might appear in a dream.

Of course, people had plenty of chances for entertainment in the earlier part of the nineteenth century—a long list of opportunities, such as vaudeville, chautauqua, the music hall, the concert hall, burlesque, and minstrelsy performances, including the genre called blackface. Some of these attracted a lower-class audience, like the music and concert halls, and some, like the vaudeville house, a slightly higher-class clientele. But even the largest of the venues, like the Palace Theater in Manhattan, could accommodate only several hundred people. Coney and its kindred parks offered something entirely new in the period, and that was mass entertainment. The time was perfectly ripe for its opening.

The ends of years make people both sad and righteously giddy. It's a time of resolutions, of lament for the past but also of a desire to make amends for the future. Janus, the two-faced god, watches intently over December 31, at midnight hour. He can afford to be judicious because he can look both ways at once—to the past and to the future. The New

Year is a new chance, a brand new opportunity to get it right. It comes upon us with a certain air of euphoria—bubbly, effervescent champagne perfectly captures the mood for the turn of the year, as the old year drifts away. It's easy enough to feel giddy and lightheaded, if only to get the last year off our backs. This year, by God, I intend to get it right. Hope springs fairly eternal.

The ends of centuries come larded with even greater expectations than the ends of years. Moving from the nineteenth into the twentieth century, people knew that something was ending, but they also felt that something not just new but actually monumental was beginning. The countdown comes with surprises. The end of the 1800s was no exception. In the century's last years, businesspeople directed a good deal of technological know-how toward changing great masses of people's attitudes toward leisure time, and more important, toward fun. Since most workers had begun to feel no more important than cogs or robots, they desperately needed recreation—one is tempted to say, re-creation. In the process, those adventurous businesspeople who turned their entrepreneurial skills to entertainment became very wealthy. Fun paid off big. (The collusion between technology and amusement would eventuate in today's own highly sophisticated computer-generated images in films, and in wildly violent, realistic, and popular video games.)

At every social level, people sought out and found new ways of amusing themselves. Thomas Alva Edison helped in a big way toward satisfying that need for entertainment. One of his inventions in particular made a remarkable impact in a fairly short time. In 1878, he received a patent for a machine he called a phonograph (sometimes referred to as a gramophone)—a talking and singing machine—which captured, through a mysterious process, the human voice on a piece of tinfoil. Some audio historians believe that a Frenchman named Édouard-Léon Scott de Martinville recorded ten seconds of "Au Claire de la Lune" almost two decades earlier than Edison, on April 9, 1860, on an instrument he called a phonautograph—an odd name suggesting the revelation of oneself through one's voice. Scott had designed a machine to record sounds visually; his machine etched sound waves onto sheets of paper that had been blackened by smoke from an oil lamp. But Scott had intended his recordings not for listening but for seeing. He sought only to create a paper record of speech, an autograph of sorts that others could later decipher and analyze if they so desired. The idea of playback did not come until Edison.

Edison's phonograph quickly got pressed into service as an instrument of entertainment, designed, as the advertisements would later claim, for "America's listening pleasure." (*Phonograph*, "writing with sound," is of course distinct from *photograph*, "writing with light.") Edison's advertisements for his new machine took people off to unimagined possibilities. Think about being able to sit in the privacy of your own living room, listening to the voices of the most famous musical stars in the world. All this for just a few dollars. Disembodied, ghostly voices need not be scary; they could be entertaining and fun. Thomas Alva Edison was a madman; he was a genius. He was the most prolific inventor in America, perhaps in the world. Above all else, in the context of the period, Edison was a consummate dreamer.

Edison came to the invention of the phonograph as a result of his work on two other machines, the telegraph and the telephone. To Edison must go the title of the king of the body snatchers, for his perception exactly matched the period's emphasis on disembodiment, developing several machines that could speak and talk without the aid of any physical body. And that's the spirit that he wished to exploit to the fullest. And so, the editors of the magazine *Scientific American,* in the December 22, 1877 issue, reported on Edison's initial and bold visit to their offices with his new talking machine: "Mr. Thomas A. Edison recently came into this office, placed a little machine on our desk, turned a crank, and the machine inquired as to our health, asked how we liked the phonograph, informed us that it was very well, and bid us a cordial good night."

Notice that the machine has at this early date already assumed human properties: The machine, or rather the crude tinfoil sheet on the machine, "inquires" and "informs" and "bids," just as we talk of our computers today as if they were in actual possession of a memory and of language. None of this, by the by, did Edison do accidentally. On January 24, 1878, he established the Edison Speaking Phonograph Company, choosing a name that suggested that the machine itself was capable of conjuring its own sentences. By this time, the average person in America had already invested machines in general with enormous power; machines could perform tasks faster and more efficiently than even the most skilled person. But here was something entirely new and frightening: This machine seemed to exhibit decidedly human attributes—speech and memory and intelligence.

The world's superstars quickly latched on to the allure of Edison's magical machine. Edison could do for singers, for instance, what Johannes Gutenberg had done for letters. Both of them made for the possibility of a lasting impression. Always on the lookout for more and inventive ways to promote herself, one day in 1879, unannounced, none other than Sarah Bernhardt showed up at the Edison factory in Menlo Park, New Jersey. Technology had early on pulled one of the world's superstars into its vortex; she simply could not resist the call of an apparatus that in effect guaranteed immortality. Sarah Bernhardt was possessed of the true celebrity's uncanny sense that, in its ability to preserve her voice for generations to come, the phonograph would become the machine of the future. But again, like the true star, she was not quite sure that the crude machine would capture the real qualities of her voice. According to the company's publicists, Edison convinced her with a well-planned demonstration that he would be producing "perfect records." Even though it took some time, Edison kept his word: The Edison company finally introduced wax cylinders in 1888, which did in fact greatly improve sound quality.

After much enticement and an intentionally undisclosed amount of money, Sarah Bernhardt signed an exclusive contract with Thomas Edison and his company. No slouch himself when it came to publicity, Edison pressed every one of his dealers to write their local newspapers with the announcement of the monumental signing, for after all, he told them, "No paper will refuse to publish the news, as everything that the immortal Bernhardt does is eagerly seized upon by the press."[9]

Edison was his own best booster. Choosing the oldest continuing literary magazine in the country, *The North American Review,* Edison wrote a letter, in the June 1, 1878 issue, pointing out the possible future uses of his invention and, in the process, revealing once again his belief that the machine had life. His first suggestion for the phonograph was for "[l]etter writing and all kinds of dictation without the aid of a stenograph." The machine itself would stand in for the stenographer, performing the work better and faster, Edison contended, than the person. He suggested many other things, including remaking clocks so that they could "announce in articulate speech the time for going home, going to meals, etc."

Edison got the idea of time correct; it does in a great sense exert control over us. The timepiece some of us wear on our wrists, the watch, carries the same name as the verb "watch." Both words come from the same Latin root, *vigilia,* which produces words like *wake,* as in the Catholic watch over the body, or to be *awake*—that is, to be "vigilant." One watches one's watch, but the watch really "watches" the person who wears it, subtly directing by indicating the exact time to be somewhere, or simply by noting the passing of time on the person's way to fame and fortune. This is not unlike the television we so blithely watch without thinking that the executives behind it all know exactly our viewing and buying and after-hour proclivities, habits, and desires. We are watching the Big Brother that is watching us.

Not only did Edison link speech with time in his talking clock, but he also proposed a further connection with another appliance, the telephone, "so as to make that instrument an auxiliary in the transmission of permanent and invaluable records instead of being the recipient of momentary and fleeting communication." With that stroke, he conceptualized the modern answering machine, turning the breathy and fleeting nature of a few brief moments of unrehearsed talking—its inherent nature of evanescence—into something of permanence. Everything melts into air, except that most fleeting of things, as far as Edison was concerned, human speech. That Edison made permanent.

As further proof that Edison liked to conflate the mechanical with the human, he affectionately referred to his talking machine as "Baby." To reinforce the idea that he had created a "Baby," the first words he recorded on the machine he took from the beginning of the most well-known nursery rhyme, "Mary Had a Little Lamb." He chose his term of endearment "Baby" well, for over the course of his career inventing things, he wanted desperately to create a lifelike talking doll and set an astonishing 250 people to working on each little creature. In another part of the factory, he had another eighteen young girls reciting nursery rhymes into phonographs. His project fit well into the tradition of the wax effigy and the automaton and Freud's notion of the "uncanny." In what amounted to an almost Doctor Frankensteinian fever pitch, Edison hope to bring to market an estimated one hundred thousand dolls a year. How many he made, no one knows, and none of the dolls has, evidently, survived.

In an interview with *Scientific American* magazine early on in his career, he referred to the human brain as a "piece of meat mechanism,"[10] nothing more than a machine that would eventually fall into decay. The real power lay with the mechanical, and someday someone, he believed, would build a mechanical brain that would outperform the human version. But in his later years, America's most prolific inventor—he and his assistants get credit for some 1,093 patents—underwent a radical change of heart. He could find no ghost in the machine, no soul in the mechanical.

The same kind of fervor he had used for inventions he now turned on the spiritualism movement and in particular Madame Blavatsky and her ideas of theosophy. He decided that personalities were just too powerful to ever disappear just because the body had decayed, and so they must attain their own immortality. He thus decided to design a high-powered electrical device that could record voices from the other side to quiet the skeptics. "We can evolve an instrument," he said, "so delicate as to be affected, or moved, or manipulated by, our personality as it survives in the next life; such an instrument, when made available, ought to record something."[11] Alas, even though he experimented with variations on the device at séances, and even with the encouragement of Houdini—who was a skeptic about the paranormal—he could not make contact with the other side.

From the seventies through to the end of the century, Edison contributed to making the nature of life certainly miraculous but at the same time also fairly odd. Machines talked, railroad cars moved great distances across steel tracks at high speeds, and people—or at least facsimiles of people—moved across movie screens. On February 14, 1876—perhaps in honor of Valentine's Day—both Alexander Graham Bell and Elisha Gray filed papers with the United States Patent Office to register their competing designs for the telephone. Bell got the patent. His telephone device allowed two people, physically removed from each other by fairly great distances, to carry on a conversation—perhaps about matters of the heart. Meanwhile, Edison's incandescent lighting was working its own miracle by pushing daylight further and further into the night. Edison received his patent for the light bulb in 1880.

In another competition, this one to see who could transport the human voice great distances at cheap prices, Western Union opened for business in 1851, in Rochester, New York, near the Eastman Kodak building. The company began transmitting messages by Morse code over wire, hand-delivering the copy by courier to its final destination. After only ten years in business, by 1861, the company had completed the first transcontinental telegraph line, which immediately put the Pony Express out of business, since Western Union could now get a message across the country in less than one day. (The Pony Express took ten days, a case of technology winning out over literal horsepower.)

At her Jubilee procession, in 1897, Queen Victoria sent a message around the world, carried through the cables that Britain had laid to reach all its outposts. In every British colony, from Asia to India to Africa, millions and millions of loyal subjects and colonial subjects heard the queen intone her royal words, intended to uplift and sanctify: "From my heart I thank my beloved people. May God bless them." It was an extraordinary historical moment, an accomplishment in which the queen's words took but two minutes, according to reports at the time, to reach a location as exotic as Tehran.[12]

Nikola Tesla, born in Croatia, also contributed to this new drive toward entertainment. In 1895, Tesla began sending radio signals over a distance of fifty miles. Two years later, in 1897, Tesla received a patent for perhaps the ultimate instrument to disembody the human voice, the radio, beating out his rival, Guglielmo Marconi. The idea of the radio was not to supply mere snippets of conversations of the sort Edison provided on the phonograph, but whole speeches and long conversations. The radio would prove to be, of course, along with the phonograph, one of the key appliances for providing entertainment in the early years of the twentieth century. While people now spend more time watching television than they do to listening to radio, television still has not dislodged the radio from homes. And we know how important it is in automobiles.

Even the automobile, perhaps the ultimate "vehicle" of entertainment, managed to slip in under the wire of the end of the century, when Gottlieb Daimler and Wilhelm Maybach, in Germany, in 1889, built the first automobile powered by a gasoline engine. Developing 1.5 horsepower out of its tiny two-cylinder engine, this crude automobile went humming along the countryside at a top speed of ten miles per hour. Its four-speed transmission made it able to climb hills and even pull a small load. The century's frenzy over technological invention and innovation prompted an apocryphal line from Charles H. Duell, commissioner of patents, who was said to argue, in 1889, that the government ought to close the Patent Office permanently on the grounds that "everything that can be invented has been invented."

On top of all the changes brought about by technology, museums and zoos opened all across this country and in Europe, so that entire families could now observe art objects and wild, exotic animals up close but decidedly out of hand's reach. The nation's first botanical garden opened in 1820 in the Washington, D.C. The haptic life seemed to be receding at a fast clip, just out of everyone's grasp. More and more experiences came to be truly disembodied ones in the period, one of the powerful legacies the nineteenth century handed down to our own century. In our own time, it is hard to imagine a more disembodied and decidedly bizarre use for Edison's telephone than the purportedly erotic pastime called "phone sex." Nicholson Baker wrote an entire novel, *Vox*, formulated around the conversations of two people who call a 976 party line at the same time, engaging in what can only be called "social intercourse," telephone to long-distance telephone sexual intimacies, or what one reviewer of Baker's novel calls "aural sex."[13]

As more and more people moved off the farm and into the city, time—both with the regular clock and the time clock—controlled more and more aspects of their lives. Imagine Edison's clock yelling at people to get out of bed and get to work, get to dinner, get to church. If they worked in factories, people's tasks turned blindingly repetitive, their every movement—and quarter-movement—measured by Frederick Winslow Taylor's new time and motion studies and his ubiquitous stopwatch. People felt more regulated, their lives more robotic. At the same time, machines seemed to take on more human qualities. The period from 1860 to the end of the century is known as the Golden Age of the Automaton. What a confusion! What a grand confusion! Working people—especially Americans, living in the heart of the growing and grinding Industrial Revolution—needed to have a serious (or more accurately, a frivolous) break, a regular break, it turns out, oddly enough, from all that pounding and dampening routine. National holidays, birthdays, and anniversaries just would not do. There had to be more, and there had to be lots more of that more.

Just when Edison brought out his phonograph, a new word, *weekend,* began to appear in dictionaries, defined as "the holiday period at the end of a week's work, usually from Saturday noon or Friday night to Monday; especially this holiday when spent away from home." The weekend provided that marvelously frivolous break, an officially designated time to forget. For those who couldn't make the trek to Coney, alcohol added a way to drown the self, easing or even erasing the bitter memories of seemingly unending hours and hours and days and days of repetitive labor. And for most people, alcohol worked as effectively as the best analgesic. If there was a buck to be made, the American businessperson could always be counted on to respond, and thus entrepreneurs opened more taverns and bars per capita during the last two decades of the nineteenth century than at any other time in the nation's history. Alcoholism, as a disease brought on by the abuse of alcohol, first appeared in medical journals mid-century. Just a decade later, local newspapers carried news of the new disease. The London *Daily News,* for example, on December 8, 1869, reported on "the deaths of two persons from alcoholism."

To enhance that feeling of a dreamy, ghostly oasis on the New York shore, Coney blazed with over one million electric bulbs (another of Edison's inventions)—so much incandescence that Edison had to build a power plant in New Jersey just to accommodate the park's enormous electrical needs. Lights adorned every building: Newspapers called it "the architecture of exhilaration."[14] Under that blinding canopy of light, for a penny or two, one could ride the world's largest and longest roller coaster, the Thunderbolt; try to survive a precipitous fall on the parachute jump ("The Eiffel Tower of Brooklyn"); climb on the back of a metal horse and race the steeplechase; turn topsy-turvy on the Loop-the-Loop; or take a spin on Mister Ferris's gigantic revolving hub, the Wonder Wheel, the first of which he had designed for the Chicago World's Fair in 1893. Sitting on top of a water slide called Shoot-The-Chutes, elephants (according to Blaine Harden's 1999 *New York Times* article "An Incandescent Coney Island of the Mind") came "thundering down, one by one, to smack the water as only falling elephants can, drenching and delighting paying customers at . . . Dreamland."

In the hands of advertisers, the Industrial Revolution had become a fanciful plaything. Coney put into action that nineteenth-century coining *analgesic,* the amusement park as pain reliever. God may have died, the general population may have lost faith, but people still knew how to have a good time; if they didn't, Coney showed them the way. Surreal clowns the size of small buildings; two-headed women and dog-headed men; midgets and dwarves dressed in outlandish costumes: The unconscious had seemingly sprung to life. Families could even sleep inside an elephant, at the Elephant Hotel, in the shape of the animal itself. According to Harden, Coney drew ninety thousand people a day at the turn of the century, when baseball games did well to grab twenty thousand.

Everywhere people walked at Coney, they could not help experiencing euphoria or vertigo—or both. Look, that's your reflection in the hall of distorted mirrors—howl over your fat self, laugh at your worst nightmare— bent totally out of recognition. Grown men and women staggered off the Thunderbolt—itself a huge scaffolding, not unlike the Brooklyn Bridge— confessing, "I was scared to death but I felt totally alive." Standing solidly on the ground again, they shouted their joyous sense of relief to the crowd. They had become, in the root sense of the word, *exhilarated,* "giddily hilarious." In that new, nineteenth-century aesthetic where danger merged with fear—the art of flirting with certain death—they found themselves, during their brief three-minute thrill ride, transformed once again into human beings, high on an infusion of adrenaline.

Promoters found other ways to scare people, while amusing them at the same time. For the first time, spectators saw mock death and destruction on the grandest of scales, played out on the most elaborately built sets. At Coney, as the evening grew dark, hundreds of players reenacted battles from the Spanish-American War, the Civil War, the Boer War. Every several hours, Tilyou's cast of characters staged the eruption of Mount Vesuvius. Sparks showered the crowd. Bombs exploded. Sirens screamed. Men and women jumped from the windows of burning buildings to the ground, seven floors below; they got blown up on the battlefield and mowed down by a firing squad. Audiences could not get their fill; they clamored for more and more. In some newspaper accounts, these spectacles attracted greater crowds than any of the thrill rides.[15]

In front of their very eyes, audiences saw performances of the kind of devestation that would later dominate video screens, on which countless numbers of human beings died virtual deaths. The first occurrence of the word *virtual* to mean a facsimile body actually comes in the nineteenth century, in 1883, and refers to the Calvinist doctrine of Christ's virtual presence in the Eucharist. *Virtual* refers to a body not exactly present— totally in keeping with the nineteenth century's sense of fading human beings dying fake deaths, or better yet, those virtual human beings parading across the movie screen.

At precisely the same time, just as people could preserve their happy moments in photographs and erase their painful ones temporarily with alcohol or amusement, Sigmund Freud seized on the self and its close ally, memory (and consciousness), as the way to bring anxiety-ridden patients back to psychic health. And while the dreamlike atmosphere of Coney Island promised to alleviate all trace of the work-weary world, Freud opted for just the opposite effect—to help people remember. In the process, however, he too would rid them of their pain. People never forget anything, Freud maintained, they just bury their most painful memories through a process called repression. By interpreting the patient's dreams with the patient, he could break into something even deeper than consciousness itself, into a subterranean, virtual layer he called the subconscious. The psychoanalyst acted as an archaeologist, digging into the patient's subconscious to retrieve lost or neglected bits and pieces of experience.

Freud would, of course, eventually map the tripartite structure that, for him, made human beings absolutely and unequivocally human, the unconscious. Like Lamarck, Mendeleev, Childe, and scores of others in the period, Freud undertook a taxonomy of that shadowy enterprise known as the mind, which he saw divided into three parts: the id, the ego, and the superego. He was absolutely certain that he had found the seat of consciousness; a good deal of the world slowly came to believe him, as well.

Freudian analysis, however, brought with it several of its own major problems. For one, while Freud's theories rested on the recovery of the self—memory required a self to activate it—the self lay hidden sometimes many layers below the level of ordinary consciousness. Excavation was a protracted, painstaking process. Analysis, the so-called talking cure, could take years and years, and Freud used several techniques. Through suggestions, the client might be prompted to remember certain childhood traumas. Since Freud thought that people revealed themselves in their most unguarded moments, he listened carefully to the jokes his patients told. But Freud believed that his patients could unlock their repressed memories most effectively by recounting their dreams. Again, Freud would listen for the castoff phrase, or the passed-over image, those unexamined gestures that we saw in a previous chapter that led to the solution of crimes, or the authentication of a particular painting.

The second problem with Freud's protracted talking cure followed on the first, but posed for many an insurmountable problem: Analysis was frighteningly expensive, which meant that only the really wealthy, those blessed with the luxury of enough "spare time" to sit in a doctor's office for an hour or more a day, week after week, could afford what we call today therapy. It should not be surprising, then, that the bulk of Freud's clients were wealthy Viennese women. Psychotherapy still remains expensive and out of reach for a great many people.

Both Freud and Coney relied for their success on the last bastion in the fight for human essence, the self. Coney worked so well by having the self evaporate, drop away, attraction by attraction. Freud, on the other hand, hoped to retrieve the self and hold it up to the bright light of logic. For the overwhelming mass of the population, well, such things just did not matter. The self remained, for the great part, the concern of intellectuals—writers and artists and the new social scientists. Even if they believed in it, few people could afford therapy of any kind. In America, particularly, where entrepreneurs developed fun to such a high art, the general public rigorously pursued popular entertainment that they considered therapy, or at least therapeutic.

Huge crowds made the weekly pilgrimage to Coney, while discovering, along the way, less elaborate forms of entertainment—drinking, dancing, attending the new burlesque houses, watching magic acts, visiting the new striptease, the Yiddish theater, and on and on. The more daring, and perhaps more desperate, could step beyond the standard anodynes, laudanum or absinthe, to a variety of new and immensely more powerful drugs, like morphine, heroin, and cocaine. And, on and off during the period, young people in particular flirted with nitrous oxide.

A new world had opened in the nineteenth century, a world of high entertainment and supreme pleasure. If one could just make it through the week, the weekend beckoned and it promised wholesale relief. Whenever they could, New Yorkers would spend their free time—their weekend time, without some professional peering over their shoulder and measuring their every move—on the boardwalks of Coney Island. Great masses of city dwellers on a Saturday or Sunday boarded the subway for one nickel in Manhattan and got off at the Stillwell Avenue station, breathed a collective sigh of relief, and smiled broadly. They had arrived.

Some newspaper reporters told a different story. They condemned Coney and its working-class crowd as a two-bit tawdry affair, dismissing the whole enterprise as nothing but one big fun zone—with the emphasis on fun. They condemned it by renaming Coney the new Sodom by the Sea.[16] But the enormous crowds paid those stories little or no mind. They forgot the critics and the naysayers as they ordered their Nathan's frankfurter, washed it down with a Nedick's orange soda, and as a grand finale finished off their ten-cent meal with one version or another of an intense sugar spectacle—toffee apples, saltwater taffy, chocolate fudge, or towers of cotton candy in every pastel shade a young person could possibly imagine.

But the true marvel of confectionery skill came as a gift from the gods, who showered good fortune on little boys and girls: a French quiescent dessert, perfected at a restaurant called Fouquet's, on the Champs-Élysées, that had arrived in America in the nineteenth century. It was called ice cream. It made Freud's theory of the pleasure principle into something startlingly alive and above all else tangible. In America, Emerson stands out as one of the most respected public intellectuals, commenting with startling insight on almost every issue and topic of the day—even ice cream. His comment on that miraculous dessert comes from "Man the Reformer," a lecture he delivered to the Mechanics' Apprentices' Library Association in 1841, a fitting image in a lecture principally about the way essence has disappeared from every person, at every level of society, from aristocrat to worker: "We dare not trust our wit for making our house pleasant to our friend, and so we buy ice-creams." As amazing and witty as ice cream was already, Coney added a radical improvement by serving huge scoops of it, in a superabundance of flavors, in a pastry cone.

Dessert had been liberated from the dining table. The main course had already been freed, with the five-cent frankfurter, or more commonly "hot dog," on the boardwalk. And then came the dessert. Yes, there was taffy and saltwater taffy, but nothing to rival the ice cream. Families walked the boardwalk on warm summer evenings, each member with an ice cream cone in hand. At no other time did one hear parents urging and encouraging their children to finish up every last bit of that runny and drippy sugar—and to get it done fast! Eat, eat! Keep licking, keep on eating. And when anyone—child or adult—finished the cone, it made apparent the real miracle—for absolutely nothing was left! No container, no utensil, no waste—everything totally and thoroughly gone. There was nothing to wash, nothing to dispose of, nothing, as we say these days, to recycle. A child could finally make "all gone."

No other dessert but the ice cream cone could serve as such a perfect nineteenth-century confection, the greatest vanishing act that ended up as a most ghostly experience. Yes, everything solid melts into air—especially, it seems, ice cream. Many years after the opening of Coney Island, the great American poet Wallace Stevens rolled Marx and Emerson into one tantalizing line in his dreamlike poem, "The Emperor of Ice-Cream," which ends with the very mysterious line, "The only emperor is the emperor of ice-cream."

• ❦ •

WHERE WOULD IT all lead? Clearly, people seem to have opted, very heavily, for entertainment. It is a multibillion-dollar-a-year conglomerate of businesses, dominated now by electronic technology. The re-creation, say, of the Boer Wars pales in the immediacy of its impact in the face of even the lowest-level software from Nintendo or Sega. No one in the nineteenth century would have suspected that people would tote their telephones around in their hip pockets, let alone snap pictures with them. They could not conceive of sending email messages through the ether, or turning on images, like water, as if from an electronic tap, in the living room, with something called a television set. And listening to an iPod: Never! By mid-nineteenth century, however, the drive toward such innovation was firmly in place, in England and particularly in America. Entertainment, fun, electronic technology—all have had a long and successful run, one hundred years or more.

Once human beings are emptied of substance, any professional—from the advertiser on Madison Avenue to George C. Tilyou on Coney Island—can fill them back up with whatever gadgets or innovations they are told they need and thus come to believe they actually want. Nowadays, someone or some agency continually has the public's ear and eye and appetite, telling each and every person what to think and whom to hate and how to react. Fear works so effectively these days because it freezes people in place, preventing them from thinking critically about any issue or problem. It's impossible, of course, to refuse or refute anything once thinking has been shut off. But we need a more substantive, more basic solution to this problem of human disappearance.

And now, now we have a new bestseller listing in *The New York Times,* one that charts the sales of self-help books. The word *self-help* enters the language in 1831, with Thomas Carlyle, who uses it in *Sartor Resartus* to refer to Ishmael: "In the destitution of the wild desert does our young Ishmael acquire for himself the highest of all possessions, that of self-help." Self-help for Carlyle is already a "possession," something to strive for and acquire—a laudable goal. Indeed, it is one of the highest of all goals.

Our contemporary articulation of self-help continues that same idea, situating the "help" in some outside agency or person as instruction or, more than likely, in some bracing reprimand to invigorate the "self." For example, one such book on "tough love" carries the title *You're Fat! Now Lose It!* Like the concept "life," the self is an entity to be molded and shaped and directed. These are books not about the help from which a person might benefit, but the help a person will require to become more productive at work, more successful with love, and, most important of all, happier with him- or herself. Self-help books resemble repair manuals: The system is down and in need of fixing.

Like any other enterprise, some of those books probably do help a few people, while a great many others of them merely cash in on people's despondency, asking their reader-clients to pay attention to what they are doing, how they are acting, and what they are feeling. All of them try to provide a level of therapy between hard covers. Some work, some do not, but the hope remains that maybe the next ones will pull off the miracle cure—and that keeps sales vital.

A 2008 *Christian Science Monitor* article points out that, while overall book sales have fallen, sales of self-help books continue to increase dramatically: "Almost half of Americans purchase at least one self-help book in their lifetimes. The genre accounted for $581 million in sales in 1998, but today that number has quadrupled to more than $2 billion."[17]

A phrase made popular by the TV series *Sex and the City,* "He's not that into you," became the title of a successful self-help book, which, in turn, became a movie. What a perfect alignment: pop psychology and mass entertainment, Freud *and* Disneyland joining forces. The ground for such a collusion was ably prepared by Doctor Phil, a self-help guru created by the staggering popularity of *The Oprah Winfrey Show,* itself a kind of performance in self-help. Doctor Phil's outspoken and recurring command to audience members (suggesting he is possessed of a self) serves as a counter to our ghostly existence: "Get real!"

SEVEN | The Draculated Cat

"When I had my Defiance given,
The Sun stood trembling in heaven;"

—WILLIAM BLAKE, 1800

N 1814, A GERMAN BOTANIST and poet named Adelbert von Chamisso published what he called a children's tale titled *Peter Schlemihl's Remarkable Story.* Like a good many stories for children, this one clearly went beyond children and carried profound meaning for adults, especially for those who had hope of understanding the period. Chamisso recounted the adventures of penniless little Peter, who wanders aimlessly and glumly around the German countryside. Head down and depressed, Peter stumbles into an unknown magician who tells Peter how much he loves his "beautiful shadow in the sun, which, with a certain noble contempt, and perhaps without being aware of it, you threw off from your feet."

The magician offers to buy Peter's shadow in exchange for a magical purse. No matter how many coins Peter might manage to withdraw from it, the purse will immediately fill back up, leaving Peter to live out his days forever wealthy, which means that he can finally stop worrying. Hungry for wealth and even hungrier for fame, Peter agrees to part with his lifelong and intimate friend, the shadow: "[W]ith wonderful dexterity, I perceived him loosening my shadow from the ground from head to foot; he lifted it up, he rolled it together and folded it, and at last put it into his pocket."

Happy at long last, Peter returns to wandering the countryside, this time as a wealthy and seemingly content little man. But, much to his shock, he slowly discovers that no one wants to talk to him and, worse yet, nobody wants to be with him. Most distressing of all, the woman he has for so long adored shuns him; this baffles Peter. For if anything, Peter realizes, he is a better, wealthier person than in the recent past.

But the lesson of the story shines clearly through: Love finds its vitality in the light, but does not shy away from the shadow. The negative emanation, to which very few if any people pay attention, is as important to the whole person as the bright and attractive side. It is the psychological equivalent of Freud's incidental gesture, a twitch or tic that speaks whole novels in a simple toss of the head or turn of a phrase. In a most significant way, a shadow is an imprint from which the loved one derives great enjoyment, meaning, and understanding. For the loved one, the shadow is the silhouette of the soul.

In the nineteenth-century drive toward essentialism, adepts in the period believed that our shadows offered observers the opportunity to see the distillation of our inner beings—a chance to examine the revelations of our deepest character. We can find this idea most wonderfully presented in the nineteenth-century fascination—practically a cult—for the silhouette. (The word *silhouette* comes from Étienne de Silhouette, a French author and politician, and enters the English language in 1798.) The place the making of silhouettes occupies is a popular precursor to photography. It is a photograph without any of the technology.

Drawing silhouettes, like the casting of shadows, offered a way to glimpse a person's soul. Both involved the casting of a negative; both involved free-floating interpretation. It makes sense, then, that silhouettes should appeal to one of the most well-known phrenologists of the period, Johann Kaspar Lavater. In 1820, Lavater began analyzing subjects through a backlit screen that revealed nothing but their outlines. By concentrating on those outlines that had no confusing details, Lavater felt enabled to make bold assertions about the subject's personality and character. The outline, he argued, eliminated everything extraneous, leaving, for Lavater, only the barest outlines of personality. Think of the shadow or the silhouette, then, as a negative from which we begin to make a positive impression slowly emerge.

Kara Walker, the contemporary African American artist, creates silhouettes of slave scenes. What motivates her art is the belief, in part, that too much has been written about slavery in this country over the past one hundred fifty years or so, while African Americans have made scant progress over that same period of time. Walker offers silhouettes—outlines of real people—which is the way most people saw African Americans in the nineteenth century, and the way most Americans perceive blacks today, and that is exactly what she is creating—"blacks." She asks us to realize that we still see African Americans in outline only, and begs her viewers to fill in the details. She believes we all know enough at this point to do just that. Out of all the millions of pages written about slavery and all the films and testimonials about black liberation, we can only "get it," finally, by filling in the details ourselves—that is, by completing the picture ourselves.

On another level, once we do fill in the details—in some sense, project ourselves into the scene—we enter into a complicity with, and a historical responsibility for, the over two hundred years of slavery in this country. All of this in art without color—and the phrase "without color" should reverberate for us—and without fine detail and description, in the strictest contrast of black and white. And isn't that the nineteenth century in America, a startling contrast of black and white? Keep in mind that in 1850 plantation slaves constituted America's largest workforce, even though fewer than 1,500 plantations owned more than one hundred slaves, only nine had more than five hundred, and only two had more than a thousand.[1]

Shadows, the negative cast by sunlight, always brings Plato's parable of the cave to life, except with a powerful psychological thrust, for my shadow is not just a mere reflection of reality in the nineteenth century—a phantasm—but reality and even much more—my *inner* reality. Who I am in the full blaze of the sun, in the clearest light of day, leaves a faint trace, which you can discover in my shadow. As the sun sets—as I grow older—I reveal more and more of myself. I am substantial and insubstantial at one and the same time. I move through the world as both positive and negative. One of the most forceful ambiguities of the period is one that sees in absence the possibility of a most powerful presence. Digital photography destroys the metaphor of photography as a way the psyche makes itself apparent. Digital photography does away with film—and negatives—just as word processing does away with paper and rough drafts.

Photographic printing techniques improved over the course of the nineteenth century. The blacks went through a process of fine gradation, making detail, especially in faces, much more finely delineated. Marina Warner goes so far as to say that the new techniques "could bestow lifelikeness on the inanimate, often to an uncanny degree." Innovations proliferated: Calotypes, salted paper prints, as well as platinum prints, in particular, allowed the lines to sink into the paper, giving the image an extraordinary depth. Warner also points to the range of nuanced color that started to emerge in the shadows— "indigo, maroon, saffron, and smoky grey." Like a silhouette, nineteenth-century photography drained reality of all color, distilling every object and detail into stark black and white. William Henry Fox Talbot, who invented the once-familiar negative in 1841, characterized photography in a phrase that tried to capture that rendering of full-color experience into a redaction of white and black, calling it, quite appropriately, the "pencil of nature."

The successor to the silhouette was a popular and innovative parlor game called the inkblot, in which people would try to find various animals, creatures, devils, and monsters in a simple blot of ink. It's the last gasp at enjoying messiness and fuzzy borders. It makes a virtue out of mistakes. A

German physician and poet, Justinus Koerner, really instigated the pastime. He began by "transforming smudges and blots on his letters to friends by doodling figures he divined in the shapes; later, he spattered ink on to paper on purpose, and then took the further step of folding it to produce a symmetrical image. He enhanced his fantasia by adding brushmarks—of eyes and other features. Skeletons, ghosts, imps, bats, and moths predominated, and he wrote whimsical verses to accompany them. Koerner suffered from very poor eyesight, so this was his way of transforming incapacitating blurs into aesthetic 'creatures of chance.'"[2]

Notice the phrase, "creatures of chance," a perfect Freudian line. Nothing is accidental, of course, for Freud. The smallest detail reveals all. And so, Justinus Koerner's simple parlor game, like Lavater's shadow and silhouette experiments, led to the very serious and elaborate Rorschach test that the Swiss psychologist Hermann Rorschach, in 1921, made into an integral part of his clinical psychiatric practice, and which later became a standard and familiar tool of diagnosis. In his clinical practice, Rorschach would present a series of inkblots to patients who had been diagnosed as schizophrenic, asking them to describe, with precise detail, what and whom they saw in each blot. Through their interpretations, Rorschach believed, he could put together a coherent narrative of his patients' problems.

By this strange and circuitous route, the common, everyday shadow moved into the scrubbed, antiseptic clinic. Schlemihl's magician may have been a doctor, then, nabbing his shadow for laboratory analysis. Working in just the opposite way, Freud attempted to take those mysterious shadows out of the bedrooms of his patients and make them disappear in the clear light of day. He wanted to shine a light on all the dark corners of the psyche. By this same psychological form of reasoning, we have to conclude that our shadows—in whatever way, in whatever system—carry great importance. We cannot hide our shadows, and we certainly cannot get rid of them, for in very significant ways, the shadow *is* the person. Without his shadow, Peter Schlemihl is simply not a person anymore.

On the most obvious psychological level, Peter's shadow represents his dark side, the shadow self that Jung described. Without acknowledging that darker side, Peter can never become a whole person; in turn, no one can love him because he cannot really embrace himself. He can only achieve psychic well-being by integrating his two sides, the two halves of his being. This theme, as we have seen, runs through a great deal of literature in the nineteenth century, from the obvious example of Doctor Jekyll and Mister Hyde to the secret sharer and the shape-shifting transformations of the wolf man.

On a psychoanalytic level, we must say that Peter Schlemihl finds himself stuck. Patients come to psychoanalysis when they keep repeating the same behavior, when they tell themselves the same stories, over and over again, about their lives. "This unconscious limiting or coercion of the repertoire of life-stories," according to Adam Phillips, "creates the illusion of time having stopped (or rather, people believe—behave as if—they have stopped time). In our repetitions we seem to be staying away from the future, keeping it at bay."[3] Freud called this particular symptom a failed attempt at doing ourselves in, a passing attraction with our own death, and concluded that such conspicuous repetitions resulted from the person's unwillingness to remember. In Freudian terms, we cannot make the sun move again except through the painful act of remembering those acts from childhood that have blocked us. Otherwise, we face a death in life.

And Schlemihl has, indeed, entered into a kind of death, where everything—not just the sun—has stopped for him. (I realize that it is the Earth that must stop and not the sun, but I adhere to linguistic conventions here: for example, "sunrise" and "sunset.") He has moved into a state where he would rather not remember much of anything. Chamisso has given us a parable about Peter's essence, and the state of the collective soul in the nineteenth century. It is not Peter's shadow that has disappeared, but, in effect, Peter himself. Take away the shadow and you take away life itself.

In 1841, the novelist Honoré de Balzac made the following, very convoluted declaration about human essence, couched in terms of a period becoming quickly dominated by the technology of the camera. That's why he made this particular declaration to the photographer Nadar, who had the great distinction of many times photographing Sarah Bernhardt. Balzac perceived that presently "each body in nature consists of a series of ghosts, in an infinity of superimposed layers, foliated in infinitesimal films, in all the directions in which optics perceive this body." He went on to apply his extended image specifically to the daguerreotype, which he believed "was going to surprise, detach and retain one of the layers of the body on which it focused . . . from then onwards, and every time the operation was repeated, the object in question evidently suffered the loss of one of its ghosts, that is to say, the very essence of which it was composed."[4]

Balzac gives new meaning to the phrase "Let me *take* your picture," which, in the context he provides, we might want to recast as "Let me take your image"—for each time I "shoot" you, in his terms, I remove one more layer of your being. Not only had human beings been reduced to ghosts, as far as Balzac could see, but now technology had begun stripping away even those ghosts, making the human being totally disappear, and leaving behind absolutely nothing.

Balzac was not alone in his fear of the great erasure of the human being. Emerson, too, compared the taking of a person's photograph with the ultimate taking—death. Caleb Crain, in a review of an exhibition at the National Gallery of Art in Washington, D.C., called The Art of the American Snapshot, 1888–1978, quotes Emerson on the subject of sitting for a portrait in the studio of a photographer. Crain observes, about the process of photography in the 1840s, that "no chemical preparation was then sensitive enough to record a person unwilling or unable to keep still. 'Were you ever daguerreotyped, O immortal man?' Emerson asked in his journal in 1841." A question on which Emerson then elaborated: "And in your zeal not to blur the image, did you keep every finger in its place with such energy that your hands became clenched as for fight or despair . . . and the eyes fixed as they are fixed in a fit, in madness, or in death?"[5] Did you put a hold on your life, Emerson wants to know, and play possum to the world? Interestingly enough, the term *rigor mortis* enters the language just a few years after Emerson's journal entry, in 1847, to describe the stiffening of the body following death.

In the nineteenth century, at least, we simply cannot separate the idea of death from the click of a camera—"shooting" holds them together. Since each photograph consists of one more ghostly version of the person, contemporary critics found the camera guilty of removing the person layer by layer, just as Balzac had insisted. Peter's shadow serves as a photograph of Peter himself, his veil or film, if you will; his loss of that shadow is, in very key ways, Balzac's statement, or Emerson's insights, recast as a contemporary children's story. It, too, casts its own shadow—in the form of a deeper meaning, of a warning to the age.

And so, on another, perhaps more important level, the story of Peter Schlemihl carries a message about the sun. Schlemihl is a schlemiel because what he really craves is a kind of Mephistophelean power: Peter wants to master time. We cast no shadow only when the sun shines directly over our heads. For Peter to live without a shadow the sun must remain forever at high noon. In Goethe's rendering of the Faust legend, Faust practically explodes with joy at one of the devil's tricks and declares that he loves it so much he never wants the moment to end: "Shall I say to the moment/'Stay a while! You are so beautiful!'" Peter could be sitting for one of those daguerreotypes that Emerson describes, sitting still forever, alive but looking very much dead.

Peter does not want the sun to move through the sky—that is, he does not want the Earth to move around the sun—which, translated, means that Peter wants to stay forever young. In effect, with that wish, Peter throws out all hope of learning, all need for experience, all desire for growing older and perhaps even wiser. And of course he throws out all possibility of pain. This is, of course, his undoing. Dorian Gray comes face to face with this very same lesson. No matter, this is what people in the period seem to crave—eternal life, eternal youth—just as people do today, as evidenced through Botox injections and cosmetic surgery of all sorts. But of course we cannot conquer time.

I should reconsider that line, "we cannot conquer time." For isn't that the inevitability of technology, the annihilation of time and speed? And that is exactly what happens with the photograph—the moment frozen forever for our delight and enjoyment. It's in the human context where things go haywire, where we lose control. Schlemihl deceives himself; he thinks that stopping time can happen. He thinks he can dispense with his shadow forever and live in the bright moment. But he gets it wrong: Our shadow sticks to us. Only in certain circumstances do we lose it, and only momentarily. In the ancient world, for example, when people cross to the other side they lose their shadow selves, their dark experiences, in the River Lethe, the river of forgetfulness. At the same time, *Shades* is another name for the realm of the underworld, the netherworld where the dead and the shadows reside—the place more commonly called Hades. In our own time, the groundhog comes out of his burrow on February 2—Candlemas—and if he sees his shadow, he must go back underground for another six weeks, when presumably it will be spring. In sidereal terms, the groundhog remains out in the open only when the sun shines directly over his head, making him lose his dreary shadow. This is the true definition of solstice— *sol* meaning "sun," and *stitium* meaning "a stoppage." The sun stands still twice a year—at each of the solstices, both summer and winter.

Another way of saying all this is that, try as we might, we cannot occupy two places at once: A person cannot both remain young (this requires stopping the sun) and, at the same time, push his or her way through the world (that is, move through time). So many people, so many creatures, in this period, however, do occupy dual categories at once—from vampires and somnambulists to patients in comas and others in anesthetized or hypnotized states. The nineteenth century exploits a very special space, a psychic hovering; the nineteenth century loves a conundrum.

Peter, however, wants nothing of ambiguity. He prefers to be all Doctor Jekyll; he wishes to rid himself of his Mister Hyde. In the very fundamental sense of the word, Peter demands clarity—a fully and continually bright-lit life. He refuses to change, to risk any experience, to jump into this life on this very Earth, which in the nineteenth century went by the name of the nether world in ancient times, the *Shades*. In Robert Louis Stevenson's story *The Strange Case of Dr. Jekyll and Mr. Hyde,* Jekyll must kill his al-ter ego Hyde, he thinks, to survive. But Jekyll commits the murder in vain. Nothing much happens from his transgression except to generate for him tremendous amounts of guilt and punishment. Stevenson's lesson seems to be not one of exclusion and elimination, but one of integration, acceptance, and embrace. Like Peter's shedding of his shadow, the death of Hyde leads to the downfall of Jekyll.

What can we conclude from all this? Can it be that we should see Count Dracula as one of the heroes of the nineteenth century, and as someone who provides a lesson for us today? Perhaps that's so, for the Count absolutely refuses to be defined, corralled, or classified. He has a presence only as a creature both dead and alive simultaneously. As Falstaff says of Mistress Quickly, "a man knows not where to have her." Doctor Frankenstein's monster, too, hovers between two categories, moving across the German countryside, at one and the same time, as both human and nonhuman. These characters, like some thoroughly baffling Zen koan, can settle into their ambiguity without needing to reach resolution. They derive their very power from that confusion and ambiguity and total disregard of logic. Such characters put the lie to all those essentialists in the nineteenth century who attempted to find the one and only basic nature of the human being.

Meanwhile, the nineteenth century was fast closing in on the goal of defining and categorizing everything in creation. Scientists and philoso-phers wanted to place every last thing in its right spot and category. They demanded that every part of the created universe must have its proper home. Taxonomies and periodic charts defined and ordered and registered every element, tree, rock, animal, and race of human being. Zoos and botanical gardens and museums helped to arrange and order the wide range of natural phenomena.

In imitation of the scientists, bureaucrats collected statistics on everything from crime rates to birthrates, from the numbers of people who died in their homes to the numbers of people in asylums or living on the street. Two historians of science, Lorraine Daston and Peter Galison, note that "the gathering of state statistics on a large scale coincides historically with the French and American Revolutions and the concerted nation building of the first half of the nineteenth century, both of which redefined the categories of putative homogeneity and heterogeneity."

As science went about its task of placing the world under its giant thumb, those things that managed to defy definition seemed all the more strange and bizarre and out of the "ordinary," where the *ordo* in *ordinary* refers to the Church's liturgical calendar, to its fine-tuning and ordering of the entire year. Under these conditions, the definition of what constitutes normalcy takes on an especial clarity, and the criminal and the deviant seem, in contrast but with equal clarity, much more aberrant. The outcast lands far outside the norm.

The narrowing of the definition of normalcy and normal behavior meant a radical and dramatic increase in the numbers of people in America, over the course of the nineteenth century, who found themselves consigned by some state agency to a mental institution or an asylum. Authorities decided who was crazy, and then coined a word, *deviant,* to describe them. Psychologists defined their behavior, and warned the public what to look out for. As the century wore on, the numbers of deviants increased dramatically. Not only did the population increase in gross terms, say, in the United States, but the per capita number of crazies increased, as well. Great Britain was the first nation to recognize the growing problem of insanity by passing an act, in 1808, establishing a public lunatic asylum. America quickly followed, and local authorities very quickly filled the beds.

The statistics are shocking. According to Nancy Tomes and Lyn Gamwell's book *Madness in America: Cultural and Medical Perceptions of Mental Illness before 1914,* "the increasing number of hospitals [in the United States] that treated the insane, from 18 in 1800, to almost 140 in 1880, reflected not only population growth, but also a greater demand for the asylum's services. The ratio of hospital beds for the insane to the adult population grew dramatically, from 1 for every 6,000 persons over age 15 in 1800, to 1 for every 750 persons in 1880." In England, according to the historian of asylums Roy Porter, "around 1800, no more than a few thousand lunatics were confined in England in all kinds of institutions; by 1900, the total had skyrocketed to about 100,000." During the period, Porter points out, the press referred to these institutions as "museums of madness."[7]

In both England and America, physicians consigned a good number of these people to asylums because they had been diagnosed with dual or split personalities, which nineteenth-century medicine chose to call a "dissociated personality": "A pathological state of mind in which two or more distinct personalities exist in the same person."[8] We might add here that split personalities competed side by side with the double for attention. But while the doppelgänger might work well inside a story or a novel, acting that way on the streets would land a person in an asylum. The word *paranoia* first appears in English in 1857 and translates *para,* "beside," and *noia,* "mind." A paranoid experiences an acute doubling—literally standing beside his or her own being.

This desire for incarceration did not let up in the twentieth and twenty-first centuries, as if each cell were a category and each person a defined villain. The focus merely shifted from the mental institution to the prison, from the insane to the criminal, from the people at the margin to the people of color. So, for instance, the United States, with only five percent of the world's population, houses twenty-five percent of the world's prisoners.

This country can boast of the highest incarceration rate per one hundred thousand people of any other developed country in the world. The United States arrests adult male African Americans at a higher rate than did South Africa during the height of apartheid.

Throughout the second half of the twentieth century, the three growth industries included hotels and gambling, but what led, usually, was the prison industry. But though the focus changed, the definition remained the same: Criminals led dual lives, with one part of their personalities out in the bright light of day and the other operating in the dead of night. Authorities still describe the criminal, today, as dissociated.

No entity in the nineteenth century relishes that definition of dissociation with more delight than a ghost. The French refer to a ghost as a *revenant,* derived from the word *revenir,* "to return," and is cognate with *revenue.* The ghost, like money, circulates, picking up more and more interest as it courses through the world. For the French literary critic Jacques Derrida, as I have said, the revenant represents the spirit of capitalist striving: "the specter is the becoming fetish of the commodity,"[9] a subject that Karl Marx takes up in his discussion of capital. Money haunts: Almost every person anticipates—expects and may even pray for—its continual appearance and reappearance. Buying a ticket in the state lottery is like attending a séance, in that the player tries to raise the ghost of wealth that lurks somewhere in the beyond, and against overwhelming odds tries and tries again. It's a game thoroughly saturated with superstition and premonition, the player searching the universe for divine signs to the right combination of numbers for the Really Big Visitation.

The revenant behaves like money in another crucial way, for some charter sects, notably the charismatic and Pentecostal traditions, instruct parishioners to give their money away—say goodbye to handfuls of tens and twenties—in the hopes that much more will come back in return. Christians call this strategy of multiplying one's wealth by giving it away the concept of seed money. The infinite bounty of seed money gets represented in the

Middle Ages by the pomegranate; while one seed will produce one only tree, each pomegranate contains thousands of seeds and there must exist in the world millions of pomegranate trees.

We greet every ghost, in our own dissociative way, with a simultaneous goodbye and hello, since every one of them comes from the land of the dead where we have said our farewells to the departed—and yet there it is, standing in front of us, forcing us to acknowledge its arrival with a reluctant hello. Like the stroke of midnight at the last moment of the year, the ghost haunts the most invisible of lines where it is no longer last year and not yet the New Year: the exact stroke situating us neither here nor there. It is the most rare moment of the year, for it leaves us hanging in time, suspended and stretched. In the nineteenth century, the ghost is the ultimate border runner.

One very radical and enormously influential scientist, Erwin Schroedinger, spent his formative years in the nineteenth century, where he absorbed the age's compulsive drive toward order and conclusiveness. Schroedinger appears to have reacted sharply to that age's stance. In the following century, Schroedinger helped found a branch of science called quantum mechanics that radically transformed the traditional way people conceived of physics. Schroedinger found the essence of all life in the cracks between categories; he went after that which could not be held within a tightly bound and logically predicated definition. He refused to accept most definitions. In his hands, physics would confirm the truth of the world that nineteenth-century literature had so desperately tried to dramatize. Erwin Schroedinger built a system of science on the idea of the defiance of categories, logic, definitions, and, perhaps most startling, common sense.

Schroedinger postulated what he called the quantum theory of super-position, which says that an object may exist in several states at once, but when a person observes that very same object it always collapses into one state. Schroedinger annoyed those outside the scientific community by arguing, for example, that his cat could be both alive and dead at the same time, but that when he looked at it, the cat always collapsed into the one state—of total aliveness. Historians of science have taken to calling this phenomenon the observer's paradox. And to name this situation that ran so counter to logic, Schroedinger paid homage to a fantastical work of nineteenth-century literature: He described the condition of his mystifying cat as Draculated. While a good many people either laughed at Schroedinger or ignored him, the Nobel Committee took him seriously enough to award him the prize in physics, in 1933, for his revolutionary and extraordinarily counterintuitive work.

Schroedinger allowed us ordinary people to believe in either/or at the same moment. People always feel great sadness on leaving the old year behind, but that gets overlaid with an overwhelmingly great excitement in moving into the new, pristine year, where anything is possible because, for that one great reason and on that one great occasion, they have not yet made any mistakes. The New Year offers every person, just like the lottery, the chance for a new beginning, an opportunity to attempt the same thing all over again, to forgive oneself, and to watch the wheel of time turn wearily around again, but with no strikes against one. It is as close as we can possibly get to the idea of a clean slate.

The guardian of the threshold into the New Year, the formidable, two-faced god Janus, is the god of either/or. He cries and laughs at the same time—the common denominator of intense crying and laughing, his tears. In Roman mythology, Janus stations himself in front of doorways, at gates, and at the entrances to bridges; he guards the threshold and sees it all and knows it all and yet, like a shadow, reveals absolutely nothing. He leaves every last bit of information to interpretation. Janus refuses to be classified, for at one and the same time, the great god says hello and he says goodbye. Classical busts depict him as two-faced but not splintered, for he is conjoined forever in marble in one dramatic head. Janus may look like he is about to split apart, but he hangs solidly together. He sharpens his gaze in particular at the beginning of every new millennium, for at those moments he must gaze into the deep past and peer into the distant future.

And so both his crying and laughing—and ours, as well—grow louder and more intense at the turn of the millennium. As 1999 rolled over into 2000, the general sadness seemed profound; after all, the century was coming to a close. Most of us had used the phrase "the twentieth century" our entire lives. And soon whatever reality the twentieth century actually possessed would be gone—totally and utterly vanished. But, at the same time, the fireworks announcing the New Year, from all reports around the world, certainly went off in the night sky with more noise and more brilliance than any display that anyone had ever witnessed before. TV stations followed the turning of the heavens, moving from country to country as the night seemed to go on and on forever.

There was, however, a rub. For that particular turn of the century, that particular passage into the millennium came freighted with an additional burden. Most of the world, it had become more and more clear, was riding into the future with the aid of computers. That New Year represented a new test for technology, and it represented a new test for the new human being—not the disembodied one, the disappeared one we have been discussing in this book, and not even the end of the nineteenth-century being that Balzac described, comprising layer upon layer of ghosts. Here was a new binary being, one made of bits and bytes, one seemingly composed totally out of an accumulation of data.

One need not belabor the point that, as human beings, our lives have been shaped and directed by the so-called revolution in technology. The computer has by now gotten under the skin of the culture and seriously shaped people's interior lives. We have now become so fastened to the image, to the simulacrum over the real, for instance, that the masters of the blogosphere—those who navigate the Internet a good portion of the day and who go by the techno-moniker "netizens"—band together as "cyber-vigilantes" to humiliate their victims on forums and chat rooms. This phenomenon started in China after the 2008 earthquake, when the cyber Klan rooted out those unsympathetic to the dead and dying. They use a strongly violent phrase when they spring into their electronic lynching mode: "Call out the human flesh search engines." Which is to say, find the actual person, discover all we can about that person, and then proceed to humiliate him or her online, including posting the person's birthday, cell phone number, and home address. Realize that in China such an onslaught can add up to 160 million so-called netizens.

While it sounds like the mob equivalent of a contract on an enemy, and in this case bloggers have to make an emphatic point in order to talk about real humans and real flesh, they still cast the threat in electronic terms. They still have a hard time breaking out of the parameters of communication. Think of the absurdity: A search engine will hunt you down and tear you up! We have become locked inside the language of the computer, a new version of the ghost in the machine.

What distinguishes this new phase of our disappearance lies in the fact that computer programs most decidedly cannot accept ambiguity. An electronic impulse cannot be both on and off at the same time. Computers run on a binary principle—on a system that is on one instant and off the next. The machine pulses with a series of ones and zeros—usually represented by 101, the same number that also happens to hang on the door to the Ministry of Love's torture chamber, in George Orwell's dystopian novel *1984*. In that room, Winston Smith will face his torturers—that is, the ministry will force him to face his own worst fears, rats. The computer cannot be on and off at the same time. Schroedinger could never describe a computer program as Draculated.

In 2008, the Science Museum in London built two replicas of the mathematician Charles Babbage's Difference Engine No. 2 from Babbage's own 1847 designs. Babbage designed the machine, which weighs five tons and has eight thousand parts, as a gear-driven calculator based on Newton's method for performing mathematical integration. Dissatisfied with his first efforts, Babbage went on to develop the more refined Analytical Engine, a programmable mechanical computer. Many technology wonks consider it the real prototype of the modern computer. J. David Bolter, in his book *Turing's Man: Western Culture in the Computer Age,* places "Babbage and his protégés, among them the Countess of Lovelace, Byron's Daughter, [as] genuine visionaries. In their writing we often find expressions of a world view fully a century ahead of its time. If the Analytical Machine had been built, it would indeed have been the first computer . . . "

•✦•

MUCH LIKE OUR COMPUTERS, we operate only with great difficulty in situations of ambiguity, or opt out of those situations entirely. We need sanctions for our every action. Even in the case of torture, we now know that several memoranda from the Justice Department gave wide latitude to the CIA to use interrogation methods that might otherwise be prohibited under international law. So while the Geneva Conventions prohibit "outrages upon personal dignity," for example, the Justice Department made clear, in several memoranda, that it had not drawn a precise line in deciding which interrogation methods would violate that standard. Those memos sound like Orwell wrote them, except this statement comes from a deputy assistant attorney general: "That fact that an act is undertaken to prevent a threatened terrorist attack, rather than for the purpose of humiliation or abuse, would be relevant to a reasonable observer in measuring the outrageousness of the act." Newspeak or Uniquack—who knows?

The text as metaphor for organizing our interior lives has been replaced by the computer screen, a medium on which we write with letters of light, which we can make totally disappear with a touch of a delete key. The computer has brought us to the completion of a cycle of disembodiment, of disappearance at perhaps a deeper level. Not only have we become ghosts, but, writing with light, we have also turned into ghostwriters. One of the most permanent of our activities, writing, is now a tenuous and tentative activity.

As a people, we have grown accustomed to the act of deletion; we use it with ease. Most insidiously, deletion has wormed its way into the language as one of its principal metaphors. Imagine anyone, after the experience of Hiroshima and Nagasaki, saying that he or she would even contemplate eliminating an entire nation—wiping it, as people say in an effort to make the reality more remote, "off the map." But that's just what Hillary Clinton said about Iran during the presidential campaign in April of 2008. Responding to a question asking how she would respond as president if Iran were to use nuclear weapons (which it does not have) on Israel (which does have them), she proudly declared that she would "totally obliterate them." I understand that answer as genocide on the largest scale—the eradication of every man, woman, and child, to say nothing of the animals and the flora and fauna—in the nation. The computer does not have a deterrence button—too bad for us—only one marked *delete*.

We can understand, quite graphically, the extent to which the computer has taken over our "lives" by looking back to the end of the year in 1999. The technological revolution unmoored the text from the book, and with it went the familiar metaphors of literacy: reading character, as Freud did in the nineteenth century; or reading minds as Houdini did during that same time; or reading movies, as contemporary audiences do. Ivan Illich points out that the "first to use writing no longer as a metaphor but as an explanatory analogy was . . . a physicist, the Jewish emigrant Erwin Schroedinger. . . . He suggested that genetic substance could best be understood as a stable text whose occasional variations had to be interpreted as textual variations. As a physicist, Schroedinger stepped completely beyond his domain formulating this biological model."[10] Maybe more than any other person, Schroedinger understood those new, post-literate people and had just the right scientific background to comment on what the future held for them.

Those metaphors of literacy slowly became disembedded from the culture during the course of the twentieth century. Such a rupture could take place because the book, as the crucible for carrying knowledge in the culture, was slowly dying out, only to be replaced by the computer and all its affiliates—Internet, websites, blogs, chat rooms, threads, and on and on. The deeply embedded metaphor for carrying knowledge—the book—gave way over the century to various kinds of screens—movie, television, computer, cell phone, and computer game consoles. In the process, people found themselves reduced to programs and data.

In the midst of that low-level and constant hum of machines, a very terrible scare marked the final years of the last century, a scare that revealed just how dependent the general population had become *on* computers, and just what kind of beings we had now become because *of* them. A small technological "glitch" threatened to make the entirety of data on which we construct our everyday lives evaporate into the ether. That disappearing act, dubbed Y2K by the technology community, was to commence at another monumental, liminal moment, midnight, January 1, 2000—the beginning of both the new century *and* the new millennium. Experts attributed the problem to a small matter in the way computers inventory time.

Let me first mention an earlier scare about the very same issue—about telling time—from the preceding century. We can think of Y2K as an electronic version of a catastrophe that threatened life from the nineteenth century. Recall that on November 18, 1883, America's railroads put the entire nation on standard time. Jack Beatty, in his book *Age of Betrayal,* probably without knowing about Peter Schlemihl, recasts the event this way: "On November 18, 1883, America's railroad corporations stopped time." The *Indianapolis Daily Sentinel* pointed to a certain natural absurdity in that temporal shift: "The sun is no longer to boss the job. . . . The sun will be requested to rise and set by railroad time. The planets must, in the future, make their circuits by such timetables as railroad magnates arrange."

Where people for centuries had experienced time mainly with the sun, they would now measure, let's say, high noon by a railroad schedule. The *New York Herald* observed that standard public time "goes beyond the public pursuits of men and enters into their private lives as part of themselves." The new time severed whatever relationship people had with the heavens. The rising and setting of the sun had determined local times for centuries; now, by tampering with the local sun, the railroads threatened to upset the natural world.

On November 17—the day before the proposed change—*The New York Times* reported that city jewelers "were busy answering questions from the curious, who seemed to think that the change in time would . . . create a sensation . . . some sort of disaster, the nature of which would not be exactly entertained." Jack Beatty relates the story of the following day, November 18, "The Day of Two Noons," as the *New York World, The Washington Post,* and the important *Boston Evening Transcript* called it: "The master clock at Chicago's West Side Union Depot was stopped at 12:00, waiting for the railroad-decreed noon." People huddled around the large clock; they talked and they debated, but mostly they waited. Finally, the long-awaited news: At precisely nine minutes and thirty-two seconds after high noon, a telegraph arrived announcing the start of 12:00 in public standard railroad time. In matters of telling time, the sun had stopped dead in its tracks across the sky, which is to say, I suppose, the Earth stood stock still.

In those nine minutes and thirty-two seconds "out of time," people feared the absolute worst. Schlemihl could not stop time; but technology seemed to have pulled it off. What would be the fallout? Ordinary nineteenth-century Americans had the Bible, Joshua 10:12–14, to frighten them: "So the sun stood still, and the moon stopped, till the nation avenged itself of its enemies, as it is written in the Book of Jashar. The sun stopped in the middle of the sky and delayed going down for about a full day." God gave Joshua a gift of time at the battle of Jericho. Believers know it as the longest day ever. And here it was, right in their midst, except big and powerful industry was intervening, not God. On top of that, the railroads had chosen to make the change on a Sunday. What could it all mean? More to the point, what *would* it all mean?

But of course nothing overtly catastrophic ensued. No disasters followed. People argued over the power of railroad magnates, but business went on as usual. For a brief time people asked, "Have you the new time?" But no one recorded any obvious major tragedies. In fact, it took until 1918 and an act of Congress for the federal government to cede time to the country's railroads.

But a severing did occur. Anyone in Chicago who was used to looking into the sky and judging high noon would find himself or herself forever off by nine minutes and thirty-two seconds. In the scheme of the universe, that does not seem like a big thing, but it does represent a shift—a small but significant shift—away from one's own place in nature to a move toward the mechanical and the commercial.

Only one person commented, and then only indirectly, on the major change. An editor of a local newspaper in Nebraska had this to say about the incursion of the railroad into people's lives, both in terms of time and space: "In a quarter of a century, they have made the people of the country homogeneous, breaking through the peculiarities and provincialisms which marked separate and unmingling sections."[11] Train travel does not represent the only erasure of the human being, but it certainly exerted a major force in eroding the differences in individuals.

After all, the railroad hauled people—one person much the same as the next—from one place to another, through those various zones of localized time. Take a load of people from New York and set them down in Chicago, say, change watch time, and, in a snap, they all suddenly emerge as Chicagoans. Only the accent—or lack of accent—would give any of them away.

Michael O'Malley opens his chapter on public standard time with the following paragraph. It so much summarizes the thrust of the age, I want to quote it in full. It also serves as a transition to Y2K, for it prepared the way for transforming time into bits: "American astronomers, drawing on technological innovations like the telegraph, had created a new understanding of time by 1880. The observatories made time a product. They captured an apparently natural phenomenon, distilled what they understood to be its essence—order—and then offered this essence for sale in tidy, attractive packages."[12]

When the ball fell on the year 1999, many experts predicted, the world would witness the worst of all manmade disasters. Unlike the temporal change in the nineteenth century, no one seriously questioned this one, which got labeled, in appropriate machine language, Y2K. America's entire financial, governmental, and social system would utterly and totally disappear into that nineteenth-century quintessential stuff, the ether. Few experts were willing to predict the extent of the devastation, but most critics described it as if a huge bomb might go off in our midst, sending shock waves and shrapnel throughout the population all over the world. No one—not a single soul—would be exempt. No one would get a free ride.

The reason for the crisis exposes the very nature of computing. From the late 1960s on, computer software stored dates with two digits rather than four in order to save memory on what were fairly expensive disks. As the nineties came to a close, computer experts realized that their programs might read double zero not as the year 2000 but as the year 1900. What an amazing irony, as if the universe were sending a message, telling us that we were forever stuck at the juncture between the close of the nineteenth century and the opening of the twentieth; that we were condemned to repeat that century because we had learned absolutely nothing from it. The film *Groundhog Day* captured the dilemma perfectly.

If that were to happen, we would inhabit two places at once: finding ourselves standing in the twenty-first century, but with all of the dates clearly pointing to the twentieth or even the nineteenth. We would be dead in this century, and alive only in the nineteenth. No matter how loud we screamed, "Look, I am alive," we could not prove that we were indeed alive. We would be in possession of no records to prove even who we actually were. Only when someone observed us would we then come alive.

Through our own inept computing designs, and our own foolhardy reliance on numbers, we would have made a seer out of Erwin Schroedinger, for we would all be fully Draculated.

Of course, we could not tolerate such a frustrating state of affairs. Computers made it a certainty that as a people we could not tolerate such ambiguity. Computers dictated that we needed but one definition, one place, one time. Schroedinger be damned! And so IT companies around the world spent billions and billions of dollars to correct the glitch. Systems application companies worked feverishly to develop compliant software to combat the problem. The race was on to try to beat the countdown to the end of the millennium. If we hoped for victory, then the technocrats of the world would have to stop time in its tracks. Of course, the poorer nations could not afford the fix, and moved into the future only with the mercy and generosity of the more wealthy countries and the aid granted by IT companies. The fear was real and the fear was widespread.

But the most potent fear by far was the loss of what went by the name of something called personal identity: Every number on which we found ourselves, the argument went, would disappear—gone would be social security numbers, bank account numbers, savings account numbers, driver's license numbers, cholesterol and blood pressure levels. Our bank deposits would be gone. The numbers of our bank accounts would no longer exist. All of our contracts, records, transcripts—everything that had been digitized would be erased just as the ball dropped in Times Square. We would no longer know who we were, for on one very crucial and decidedly deep level, at least, we are nothing but a string of integers.

The ball fell, the numbers turned over, and, well, nothing happened except for the new morning—all foreplay and no climax. The sun did not stop in the sky and the crisis did not end on January 1, 2001. For Y2K was but a prelude, a brief prelude, to a more recent and terrifying loss of self, total identity theft—or what I choose to call electronic cloning. The self had fallen into the flimsiest of constructions—of little or no use any longer.

Our identities can be eradicated in an instant with a simple hack of any corporate computing system, or even of our own personal computers. On the Internet, we can become anything we want; we can use any name we choose; we can construct any identity we prefer. The self is as slippery and elusive as one wishes it to be.

The most ordinary people take on the wildest new identities on the Internet, construct entirely fanciful lives on the World Wide Web. Such is the nature of the postmodern, protean self. In the digital age, we can deconstruct the self with utter ease, and reconstruct with that same ease. We can split ourselves into many different voices without fearing the punishment of the insane asylum. As the old joke goes, On the Internet, no one knows you're a dog.

It does little good to say, "This is who I am," and then offer up a name, an address, a zip code, as if we were the product of a self-interrogation. In a sense, we all now carry fake IDs. Besides, you can find me, or a facsimile of me, on MySpace or Facebook. How *do* we, then, talk about who we are, about what makes us human in this, the twenty-first century, and about what place we occupy in the grander scheme of things? How do we stop the disappearing act that began in the nineteenth century and which continues to rush on through our own time?

In another century, Poe warned that people were being buried alive; Emerson countered, No, they just needed to take deeper breaths to find out that they were very much alive; he pointed to the ultimate power of the self. Oscar Wilde exposed society's criminal underbelly; the reverend Henry Ward Beecher revealed society's magnificent soul. Oliver Wendell Holmes condemned people's greed; Darwin celebrated humankind's roots. Some warned about losing humanness, while others showed the way back to power and strength and autonomy. In the end, however, very few people listened. They took the subway to Coney; they had a drink; they watched a movie; they turned on TV; they played a video game. They had fun. The questions linger, and they constitute our legacy: What is essential? What is of meaning? Of permanence? What allows us, as human beings, not merely to endure, but to prevail?

I certainly offer no definitive answer; that would be presumptuous and even arrogant. In the end, people must find their own solutions. They first have to think that a problem exists. But framing the question correctly can sometimes prove helpful. The answer will undoubtedly be different for each person. It may be love, friendship, family, but each response rests on a powerful belief in real, live people. We can find no solution to any of our grand contemporary problems—war, terrorism, global warming—without first participating in this most basic project: the recovery of the human being. By lifting the veil, we can, hopefully, become more than spectators at a deposition.

Any solution to the vitality of our own being, I believe, now requires slipping out from a system that does not admit of ambiguity; that wants to keep us tightly and solidly defined. People struggle, it seems, to regain some of that ambiguity on the very machine that robs them of it—by spinning new selves on the web. There is tremendous irony here, for they are being forced into that kind of splintering just to feel whole and alive—and trying to feel more real on a virtual canvas called the monitor. This is part of the great appeal currently of the work of Patricia Highsmith, and in particular of her novel *The Talented Mr. Ripley*. To assume another identity, as young Tom Ripley does, with such audacity takes a great act of bravery and great exercise of will. One has to assert one's entire being in just being.

In the broadest outlines of the story, Tom kills the man whose identity he assumes, Dickie Greenleaf, so that he can inherit his enormous wealth. The false Dickie—Tom—then disappears, leaving a "suicide" note that praises Tom for his valor and self-righteousness. From that point on, Tom haunts the novel with a most ghostly presence: People discuss his character, wonder about his whereabouts, and attempt to make contact with him. But he is essentially gone—sort of.

And then, like any good revenant, Tom reappears, having left Italy for some undisclosed location, somewhere in Greece. Highsmith gives us two Toms—Tom as Tom and Tom as Dickie—just as Twain gives us two Hucks—Huck as Huck and Huck as any number of other personalities, even a young girl. Huck leaves a similar suicide note at the very outset of the novel, only to resurface toward the end of the story as the real live Huckleberry Finn. In *Mr. Ripley*, Tom holds a powerful but unspoken sexual fascination for Dickie; in the film, they look slightly alike and exchange provocative glances. At any rate, Highsmith clearly wants the reader to see the two young men as doubles, with Tom of course as the darker side willing to kill for what he wants.

Like someone taking off a jacket and having the sleeves turn inside out, the demimonde of the nineteenth century, like Tom, has come to the surface of our period and threatens to dominate it. I think this is the current fascination with the thug and gangster aesthetic—prison clothing, tough-guy talk in music, tough-guy assassinations, prison haircuts, song lyrics, and on and on. I put those things in the same category as bodybuilding, tattoos, and steroids, attempts to take up more space, to "live large and in charge." They constitute attempts to come alive; they make obvious the problem at a visceral level—people wanting to be fully alive. And one gets little instruction on how to plunge safely into life. (I do not count Doctor Phil as an instructor here.)

In the context of a culture dominated by the programmatic rule of either/or, I find the most promising examples in people allowing themselves to break out of that binary bind by overthrowing the categories of gender. Movements that remove people from easy categorization—gender being the prime example—have supplanted the protest and liberation movements of the fifties and sixties. Identity politics, including the switching of gender roles, cross-dressing, the transition into something called transgender identification, and many other permutations—represent today's attempt, on one very powerful level, for some people who are trying to maintain their basic essence and humanity. I refer here to people trying to discover who they really are. Of course, this appeals to only a small part of the population. The great majority of people must find their own way. But those who think of themselves in this new sexual revolution may serve as a model. After several centuries of moving toward essentialism, this can truly be called antiessentialist; and that is a good part of its power and appeal.

These movements toward gender liberation resemble the permutations of the self of the Internet, but with this difference: Those identities arise from deep inside the fleshy and sensual body. What we see in contemporary gender politics is a definite move toward embodiment and a curious kind of ownership. A bumper sticker reads, KEEP THE US OUT OF MY UTERUS. Pro-choice offers a chance at this kind of ambiguity if only because it demands that the person *make* a choice, and the choice is not always easy—not always, as they say, so black and white. What takes place here is a different enfleshing impulse, it seems to me, from bodybuilding and anabolic steroids. People here do not wish to merely take up space or to look powerful or even scary. Instead, they prefer to be enfleshed, to be alive, to feel alive.

The literary critic Marjorie B. Garber published a crucial book, in 1991, entitled *Vested Interests: Cross-Dressing and Cultural Anxiety*, in which she makes the offhand comment that the transvestite has the power "to unsettle assumptions, structures and hierarchies." Commenting on her book, Adam Phillips notes that the "transvestites' power to unsettle is proof, if we needed it, of how precarious our categories are, and how uncertain we are as the makers of categories . . . dressing up and cross-dressing reveal something of the bizarre logic of our senses of identity; and how a world of entitlement—of privileged positions and secure identities—conceals an underworld of (sometimes desperate) improvisation."[13]

We can only thrive in the midst of confusion and ambiguity if we have our shadows returned to us—which is to say that we need to embrace the darkest sides of our personality. We must refuse to be defined in one way only. We must refuse the desire to have the sun shining brightly, directly overhead, as the transhuman movement so desperately seems to want. In "The Man Who Could Work Miracles," and in *The Time Machine,* H. G. Wells plays with time, moving clocks forward and moving them backward. And once again, as with so much other literature in the period, the experiments backfire and fall apart into rank disasters.

In one of the supreme reversals of literary history, those horrible monsters of the nineteenth century that frighten us and give us chills—Dracula, Frankenstein's creation, Mister Hyde, Raskolnikov, ghosts and ghouls in general—may really hold the answer to our own contemporary existence. Every one of those creatures from the nineteenth century derives its power and strength from its ambiguity. Each one of them can comfortably occupy two definitions at once. Indeed, none of them can stand to occupy a discrete category. The idea of the double is buried deep in the name Raskolnikov: *raskol,* Russian for "splitting" or "schism." Even the subtitle of Mary Shelley's *Frankenstein,* as we have seen, invokes not just Prometheus but by association also his twin, Epimetheus—in a powerful mythological doubling, an amalgam of what those two fallen gods stand for: foresight and hindsight.

One of those doubles is the zombie, who on close inspection looks very much like Schlemihl, but instead of buying a shadow, a magician has stolen the zombie's soul. As the writer Marina Warner points out,

> Unlike phantoms, who have a soul but no body, zombies and vampires are all body—but unlike the vampire who has will and desire and an appetite for life (literally), a zombie is a body which has been hollowed out, emptied of selfhood. The word 'zombie' derives from 'jumbie,' one of the most common words for 'spirit' in the Caribbean, appearing frequently in ghost stories, folk-tales, and documentary accounts of the archipelago throughout the last century.[14]

But buried in the story of the zombie is a potent reversal. The word first comes into the English language with the poet Robert Southey in his

History of Brazil (1810), where Southey gives the name to a revolutionary hero who led an uprising against Portuguese rule in Brazil. According
to Southey: "Zombi, the title whereby he [chief of Brazilian natives] was
called, is the name for the Deity, in the Angolan tongue. . . . N*Zambi* is
the word for Deity." (Compare the name of the African nation Zambia.)
Zombi, who stands at the opposite end of Schlemihl, would rather die than
live as a slave.

But then the *zombie* falls from its lofty position. Because of the abolition of slavery and then its reinstatement, the so-called zombies came to be
associated not with those who had achieved liberation, but with those who
found themselves, once again, enslaved and "hollowed out," with those
who found themselves forced to live without a sense of the self. That's
when the zombie took on the character, as all slaves ultimately do, of the
walking dead.

Marina Warner insists that "[z]ombies embody the principal ghostly
condition of our time . . . Soul-theft is a master plot that readers began
to recognize in the nineteenth century." We must keep in mind, however,
the zombie's potential, what it once had been, and what it can become.
Odd as it may seem, such a bizarre creation may hold key lessons for us
today. It may be time for us to learn from the so-called darker creatures
of the nineteenth century, those who traditionally give people the creeps.
For one of the great painters of the late nineteenth century, Gustav Klimt,
boundaries and categories dissolve allowing creatures to melt and fall
away and come back together again. Carl E. Schorske, musing on Klimt,
offers the following: "The snake, amphibious creature, phallic symbol
with bisexual associations, is the great dissolver of boundaries: between
land and sea, man and woman, life and death. This character accords well
with the concern with androgyny and the homosexual reawakening of the
fin-de-siècle."[15]

It may be time to see all those nineteenth-century dream monsters for
what they are, creations from fantastical writers and artists who push their

characters and images in one way or another to shed the stultifying world of category and definition and to find, once more, the true sense of self and thus of life.

ENDNOTES

INTRODUCTION | Pictures at a Deposition

1. Virginia Woolf, *Mr. Bennett and Mrs. Brown* (London: Hogarth, 1924), page 4.

2. Tony Judt, "Goodbye to All That?" *The New York Review of Books,* September 21, 2006.

3. Cited in Kenneth Silverman, *Lightning Man: The Accursed Life of Samuel F. B. Morse* (New York: Da Capo, 2004).

4. Silverman, *Lightning Man.*

5. Cited in Paul Hill, "Natural Magic and Moonlight," June 2008, in Henry Iddon, *Spots of Time: The Lake District Photographed by Night* (London: Wordsworth Trust, 2008), foreword.

6. Jean Baudrillard and Enrique Valiente Noailles, *Exiles from Dialogue* (Paris: Les Éditions Galilée, 2005).

ONE | What Is Life?

1. Georg Simmel, *Simmel on Culture: Selected Writings,* David Frisby and Mike Featherstone, eds. (New York: Sage Publications, 1998), passim.

2. *The Lumière Brothers' First Films,* dir. Bernard Tavernier.

3. Carmine Di Biase, "New Kid off the Old Block," *TLS* (March 21, 2008), page 22.

4. Martin Booth, *Opium: A History* (New York: St. Martin's Press, 1998), pages 22–23.

5. Ibid., page 69.

6. Cited on www.general-anaesthesia.com/images/Robert-southey.html.

7. Henry Smith Williams, *A History of Science,* Volume 4 (South Carolina: Bibliobazaar, 2007).

8. Quoted in Laurence K. Altman, "When the Doctors Are Their Own Best Guinea Pigs," *The New York Times,* October 9, 2005.

9. From www.chm.bris.ac.uk/motm/n20/n20c.htm.

10. Colin Evans, *The Father of Forensics: The Groundbreaking Cases of Sir Bernard Spilsbury* (New York: Berkley Publishing Group, 2006).

11. Sigmund Freud, *The Interpretation of Dreams,* trans. James Strachey (New York: HarperCollins, 1998), passim.

12. Daniel J. Kevles, *In the Name of Eugenics: Genetics and the Uses of Human Heredity* (Cambridge, MA: Harvard University Press, 1995).

13. Stephen Jay Gould, *The Mismeasure of Man* (New York: W. W. Norton, 1996).

14. Peter Burke, *Popular Culture in Early Modern Europe* (New York: HarperCollins, 1978).

15. Carl E. Schorske, *Fin-de-Siècle Vienna: Politics and Culture* (New York: Alfred A. Knopf), pages 8–9.

16. Karl Marx, speech at the anniversary of the *People's Paper,* 1856.

17. Marshall Berman, *All That Is Solid Melts into Air: The Experience of Modernity* (New York: Simon and Schuster, 1986), page 19.

18. Cited in Charles S. Whitney, *Bridges: Their Art, Science and Evolution* (New York: Greenwich House, 1983).

TWO | When Death Died

1. Quoted in Drew Gilpin Faust, *This Republic of Suffering: Death and the American Civil War* (New York: Alfred A. Knopf, 2008), page 58. I am indebted to Faust for information for this chapter.

2. James M. McPherson, "Dark Victories," *The New York Review of Books,* April 17, 2008.

3. From Plague in Gotham! Cholera in Nineteenth-Century New York, New-York Historical Society exhibition, June 2008.

Endnotes

4. Steven Johnson, *The Ghost Map: The Story of London's Most Terrifying Epidemic—and How It Changed Science, Cities, and the Modern World* (New York: Riverhead Books, 2006), page 13.

5. "Brady's Photographs: Pictures of the Dead at Antietam," *The New York Times*, October 20, 1862.

6. *Encyclopedia Britannica*, eleventh edition (1910–1911).

7. Faust, *This Republic of Suffering*, page 69.

8. See McPherson, "Dark Victories."

9. Gary Wills, *Lincoln at Gettysburg: The Words That Remade America* (New York: Simon and Schuster, 1992).

10. Faust, *This Republic of Suffering*, page 57.

11. Ibid., page 57.

12. Ibid., page 57.

13. Ibid., pages 66–67.

14. See Adam Gopnik, "In the Mourning Store," *The New Yorker*, January 21, 2008.

15. Faust, *This Republic of Suffering*, page 93.

16. Ibid., page 87.

17. Jan Bondeson, *Buried Alive: The Terrifying History of Our Most Primal Fear* (New York: Diane, 2004), page 221.

18. Faust, *This Republic of Suffering*, page 57.

19. Ibid., page 66.

20. Ibid., page 57.

21. Ibid., page 10.

22. Ibid., page 55.

23. Ibid., page 59.

24. Russell Baker, "The Entertainer," *The New York Review of Books*, November 3, 2005.

25. Ibid., page 39.

26. Human Rights Watch, "Torture in Iraq," *The New York Review of Books*, November 3, 2005.

27. Ivan Illich, "Death Undefeated," privately circulated.

THREE | A Couple of Sarahs Later

1. John Strausbaugh, "When Barnum Took Manhattan," *The New York Times,* November 9, 2007.

2. Ibid.

3. Quoted in Stephen Jay Gould, "The Hottentot Venus," in *The Flamingo's Smile: Reflections in Natural History* (New York: W. W. Norton, 1985), page 294.

4. Mike Hawkins, *Social Darwinism in European and American Thought, 1860–1945* (Cambridge: Cambridge University Press, 1997), pages 201–203.

5. Source for newspaper and Morton accounts is Gould, "The Hottentot Venus," page 294.

6. Robert W. Rydell, "'Darkest Africa': African Shows at America's World Fairs, 1893–1940," in Bernth Lindfors, ed., *Africans on Stage: Studies in Ethnological Show Business* (Bloomington and Indianapolis: Indiana University Press, 1999), page 145.

7. Gould, "The Hottentot Venus," page 293.

8. *The Life and Times of Sara Baartman,* dir. Zola Maseko, 1998.

9. Ibid.

10. Gould, "The Hottentot Venus," page 292.

11. Ibid., pages 298–299.

12. Letter from Sigmund Freud to Martha Bernays, November 8, 1885, (New York: Basic Books, 1975).

13. Ibid.

14. Robert Fizdale and Arthur Gold, *The Divine Sarah: A Life of Sarah Bernhardt* (New York: Alfred A. Knopf, 1991), page 221.

15. Ibid., page 220.

16. Quoted in Edward Rothstein, "Celebrity So Extraordinaire She Rivaled the Eiffel Tower," *The New York Times,* December 2, 2005.

17. Toni Bentley, *Sisters of Salome* (Lincoln and London: University of Nebraska Press, 2005), page 27.

18. Ibid., page 207.

19. Ibid., page 207.

20. Fizdale and Gold, *The Divine Sarah*, page 200.

21. Ibid., page 201.

22. Bentley, *Sisters of Salome*, page 36.

23. Ibid., page 31.

24. Carl Gustav Jung, *Man and His Symbols* (New York: Anchor Press, 1964), page 208.

25. Berman, *All That Is Solid Melts into Air*, page 109.

26. Gould, "The Hottentot Venus," page 298.

27. Friedrich Nietzsche, *The Gay Science*, trans. Walter Kaufmann (New York: Vintage Books, 1974), page 92.

FOUR | No One's Dead

1. Mary Shelley, *Frankenstein* (New York: Norton, 1995), Introduction.

2. Jim Steinmeyer, *Hiding the Elephant: How Magicians Invented the Impossible and Learned to Disappear* (New York: Carroll and Graf, 2003), page 23.

3. Ibid., page 31.

4. Ibid., page 41.

5. Rebecca Solnit, *River of Shadows: Eadweard Muybridge and the Technological Wild West* (New York: Penguin, 2004), page 183.

6. Quoted in Jay Leyda, *Kino: A History of the Russian and Soviet Film* (London: Allen and Unwin, 1960), page 407.

7. Quoted in Geoffrey Wolff, "'Mark Twain': Voice of America," *The New York Times*, October 2, 2005.

8. Quoted in Mark B. Sandberg, *Living Pictures, Missing Persons: Mannequins, Museums, and Modernity* (Princeton and Oxford: Princeton University Press, 2003), page 21.

9. Quoted in Vanessa R. Schwartz, *Spectacular Realities: Early Mass Culture in Fin-de-Siècle Paris* (Berkeley and Los Angeles: University of California Press, 1998), page 53.

10. Helen MacDonald, *Human Remains: Dissection and Its Histories* (New Haven and London: Yale University Press, 2005), page 11.

11. Stewart Evans and Paul Gainey, *Jack the Ripper: First American Serial Killer* (New York and Tokyo: Kodanska International, 1995), page 21.

12. Joyce Carol Oates, "'I Had No Other Thrill or Happiness,'" *The New York Review of Books,* March 24, 1994.

13. Ibid.

14. Joel Norris, *Serial Killers: The Growing Menace* (New York: Bantam, 1988), page 53.

15. MacDonald, *Human Remains,* page 17.

16. Deborah Blum, *Ghost Hunters: William James and the Search for Scientific Proof of Life After Death* (New York: Penguin Press, 2006), page 22.

17. See Wolfgang Schivelbusch, *The Railway Journey: The Industrialization of Time and Space in the Nineteenth Century* (Berkeley: University of California Press, 1986), for an extended discussion of this phrase.

18. Solnit, *River of Shadows,* page 11.

19. Ibid., page 18.

20. Solnit, *River of Shadows,* page 18.

21. Ibid., page 22.

22. Ibid., pages 41–42.

23. Tom Lutz, *American Nervousness, 1903: An Anecdotal History* (New York: Cornell University Press, 1993).

FIVE | There Is Only Life

1. Quoted in Jack Beatty, *Age of Betrayal: The Triumph of Money in America, 1865–1900* (New York: Vintage, 2007), page 302.

2. Ibid., page 192.

3. Ivan Illich, "The Institutional Construction of a New Fetish: Human Life," presented on March 29, 1989, Evangelical Lutheran Church of America meeting, Chicago.

4. Ibid.

5. Ibid.

6. Ivan Illich, "Brave New Biocracy: Health Care from Womb to Tomb," *New Perspectives Quarterly,* Winter 1994.

7. Illich, "The Institutional Construction of a New Fetish."

8. Illich, "Death Undefeated."

9. Anthony Kenny, "Life Stories," *Times Literary Supplement*, March 29, 2005.

10. "Dutch Ponder 'Mercy Killing' Rules," CNN, December 2, 2004.

11. Waldby quoted in Nikolas Rose, "The Value of Life: Somatic Ethics and the Spirit of Biocapital," *Daedalus*, Winter 2008, pages 36–48.

12. Ibid.

13. Quoted in George Johnson, *Miss Leavitt's Stars: The Untold Story of the Woman Who Discovered How to Measure the Universe* (New York: W. W. Norton, 2005).

14. Illumina, Inc., www.illumina.com.

15. Baudrillard and Noailles, *Exiles from Dialogue*, pages 33–34.

16. Ibid., page 34.

17. John Tierney, "The Future Is Now? Pretty Soon, at Least," *The New York Times*, June 3, 2008.

18. Personalized Medicine Coalition, www.personalizedmedicinecoalition.org.

19. Baudrillard and Noailles, *Exiles from Dialogue*, page 35.

20. Rose, "The Value of Life," page 40.

21. Genentech, www.gene.com.

22. Paul Kramer, "The Water Cure: Debating Torture and Counterinsurgency—A Century Ago," *The New Yorker*, February 25, 2008, page 56.

23. Ibid, pages 57–58.

SIX | Coney Island and the Mind

1. Friedrich Nietzsche, *Thus Spake Zarathustra* (New York: Random House, 1960), page 305.

2. Freud, *The Interpretation of Dreams*, page 41.

3. Adam Phillips, *On Flirtation: Psychoanalytic Essays on the Uncommitted Life* (London: Faber and Faber, 1994), page 25.

4. Sigmund Freud, "Screen-Memory," *The Standard Edition of the Complete Psychological Works of Sigmund Freud*, ed. James Strachey (London: Hogarth Press, 1953–1974), page 562.

5. Phillips, *On Flirtation*, page 67.

6. See John F. Kasson, *Amusing the Million: Coney Island at the Turn of the Century* (New York: Hill and Wang, 1978), page 52.

7. See Michael Immerso, *Coney Island: The People's Playground* (New York: Rutgers, 2002), passim.

8. Ralph Waldo Emerson, "Man the Reformer," in *Essays and Lectures* (New York: Library of America, 1983).

9. Randall Stross, "Edison the Inventor, Edison the Showman," *The New York Times*, March 11, 2007.

10. Edward Marshall, "'No Immortality of the Soul' Says Thomas A. Edison," *The New York Times*, October 2, 1910.

11. Neil Baldwin, *Edison: Inventing the Century* (Chicago: University of Chicago Press, 2001), page 317.

12. "Key Inventions of Nineteenth Century," *Economist*, December 20, 1997.

13. Richard Stengel, "1-900-Aural Sex," *Time*, February 3, 1992.

14. Reported by Blaine Harden, "An Incandescent Coney Island of the Mind," *The New York Times*, August 28, 1999.

15. Baldwin, *Edison*, page 401.

16. Ibid., page 452.

17. Caitlin Carpenter, "Self-Help Books Get the 'Tough Love' Treatment," *Christian Science Monitor*, February 7, 2008.

SEVEN | The Draculated Cat

1. Francis Adams and Barry Sanders, *Alienable Rights: The Exclusion of African Americans in a White Man's Land, 1619–2000* (New York: HarperCollins, 2004), passim.

2. Marina Warner, *Phantasmagoria: Spirit Visions, Metaphors, and Media into the Twenty-First Century* (New York: Oxford University Press, 2006), page 309.

3. Phillips, *On Flirtation*, page 153.

4. Rosalind Krauss, "Tracing Nadar," *October*, No. 102, 1978.

5. Caleb Crain, "The Art of the American Snapshot, 1888–1978, From the Collection of Robert E. Jackson," *The New York Review of Books*, May 1, 2008.

6. Lorraine Daston and Peter Galison, *Objectivity* (New York: Zone, 2007), passim.

7. Roy Porter, *Madness: A Brief History* (New York: Oxford University Press, 2003), pages 142–143.

8. Nancy Tomes and Lyn Gamwell, *Madness in America: Cultural and Medical Perceptions of Mental Illness before 1914* (New York: Cornell University Press, 1995), page 145.

9. Jacques Derrida, *Specters of Marx: The State of the Debt, the Work of Mourning, and the New International* (New York: Routledge, 2006), page 247.

10. Ivan Illich, "A Plea for Body History," March 1986, privately circulated.

11. Quoted in Michael O'Malley, *Keeping Watch: A History of American Time* (New York: Penguin, 1990), page 128.

12. Ibid., page 99.

13. Phillips, *On Flirtation*, page 127.

14. Warner, *Phantasmagoria*, page 357.

15. Schorske, *Fin-de-Siècle Vienna*, page 240.

SELECTED BIBLIOGRAPHY

Aczel, Amir D. *Pendulum: Leon Foucault and the Triumph of Science.* Atria Books: New York and London, 2003.

Adams, Francis and Barry Sanders. *Alienable Rights: The Exclusion of African Americans in a White Man's Land, 1619-2000.* Harper Collins: New York, 2004.

Altick, Richard. *The Shows of London.* Harvard University Press: Cambridge, Massachusetts, 1978.

Bajac, Quentin. *The Invention of Photography.* Harry N. Abrams, Inc., Publishers: New York, 2002.

Barber, X. Theodore. "Phantasmagorical Wonders: The Magic Lantern Ghost Show in Nineteenth-Century America." *Film History*, 3, 2 (1989), 73-86.

Barrow, Logie. *Independent Spirits, Spiritualism, and English Plebeians, 1850-1910.* Routledge and Kegan Paul: London, 1986.

Baudrillard, Jean. *The Spirit of Terrorism.* Trans. Chris Turner. Verso: London and New York, 2002.

Baudrillard, Jean and Enrique Valiente Niailles. *Exiles From Dialogue.* Trans. Chris Turner. Polity Press: Cambridge and Malden, Massachusetts, 2007.

Beatty, Jack. *Age of Betrayal: The Triumph of Money in America, 1865-1900.* Vintage Books: New York, 2008.

Beckman, Karen. *Vanishing Women: Magic, Film, and Feminism.* University of North Carolina Press: Durham, North Carolina, 2000.

Benjamin, Walter. *On Hashish.* Trans. Howard Elland. Harvard University Press: Cambridge, Massachusetts, 2006.

Bentley, Toni. *Sisters of Salome*. University of Nebraska Press: Lincoln and London, 2005.

Bergson, Henri. *Dreams*. Trans. Edwin E. Slosson. B.W. Huebsch: New York, 1914.

Berman, Marshall. *All That Is Solid Melts Into Air: The Experience of Modernism*. Penguin Books: New York, 1982.

Blaise, Clark. *Sir Sandford Fleming and the Creation of Standard Time*. Wiedenfeld and Nicolson: London, 2000.

Bloom, Harold. *Omens of Millennium: The Gnosis of Angels, Dreams, and Resurrection*. Riverhead Books: New York, 1997.

_____. *Romanticism and Consciousness: Essays in Criticism*. W.W. Norton and Company: New York, 1970.

Blum, Deborah. *Ghost Hunters: William James and the Search for Scientific Proof of Life After Death*. The Penguin Press: New York, 2006.

Bolter, J. David. *Turing's Man: Western Culture in the Computer Age*. The University of North Carolina Press: Chapel Hill, 1984.

Booth, Martin. *Opium: A History*. St. Martin's Press: New York, 1996.

Brandon, Ruth. *The Spiritualists: The Passion for the Occult in the Nineteenth and Twentieth Centuries*. Prometheus Books: New York, 1984.

Brinton, Crane. *English Political Thought in the Nineteenth Century*. Harper Torchbook: New York, 1962.

Brown, Nicola. *Fairies in Nineteenth-Century Art and Literature*. Cambridge University Press: Cambridge, 2001.

Brown, Stephen R. *A Most Damnable Invention: Dynamite, Nitrates, and the Making of the Modern World*. St. Martin's Press: New York, 2005.

Buse, Peter and Andrew Stott, Eds. *Ghosts: Deconstruction, Psychoanalysis, History*. Oxford University Press: London, 1999.

Bynum, W.F. *Science and the Practice of Medicine in the Nineteenth Century*. Cambridge University Press: Cambridge, 1994.

Cabinet Magazine. Issue 24, Winter 2006-7. Issue on Shadows.

Carroll, Lewis. *Alice's Adventures in Wonderland and Through the Looking-Glass*. Penguin Books: New York, 1998.

_____. *Phantasmagoria and Other Poems*. MacMillan and Company: London, 1911.

Cayley, David. *The Rivers North of the Future: The Testament of Ivan Illich.* House of Anansi Press: Toronto, Canada, 2005.

Chamisso, Adelbert von. *Peter Schlemihl, The Shadowless Man.* Trans. Sir John Bowering. Kessenger Publishing: Whitefish, Montana, 2004.

Charney, Leo and Vanessa R. Schwartz, Eds. *Cinema and the Invention of Modern Life.* University of California Press: Berkeley and London, 1995.

Connor, Stephen. *Dumbstruck: A Cultural History of Ventriloquism.* Oxford University Press: Oxford, 2000.

Crary, Jonathan. *Techniques of the Observer: On Vision and Modernity in the Nineteenth Century.* Harvard University Press: Harvard and Oxford, 1990.

Crowe, Michael J. *The Extraterrestrial Life Debate: 1750-1900.* Dover Publications: Mineola and New York, 1999.

Curtis, Edward S. Ed. Christopher Cardozo. *Edward S. Curtis: Hidden Faces.* Little Brown and Co.: Boston, 1997.

Davidson, Cathy N., Ed. *Reading in America: Literature and Social History.* The Johns Hopkins University Press: Baltimore and London, 1989.

Davies, Rodney. *The Lazarus Syndrome: Buried Alive and other Horrors of the Undead.* Barnes and Noble Publishing, 1998.

Denson, Charles. *Coney Island Lost and Found.* Ten Speed Press: Berkeley and Toronto, 2002.

Derrida, Jacques. *Spectres of Marx: The State of the Debt, the Work of Mourning and the New International.* Routledge: New York, 2006.

Douglas-Fairhurst, Robert. *Victorian Afterlives: The Shaping of Influence in Nineteenth-Century Literature.* Oxford University Press: Oxford, 2002.

Doyle, Sir Arthur Conan. *The Adventures of Sherlock Holmes.* Penguin Books: London, 1981.

_____. *The Coming of the Fairies.* University of Nebraska Press: Nebraska, 2006.

_____. *The History of Spiritualism.* Hesperides Press: New York, 2008.

_____. *The Memoirs of Sherlock Holmes.* Oxford University Press: London and New York, 1993.

_____. *The Return of Sherlock Holmes.* Pan Books: London and Sydney, 1974.

_____. *Wanderings of a Spiritualist.* Bibliobazaar: New York, 2008.

Dulken, Stephen Van. *Inventing the Nineteenth Century: 100 Inventions that Shaped the Victorian Age, From Aspirin to the Zeppelin.* New York University Press: New York, 2001.

Emerson, Ralph Waldo. *The Essential Writings of Ralph Waldo Emerson.* Ed. Brooks Atkinson. The Modern Library: New York, 2000.

Enright, D. J., Ed. *The Oxford Book of the Supernatural.* University of Oxford Press: Oxford, 1995.

Evans, Colin. *The Father of Forensics.* Berkley Books: New York, 2006.

Evans, Stewart and Paul Gainey. *Jack the Ripper: First American Serial Killer.* Kodansha International: New York and Tokyo, 1998.

Faust, Drew Gilpin. *This Republic of Suffering: Death and the American Civil War.* Alfred A. Knopf: New York, 2008.

Fiedler, Leslie. *Freaks: Myths and Images of the Secret Self.* Simon and Schuster: New York, 1978.

Fizdale, Robert and Arthur Gold. *Divine Sarah: A Life of Sarah Bernhardt.* Vintage Books: New York, 1992.

Florey, Kitty Burns. *Sister Bernadette's Dog Barking: The Quirky History and Lost Art of Diagramming Sentences.* Melville House Publishing: Hoboken, New Jersey, 2005.

Foucault, Michel. *Health and Medicine.* Eds. Alan Petersen and Robin Bunton. Routledge: London and New York, 1997.

Foy, Jessica H. and Thomas J. Schlereth, eds. *American Home Life, 1880-1930: A Social History of Spaces and Services.* The University of Tennessee Press: Knoxville, 1992.

Freud, Sigmund. *The Interpretation of Dreams.* Trans. A. A. Brill. Barnes and Nobles Classics: New York, 2005.

_____. *The Uncanny.* Trans. David McClintock. Penguin: London, 2003.

Gauld, Alan. *The Founders of Psychical Research.* Schocken Books: New York, 1968.

Gay, Peter. *Weimar Culture: The Outsider As Insider.* W.W. Norton and Company: New York, 2001.

German-Carton, Janis, Carol Ockman and Kenneth Silver. *Sarah Bernhardt: The Art of High Drama.* Published in Association with the Jewish Museum, New York, 2005.

Gilfoyle, Timothy J. *A Pickpocket's Tale: The Underworld of Nineteenth-Century New York*. W.W. Norton and Company: New York, 2006.

Gombrich, E. H. *Shadows: The Depiction of Cast Shadows in Western Art*. Yale University Press: London and New Haven, 1995.

Gould, Stephen Jay. *The Flamingo's Smile: Reflections in Natural History*. W.W. Norton and Company: New York, 1985.

_____. *Mismeasure of Man*. W. W. Norton and Company: New York, 1996.

Green, David, Ed. *Where Is The Photograph?* Photoworks: Brighton, England, 2002.

Gresham, William Lindsay. *Houdini: The Man Who Walked Through Walls*. MacFadden-Bartell Books: New York, 1961.

Gunning, Tom. "Haunting Images: Ghosts, Photography and the Modern Body." Exhibition Catalog, Disembodied Spirit.

Haining, Peter. Ed. *Zombie! Stories of the Walking Dead*. Target Books: New York, 1985.

Halttunen, Karen. *Confidence Men and Painted Women: A Study of Middle-Class Culture in America, 1830-1870*. Yale University Press: New Haven and London, 1982.

Hamblyn, Richard. *The Invention of Clouds: How an Amateur Meterologist Forged the Language of the Skies*. Picador: London, 2002.

Hecht, Herman. "The History of Projecting Phantoms, Ghosts and Apparitions." *NMLJ* 3, no. 1 (Feb, 1984) and no. 2 (Dec. 1984).

Herdman, John. *The Double in Nineteenth-Century Fiction*. St. Martin's Press: New York, 1991.

Hodgson, Barbara. *Opium: A Portrait of the Heavenly Demon*. Souvenir Press: London, 1999.

Hoffmann, E. T. A. Ed. E.F. Bleiler. *The Best Tales of Hoffmann*. Trans. Alfred Packer. Dover Publications: New York, 1967.

Humphrey, Derek. *Dying With Dignity: Understanding Euthanasia*. Carol Publishing Group: New York, 1992.

Ifrah, Georges. *The Universal History of Computing: From the Abacus to the Quantum Computer*. John Wiley and Sons: New York, 2001.

_____. "The Institutional Construction of a New Fetish: Human Life." Paper Delivered at the Evangelical Lutheran Church Conference in America, March 29, 1989, Chicago.

James, Henry. *The Turn of the Screw and Other Stories*. Penguin Books: New York, 1977.

James, William. *Essays in Psychical Research*. Harvard University Press: Cambridge, 1986.

_____. *The Varieties of Religious Experience: A Study in Human Nature.* Modern Library: New York, 1902.

Jensen, Derrick. *The Culture of Make Believe*. Chelsea Green Publishing Company: New York, 2004.

Johnson, Steven. *The Ghost Map: The Story of London's Most Terrifying Epidemic—and How It Changed Science, Cities, and the Modern World.* Riverhead Books: New York, 2006.

Kalush, William and Larry Sloman. *The Secret Life of Houdini: The Making of America's First Superhero*. Atria Books: New York and London, 2006.

Kasson, John F. *Houdini, Tarzan and the Perfect Man: The White Male Body and the Challenge of Modernity in America*. Hill and Wang: New York, 2001.

_____. *Amusing the Million: Coney Island at the Turn of the Century*. Hill and Wang: New York, 1978.

Larson, Erik. *The Devil in the White City: Murder, Magic, and Madness at the Fair that Changed America*. Random House: New York, 2004.

Lavi, Shai J. *The Modern Art of Dying: A History of Euthanasia in the United States*. Princeton University Press: Princeton and Oxford, 2005.

Lears, Jackson. *No Place Of Grace: Antimodernism and the Transformation of American Culture, 1880-1920*. Pantheon Books: New York, 1981.

Lienhard, John H. *Inventing Modern: Growing Up with X-Rays, Skyscrapers, and Tailfins*. Oxford University Press: London and New York,

Lightman, Bernard, Ed. *Victorian Science in Context*. University of Chicago Press: Chicago, 1997.

Lutz, Tom. *American Nervousness, 1903: An Anecdotal History*. Cornell University Press: Ithaca and London, 1991.

MacDonald, Helen. *Human Remains: Dissection and its Histories.* Yale University Press: New Haven and London, 2005.

Malson, Lucien. *Wolf Children and the Problem of Human Nature.* Monthly Review Press: New York and London, 1972.

Melville, Herman. *The Confidence Man: His Masquerade.* W.W. Norton and Company: New York, 1971.

Menand, Louis. *The Metaphysical Club: A Story of Ideas in America.* Farrar, Straus and Giroux: New York, 2001.

Meyerson, Joel, ed. *A Historical Guide to Ralph Waldo Emerson.* Oxford University Press: Oxford and New York, 2003.

Millar, David, Ian, John, and Margaret. *The Cambridge Dictionary of Scientists.* Second Edition. Cambridge University Press: Cambridge and New York, 2002.

Newitz, Annalee. *Pretend We're Dead: Capitalist Monsters in American Pop Culture.* Duke University Press: Durham, North Carolina and London, 2005.

Nissenbaum, Stephen. *The Battle for Christmas: A Cultural History of America's Most Cherished Holiday.* Vintage Books: New York, 1996.

O'Malley, Michael. *Keeping Watch: A History of American Time.* Viking: New York, 1990.

Perez, Gilberto. *The Material Ghost: Films and Their Medium.* The Johns Hopkins University Press: Baltimore, Maryland, 1998.

Phillips, Adam. *On Flirtation.* Faber and Faber: London and Boston, 1994.

Poe, Edgar Allan. *The Complete Tales.* Ed. Alix Perry. Random House: New York, 1981.

Powell, Marilyn. *Ice Cream: The Delicious History.* The Overlook Press: Woodstock, New York, 2006.

Price, Harry. *Confessions of a Ghost Hunter.* Time-Life Medical: New York, 1983.

Richardson, Robert D. *William James: In the Maelstrom of American Modernism.* Houghton Mifflin: New York, 2006.

Roach, Mary. *Spook: Science Tackles the Afterlife.* W.W. Norton and Company: New York, 2005.

_____. *Stiffed: The Curious Lives of Human Cadavers.* W.W. Norton and Company: New York, 2003.

Royle, Nicholas. *The Uncanny: An Introduction*. Routledge: Manchester, 2002.

Ruffles, Tom. "Phantasmagoria Ghost Shows." *Udolpho*, 30 (Autumn 1997).

Rybczynski, Witold. *One Good Turn: A Natural History of the Screwdriver and the Screw*. Scribner: New York, 2000.

Sandberg, Mark B. *Living Pictures, Missing Persons: Mannequins, Museums, and Modernity*. Princeton University Press: Princeton and Oxford, 2003.

Schmitt, Jean-Claude. *Ghosts in the Middle Ages*. Trans. Theresa Lavender Fagan. University of Chicago Press: Chicago, 1998.

Schoonover, Karl. "Ectoplasms, Evanescence, and Photography." *Art Journal*, 62, 3 (Fall 2003).

Schorske, Carl E. *Fin-De-Siècle Vienna: Politics and Culture*. Vintage Books: New York, 1981.

Schwartz, Vanessa R. *Spectacular Realities: Early Mass Culture in Fin-de-Siècle Paris*. University of California Press: Berkeley and Los Angeles, 1998.

_____ and Leo Charney, Eds. *Cinema and the Invention of Modern Life*. University of California Press: Berkeley and Los Angeles, 1995.

Sconce, Jeffrey. *Haunted Media: Electronic Presence from Telegraphy to Television*. University of North Carolina Press: Durham, North Carolina, 2000.

Shattuck, Roger. *Forbidden Knowledge: From Prometheus to Pornography*. St. Martin's Press: New York, 1996.

Shelley, Mary. *Frankenstein, or The Modern Prometheus*. Penguin Classics: New York, 2003.

_____. *Transformation*. Hesperus Classics: London, 2005.

Shteir, Rachel. *Striptease: The Untold Story of the Girlie Show*. Oxford University Press: Oxford and New York, 2004.

Silverman, Kenneth. *Lightning Man: The Accursed Life of Samuel F. B. Morse*. Da Capo Press: New York, 2004.

Smith, Daniel B. *Muses, Madmen, and Prophets: Rethinking the History, Science, and Meaning of Auditory Hallucinations*. The Penguin Press: New York, 2007.

Solnit, Rebecca. *River of Shadows: Eadweard Muybridge and the Technological Wild West*. Penguin Books: New York, 2003.

Starr, Paul. *The Social Transformation of American Medicine: The Rise of a Sovereign Profession and the Making of a Vast Industry*. Basic Books: New York, 1982.

Steinmeyer, Jim. *Hiding the Elephant: How Magicians Invented the Impossible and Learned to Disappear*. Carroll and Graf Publishers: New York, 2003.

Stevenson, Robert Louis. *The Strange Case of Dr. Jekyll and Mr. Hyde and Other Tales of Terror*. Penguin Classics: New York, 2003.

Stoichita, Victor. *A Short History of the Shadow*. Reaktion Books: London, 1997.

Stoker, Bram. *Dracula*. Bantam Books: New York, 1987.

Stratmann, Linda. *Chloroform: The Quest for Oblivion*. Sutton Publishing: New York, 2003.

Thornton, Tamara Plakins. *Handwriting in America: A Cultural History*. Yale University Press: New Haven and London, 1996.

Tussaud, John Theodore. *The Romance of Madame Tussaud's*. Odhams: London, 1920.

Von Franz, Marie-Louise. *Shadow and Evil in Fairy Tales*. Shambhala: Boston and London, 1995.

Warner, Marina. *Phantasmagoria: Spirit Visions, Metaphors, and Media into the Twenty-First Century*. Oxford University Press: Oxford and New York, 2006.

Wassermann, Jakob. *Caspar Hauser: The Inertia of the Heart*. Penguin Books: New York, 1991.

Weisberg, Barbara. *Talking to the Dead: Kate and Maggie Fox and the Rise of Spiritualism*. Harper San Francisco: San Francisco, 2004.

Wells, H.G. "The Invisible Man." Dover Publications: New York, 1992.

_____. *The Time Machine*. Penguin: London, 2005.

Whitney, Charles S. *Bridges: Their Art, Science and Evolution*. Crown Publishers: New York, 1983.

Wilde, Oscar. *The Picture of Dorian Gray and Other Writings*. Bantam Books: New York, 1982.

Wilson, A.N. *God's Funeral*. W.W. Norton, Company: New York, 1999.

Winwar, Frances. *Oscar Wilde and the Yellow 'Nineties*. Blue Ribbon Books: Garden City, New York, 1940.

Zizek, Slavoj. *Iraq: The Borrowed Kettle*. Verso: New York and London, 2004.

INDEX

Index

Index

Index

Index

270; as key to human essence, 37; vs. "normal," 140; and serial killing, 203; sexual, 155; and "underground" pursuits, 40

The Devil in the White City: Murder, Magic, and Madness at the Fair That Changed America (Larson), 62

Dickens, Charles, 141–142

digital photography, 310

dioramas, 195

Dircks, Henry, 179–181

disappearance: in fiction, 189–194; of the human being, 1, 4, 7, 19; missing persons, 200–201; of perceived reality, 214–215; as performed by illusionists, 186, 187; recording, 19; of Salomé, 161

disaster, numbness to, 4

disease, 203–204

Disney amusement parks, 284

doctors, 44, 252

dog tags, 110

dolls, Edison's, 294

"The Domain of Arnheim" (Poe), 193

doppelgänger (double-walker), 43

Dostoevsky, Fyodor, 31, 43

Double (Dostoevsky), 43

Douglas, Lord Alfred, 150

Dracula: death as conquered by, 262; as embodying paradox, 316; as a parasite, 205

"Dream of Duncan Parrenness" (Kipling), 43

dreams: as altered states, 278–279; at amusement parks, 288; consciousness in, 281–282; embracing creatures from, 336–337; Freud on, 278, 279–280, 282; 19th century as viewed through, 276–277; self-expression in, 283; typical, 288–289

Dreser, Heinrich, 50

"Dr. Heidegger's Experiment" (Hawthorne), 191

drones, 94–95

drug experimentation: cocaine, 50–51, 275; ether, 54–55; to find the essence of life, 37–38; heroin, 50; morphine, 48; 19th-century, 278–279; nitrous oxide, 51–53; opium, 46–48

Duell, Charles H., 297

Dumas, Alexandre, 148, 178

Dumas, Jean, 55

Dupin, C. Auguste, 1

dynamo, the, 54

E

Eastman, George, 220–221

Ecce Homo (Nietzsche), 28

economic efficiency, 217

Edison, Thomas, 26, 184, 209, 290–295

Edison Speaking Phonograph Company, 292

education: as building character, 78; on creationism, 77; kindergarten, 73–74

electrotherapy, 226

Eliot, T. S., 256

Ellis, Havelock, 35

embalming, 102–103, 198, 199

embryos, 250, 265

Emerson, Ralph Waldo, 242, 284–286, 303, 313

emotions, 38

"The Emperor of Ice-Cream" (Stevens), 304

enemy combatants, 119

Engels, Friedrich, 83

England: bans *Salomé*, 159; folklore study, 74; freak shows, 140; London cholera epidemic, 83; nitrous oxide experimentation, 51–53; opium use in 19th-century, 46–47; Sarah Baartman in, 143–145

entertainment: actor as author, 157–158; at amusement parks, 283–284; life through, 282; modern, 304; at the morgue, 197–198; new identities through, 137; 19th-century, 289, 302; racist freak shows, 140–142; by the supernatural, 178–181, 186–187; technology for, 290

Epimetheus, 42, 335

Eremozoic age, 7

Esfandiary, F. M., 264–265

ether, 54

ethnic cleansing, 68

eugenics, 67, 266

euphoria, 48, 299

euthanasia, 110, 251–253, 255–256

evangelical Christianity, 117

Index

Index

Index

Index

Index

Index

soul, the: and life, 42; in life and death, 105; mechanical, 294; shadow and, 308, 312, 315, 335; as stolen from zombies, 335, 336; as suspended in surgery, 125–128
Southey, Robert, 52, 335–336
South Street Seaport Exhibition Centre, 200
space: annihilation of, 216, 217; and Froebel's blocks, 73; life/death as located in, 130; redefining human notions of, 26
special effects, 188
Speed and Politics (Virilio), 94
Spencer, Herbert, 58
Spilsbury, Sir Bernard, 64–65
spiritualism, 117–118, 208–211, 294–295
split personalities, 318
Spook: Science Tackles the Afterlife (Roach), 212
Stanford, Leland, 181–182
statistics: categories of, 317; of Civil War dead, 95; of Holocaust victims, 2–3; of U.S. incarceration, 318–319; of U.S. mental patients, 318; of U.S. serial killers, 203; *see also* numbers
status quo, questioning the, 33–34
stem cell research, 250
stereotypes, criminal, 34
Stevens, Wallace, 304
Stevenson, Robert Louis, 43, 316
Stoicescu, Dr. Dan, 259, 261, 263
Stoker, Bram, 262
The Strange Case of Dr. Jekyll and Mr. Hyde (Stevenson), 43, 316
Stratmann, Linda, 55
Strausbaugh, John, 138
strength, 79
stress, 229
strikes, labor, 238–239
striptease, the, 160–161, 168
strongmen, 233–234
structuralism, 74
Studies in Motion: The Hauntings of Eadweard Muybridge (Kerr), 184
"The Subjective Effects of Nitrous Oxide" (James), 51
suicide bombers, 267–268
Sumner, Senator Charles, 98

The Sun Also Rises (Hemingway), 127, 128
surgery: anesthesia for, 53, 54–55; McMurtry on, 126–127; suspension of life in, 123
suspended animation, 9, 208, 255
suspension bridges, 79–80
Swift, Gustavus, 103
syphilis, 205
syringe, hypodermic, 49

T

Talbot, William Henry Fox, 18, 220, 310
The Talented Mr. Ripley (Highsmith), 332–333
Tales of the Dead, 174
Tammuz, 162
taphophobia, 106
tattooing, 233
taxidermy, 196
Taylor, Frederick Winslow, 228–229
technology: as defining human experience, 134; of embalming, 102–103; for entertainment, 287, 290; genetic engineering, 266; genetic sequencing, 259–261, 263; influence on death, 86; loss of control to, 215, 218; meat-packing, 103; military, 88, 91–94; nervous tension from, 226–227; 19th-century evolution of, 26; power of, 222–223, 258; and self-perception, 76; transhumanists on, 262, 264; and virtual death, 130–131; war is not ended by, 15–16; Y2K, 322, 326, 329–330; *see also* machines
telegraphs, 291, 295–296
telephones, 291, 293–294
television, 214, 296
terminology: architectural, 78; drug "highs," 49; "euthanasia," 251; "folk," 73; "freak," 30; "human being," 240–244; of human extermination, 3; "immigrant," 11–12; Iraq War, 13–14; "life," 5, 239, 244; "scientist," 7; "snapshot," 17; "veil," 164; wartime, 10, 100; "watching" time, 293
Tesla, Nikola, 296
test tube babies, 265

Index

Printed in the United States
by Baker & Taylor Publisher Services